THE REALITY OF RESEARCH
WITH CHILDREN
AND YOUNG PEOPLE

THE REALITY OF RESEARCH WITH CHILDREN AND YOUNG PEOPLE

EDITED BY

Vicky Lewis
Mary Kellett
Chris Robinson
Sandy Fraser
Sharon Ding

SAGE Publications
London • Thousand Oaks • New Delhi

In association with

The Open
University

First published 2004

 SAGE Publications Ltd
6 Bonhill Street
London EC2A 4PU

SAGE Publications Inc.
2455 Teller Road
Thousand Oaks, California 91320

SAGE Publications India Pvt Ltd
B-42, Panchsheel Enclave
Post Box 4109
New Delhi 100 017

British Library Cataloguing in Publication data

A catalogue record for this book is available from
the British Library

ISBN 0 7619 4378 1
ISBN 0 7619 4379 X (pbk)

Library of Congress Control Number: 2003104749

Typeset by C&M Digitals (P) Ltd., Chennai, India
Printed and bound in Great Britain by Athenaeum Press, Gateshead

Contents

Contributor Affiliations

Jane Aldgate Professor of Social Care, School of Health and Social Welfare, The Open University, England, UK.

Alison Clark Research Officer, Institute of Education, University of London, England, UK.

Elizabeth Coates Lecturer, Institute of Education, University of Warwick, England, UK.

Daphne Evans Senior Research Officer, Psychology Department, University of Wales Swansea, Wales, UK.

Dev Griesel Research Professor, School of Psychology, University of Natal, Pietermaritzburg, South Africa.

Lynda Ince Senior Lecturer, University of Hertfordshire, England, UK.

Vicky Lewis Professor of Education, Centre for Childhood, Development and Learning, Faculty of Education and Language Studies, The Open University, England, UK.

Marina Monteith Research Fellow, Institute of Child Care Research, Queen's University, Belfast, Northern Ireland, UK.

William Pickett Associate Professor, Faculty of Health Sciences, Queen's University, Kingston, Ontario, Canada.

Samantha Punch Lecturer in Sociology, Department of Applied Social Science, University of Stirling, Scotland, UK.

Naz Rassool Reader in Education, Institute of Education, University of Reading, England, UK.

Jon Sutton Editor of *The Psychologist*, The British Psychological Society, UK; Honorary Lecturer, Glasgow Caledonian University, Scotland, UK.

Wataru Takei Associate Professor, Faculty of Education, Kanazawa University, Japan.

Barrie Thorne Professor of Sociology and Women's Studies, University of California, Berkeley, USA.

Acknowledgements

A great many people contributed to this edited collection of articles and commentaries and we are grateful to them all: Peter Barnes, Liz Benali, Rachel Burr, Ann Brechin, Louise Delaney, Ronny Flynn, Maria Francis-Pitfield, Liz Freeman and colleagues in co-publishing at the Open University, Chris Golding, Andy Grayson, Roger Hancock, Mary Jane Kehily, Alison Poyner and colleagues at Sage Publications, Iris Rowbotham, Indra Sinka, Will Swann, Nigel Thomas, Steph Withers and Martin Woodhead. We would also like to thank all the contributors whose articles and commentaries appear in this book. If they had not carried out their research and had not been willing to comment on how they went about the research and to reveal some of the difficulties which arose, there would have been no book.

The authors and publishers wish to thank the following for permission to use copyright material:

Paper 2: Taylor & Francis Ltd (http://www.tandf.co.uk/journals) for Elizabeth Coates (2002) '"I Forgot the Sky!" Children's Stories Contained Within Their Drawings', *International Journal of Early Years Education*, **10**(1), pp. 21–35.

Paper 3: Blackwell for Wataru Takei (2001) 'How do Deaf Infants Attain First Signs?', *Developmental Science*, **4**, pp. 71–78.

Paper 4: The British Psychological Society for Jon Sutton, Peter Smith and John Swettenham (1999) 'Social Cognition and Bullying: Social Inadequacy or Skilled Manipulation?', *British Journal of Developmental Psychology*, **17**, pp. 435–450.

Paper 5: HMSO for Jane Aldgate and Marie Bradley (1999) *Supporting Families Through Short Term Fostering*.

Paper 6: Taylor & Francis Ltd (http://www.tandf.co.uk/journals) for Samantha Punch (2001) 'Negotiating Autonomy: Children's Use of Time and Space in Rural Bolivia', in L. Alanen and B. Mayall (eds) *Conceptualising Child-Adult Relations*; and Hodder Arnold for Samantha Punch, 'Multiple Methods and Research Relations with Children in Rural Bolivia', in M. Limb and C. Dwyer (eds) *Qualitative Methodologies for Geographers*, Arnold (2001), © 2001 Arnold. Reprinted by permission of Hodder Arnold.

Paper 7: AMA for Will Pickett, Holger Schmid, William Boyce, Kelly Simpson, Peter Scheldt, Joanna Mazur, Michel Olcho, Mathew King, Emmanuelle Godeau, Mary Overpeck, Anna Aszmmann, Monica Szabo and Yossi Harel (2002) 'Multiple Risk Behaviour and Injury: An International Analysis of Young People', *Archive of Paediatric and Adolescent Medicine*, **156**, pp. 786–793.

Paper 8: Alison Clark's 'The Mosaic Approach and Research with Young Children' was especially commissioned by the Open University.

Paper 9: Marina Monteith (1999) 'Making Progress? The Transition to Adulthood for Disabled Young People in Northern Ireland', was reproduced from *Child Welfare Policy and Practice* edited by Dorota Iwaniec and Malcolm Hill with permission from Jessica Kingsley Publishers. Copyright © 2000 Jessica Kingsley Publishers.

Paper 10: Daphne Evans and Paul Norman (2002) 'Improving Pedestrian Road Safety Among Adolescents: An Application of the Theory of Planned Behaviour', in D. Rutter and L. Quine (eds) *Changing Health Behaviour* (2002), Open University Press; and Rutter, D. and Quine, L. (2002) 'Social Cognition Models and Changing Health Behaviours' in D. Rutter and L. Quine (eds) *Changing Health Behaviour* (2002), Open University Press.

Paper 11: BAAF Publications for Lynda Ince (1999) 'Preparing Young Black People for Leaving Care', in R. Barn (ed.) *Working with Black Children and Adolescents in Need*; and BAAF Publications for Lynda Ince (1998) *Making it Alone*.

Paper 12: Taylor & Francis Ltd (http://www.tandf.co.uk/journals) for Naz Rassool (1999) 'Flexible Identities: Exploring Race and Gender Issues Amongst a Group of Immigrant Pupils in an Inner-city Comprehensive School', *British Journal of Sociology and Education*, **20**(1), pp. 23–26.

Paper 13: Rutgers University Press for Barrie Thorne (1993) *Gender Play: Girls and Boys in School*.

Paper 14: Sage Publications for Dev Griesel and Jill Swart-Kruger (2002) 'Children in South Africa can make a Difference: An Assessment of "Growing Up in Cities" in Johannesburg', *Childhood*, **9**(1), pp. 83–100.

1 The Reality of Research: An Introduction
VICKY LEWIS

Research is an exciting activity. It provides a wonderful opportunity to explore ideas and theories, discover new things, confirm facts and identify further questions in need of answers. However, there is another side to research which is often not discussed. It can be very stressful, lonely and frustrating. Things may not go according to plan. You may have to make changes part way through a piece of research for reasons beyond your control. Some parts of the research may take much longer than you anticipated at the outset. And so on.

There are many books on how to do research which explore topics such as asking research questions, designing a study, selecting a method, collecting data, analysing data, etc. In this edited book we have not attempted to cover these sorts of topics. Rather, we have brought together 13 pieces of research which have either been published as reproduced here or adapted slightly, edited from longer publications or specially commissioned. The focus of each paper is either children or young people and together they represent a range of qualitative and quantitative research methodologies within Education, Health, Social Welfare, Psychology, Sociology and Anthropology. However, published papers, such as the 13 included in this book, seldom reflect the process of research. In such papers researchers generally refrain from commenting on the origins of the research questions, the difficulties experienced or the things that went wrong. Published papers are generally a polished account of research.

Our aim in putting this book together was to get at the side of research which is rarely evident from the final publication. In order to achieve this we asked the first author of each paper to write a commentary on the various stages of carrying out the research, from the origins of the ideas for the research to writing up. These commentaries follow each paper. They provide a rich addition to the reported research, illuminating the reality of doing research. The approach of providing a paper *and* a commentary on the process makes this book distinctively different from other books on doing research. We have deliberately put the commentaries after the papers so that you first encounter the polished account and then hear about the process.

When we embarked on this book with the idea of asking researchers to write a commentary on the process of carrying out their research we had several concerns. One was whether or not researchers would be prepared to engage with this sort of self-reflection. Another was whether we would get 13 commentaries which said much the same things albeit in slightly different ways. We did not know most of the researchers at the outset so we had no way of judging if our concerns were justified. We had chosen the research 'stories', as they became known, because we felt that together they covered the disciplines and methodologies we wanted to illustrate. We hadn't selected the stories because we felt the researchers would have the ability to reflect on their research and would bring distinct perspectives. Our concerns were soon dispelled when the commentaries began to come in. Everyone was able to engage with this process. Some commented on how much they had enjoyed writing about doing their research, almost as though no one had ever asked them about it. Others commented on how easy it was to do. Likewise, although we asked most of them to comment on similar things such as access, ethics, choosing a methodology and so on, the commentaries were very different from one another. Nevertheless, one thing did surprise us. And this was how much additional insight into the research process these commentaries brought.

We hope that you will find the papers and commentaries helpful for your research, whatever stage you are at. This volume was put together in conjunction with a companion volume, *Doing Research with Children and Young People* (Fraser, Lewis, Ding, Kellett & Robinson, 2004). The contributors to that book discuss a number of critical issues which arise in the planning, carrying out and dissemination stages of research. Many of the issues and questions they discuss are also evident in the commentaries and papers in the present volume. In the remainder of this chapter we have provided an overview of the 13 research 'stories' in terms of how they fit various categories into which research can be grouped. Depending on your interests this may help you select particular 'stories' on which to focus. There is no need for you to read the stories in sequence.

When we began to consider potential research stories our selection criteria included that the content should be engaging, the approach taken should be representative of different disciplines, the research should involve children and young people of varying ages, should have been carried out in different countries and should utilise a range of different research tools.

We certainly hope that the content of the research of all the papers is engaging, although we expect some to be more engaging than others. They are certainly very varied in the topics studied, as the following snapshots hopefully demonstrate. Liz Coates examined how children's drawings can be supplemented and enriched by what they say to themselves and to others as they draw, while Wataru Takei observed the hand gestures of two deaf infants in the period before they began using Japanese Sign Language. Jon Sutton and his colleagues addressed the question of whether children who bully have an especially sophisticated understanding of what others are thinking and feeling. Jane Aldgate and Marie Bradley studied children's views of short-term accommodation away from their families, whereas Samantha Punch focused on the lives of children in a rural community in Bolivia. Will Pickett and his colleagues looked at the behaviours which increase young people's likelihood of injury, and Alison Clark explored young children's views of their school nursery. Marina Monteith examined the transition to adulthood for disabled young people, and Daphne Evans and Paul Norman reported an intervention study aimed at improving attitudes to road safety. Lynda Ince carried out a study of young black people leaving care, and Naz Rassool examined race and gender issues among immigrant pupils. Barrie Thorne studied gender relations in school and Dev Griesel and colleagues evaluated the effect of involving South African children in improving their environment.

In terms of our other criteria, there are research stories from Education (Coates; Clark), Psychology (Takei; Sutton et al.; Griesel et al.), Social Care (Aldgate & Bradley; Ince), Anthropology (Punch), Sociology (Rassool; Thorne), and Health and Social Welfare (Pickett et al.; Monteith; Evans & Norman). The studies involve children and young people across a wide age range from the first year (Takei), three to seven years (Coates; Clark), seven to ten years (Sutton et al.; Thorne), 10 to 21 years (Pickett et al.; Monteith; Evans & Norman; Ince; Rassool; Griesel et al.) and two of the papers span several age groups (Aldgate & Bradley; Punch). In addition, within the research stories are studies of disabled children and young people (Takei; Monteith), young black people (Ince; Rassool; Griesel et al.) and gender differences (Thorne).

A majority of the papers are from the UK, although papers are included from Japan (Takei), Bolivia (Punch), South Africa (Griesel et al.), and America (Thorne), while one paper includes young people from 12 different countries including Canada, Estonia, Lithuania and Sweden (Pickett et al.). The studies also vary enormously in the number of children or young people involved. At one extreme is Takei's observations of two infants and at the other is Pickett et al.'s report of findings from almost 50,000 young people. The remaining papers involved between 10 (Ince) and 242 (Evans & Norman) children and young people.

A wide range of research tools are used. Several rely on naturalistic observations and of these four researchers simply kept notes of their observations (Coates; Punch; Clark; Thorne) whereas one made video recordings of everyday situations which were later coded (Takei). Questionnaires were used by Sutton et al., Pickett et al., Evans and Norman, and Griesel et al. Sutton et al. and Punch used specially designed tasks, and Sutton et al. and Griesel et al. administered standardised psychometric tests. Clark used a range of methods, including the children taking photographs, and escorting the researcher around the nursery. Clark also interviewed the children, and interviewing was employed in a number of the other studies (Aldgate & Bradley; Punch; Monteith; Ince; Rassool) and Griesel et al. used discussion groups. Rassool asked the young people to construct a personal life history and Ince examined casework files to support her research.

We were also clear from the outset that we wanted research stories which illustrated both qualitative and quantitative research and this is reflected in the 13 we have selected. Thus, six are qualitative (Coates; Punch; Clark; Ince; Rassool; Thorne), two draw on both qualitative and quantitative data (Aldgate & Bradley; Griesel et al.), and five present quantitative data (Takei; Sutton et al.; Pickett et al.; Monteith; Evans & Norman). Within the papers presenting quantitative data, three give descriptive statistics such as means and percentages but do not carry out any statistical analyses (Takei; Aldgate & Bradley; Monteith), whereas the other papers make use of a range of statistical procedures including χ^2 (Sutton et al.), analysis of variance (Sutton et al.; Evans & Norman; Griesel et al.), analysis of covariance (Sutton et al.), Wilcoxon signed-ranks tests (Evans & Norman), correlation, including partial correlation (Sutton et al.; Pickett et al.), and logistic regression (Pickett et al.).

There are also other interesting contrasts which are evident in our final selection. For example, three of the studies are longitudinal, involving observations over a period of time (Takei; Punch; Thorne) and two involve observing and assessing children and young people before and after an intervention (Aldgate & Bradley; Evans & Norman). The remaining stories are representative of cross-sectional research, involving observation or assessment of children and young people at one moment in time.

Three of the studies took an experimental approach (Sutton et al.; Evans & Norman; Griesel et al.). Sutton et al. grouped children on the basis of their involvement in bullying and then compared the groups in terms of their understanding of other people's thoughts and feelings. Evans and Norman compared the attitudes towards road safety of two groups, one of whom had watched a drama on road safety, while the other group had not. Likewise, Griesel et al. compared groups of young people who differed in terms of whether they had been involved in a programme to improve their community.

The studies also represent different stages of research. For example, Coates and Ince describe their studies as pilot studies, whereas the study by Pickett et al. is part of an ongoing multinational epidemiological health study which is repeated every three or four years involving tens of thousands of young people. Some of the other papers are part of ongoing research programmes, as indicated in the authors' commentaries, whereas others are one-off studies examining a particular question.

The above account of the 13 research stories within this book demonstrates the variety of information which is available. We hope that the final selection has largely met our original criteria and more besides, although we would be the first to acknowledge that we have achieved some criteria to a greater extent than others. However, in each case the commentaries provided by the authors further elucidate the process of doing research with children and young people. We hope you find them as illuminating as we have.

2 'I forgot the sky!' Children's Stories Contained within Their Drawings
ELIZABETH COATES

This paper was originally published as Coates, E. (2002) '"I forgot the sky!" Children's stories contained within their drawings', *International Journal of Early Years Education*, **10**(1): 21–35.

Abstract

What stories do young children's drawings contain? So often children's free drawings are not held in high regard but are seen as an activity which is undertaken outside lesson time or as an illustration to some prescribed task. However, the concentration and care with which some children undertake a drawing suggests that the content has real significance and that the drawing has not been undertaken lightly. This small-scale study arose from observations in a school setting of young children talking to themselves as they drew pictures. Often it seemed that this talk was a rehearsal for the drawing and it was this link that the project set out to explore. Children aged from 3 to 7 years were studied in their classrooms where they were participating in a free choice of activities. This paper examines the drawings collected together with transcriptions of the children's descriptions of their drawings. It looks at the symbolism contained within the pictures and the stories woven within each one. The study is intended as a pilot for a longitudinal research project focusing not only on children's drawings and accompanying narrative but extending to an exploration of emergent writing.

Introduction

For the young child the very process of making marks may be seen as part of their play, an exploration of the way surfaces can be transformed through their actions. Observations of 2-year-old children at a local nursery showed their absorption in a tray of damp sand using their fingers to investigate its texture, making grooves and squiggles in its smooth surface. At this stage such experimentation, whether it be with sand, paint or crayon, would seem to be the enjoyment of mark making for its own sake. However,

Gentle (1985) suggests that in fact a child's mark making progresses through a store of marks and schemata common to children worldwide. Research undertaken in the 1950s by Rhoda Kellogg provides a basis for such an assumption, since her study of more than 100,000 drawings led her to conclude that between the ages of 2 and 3, children repeatedly make a number of definite marks (Kellogg, 1955). These she categorised into 20 basic scribbles, examples of which can be seen either by themselves or in combination as we study young children's drawings today. To the uninitiated such scribbles may appear to be meaningless, except as an indication of developing manipulative skills, but Kellogg intimates that this may be because the work is being viewed from an adult's perspective. To the child, she feels, each scribble has particular significance and those observing young children may gain insights by listening to the child's simultaneous utterances. This notion is given further credence by the work of Nutbrown (1999) whose study of schema led her to propose: 'given that children working on particular patterns of thought can represent their schemas through making marks and talking as well as through their actions, it may follow that "vertical" and "back and forth" schemas emerge before "enclosing and enveloping" schemas'. If one accepts this hypothesis then it follows that these very early drawings form an important part of children's learning. Such activities allow rules to be explored, the child choosing the direction, shape and format appropriate to that moment (Matthews, 1994). The spontaneity of these drawing episodes might lead the adult to consider connections between recent events and their content, and whereas it might seem logical to relate a lively combination of scribbles to a visit to the seaside, without knowledge of the child's internal thought process we cannot be certain. Observations of the child in other contexts may suggest an exploration of a particular schema allowing an entirely different interpretation to be made (Cooke et al., 1998; Malchiodi, 1998; Nutbrown, 1999). Asking the very young child to talk about the drawing can lead to unexpected results, for whereas the child might seem engrossed in the activity, once he has finished interest is frequently lost. How completely this interest disappears was illustrated for me by my son (Figure 2.1) who at 2 years 2 months drew a complicated and vigorous mixture of scribbles which I felt must surely have real significance. When asked what it was, he replied 'a drawing'. To the question: what is it a drawing of? he answered, 'a picture'.

At this stage, Matthews (1994) feels the child's drawings are personal and not intended to communicate or be shared with others. As Jameson (1968) says, what the child really wants to do is to talk to himself in pictures, which suggests that the child weaves stories around the marks being made, each scribble having particular meaning dictating the story's direction so that the whole turns into a fantastical journey, a parallel for active fantasy play. To anyone living or working with young children this must seem a familiar idea, for they will almost certainly talk to themselves all the time they are drawing. It is not often, however, that adults pay attention to the content of this talk and much of the literature written about art education and the

Figure 2.1   Bruce, aged 2 years 2 months. 'A drawing.'

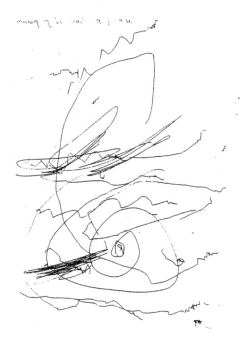

drawings of young children focuses far more on the developmental aspects, missing what to me seems an essential ingredient. Indeed at times it seems as though it is only the product that is being interpreted whilst utterances which could aid understanding are ignored (Kress, 1997).

Mark making and emergent writing

Consideration of children's utterances whilst drawing is more likely to be found in text relating to pre-literacy, where links are made between mark making and emergent writing. Pahl (1999) suggests that drawing helps the child externalise a thought and is a first step in creating symbols to represent real objects. Kress (1997) in *Before Writing* goes further, seeing the form and content of drawings as being as powerful as composing and writing. My own experience both as a parent and a teacher of young children confirms this, for the progression from scribbles to forms recognisable to others paves the way for a dialogue which aids understanding of the child's perception of the world (Coates, 1993). There is a danger, however, that in our eagerness to respond to perceived images we put our own interpretations on them, seeing and labelling figures, for instance, as 'Daddy', 'Mummy' or brother or sister. If we accept Kellogg's (1969) claim that children accept adults' responses even though they may not be a true interpretation then we can begin to understand why the description of the drawing's content once completed differs from the narrative which the child told to himself as he drew. If this is the case then it is possible that children from an early age are being conditioned into the format so familiar in educational settings. They come to expect to be asked about the drawing's content and a routine of drawing, telling the adult about the picture and the adult writing a sentence about it, is established. Browne (1996) stresses that this is no longer sufficient as an introduction to writing, for the expectation that the child will copy the adult's writing denies him the opportunity to show how much he already understands. For some children, however, Jameson (1968) feels this is necessary, for the adult's writing creates a link between the written and spoken word in the context of drawing. Within today's print-laden society it is difficult to imagine young children being unaware of the symbolic nature of writing, and many of the spontaneous drawings I have examined contain evidence of graphemes scattered across the page or lines of loops and zigzags resembling an adult's hand. When such signs first appear it is difficult to say with any conviction that there is a distinction being made between drawing and writing: certainly unless the child's spoken discourse provides a clue. I would agree with Kress (1997) that the 'child is (either) "drawing" both the print and the image or "writing" both print and image' (p. 61). Bruce's

Figure 2.2   Bruce, aged 3 years 4 months. 'Hey, Diddle, Diddle.'

drawing of the nursery rhyme 'Hey, Diddle Diddle' (Figure 2.2) illustrates this point well, for he sang as he drew and the letter-like shapes, which may include his initials (B.C.), appeared to be an extension to the drawing rather than a separate entity.

Drawing and language within nursery

The concentration within English nursery and infant schools today on developing children's literacy skills seems to have moved the emphasis away from spontaneous drawing to the more formal pursuit of using it as source material for copy writing, until by the age of 7 writing takes precedence, with drawing used to illustrate. It was an awareness that even in some of our nursery schools 3-year-old children were spending time copying letter shapes and tracing over writing with little opportunity for free drawing that led to this small-scale study. While observing student teachers I had become very conscious of the different values placed on children's drawing as they progressed from nursery to the top of the infant school. I felt that often the role of the teacher and early years practitioner precluded their sitting to observe children during free-choice activities and therefore valuable links between talk and drawing were being missed. To explore this further a decision was made to set up a pilot study which allowed time to be spent looking at children across the 3–7 age range. From this it was hoped to construct a sound basis for a longitudinal project not only focusing on children drawing and the accompanying narrative, but extending to an exploration of emergent writing.

The pilot study – observations

Twenty children in three settings were observed: four 4-year-olds (nursery setting), eight 5-year-olds, four 6-year-olds and four 7-year-olds (in two primary school settings). Because of the nature and organisation of some of the classrooms it was not always possible to set up a drawing area within them and some observations took place in the activity area outside. Although it was originally intended to spend several sessions with each age group this proved impossible, so one morning was spent observing each age group instead.

It was apparent to me prior to this study that there was often a dichotomy in nursery and reception classes between the child's narrative during each spontaneous drawing episode and the off-task talk which arose as they laboriously traced sentences dictated previously to their teacher. These sometimes stilted and short descriptions contrasted with the lively dramatisation that occurred as children took on the role of the characters being drawn. As Cox (1992) suggests, although the marks may not look like the objects involved, it may be the movement or functional aspects of these objects that are being represented. Observations in my first setting, a large nursery, seemed to support this idea.

The 3- and 4-year-olds

Although much emphasis was put on developing formal literacy skills there was a drawing area set up as a free choice activity. Thomas's drawing of a 'dog factory' (Figure 2.3) was accompanied by a commentary on the route the ingredients took. As he drew each part he said 'in there', 'down there', 'down there', 'down there', 'here!' Although his description of his drawing was phrased in a more conventional format, 'A dog factory. The ingredients go in here then they go down the pipes, round there and come out here', it was obvious that his commentary had been integral to his completed picture. My second example (Figure 2.4) is another 4-year-old, Jack, whose approach initially was similar in that he named each part as he drew it. However, far from drawing the head shape and then adding the features, his starting point was the eyes, saying 'one eye, two eye' followed by the nose, which he didn't name but called 'massive' (see Figure 2.4). The jaw and top of head were added separately and the drawing was abandoned when he drew the second ear piece 'too long'. This drawing, which he gave to me, he labelled a clown but immediately started another 'clown' drawn in the same way but to which he added a very small body. As he drew this part he laughed and said, 'Has a big head, when he sits on the settee his head is bigger than the settee. When he goes to bed his head is bigger. He needs an enormous pillow.' This again was labelled 'a clown' with no more details. Jack set about his drawings in a very deliberate fashion, the repetition in exactly the same order of the clown's head suggesting that he had a particular plan in mind. It would have been interesting to see if this was peculiar to the clown or whether this order occurred in other figure drawings, supporting Goodnow's (1977) contention that young children are remarkably consistent in their drawing sequences. To the adult seeing only the completed picture, Jack's particular and perhaps unconventional order would not have been obvious. Certainly they would not have been aware that his narrative for the second drawing echoed Kellogg's (1969) claim that children are well aware when their pictorial representations are out of proportion. Although I was present when both Thomas and Jack were drawing and therefore aware of the precise circumstances in which they took place, as Pahl (1999) points out, the observer is not in a position to know the thinking behind them. Without knowledge of the social and emotional factors at play and an understanding of the culture surrounding the two boys it is possible only to surmise about their subject choices. Neither of the remaining two nursery children observed stayed for any length of time. It was obvious that drawing for them at that time was only a transitory affair, for they talked steadily to other children, made cursory marks on paper and then threw them in the bin after no more than three minutes.

Figure 2.3 Thomas, aged 4 years 6 months 'A dog factory. The ingredients go in here, then they go down the pipes, round there and come out here.'

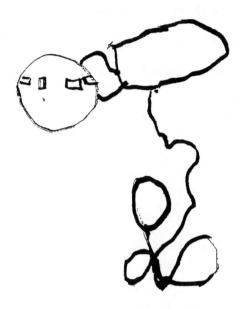

Figure 2.4 Jack, aged 4 years 10 months. 'A clown.' Drawing sequence: 1. eyes; 2. nose; 3. jaw; 4. moustache; 5. top of head; 6. mouth; 7. glasses–ear pieces.

The 5-year-olds

In the two primary schools, observations were made of four children at a time. There were similarities between the two groups of 5-year-old children in that all eight drawings contained the stereotypical houses described by Kellogg (1969) and Duffy (1998) and, unlike the 4-year-olds, these children discussed their drawings, announcing what they intended to draw and adding details as ideas came up in the conversation. The first group, which consisted of two boys and two girls, showed different approaches. The two girls talked throughout about their drawings, mentioning each new detail and competing with each other, as this extract shows:

Tamara: I'm going to do a doorbell. I'm going to put a road. [*talks as she draws these*]
Tom: I've already put one in. [*doorbell*]
Shannon: I'm doing one as well. [*adds road*]
Tamara: You're copying me!
Shannon: I've made a road like you.
Tamara: I'm putting lines on.
Shannon: I'm going to do a kennel.
Tamara: I'm going to do one as well.
Shannon: You've got to do a roof. [*to Tamara*]
Shannon: Look, I've done a sun.
Tamara: I'm going to do one.
Shannon: I'm going to do a moon.
Tamara: I'm going to do a moon as well.
Tom: You can't have the sun and the moon at the same time.
Tamara: I have in my drawing.

One of the interesting aspects of this exchange is the reversal of roles. Part way through, Shannon initially accused of copying becomes the source of the sun and moon images as well as the kennel. The finished pictures (Figures 2.5 and 2.6) do appear similar in the central placing of the house and road. Both contain elements of writing placed strategically and appearing, as Kress suggested, an essential part of the drawing rather than as a separate entity. Tamara's 'emforty5' refers to the motorway near her home, and Shannon's writing forms part of her address. Whilst Tamara was happy to talk about her completed drawing (see Figure 2.5), Shannon, like some of the children in Matthews's (1994) research, wanted to move on to another activity rather than describe her work. Neither of the two boys really joined in the conversation although it was clear from Tom's description of his drawing that he had been listening to the girls and some of the details suggested appear in his drawing. When Tamara realised she had forgotten the sky, Tom echoed 'I've forgotten it as well' and coloured a broad patch of blue at the top of his paper saying, as he coloured round the sun, 'The sun's going, it's getting to the evening.' Examining the children's descriptions of their drawings (see Figures 2.7 and 2.8 for Tom's & Charlie's) they seem to form a pattern. Rather than a continuous narrative they follow the familiar naming of items format which Browne (1996) warns us against. Having said that, however, the dialogue between the two girls follows a similar path for there is no story as such, only a detailing of each item being drawn.

The combination of Charlie's narrative and drawing (Figure 2.8) tells us a great deal about his level of understanding. His van, drawn accurately with just two wheels visible, not only stands firmly on a road but the actual

Figure 2.5 Tamara, aged 5 years 1 month. 'That's the M45 [points to road]. That's a house with lots of people together. That's the sun and that's the moon and "Oh", I've forgotten something. I forgot the sky [starts to draw it as a blue line] now I've got to tell you about the sky. That's the sky.'

Figure 2.6 Shannon, aged 5 years and 4 months (no narrative offered).

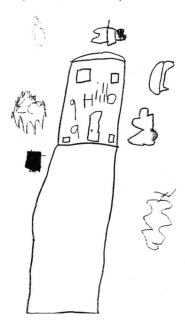

Figure 2.7 Tom, aged 5 years 8 months. 'The sun's going, it's getting to the evening' (as he adds the sky and the sun). Description: 'It's a house with the sky. A green door. That's a butterfly and that's a dog kennel' (points to each item as he speaks).

road is identified, as 40 (the M40 is the nearest motorway). Charlie's name appears on the side of the van as a reversal and one gets the impression of a potential storyline as the van heads away from his house (identified as number 10). Although it is possible to gain some insights, through observation, into the drawing's content, as Pahl (1999) states, so much more could be gained from a knowledge of the culture within which the child lives.

The dialogue between the other group of 5-year-olds followed a similar pattern. Haas Dyson (cited in Pahl, 1999, p. 4) in her studies of children of this age talks about the complexities of these discussions and how the children support each other, stimulating and extending their compositions. I could relate her findings to my study groups. However, there was a distinct difference in the way these two groups talked about their drawings once completed. Whereas the first group described their pictures, the second group offered definite storylines instead. Kress (1997) suggests that

Figure 2.8   Charlie, aged 5 years. 'A butterfly on the top of the house. There's a house underneath it. That's the van with my name on it and two letters. There's a door with number 10. There's a road under the van. There's a tree by the house. That's the sun on top of the tree. There's a cake on top of the house and that's all.'

children typically produce a stage set of figures and objects which serve as prompts for their verbal narrative; certainly one could read this group's drawings in this way. Melissa, whose drawing (Figure 2.9) conforms to Kellogg's human, vegetation and buildings groupings (1969, p. 114), uses the characters to 'tell a story', referring to all the items drawn: 'She's going to climb the tree to pick some blue berries and red berries and then she is going into the house to put her berries in the basket and then she's going to pick some flowers to put as decoration in her bedroom.'

The 6-year-olds

Observations of the 6-year-olds again showed a brisk exchange of ideas after an initial stating of intention. Unlike the last two groups, the two boys dominated the conversation, with contributions from the girls. As they started, Daniel stated that 'girls draw the same things boys draw the same' which in this instant was true, for the girls focused upon house and pictures and the boys on Pokémon characters. The two boys worked closely, naming characters, singing songs and discussing the features of each one. They seemed to be entering into the spirit of the drawing, making appropriate noises and movements, thereby dramatising their creation. Once again the

Figure 2.9 Melissa, aged 5 years 9 months. 'She's going to climb the tree to pick some blue berries and red berries and then she is going into the house to put her berries in the basket and then she's going to pick some flowers to put as decoration in her bedroom.'

dialogue was more involved than the description given at the picture's completion. The following extract gives a flavour of their discussion and comes halfway through the session.

Craig:	I'm going to draw Charzard.
Daniel:	He's the biggest one.
Craig:	Mine's saying Charzard come here. Charzard has a really, really long tail.
Daniel:	He has such a long tail doesn't he?
Daniel:	Yes, but he has a really fat tail.
Craig:	Pikachu is really, really little.
Daniel:	Do some fire on his tail.
Craig:	He has fire in his mouth.
Daniel:	I'm going to do Charzard red. Who's that one who is red?
Craig:	Oh, that's the baby Charzard. Right here comes the fire! [*draws fire*] Here's the baby, the baby can't fly, can he?
Daniel:	I like the baby Charzard
Jodie:	The baby has fire, doesn't he?
Craig:	No, the baby Charzard doesn't.

Compare this with Craig's description of his drawing which he gave as he was adding the last figure:

> Pikachu's in it, Charzard and there's going to be Baby Charzard and Squirtle and I'm going to have one more and that's called Charmander. I'm going to do one more and that's going to be Bulbasaur.

and Daniel's comment: 'Mine's the same as Craig's.'

Although one of the girls offered a similar descriptive passage, the other girl whose picture showed an awareness of composition indicated the beginnings of a storyline (Figure 2.10) with:

> A cottage in the wood, and some mountains in the distance and there's the stars cos it's night-time. There's a rabbit popping out of his hole.

The picture itself was interesting for the way it had been laid out, as it took the observer's eye straight along the path to the house whilst the surrounding dark blue focused the action on the lighter central area. The black and white version does not do the drawing justice for the stars and moon, both essential elements, are yellow – a colour that will not reproduce in this circumstance. It felt as if Jodie was not only beginning to understand composition but also had a sense of an audience, seeking to involve the viewer in her story. Such supposition, of course, can only be raised as an idea, for without knowledge of her background and many more observations it is impossible to draw more positive conclusions.

Figure 2.10   **Jodie, aged 6 years 6 months. 'A cottage in the wood and some mountains in the distance and there's the stars cos it's night-time. There's a rabbit popping out of his hole.'**

The 7-year-olds

The last group to be observed again consisted of two girls and two boys. These were in their last year in the infant department and would be moving to the other side of the building housing the junior children after the summer break. To begin with, the children drew in silence, Matthew taking his inspiration from a circus poster on the wall, including a clown and a cannon in his drawing. The cannon obviously triggered a memory for him since his last comment: 'Sam, I do like the gun on fire, like the boy who set the cannon on fire' started a long discussion about Florence Nightingale, a drummer boy and how cannon balls can shoot your legs off. Conversation was sporadic and although occasionally it focused upon the drawings, generally the talk was about issues related to television, guns and James Bond. Although all four children had chosen to draw they seemed to treat this as an opportunity to socialise rather than concentrate on the activity. This was reflected to a certain extent in the finished pictures and descriptions, which lacked the detail and depth of content of those produced by most of the younger children. Again, a series of observations might have contradicted this but, given the prescriptive nature of the curriculum generally offered to 7-year-old children in the English school system, it seems a reasonable assumption. Gentle (1985) suggests that by the age of 7 children are able to stand back from their experiences; their drawings may register this change in their seeing and thinking. By this age, too, many children have become critical of their attempts at representation, aware that they fall short of the real object, and this can have the effect of inhibiting them. Two of the completed pictures were of clowns juggling from the circus poster, but whereas Evie included a flower and butterfly with the clown in the foreground, Matthew (Figure 2.11) placed the clowns in context and explained the action happening in his picture. Both Matthew and Sam (Figure 2.12) included speech in their drawing and their narrative shows an element of wit, with Matthew's 'help me' as he shows a person flying in the air after touching the hot cannon and Sam's monkey in the tree saying 'hello' to the panda as he walks past.

Sam's drawing is very regimented, with the three trees set at intervals and the pandas spaced carefully between – again, one might suggest, relating to the stage set referred to by Kress (1997). The technique Sam used in his drawing of the trees was very different from the way any of the other children attempted them. He started by drawing brown blocks one on top of the other until Matthew asked what they were and suggested, 'If you put a top on them it could be a trampoline'. Sam then proceeded to put green ball shapes on the top and responded to Matthew's 'What is that?' with 'They're trees.' It seemed that everything he did was very deliberate and he spent time thinking about each aspect before drawing it.

Sophie, the fourth member of this group was noticeably quiet throughout the session and her drawing was quite different. Her picture (Figure 2.13) was dominated by two arched doors. These, she said, were part of the old

Figure 2.11 Matthew, aged 7 years 8 months. 'He says "help me". He files in the air because he touched the cannon and it's on fire. They're the people [points to faces]. They're the only ones you can see.'

Figure 2.12 Sam, aged 7 years 8 months. 'They're panda bears going for a walk in the woods. There's a monkey up in the tree saying "hello".'

Figure 2.13 Sophie, aged 7 years 9 months, 'I'm drawing the old school. That's Mrs Chapman's and that's Mrs Harrison's.'

school and she named the teachers who had classes there. Whether this draw-ing was a result of her imminent move to the juniors or whether a sibling was about to go into one of these classes it is difficult to know. Without more knowledge of Sophie one can only surmise but the old building is a promi-nent part of the school and houses the two oldest classes.

Concluding discussion

Despite the fact that this was only a small-scale study, the children's drawings and accompanying narrative offered tantalising glimpses of their differing approaches. The progression through drawing styles from figures, houses and vegetation to culturally specific objects such as Pokémon, school build-ings and motorways gives credence to the findings of Kellogg so many years ago and shows why her work is still important. There did appear to be a change in the accompanying narrative as the age group changed. The youngest children communicated to themselves as they worked through their drawings and there seemed to be a definite link between the direction these took and this self-talk. One of the most obvious and frequent findings was the descriptive nature of the children's narratives about their com-pleted pictures. It did seem as though they were working to a particular formula similar to that referred to by Browne (1996) and one which they had realised was acceptable to adults. There were instances, however, where a real storyline emerged and the drawing could be seen to illustrate and enhance this. This was not necessarily restricted to the older children;

although the 7-year-olds did seem to have moved away from the descriptive, one group of 5-year-olds also told stories in relation to their pictures. As all these children were firmly established in the school system this might have something to do with teacher expectation, as the two groups of 5-year-olds were from different schools. The other common feature of these groups of children was their interaction, following the pattern described by both Kress (1997) and Haas Dyson (cited in Pahl, 1999). There was evidence of the stated intention and the influence of peers altering both content and direction of drawings. There were also occasions when the children's enthusiasm for their characters (in particular Craig and Daniel's drawings of Pokémon) led to dramatisation, as sounds and movements were introduced into the conversation.

As an exploratory study, observation of these children highlighted many areas for future research. Talk and drawing certainly did seem to go hand in hand but it seemed that the self-talk of the 4-year-olds added an extra dimension which would bear closer scrutiny. At what point do children move away from this communication form to the interactive peer discussions and will there be evidence of emergent writing as they become more aware of the print around them? Will there be progression through humans, animals, buildings and vegetation, as Kellogg suggests? The questions are countless and such a small study can only hope to raise more rather than give soundly based answers.

References

Browne, A. (1996) *Developing Language and Literacy 3–8*, London, Paul Chapman.

Coates, E. (1993) 'The language of appreciation through talking and making'. *Educational Review*, **45**(3), pp. 251–252.

Cooke, G., Griffin, D. & Cox, M. (1998) *Teaching Young Children to Draw*, London, Falmer Press.

Cox, M. (1992) *Children's Drawings*, Harmondsworth, Penguin.

Duffy, B. (1998) *Supporting Creativity and Imagination in the Early Years*, Buckingham, Open University Press.

Gentle, K. (1985) *Children and Art Teaching*, London, Croom Helm.

Goodnow, J. (1977) *Children's Drawing*, Oxford, Fontana.

Jameson, K. (1968) *Pre-school and Infant Art*, London, Studio Vista.

Kellogg, R. (1955) *What Children Scribble and Why*, Palo Alto, N.P. Publications.

Kellogg, R. (1969) *Analyzing Children's Art*, Palo Alto, National Books.

Kress, G. (1997) *Before Writing: Rethinking the paths to literacy*, London, Routledge.

Malchiodi, C. (1998) *Understanding Children's Drawings*, London, Jessica Kingsley.

Matthews, J. (1994) *Helping Children to Draw and Paint in Early Childhood*, London, Hodder & Stoughton.

Nutbrown, C. (1999) *Threads of Thinking*, 2nd edn, London, Paul Chapman.

Pahl, K. (1999) *Transformations*, Stoke, Trentham Books.

Commentary: Elizabeth Coates

Starting points

For the past fifteen years I have worked at the University of Warwick, Institute of Education as a Lecturer in Education. My interest in the 0–8-year-old age group arose from many years spent as an infant teacher in Birmingham working mainly with reception age children.

Throughout my adult life I have been interested in the twin strands of art and language. While working with children who were just beginning to write I found instances of self-talk as they wrote a few words, read them back, added a couple of words and then wrote them down, carrying on in this fashion until the sentences were complete. Their concentration was intense and this 'thinking aloud' process provided real insights, not only into the way sentences were constructed but also into the decision making about the actual content.

Observing teacher training students in nursery and reception classes gave me an opportunity to watch children drawing. Many of them talked steadily as they drew, sometimes to each other but more often to themselves. Was it possible that the talk was a rehearsal for the drawing? Would it tell the listener the story behind the drawing or the thought process that the child was going through as the drawing took shape? The tradition of children dictating a sentence to be written by a practitioner under the drawing has always seemed limiting, both in terms of the time afforded to each child and in the ephemeral nature of the child's interest. The actual completion of the drawing seems sufficient for most young children, and one might question whether they really want to stop and talk about it or move on to something new. It was these dilemmas which caught my interest – particularly when I observed children laboriously working on a picture, muttering furiously all the time, only to look blankly at the adult who asked about the end product.

Formulation of hypothesis/research questions

A study like this begins because the researcher is curious, wants to know how, why and what if; the motivation to do this work coming from within oneself rather than from outside funding or commissioning agencies. Reflecting upon my classroom observations, I began to speculate: what did I really want to find out and, given that my abiding interest lay in the links between language and drawing, how was I going to set out to satisfy my curiosity? The following hypothesis became the starting point for the study:

Talk when young children are drawing is inextricably linked to it, telling its story and dictating its content.

From this it became possible to formulate research questions, although these were refined at the writing-up stage and new ones suggested.

- Was the child's talk a rehearsal for each stage of the drawing?
- Did the talk tell the story behind the drawing?
- How different was the child's description of the completed drawing from the talk which accompanied the activity?

Early thinking processes

If I was to be able to test my hypothesis then I required schools where children had the opportunity to undertake free drawing rather than operating solely under the restrictions of the Literacy or Numeracy Hour. I opted for schools where I had already worked as a link tutor. This had another advantage in that head and class teachers knew me and were sympathetic to my request.

The three school settings all had free drawing and writing areas, therefore the decision about which children I observed was not mine but depended on which children chose to work there. The tables contained materials for a group of four to draw together. The crowded nature of the average classroom makes it difficult to be unobtrusive as an observer so the early part of each morning was spent just being in the room in the hope that this would make me seem less of an outsider.

As anyone familiar with infant or nursery classrooms will know, the introduction of a video camera causes maximum disruption, whilst tape recorders pick up so much extraneous sound that it is often difficult to distinguish who is talking, particularly if the children in question are unfamiliar to you. With this in mind, it seemed more appropriate to make notes since this also allowed for information about the drawing sequence and interaction to be recorded.

Methodology

I had two purposes in mind as I approached the research: one major, that of conducting a pilot, the other minor, but equally interesting to me, of exploring the possibilities of the issues involved. It has always seemed to me that definitions of research terminology vary according to the individual and even texts which focus upon such areas do not always agree on the finer points.

Aspect one: The pilot

Having formulated a hypothesis and identified initial research questions the reality of project design and selecting appropriate methods had to be addressed. I was using the pilot to tell me several things:

- Would a free drawing area within each classroom generate sufficient interest to ensure children came and worked there?
- Would observer notes provide enough information to enable the research questions to be adequately addressed?
- Was it possible for an observer to make accurate notes of all the children's narratives or would a tape recorder give a better result?
- Was the qualitative form of analysis the most appropriate one to use?
- How did one elicit narrative from the children about their finished product?
- And most importantly, was there sufficient mileage in the hypothesis to make a large scale project worthwhile?

I regarded the pilot as a means of testing the nuts and bolts relating to the research framework.

Aspect two: The exploratory

This aspect explores the issues surrounding the project. It suggests further possibilities or different directions a larger project might take. As well as testing the hypothesis it raises questions such as 'Yes, that is happening but have you thought about...?' or 'I hadn't realised that might occur, should I extend my research to include it?' Through considering the observations, notes made and other data collected, and revisiting the initial research questions, it is possible, through what I consider to be an exploratory study, to revise one's thinking and redefine the focus of the next stage.

Qualitative methods and data collection

With such a small sample and the nature of the task being undertaken it seemed that a qualitative approach was the only feasible method to use. If the aim of the research method is to gain as full and rich a picture of what is happening as possible then making anecdotal observation notes should provide valuable information. This type of note taking also allows for the inclusion of the unexpected, which may have a bearing on the interpretation of data collected. Initially though it was consideration of the hypothesis and the identified research questions which drove the choice of method.

A real concern that arises with qualitative research, especially when there is such a close focus on a relatively small number of children, relates to ethical issues. Whose permission do you need to undertake this kind of observation and if you explain to the children exactly what you are doing will they really understand? My initial approach was to the schools concerned, explaining what I wanted to do and how I was intending to do it. Through the head teachers, parents were informed that I was going to be in the class and that their children might be involved in my research, the nature of which was also explained. Because it was stressed that this was not a 'test' and in no way was judgmental, the reaction of parents was that of interest and no problems arose. I promised to give copies of any papers prepared for publication to the schools to vet before submission to a journal was made. This was done and teachers provided valuable feedback. Violating the children's space is an ethical issue that I found more difficult to solve. It was another reason not to use video or audio tape recording, because note taking allowed for some behaviour/interactions to be ignored and made it possible for the children to remain anonymous. If they asked me what I was doing then I explained but I did not tell them beforehand since I thought that might affect their inter-actions. Seeking permission to keep the children's drawings was done in conversation when they were describing their pictures to me and they were also asked if I might share them with other people.

At the end of the research I was left with three sets of data for each child:

- the interaction/narrative taking place during the drawing process;
- the finished drawing;
- the description of the completed work.

Because of the small number involved, the most obvious way forward was to examine everything, separating data into age-specific sections. Starting with the youngest children, I collated all their material and analysed it to build up a picture of what had happened during their drawing episodes. As I pro-gressed through the age groups, reconstructing scenarios, the work became more and more fascinating as differences appeared: the self-talk of the 4-year-olds giving way to dialogue with the 5- and 6-year-olds and on to the often 'off-task' interaction of the 7-year-olds. The analysis sought to address the research questions which focused upon the relationship between them.

Drawing conclusions and writing up

Reading through the data analysis and cogitating upon the literature I had examined as a prerequisite for this research, there seemed to be support for my hypothesis, which encouraged me to consider the next stage. There were some surprises, particularly in the clear demarcation between the dialogue and the drawings of the 7-year-olds and the difference in emphasis between the 4-year-olds and the next age group. On reflection, this was to be expected but really highlights the need for a much larger sample to be examined. There were frustrations too, mainly in relation to time constraints: I knew that a series of observations in each school would have enabled more sustainable conclusions to be drawn; but also in terms of interruptions from other pupils or staff which disturbed the children's concentration.

The writing-up process offers the writer an opportunity to think deeply about what they have done and throws up issues for future consideration. How does one set about writing this kind of paper? In my case I always start with a plan, reflecting upon the sequence of events, and how to offer the reader sufficient insights into the underlying research process to enable them to understand my thinking. To this end I feel that it is important to set a context by surveying relevant literature and discussing related issues. This provides evidence of the reasoning underlying the research hypothesis and leads smoothly on to the study itself whilst also furnishing material for the concluding discussion. Inevitably this process led to a reappraisal of my research questions, although the initial hypothesis still holds.

Where to next?

The next project is still in the planning stage but is likely to have two main strands:

- observation of free drawing areas within Foundation Stage classrooms over the period of a year – focusing upon drawing and accompanying narrative;
- the development of children's drawing from 3 to 5 years old – a longitudinal study following a class of children from their arrival in the nursery setting through to their move into Key Stage One. This will include noting evidence of emergent writing.

Hindsight reflections

Looking back on this study, I realise that I am now more committed to extending the research. I do regret that time and work constraints limited what I could actually carry out but the value of running a small scale pilot project as a precursor to further work is immeasurable.

3 How Do Deaf Infants Attain First Signs?
WATARU TAKEI

This paper was originally published as Takei, W. (2001) 'How do deaf infants attain first signs?' *Developmental Science*, **4**: 71–78.

Abstract

In this study the development and alternation of nonreferential gestures were examined longitudinally in terms of the acquisition of Japanese sign language. Parent–child free-play sessions in their home were videotaped at every monthly visit. Hand activities produced by two deaf infants of deaf parents are described and analyzed. Nonreferential gestures were observed frequently just before the occurrences of the first signs. They consisted of many rhythmic and repetitious movements. Nonreferential gestures became more complex and the number of them also increased as infants grew up. The comparison of nonreferential gestures and first signs revealed the continuity between them in terms of movements. In conclusion, nonreferential gestures are equivalent to a manual analog of vocal babbling.

Introduction

Japanese sign language (JSL) is a visual-gestural language created by deaf people and used by approximately 200,000–300,000 Japanese of all ages. It is evident from many linguistic studies that sign language is a fully grammaticized language, not a pantomimic communication system (Klima & Bellugi, 1979; Wilbur, 1987). Sign language is in many ways like spoken language in its acquisition, and in its role as a purveyor of identity, values and information. It is, of course, different in its form. Spoken Japanese and JSL are quite different: e.g. one makes audible words using the small muscles and articulators of the mouth and throat; the other makes visible words by moving the larger articulators of the limbs and body in space.

The acquisition of sign language in deaf infants of deaf parents occurs just as does the acquisition of spoken language by hearing infants of hearing parents with the same maturation timetable (Abrahamsen, Cavallo & McCluer, 1985;

Newport & Meier, 1985; Meier, 1991). First recognizable signs in deaf infants of deaf parents emerge from 8 months to 12 months, and two-sign combinations are produced at about 18 months. The course of sign language acquisition parallels very closely that of spoken language after the emergence of first words or signs.

In the case of spoken language, vocal babbling is observed before infants are able to utter recognizable words. How about the case of sign language? It is difficult to believe that deaf infants instantly produce first signs without any preparation. Deaf infants should be doing something to attain early expressive milestones before the occurrence of first signs.

Prinz and Prinz (1979) observed a hearing infant who had a deaf mother from 7 months to 21 months. The infant exhibited a type of manual babbling behavior in that she would wave her hands around in apparent imitation of signs produced by her parents. Griffith (1985) also reported the existence of manual babbling in a hearing infant who had deaf parents in transition from a prelexical to a lexical form in both speech and sign mode. The infant clapped and rubbed his hands in a circular motion while the investigator and his mother conversed in sign and speech and watched him. But neither Prinz and Prinz nor Griffith revealed details on manual babbling such as its phonological aspects, its qualitative alternations or continuation to first signs.

Petitto and Marentette (1991) were the first to report a manual analog of vocal babbling systematically. They described and analyzed manual activities of five infants. Two of the five were deaf infants of deaf parents; the rest were hearing infants with no exposure to sign language. Data were collected from the five participants at 10, 12 and 14 months. From this study, Petitto and Marentette came up with their definition of manual babbling, which is as follows. Manual babbling (a) was produced with a subset of combinational units that were members of the phonetic inventory of sign language, (b) demonstrated syllabic organization seen only in sign language, and (c) was produced without meaning or reference. It is interesting that manual babbling was reported to occur in deaf infants exposed to sign language much more frequently than in hearing infants. Petitto and Marentette concluded that manual babbling is a product of amodal brain-based language capacity.

However, one question arises. If manual babbling is innate, both deaf and hearing infants should show it in the same quantities and qualities. Otherwise, manual babbling must be influenced by linguistic input and not be a pure product of brain-based language capacity.

Other researchers, Meier and Willerman (1995), doubted whether manual babbling of deaf infants was different from that of hearing infants. They videotaped three deaf girls and two hearing boys at 2-week intervals from 7 months to 15 months. The children's manual activities were divided into three basic categories: (a) communicative and/or meaningful gestures such as points, reaches, waves and symbolic gestures; (b) gestures that on the basis of both form and usage can be identified as signs of American Sign

Language (ASL); and (c) meaningless, nonreferential gestures. The class of nonreferential gestures may turn out to be a superset of the class of canonical manual babbles. Results revealed that there was no sharp distinction between the deaf and hearing groups in the overall proportion of nonreferential gestures used out of the whole set of gestures. However, all three deaf infants used a higher proportion of multicycle, nonreferential gestures than their hearing counterparts. The crucial point here is what deaf infants do so as to produce the first signs.

The present paper describes the acquisition processes of JSL as a first language by two deaf infants of deaf parents, focusing on the prelinguistic and one-word stages.

Method

Participants

The participants were two deaf infants of deaf parents. One was a girl (participant A), the other was a boy (participant B). JSL was the principal means of communication within their home. Both infants had been receiving JSL input from their parents since they were born. Participants A and B began their participation at 5 months and 7 months of age, respectively. Participant B had an older brother who was also deaf. Table 3.1 shows the descriptions of participants and details of observations.

Table 3.1   Description of participants

Participant	Sex	Birth order	Number of visits	Child's age at home visit (months : days)
A	Female	1st	11	4:28 6:10 6:25 7:29 8:12 9:25 10:23 11:20 12:18 13:21 15:3
B	Male	2nd	8	7:26 8:25 9:22 10:18 11:24 13:1 14:7 15:20

Procedure

The major source of data was observations during monthly home visits, each of which lasted about an hour. When the researcher started observations, neither of the infants had produced signs or nonlinguistic communicative gestures.

Parent–child free-play sessions were videotaped in their home at every visit. To prevent the infants from being nervous, toys and books with which the infants were accustomed to playing were used. The sessions of participant A occurred for a total of 11 visits and of participant B for 8 visits.

After free-play sessions, the parents were asked what the infants had done during the past month. Interviews with the parents enhanced my knowledge of the signs and communicative gestures produced by the infants.

Scoring

All hand activities produced by participants A and B were transcribed and divided into the following four basic categories.

(a) *Signs:* gestures that can be identified as JSL signs on the basis of both form and content.

(b) *Communicative gestures:* gestures that are used communicatively and stand for objects, people, places and the like in the surroundings. Communicative gestures consist of three subcategories: (b–1) reaching, (b–2) pointing and (b–3) symbolic gesture. Reaching is an activity of unsuccessful direct attempts to grasp or reach for an object, but it also includes a gesture that stands for request or demand. Pointing is a deictic gesture produced with index finger extended, to single out objects, people and places. Symbolic gesture is the stylized pantomime whose iconic forms varied with the intended meaning of each gesture. Gestures that not only deaf but also hearing infants usually use, such as 'Bye-bye' or 'Give it to me', were coded as symbolic gestures.

(c) *Manipulating:* hand motions to grasp or handle an object. It included playing with toys. Manipulating has two subcategories: (c–1) manipulating and (c–2) giving.

(d) *Nonreferential gestures:* gestures that elude semantic interpretation. Nonreferential gestures may be produced in a communicative context of parent–child interaction, but no meaning or reference can be assigned to them. It is likely that nonreferential gestures contain manual babbling, as suggested by Petitto and Marentette (1991). In this study, however, a category of 'manual babbling' was not used because precise phonetic criteria for identifying manual babbling are very difficult to determine. It is questionable whether the definition of babbling in the vocal mode can be applied to that in the manual mode. I decided to use the wider category of 'nonreferential gestures', which is the rest excluding (a) signs, (b) communicative gestures and (c) manipulating.

All of the hand activities were transcribed by two independent coders. The agreement between them averaged 89%.

After making transcriptions of all hand activities, the precise physical forms of nonreferential gestures produced by the infants were coded with symbols that represented internal features of the hand or hands, such as their handshapes and location in space. Movement of the hand or hands was also coded, and it was analyzed to examine how many times it was repeated.

Results

Sign and nonreferential gesture

Figures 3.1 and 3.2 show the number of signs, symbolic gestures and non-referential gestures produced by participants A and B as a function of age. Participant A was found to produce her first recognizable signs at 11 months. Participant B's first sign production occurred at 13 months. In large-scale studies of children's spoken language development, it was reported that the appearance of the first spoken word occurred at 11–14 months (Capute et al., 1986). Participants in this study attained their first sign in accordance with the timetable for hearing infants.

In the case of participant A, nonreferential gestures started to be observed at 7 months. There was a gradual increase to 10 months, but the frequency of them rapidly declined after 10 months. Interestingly, participant A's first signs occurred just after the decrease of nonreferential gestures. Participant B started to express nonreferential gestures at 7 months. There was a slight increase to 10 months and the number of nonreferential gestures gradually declined except at 14 months. Participant B produced first signs at 14 months. Participant B also produced nonreferential gestures frequently before the onset of signs.

Hearing infants begin to produce syllabic vocal babbling between 6 and 10 months of age (Oller, 1986; Oller & Eilers, 1988). Both participants A and B also began to produce nonreferential gestures during that time.

There was a second marked increase in the frequency of nonreferential gestures in both participants A and B at the onset of signs. Nonreferential gestures produced at and after the onset of signs included some sign-like features, which are different from previous ones in two respects. First, frequencies of nonreferential gestures were not so high, but each nonreferential gesture had many movement cycles. Second, the infants looked at their parents after the production of nonreferential gestures. These features were present in nonreferential gestures that were produced with signs, not in nonreferential gestures produced before the infants produced signs.

Qualitative alternations of nonreferential gestures will be examined next.

Handshape in the nonreferential gestures

Figure 3.3 indicates the handshape repertory of nonreferential gestures produced by participants A and B. Seven handshapes were observed in

Figure 3.1   Number of nonreferential gestures and signs in participant A (age along the horizontal axis is given in years: months: days).

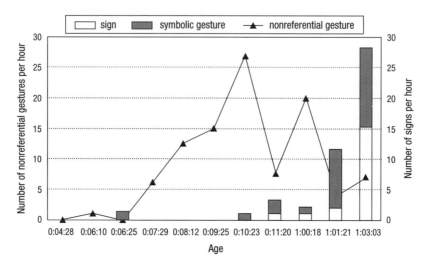

Figure 3.2   Number of nonreferential gestures and signs in participant B (age along the horizontal axis is given in years: months: days).

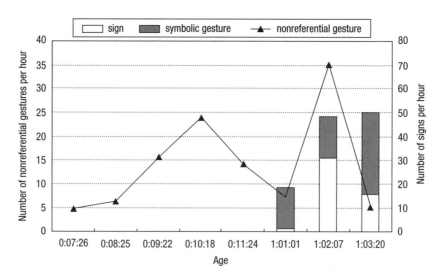

nonreferential gestures produced by participant A and five handshapes were observed in those produced by participant B. Flat hand (B handshape) was used 75% of the time. The participants in this study were probably able to perform all these handshapes before they were ready to start symbolic communication.

Figure 3.3   **Handshape repertory of nonreferential gestures produced by participants (Ø indicates a category of nonreferential gesture in which handshapes were not involved e.g. head nodding).**

	Type of Handshape	Participant A	Participant B
B		75%	75%
b0		11%	2%
A		9%	8%
B←→A		2%	3%
G		1%	3%
E		1%	0%
C		1%	0%
Ø		0%	8%
		100%	100%

Movement in the nonreferential gestures

Figure 3.4 shows movements used in nonreferential gestures which were observed more than twice at each month of age with participants A and B. In the case of participant A, the infant used the 'banging' movements and 'up and down' movements at the age of 8 months. At about 10 months, 'right and left' movements and 'clapping' were added to the movement repertoire of nonreferential gestures. After 12 months, she produced many different movements in nonreferential gestures. For example, she used 'elbow rotation', 'up and down movement with linking hands' and so on. These are often observed in signs of JSL. Nonreferential gestures produced after 12 months of age looked like self-talk in the manual mode, but it was hard to interpret their meaning. In the case of participant B, 'banging' and 'right and left' movements were often observed in nonreferential gestures

Figure 3.4   Movement repertory of nonreferential gestures produced by participants (○ and ● indicate that each type of movement was observed more than twice at that age).

Type of Movement	Participants	7	8	9	10	11	12	13	14	15
Banging	A	●	●		●			●		
	B		○	○	○	○				
Up and down	A		●	●	●	●	●	●		●
movement	B				○			○		
Right and left	A			●	●	●	●	●		●
movement	B	○		○	○	○		○	○	
Clapping	A			●	●	●				
	B					○		○	○	
Wrist flexing	A				●					
	B									
Forward and	A				●		●			
backward movement	B			○					○	
Up/down movement	A				●		●			
with hands linking	B									
Elbow rotation	A				●	●	●			●
	B									
Face touching	A									
	B							○	○	○
Stamping	A									
	B					○		○	○	○

before 12 months of age. In addition to these movements, the infant started to produce 'face touching' and 'stamping' movements after 12 months, which are more complex than previous movements observed.

As the infants grew up, movements used in nonreferential gestures got more complex and varied. Movements observed at an early stage were produced by using only a shoulder joint like 'banging' movements and 'up and down' movements. But movements observed after 12 months needed to use not only shoulder joints but also an elbow-wrist and finger joint like 'elbow rotation' movements and 'face touching' movements. In other words, the participants evolved from nonreferential gestures constructed from large movements to ones that needed fine adjustments.

Repetition of movement in the nonreferential gestures

Some of the nonreferential gestures produced by participants A and B had repeated movement. Figures 3.5 and 3.6 indicate the mean number of movement cycles comprising the nonreferential gestures of participants A and B. The average number of movement cycles rose sharply until 9 months and gradually declined after 10 months in nonreferential gestures produced by participants A and B. In the case of participant B, the average number of movement cycles rose slightly until 11 months and decreased gradually except at 7 months. All nonreferential gestures produced at 7 months were 'banging' gestures, which usually had many movement cycles.

Figure 3.5 Average of movement cycles in nonreferential gestures produced by participant A (age along the horizontal axis is given in years: months: days).

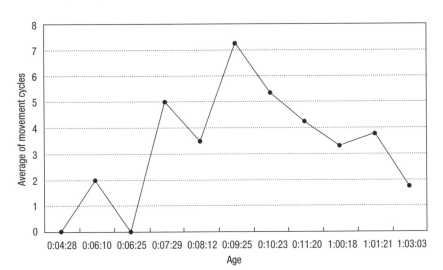

The maximum number of cycles in a nonreferential gesture was 17. Meier and Willerman (1995) reported that deaf infants showed a higher proportion of multicycle, nonreferential gestures than their hearing counterparts. The participants in this study also showed great cyclicity of nonreferential gestures. Nonreferential gestures with highly multicycle movement were observed just before the infants produced first signs. The linguistic environment may help multicycle nonreferential gestures. Multicycle nonreferential gestures influenced by linguistic input may perhaps contribute to the production of first signs.

Continuity between nonreferential gestures and signs

Participant A had attained a vocabulary of seven different signs by 15 months. They were as follows: NONE, DELICIOUS, EAT, CAR, DRINK, FINISH and SLEEP. All the handshapes produced by the participant in signs had been observed in nonreferential gestures before. But most of the handshapes in signs were flat hand (B handshape). Handshapes in signs did not necessarily play an important role in conveying the meaning for young infants because flat hand was not made consciously but naturally.

In the case of participant A, there were similarities between nonreferential gestures and signs especially in the component of movement. Participant A produced signs for DELICIOUS and NONE at 15 months. Those signs consisted of right and left movement, which was observed frequently in nonreferential gestures at about 10 months.

Figure 3.6 **Average of movement cycles in nonreferential gestures produced by participant B (age along the horizontal axis is given in years: months: days).**

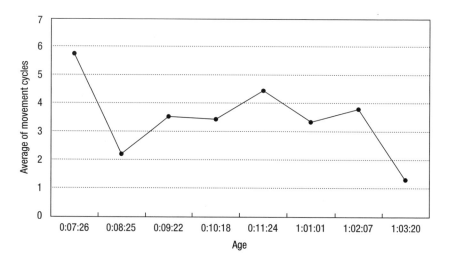

There are several other examples. Participant B had attained a vocabulary of nine different signs by 15 months. They were EAT, BIRD, DOG, HOT, DANGEROUS, ONCE AGAIN, FEARFUL, FINISH and ME. Participant B produced the sign for ME, which was expressed by pointing to the signer's nose, when he was 15 months old. Before the production of signs, similar movements, namely touching his temple with his index finger repeatedly, were observed in nonreferential gestures. It is likely that nonreferential gestures with such movements were altered into the sign for ME.

The sign for CAR was produced when participant A saw a picture of cars in a book at 15 months. She used the elbow rotation movement in the sign. Elbow rotation movement was used as a component of nonreferential gestures before the onset of signs. Interestingly, her parents never used elbow rotation when they produced the sign for CAR to her. Figure 3.7 shows a nonreferential gesture using an elbow rotation movement, the sign for CAR produced by participant A and the adult sign for CAR. These illustrations suggest that deaf infants do not only imitate signs produced by their parents. It follows from what has been said that deaf infants select a movement from the limited movement repertory that they have already acquired to express the acts and objects to which they wish to refer.

Discussion

The study of the acquisition process in the prelinguistic stage has shown two features of nonreferential gestures produced by deaf infants exposed to sign

Figure 3.7   Example of similarity between nonreferential gesture and sign.

Nonreferential gesture	Participant A-produced sign	Adult sign
Elbow rotation	[CAR]	[CAR]

language. To begin with, nonreferential gestures were observed 3 or 4 months before the onset of signs. In the vocal mode, canonical babbling is observed a few months before the first word is produced. The relation between non-referential gestures and signs is quite similar to the case in the vocal mode. Next, nonreferential gestures consisted of multicycle movements. In other words, nonreferential gestures demonstrate the syllabic organization seen in sign language. Canonical vocal babbling is also characterized by syllabic organization. In these circumstances, we can be fairly certain that nonreferential gestures play the role of babbling in the manual mode and contribute to the onset of hands being used as a means of communication.

It is instructive to compare each component of nonreferential gestures with the phonetic inventory of adult JSL. Yonekawa (1984) suggested the number of primes in each parameter such as handshape, movement and location. Handshape, movement and location parameters were 21, 45 and 21, respectively. In the case of participant A, 29% of handshape (six of 21) and 53% of movement inventory (24/45) in adult JSL were used in non-referential gestures until participant A became 15 months old.

Petitto and Marentette (1991) showed that 32% of the handshape (13/40) and 54% of the movement that made up the phonetic inventory of adult ASL were observed in manual babbling, which is similar to the results in this study. Half of the movements in the phonetic inventory of adult sign language have already been used in meaningless, nonreferential gestures produced before the onset of signs.

Language has two features: form and content. It is likely that nonreferential gestures contribute to the acquisition of forms in sign.

This study examined hand activities of two deaf infants at the prelinguistic stage. The results showed that nonreferential gestures were produced before the onset of signs. The results also suggested that there was continuity between nonreferential gestures and first signs in terms of handshape and movement. Taken together, it is clear that nonreferential gestures serve as a manual analog of vocal babbling. We can say that babbling is not restricted to the vocal modality. It is, instead, an amodal phenomenon that helps infants to acquire the finite inventory of phonetic parameters in sign language such as handshape, movement and location. More data and studies about hearing and deaf infants without a sign language environment will support the results of this study.

Acknowledgements

This study was supported by a grant from the Ministry of Education, Science, Sports and Culture of Japan (H10–6822). I am grateful to the infants and their mothers for their participation in this study. I also thank Akira Yokkaichi, Sawa Saito and Takashi Torigoe for their valuable comments.

References

Abrahamsen, A., Cavallo, M.M. & McCluer, LA. (1985) Is the sign advantage a robust phenomenon? From gesture to language in two modalities. *Merrill-Palmer Quarterly*, **31**(2), 117–209.

Capute, A.J., Palmer, F.B., Shapiro, B.K., Wachtel, R.C., Schmidt, S. & Ross, A. (1986) Clinical linguistic and auditory milestone scale: prediction of cognition in infancy. *Developmental Medicine and Child Neurology*, **28**, 762–771.

Griffith, P.L. (1985) Mode-switching and mode-finding in a hearing child of deaf parents. *Sign Language Studies*, **48**, 195–222.

Klima, E. & Bellugi, U. (1979) *The signs of language*. Cambridge, MA: Harvard University Press.

Meier, R.P. (1991) Language acquisition by deaf children. *American Scientist*, **79**, 60–70.

Meier, R.P. & Willerman, R. (1995) Prelinguistic gesture in deaf and hearing infants. In K. Emmorey and J. Reilly (Eds), *Language, gesture and space* (pp. 391–409). Hillsdale, NJ: Erlbaum.

Newport, E.L. & Meier, R.P. (1985) The acquisition of American sign language. In D.I. Slobin (Ed.), *The cross linguistic study of language acquisition*, Vol. 1: *The data*. Hillsdale, NJ: Erlbaum.

Oller, D.K. (1986) Metaphonology and infant vocalization. In B. Lindblom & R. Zetterstrom (Eds), *Precursors of early speech*. New York: Stockton Press.

Oller, D.K. & Eilers, R.E. (1988) The role of audition in infant babbling. *Child Development*, **59**, 441–466.

Petitto, L.A. & Marentette, P.F. (1991) Babbling in the manual mode: evidence for the ontogeny of language. *Science*, **251**, 1493–1496.

Prinz, P.M. & Prinz, E.A. (1979) Simultaneous acquisition of ASL and spoken English: Phase 1: early lexical development. *Sign Language Studies*, **25**, 283–296.

Wilbur, R. (1987) *American sign language: Linguistic and applied dimensions*. Boston, MA: Little, Brown.

Yonekawa, A. (1984) *Shuwa gengo no kijutsuteki kenkyu* [*A descriptive study of Japanese Sign Language*]. Tokyo: Meiji-shoin.

How did I study the acquisition of sign language?

I wrote the paper 'How do deaf infants attain first signs?' in 2001 and in it reported some research from my doctoral dissertation. Recent linguistic research on the structure of sign languages has revealed that they are fully fledged languages, comparable to spoken language. However, in sign languages linguistic information is conveyed through movements of the hands, the face and the body and these movements are perceived visually by deaf people. The gestures in sign language, which are called 'signs', are a special set of rule-governed behaviours (Baker & Cokely, 1980). Sign languages are therefore often described as visual-gestural languages.

My interest in the acquisition process of Japanese Sign Language stemmed from personal experience. Although I can hear, both my parents are deaf and as a consequence Japanese Sign Language is one of my mother tongues, the other being spoken Japanese. I cannot remember anything about how I learned Japanese Sign Language and this prompted me to want to study the acquisition of sign language as a graduate student. I was also interested in the extent to which the ability to communicate and to use a language is innate. If language is a learned ability then deaf children will not be able to acquire the lexicon and syntax of sign language without appropriate teaching. However, if the ability to acquire language is innate then all that may be necessary is to provide deaf children with opportunities to communicate with others in sign. In order to explore these questions my colleagues and I investigated two deaf adults who had grown up with little contact with the Deaf community (Torigoe, Takei & Kimura, 1995; Torigoe & Takei, 2001). They lived on an isolated island which is part of the Okinawa Islands just south of mainland Japan. They had no access to a conventional sign language, such as Japanese Sign Language, but nevertheless communicated with one another and with familiar hearing people using a shared system of signs. This home sign system was established through interactions among the two deaf people, their hearing families and neighbours. No one taught the home sign system to the deaf people, but they used it fluently, and it looked like a conventional sign language. Clearly in the absence of spoken language these deaf adults had developed an alternative sign system, which supports the idea of an innate capacity for developing a communication system.

At the outset of my doctoral research I reviewed numerous studies on language acquisition and education for deaf children in order to find out what was already known. A great deal of effort has been put into investigating the acquisition of a spoken language by deaf infants and children. Most studies report that deaf infants and children have difficulty learning spoken language. However, other studies report that they have no difficulty in acquiring sign language because their access to the signed input is not limited.

Over the past few decades, a considerable number of studies have demonstrated that the acquisition of sign language in deaf infants and children follows much the same pattern as the acquisition of spoken language in hearing children. However, perhaps surprisingly, few studies have investigated the period before the first recognisable signs are produced. How deaf infants attain their first signs remains an unanswered question.

Hearing children produce vocal babbling before they utter recognisable words and I was interested in discovering whether something equivalent might be observed in deaf children. In order to investigate this I decided to observe deaf infants of deaf parents since such infants are usually raised in a sign language environment.

One of the problems with this approach is that it is hard to find deaf infants of deaf parents because 90% of deaf people have hearing parents. In other words, most individuals within the community of deaf people do not join deaf culture at birth, whereas hearing infants with hearing parents are exposed to spoken language from birth. One of the characteristics of sign languages in comparison to spoken languages is that they are often restricted to specific communities such as schools for the deaf.

Only 10% of deaf infants receive sign language input from birth. In order to answer my research question I had to find deaf infants with deaf parents before their first birthday. This was more difficult than we anticipated. Deaf children of 3 years old will never become one year old even though deaf children of one year surely become 3 years old. If you want to study the acquisition process of sign language, especially focusing on the period before the occurrence of the first signs, you must find the youngest deaf children possible.

I overcame this problem by finding deaf women who were going to have babies. The rationale was that although the babies might or might not be born deaf they would nevertheless be exposed to Japanese Sign Language and acquire it as their first language. I located four deaf couples who were going to have a baby. One couple were personal friends and the others were introduced to me by teachers who worked at the National School for the Deaf. They had graduated from the school for the deaf a few years before and married recently. I explained the aims of my research. I felt it was important to talk with them personally in their own language, Japanese Sign Language, rather than writing to them or talking to them through an interpreter and, given my background, I could obviously do this. Fortunately, all the couples were very cooperative.

All the parents agreed to participate in the study which involved me observing the mother and the infant interacting once a month. The research on the acquisition process of Japanese Sign Language focused on the period before the first signs appeared. Two of four infants were deaf and the rest could hear. In the paper 'How do deaf infants attain first signs?' I report the findings for the two deaf infants.

I chose the observational method for the study because I wanted to examine how the deaf infants and their parents interacted in a natural setting. I could have adopted an experimental method, but I rejected it for three reasons. First, it is difficult to collect longitudinal data using experiments since a technique which is appropriate at one age may be inappropriate at a different age, especially during the prelinguistic stage when development is so rapid. In my view, experiments are not suitable for capturing changes in development. Second, since only two deaf infants were available to participate in the study I felt that it would be difficult to draw any general conclusions from experimental results. It is true that the same criticism can apply to observational studies but an observational method enabled me to looked at changes over time using the same approach. Third, I felt that an experimental setting might be a burden to both the infants and parents.

I visited their homes every month and videotaped the parent–infant free play sessions without giving them any particular instruction. After videotaping, I talked informally with the parents. We talked about changes in the infants during the past month, experiences the infants had had, daily happenings and so on and these informed my observations.

After the two infants had been identified, the data could be collected with ease, but I was faced then with another difficult problem. Few researchers have observed and reported data on the manual babbling of deaf infants, and opinions are divided among researchers on how to define manual babbling. I could not, therefore, use existing definitions to distinguish manual babbling from other hand activities.

It was inconceivable to me that deaf infants would produce their first signs without any prior attempts to produce signs used by their parents. I was sure that there was a manual analogue of vocal babbling in deaf infants being reared within a sign language environment as they developed from a prelexical to a lexical stage. I transcribed all hand activities and assigned them to one of four categories: signs; communicative gestures; manipulating actions; and nonreferential gestures. Signs and communicative gestures are produced with some intention to convey something to another, such as a pointing gesture to request something. They are definitely not manual babbling. Manipulating actions are also different from manual babbling since such actions have the specific aim of, for example, playing with toys. Nonreferential gestures are hand activities that do not belong to the other three categories and are gestures that elude semantic interpretation. Manual babbling could be included in nonreferential gestures.

Video analysis of the hand activities of the participants was hard and stressful work. I watched the video data over and over again in order to transcribe and categorize the hand activities of the infants. I often checked the data repeatedly in slow motion. It took more than 20 hours to analyse one hour of video. There was no window in the room for the video analysis at the university. This meant that I could pay attention to analysing the data without anyone interrupting me, but the video analysis was exhausting when done for a long time. To make the analysis efficient and comfortable, I gave myself rewards such as a cup of coffee and listening to the band Aerosmith as frequently as once every 20 minutes. Thanks to numerous cups of coffee and Aerosmith, 19 tapes, 15 hours in all, were coded in two months. Then, I asked another graduate student who knew sign language to code the hand activities independently. The agreement between us was about 89%. When we disagreed we discussed the hand activity until we reached agreement. In a few cases we were unable to agree and these were discarded from the analysis.

The analysis produced some surprising results. Nonreferential gestures were often observed between 7 and 12 months. This period when deaf infants produced nonreferential gestures was almost the same as when hearing infants are producing vocal babbling. The occurrence of the first signs occurred at about the same time as the development of spoken language in hearing infants. A similarity between nonreferential gestures and the first signs was also observed. In addition, nonreferential gestures consisted of multicycle repetitive movements, similar to the characteristics of vocal babbling of hearing infants which have syllabic organisation like 'mama'.

This study is important because it shows that the acquisition process of sign language parallels the acquisition process of spoken language even before the first signs/words are produced.

When I delivered a paper on the manual babbling of deaf infants to a conference in 1998, I received many encouraging comments. This motivated me to write the paper, 'How do deaf infants attain first signs' for *Developmental Science*. It is important to report the findings of research in journals in order to disseminate the results. It is also a way of repaying the cooperation and kindness of the participants. The paper in *Developmental Science* is the first I have written in English. I am not a native speaker of English, so this was painful and difficult.

I continue to be interested in the question of why deaf infants of deaf parents produce nonreferential gestures. To answer this question, it is necessary to analyse the hand activities of hearing infants of deaf parents, deaf infants of hearing parents, and hearing infants of hearing parents. If nonreferential gestures are observed in deaf infants of hearing parents, the production of them may derive from the hearing loss and have nothing to do with sign language input. On the other hand, if they are found in hearing infants of deaf parents, signing to infants by deaf parents may encourage infants to produce them. It may also be possible to explore the origins of nonreferential gestures through study of hearing infants of hearing parents.

The production mechanism of nonreferential gestures can be explored by studying hearing infants of deaf parents and deaf infants of hearing parents. Having finished writing the paper on the deaf infants of deaf parents I am now analysing the data from hearing infants of deaf parents and hearing infants of hearing parents. 'How do deaf infants attain first signs?' is not an end, only a beginning.

References

Baker, C. & Cokely, D. (1980) *American sign Language: A teacher's resource text on grammar and culture.* Maryland: T. J. Publishers.

Torigoe, T. & Takei, W. (2001) A descriptive analysis of early word combinations in deaf children's signed utterances. *Japanese Psychological Research*, **43**, 156–161.

Torigoe, T., Takei, W. & Kimura, H. (1995) Deaf life in isolated Japanese island. *Sign Language Studies*, **87**, 167–174.

4 Social Cognition and Bullying: Social Inadequacy or Skilled Manipulation?
JON SUTTON, PETER SMITH AND JOHN SWETTENHAM

This paper is an abridged version of Sutton, J., Smith, P.K. & Swettenham, J. (1999) 'Social cognition and bullying: Social inadequacy or skilled manipulation?' *British Journal of Developmental Psychology*, **17**: 435–450.

Abstract

In contrast to the popular stereotype and research tradition of the 'oafish' bully lacking in social skills and understanding, the bully may be a cold, manipulative expert in social situations, organizing gangs and using subtle, indirect methods. Performance on a set of stories designed to assess understanding of cognitions and emotions was investigated in 193 7–10-year-olds in relation to their role in bullying. Ringleader bullies scored higher than 'follower' bullies (those who helped or supported the bully), victims and defenders of the victim. Results are discussed in terms of the need for further research into cognitive skills and emotion understanding in children who bully, the possible developmental pathway of social cognition in bullying and important implications for intervention strategies.

Introduction

As many as one in four primary school children in the UK report being bullied at least 'sometimes' during the last school term (Whitney & Smith, 1993). Although intervention projects have had some success (Olweus, 1993; Smith & Sharp, 1994), none of these school-based programmes have reduced bullying by more than about 50%. Evidence from individual schools and reports from teachers in such projects (e.g. Eslea & Smith, 1998) suggest that there are a 'hard core' of children who bully. Academics and practitioners may need to consider in more detail the cognitive style and skills associated with such persistent bullying or victimization. This study considers the social cognition or 'theory of mind' abilities of children involved in bullying: how well do they understand the mental states, beliefs and emotions of others?

It has been argued (Sutton, Smith & Swettenham, 1999) that despite the popular stereotype of a bully as physically powerful yet intellectually simple or backward, there is little empirical evidence to support this view. Randall (1997) claims that 'bullies do not process social information accurately' (p. 23), describing them as 'socially blind'. Hazler (1996) suggests that bullies 'need to recognize information about how others perceive the situation' (p. 98). But considering the social context and nature of bullying, it would seem plausible that many children who bully can actually process such social information very accurately, and they may use this skill to their advantage.

Sutton et al. (1999) argued that views of children who bully as lacking in social perspective-taking skills have not been based on empirical work involving bullies: instead, theory and equivocal evidence from research using aggressive or conduct-disordered children may have formed their basis. For example, the social skills model of aggression (Dodge et al., 1986; updated by Crick & Dodge, 1994) has been influential in explaining childhood aggression in terms of social information processing biases or deficits at one or more points in a five-stage process of assessing and responding to social situations: social perception, interpretation of social cues perceived, goal selection, response strategy generation and response decisions. Several studies have found that aggressive children tend to attribute hostile intent to the actions of others more frequently than do non-aggressive children (Feldman & Dodge, 1987; Gibbins & Craig, 1997; Guerra & Slaby, 1989; Steinberg & Dodge, 1983). However, Dodge (1991) distinguishes between reactive aggression (occurring in the context of a negatively affectively-charged, high conflict relationship) and proactive aggression (coercive behaviour observed in the domination of a peer), and hypothesises that 'the processing patterns at each step might be more strongly associated with one type of aggression than the other' (p. 211). Crick & Dodge (1996) note that proactive aggressors are not particularly vulnerable to attributional biases, and Boulton & Smith (1994) note that it is only proactive aggression that includes bullying.

A recently dominant paradigm in the study of social cognitive abilities is that of 'theory of mind': the ability of individuals to attribute mental states to themselves and others in order to explain and predict behaviour (Premack & Woodruff, 1978; for a recent review, see Taylor, 1996). Theory of mind has only recently been considered in relation to social maladjustment and anti-social behaviour. Thus, Happé & Frith (1996) found that children with conduct disorder passed two standard first-order false belief tasks but showed impairments of social insight in real life behaviour as measured by the Vineland Adaptive Behaviour Scale (Sparrow, Balla & Cicchetti, 1984).

Bullying can be defined as 'the systematic abuse of power' (Smith & Sharp, 1994). This inequality of power implies dominance, which is often associated with social skills and manipulation of belief. For example, Keating & Heltman (1994) found that pre-school children who deceived successfully also tended to be those who terrorised the playground and were rated as dominant.

Bullying occurs within social relationships (Lagerspetz, Bjorkqvist, Berts & King, 1982) and usually with peers present (Pepler & Craig, 1995). These peers may take on several roles, in addition to Bully and Victim: they may help the bully (Assistant), or reinforce the bully through watching, laughing and shouting encouragement (Reinforcer). Alternatively, they may stick up for the victim (Defender), or remain resolutely uninvolved (Outsider). Using this Participant Role Scale approach (PRS), Salmivalli, Lagerspetz, Bjorkqvist, Österman & Kaukiainen (1996) found that it was possible to assign one of these roles to 87% of 11 to 13-year-old Finnish children. Having a grasp of the internal mental states of those involved, along with an ability to manipulate these thoughts and beliefs, may be crucial for the bully in developing and maintaining such inter-role relations. A Bully would be at a social advantage if he or she were to possess social cognition skills that were superior to the Followers' (Assistants' and Reinforcers') and the Victims'.

The use of social cognition skills in bullying may also relate to the type of bullying. Indirect or relational forms of aggression (Crick & Grotpeter, 1995) such as social exclusion (Bjorkqvist, Lagerspetz & Kaukiainen, 1992) often require a manipulation of the mental states and beliefs of others in the form of gossip, rumours and lies. Indeed, indirect aggression has been found to be positively correlated with peer-rated social intelligence in groups of 8-, 12- and 14-year-olds, whereas physical and verbal aggression were not (Kaukiainen et al., 1999). Indirect bullying is also relatively more frequent in girls than boys (Bjorkqvist, Lagerspetz & Kaukiainen, 1992; Rivers & Smith, 1994), and a recent study found a theory of mind superiority among girls (Baron-Cohen & Hammer, 1996). In contrast, it may be that a theory of mind is not necessary for purely physical bullying: hitting or kicking someone would seem to be a non-mental event, and consequently one may not necessarily expect physical bullying to be related to theory of mind.

Sutton et al. (1999) suggested distinguishing different types of bullies, and measuring different aspects of theory of mind ability. In the present study the PRS approach was used in conjunction with social cognition measures to investigate the following hypotheses:

(a) that Bullies will score significantly higher than Victims on a set of stories measuring social cognition;

(b) that Bullies will score significantly higher than Followers (a combined group of Reinforcers and Assistants) on a set of stories measuring social cognition; and

(c) that extent of teacher-rated indirect bullying will be positively correlated with total social cognition score when physical and verbal bullying are partialled out.

The study intends to discriminate clearly between two alternative predictions. The social skills deficit model (Crick & Dodge, 1994) should predict that bullies would score lower than other children on theory of mind tasks; this would follow from the view of deficits and biases in perceiving and interpreting the situation, and choosing and reporting responses to it. By contrast, the present authors' prediction is that on a test of theory of mind, Ringleader Bullies would score higher than Followers (hypothesis A) or Victims (hypothesis B), and possibly higher than non-involved children.

Method

Participants

The authors approached all the children in eight classes from four south-east London schools, a total sample pool of 206. Children who refused to give consent or had a parent refuse consent at the start of the study were not included (N = 13). The final sample was 193 children (102 girls and 91 boys) aged between 7 years 7 months and 10 years 8 months (mean 9 years 0 months). Although socio-economic measures were not taken, the school catchment areas were lower- to middle-class. The ethnic mix was 38.3% White, 45.4% African-Caribbean, 10.2% Asian, 1.5% Mediterranean, and 4.6% of mixed ethnic origin. Class sizes varied from 20 to 29 pupils (M = 25).

Measures

Verbal ability

The short form of the British Picture Vocabulary Scale (BPVS) (Dunn, Dunn, Whetton & Pintilie, 1982) was included as a control measure to ensure that any difference in theory of mind was not explained by differences in understanding the language of the stories.

Role in bullying

A shortened version of the PRS (Salmivalli et al., 1996) was presented as a self/peer nomination interview rather than the questionnaire format of the original, because this method was found to be more suited for use with 7 to 10-year-olds (see Sutton & Smith, 1999, for details of this adapted version). Peer and self-nominations were given for a set of behaviour descriptions in each of the following roles:

Bully: active, initiative taking, leader-like behaviour
Assistant: active, but more follower than leader-like

> *Reinforcer:*   inciting the bully, providing an audience, etc.
> *Defender:*   sticking up for or consoling the victim
> *Outsider:*   doing nothing in bullying situations, staying away
> *Victim:*   nominated in 'gets bullied' by 30% of same sex classmates.

The internal reliability for these six subscales was moderate to good (Cronbach's alphas: Bully $\propto$ 0.85, Reinforcer $\propto$ 0.88, Assistant $\propto$ 0.67, Defender $\propto$ 0.80, and Outsider $\propto$ 0.55). These nominations were used to calculate:

(a) *Role Scores* for each child. There were 21 items or behaviours on the PRS (e.g. 'gets others to join in bullying' and 'isn't usually there, stays away'). A nomination for 'sometimes' showing a behaviour was scored as one, and 'often' was scored as two. The number of nominations within a role was then divided by the number of nominators and multiplied by 100. The highest possible 'role score' for each role was therefore 200, indicating that the child and each of their same sex classmates nominated them as 'often' showing each behaviour within that role.

(b) A *Participant Role* for each child on the basis of their highest role score. The exception was that a child was assigned to the 'Victim' role if 30% or more of their classmates nominated them for the 'Gets bullied' behavioural description, regardless of other role scores (as in Salmivalli et al., 1996).

Assessment of social cognition

Children were read 11 short stories designed to test understanding of mental states or emotions. Two full examples are shown below.

Cognitive story: Double bluff (Happé, 1994)

During the war, the Red army captured a member of the Blue army. They want him to tell them where his army's tanks are; they know they are either by the sea or in the mountains. They know that the prisoner will not want to tell them, he will want to save his army, and so he will certainly lie to them. The prisoner is very brave and very clever, he will not let them find his tanks. The tanks are really in the mountains. Now when the other side asks him where his tanks are, he says, 'They are in the mountains.'

> *Control question:*   Is it true what the prisoner said?
> Where will the other army look for his tanks?
> Why did the prisoner say what he said?

Emotion story (Sutton, unpublished)

Mike wants to go out with his friends, but he has a really bad tummy ache. He knows that if his Mum notices he is ill, she won't let him go out to play. Mike goes downstairs and asks his Mum, 'Can I go out to play please?'

Control question: Which picture shows how Mike really feels?
Which picture shows how Mike will look when he talks to his Mum?

In addition to the control question based on the content of the story, answers to the questions at the end of these stories assessing understanding of mental states were scored as zero (fail), one (pass but without reference to a mental state or belief), or two (pass including reference to a mental state or belief). For example, an answer to the double bluff story above rated as two may have been 'They will look by the sea because they think that the prisoner is lying to them'. For the emotion story, a child scoring two would have selected either of the bottom two pictures (see Figure 4.1)

Figure 4.1   Emotion story responses

(neutral or happy), indicating that he or she recognized that the boy would try not to show his real feelings, along with a justification referencing the mum's mental states (e.g. 'He'll try to look happy so that his Mum doesn't know that he's ill'). Inter-rater reliability assessment of responses to the stories produced an alpha coefficient of 0.87, indicating good agreement.

The stories were also given to 21 independent raters to determine whether an understanding of emotions was crucial in order to answer the question at the end. Majority opinion supported the view that this understanding was not crucial for the first four stories (mean agreement 79%), but was for the remaining seven (mean agreement 92%). On the basis of this, each child gained a cognitive score based on the first five stories (maximum 10), an emotion score based on the others (maximum 12), and total social cognition score (maximum 22).

Assessment of type of bullying and motivation to bully

Teachers completed short questionnaires for each child who scored above the average 'Bully' role score for their school class and gender (N = 67). Questions were on a three-point scale of 'never', 'sometimes', and 'often', covering:

(a) physical bullying: 'Direct physical, e.g. hitting and kicking';
(b) verbal bullying: 'Name calling' and 'Teasing/ridiculing'; and
(c) indirect bullying: 'Excluding from social groups or activities' and 'Spreading lies or rumours about the victim'.

From this sample, a sub-sample (N = 42) were taken who the class teachers agreed were involved in bullying others more than average for their class/gender. This was to ensure that teachers were only rating bullying of which they were aware.

Procedure

After obtaining both parental and individual consent, children were tested individually away from the classroom, whenever possible in a quiet room. There were four sessions with each child: the BPVS, six of the social cognition stories, the PRS interview (see Sutton & Smith, 1999, for full details of procedure), and finally the remaining five stories.

Results

Results are presented using the categorical measure of 'Participant Role' to compare group means in social cognition, and the continuous measure of 'Role Scores' to test for correlations between social cognition and the extent of different types of behaviour in the whole sample.

Table 4.1 Numbers and participant characteristics of each role

Participant Role	Numbers in each role (% of sample)		% of total sample by gender		Age (months)		Verbal ability (BPVS score)	
			Boys	Girls	Mean	(SD)	Mean	(SD)
Bully	25	(13.0)	11.0	14.7	108	(9)	91	(14)
Reinforcer	15	(7.8)	8.8	6.9	103	(8)	92	(19)
Assistant	12	(6.2)	6.6	5.9	107	(8)	90	(15)
Defender	85	(44.0)	36.3	51.0	106	(9)	95	(17)
Outsider	21	(10.9)	12.1	9.8	110	(9)	95	(22)
Victim	35	(18.1)	25.3	11.8	110	(10)	93	(18)

Participant Roles and characteristics

The distribution of the 193 children across the six Participant Roles is shown in Table 4.1. There was no significant association between sex and Participant Role ($\chi^2(5) = 8.22$, ns). There were no significant differences between roles in terms of verbal ability ($F(5,187) = 0.38$, ns), but a significant main effect of role on age was found ($F(5,187) = 2.21$, $p < 0.05$). Follow-up t-tests showed that Reinforcers were significantly younger than both Outsiders ($t(34) = -2.62$, $p < 0.05$) and Victims ($t(48) = -2.28$, $p < 0.05$). To exercise caution, both age and verbal ability were controlled for in further analyses.

Participant Roles and social cognition

From a total of 2,123 responses (11 stories each for 193 children), there were 40 cases (less than 2% of the total number of responses) when a child got a control question wrong. In all cases the question was repeated and was then answered correctly. Errors also did not appear to be clustered in any particular Participant Role group: 18 Defenders, 6 Victims, 5 Bullies, 2 Outsiders, 2 Assistants and 1 Reinforcer failed a control question, figures in line with the differences in the sizes of the groups. For these reasons, control questions are excluded from further analysis.

Table 4.2 shows the mean percentage of correct responses over cognitive and emotion stories, and overall social cognition performance for the six participant groups. As a group, Bullies score higher on total social cognition score than any other group. A one-way analysis of covariance was performed to investigate the effect of Participant Role on total social cognition score. Age and verbal ability were entered as covariates. There was a significant effect of Participant Role on total social cognition score ($F(5,192) = 2.29$, $p < 0.05$).

Table 4.2   Participant Role and mean percentage social cognition scores

Participant Roles	Mean % cognitive score (SD)	Mean % emotion score (SD)	Mean % total social cognition score (SD)
(For whole sample)	40.09 (23.59)	39.56 (13.85)	39.59 (14.74)
Bully	48.00 (23.57)	44.29 (11.48)	45.64 (13.60)
Reinforcer	35.00 (20.70)	32.38 (17.68)	33.64 (16.99)
Assistant	38.54 (27.93)	37.50 (12.97)	37.88 (14.29)
Defender	38.53 (20.70)	39.41 (12.93)	38.98 (12.01)
Outsider	45.83 (26.61)	42.18 (15.47)	43.51 (18.16)
Victim	37.50 (27.45)	38.78 (14.42)	37.53 (17.37)

As there were only two *a priori* comparisons, standard follow-up *t*-tests were used with a more conservative level of α to control the family wise error rate. These supported the hypotheses predicting social cognition differences between individual roles. Bullies score significantly higher than Victims (hypothesis A: $t(58) = 1.94$, $p = 0.025$). Bullies score significantly higher than the Follower group (hypothesis B: $t(50) = 2.50$, $p < 0.01$). *Post hoc t*-tests also revealed that Bullies score significantly higher than Defenders ($t(108) = 2.36$, $p < 0.05$), but not significantly higher than Outsiders ($t(44) = 0.45$, ns).

When cognitive score and emotion score are analysed separately, the only significant difference between groups is between Bullies and Followers on the emotion score ($t(50) = 2.51$, $p < 0.05$).

Role scores and social cognition

Table 4.3 indicates two-tailed partial correlation coefficients (controlling for age and verbal ability) between social cognition and actual *extent* of different types of behaviour, using the whole sample.

The initiative-taking, ringleader behaviour of the Bully role is the most highly correlated with total social cognition score, whereas Victim score is significantly negatively correlated with total social cognition score. Role scores representing involvement in bullying (Bully, Reinforcer and Assistant) are all significantly positively correlated with cognitive score, whereas Defender role score is uncorrelated and the Outsider and Victim role scores are significantly negatively correlated with cognitive score. Bully score is also positively correlated with emotion score.

Type of bullying

Hypothesis C was not supported: a partial correlation between total social cognition score and teacher-rated extent of indirect bullying (controlling for age, verbal ability and both physical and verbal bullying) was not significant

Table 4.3 Partial correlations of individual role scores and social cognition

	Role score					
Social cognition score	Bully	Reinforcer	Assistant	Defender	Outsider	Victim
Cognitive	0.32***	0.28***	0.19**	0.01	−0.16*	−0.16*
Emotion	0.17*	0.07	−0.01	−0.01	−0.02	−0.06
Total score	0.29***	0.21**	0.11	0.01	−0.10	−0.15*

***$p < 0.001$; **$p < 0.01$; *$p < 0.05$

($r(36) = −0.11$, one-tailed $p = 0.25$). In an equivalent analysis for physical bullying, there was a non-significant trend ($r(36) = −0.24$, $p = 0.14$), whereas there was a significant positive partial correlation between verbal bullying and total social cognition score ($r(36) = 0.43$, $p = 0.007$).

Discussion

The results of this study clearly do not support an application of the social skills deficit model of aggression (Crick & Dodge, 1994) to children who bully others in school, or the view of the child who bullies as 'oafish' and stupid. There was a significant effect of Participant Role on total social cognition score. Bullies scored significantly higher on the stories than all other groups in the bullying process (if it is accepted that Outsiders are not involved). In support of hypotheses A and B, Bullies scored higher than both Victims and Followers (Assistants plus Reinforcers). An unexpected finding was that Bullies scored higher than Followers on the emotion stories.

As for the continuous measure indicating extent of the different behaviours in the whole sample, role scores showing involvement in bullying others were positively correlated with total social cognition score, whereas Outsider and Defender role scores were not correlated and Victim score was negatively correlated with total social cognition score. Roles involved in bullying others were significantly correlated with a cognitive score, whereas Defender role score was not correlated and Outsider and Victim scores were negatively correlated with cognitive score. The Bully role score was also positively correlated with the emotion score.

The positive correlation between teacher-rated verbal bullying and theory of mind was not predicted. However, it may well be that the ability to understand the mental states and emotions of others is a very adaptive one in teasing somebody effectively, or knowing what names will be most hurtful. In fact, despite the negative trend found between teacher-rated physical bullying and theory of mind, it could be argued that even in purely physical bullying, social cognition will still be of use in avoiding detection, or choosing the most effective time and method for each situation in terms of maximizing the victim's vulnerability and minimizing chances of hurt to themselves. A single bully and his or her chosen victim often appear to have a bizarre dyadic relationship (Randall, 1997), in which there may be more consideration of mind than is immediately evident in the bully's behaviour.

However, the treatment of 'bullies' as a single category was a limitation of the study. Further research is needed into the link between theory of mind and different types of bullying, particularly using information from peers on the methods used. This may overcome the problem of using teacher questionnaires (Ahmad & Smith, 1990), which may go some way to explaining the absence of a link between indirect bullying and theory of mind. There is evidence that teachers do include examples of indirect and direct forms in their views of what bullying is (Boulton, 1997), and analyses in the present study were limited to children about whom teachers agreed regarding their overall level of bullying. However, there may still be an underestimation of the more covert and indirect methods. A larger sample utilizing peer information on the type of bullying may possibly reveal a bi-modal distribution of social cognition scores in bullies, with a socially skilled group and a group using predominantly physical methods performing less well on the stories.

In general, these results support the view presented that bullies may be at an advantage if they possess theory of mind skills superior to those of their followers and their victims. This study has identified their superior performance on a small set of stories, distinguishing between cognitive and emotion understanding. Three of the stories were Happé's (1994) stories: these have been shown to be sensitive enough to identify the mentalizing deficit in autistic participants who pass all standard false belief tasks, and for use in the identification of the neural substrate of the ability to mentalize through functional neuroimaging (Fletcher et al., 1995). The remaining stories were similar in structure and style, and the absence of ceiling-level performance on the whole set of stories suggests they are age-appropriate. However, a more fine-grained analysis using a wide range of tests and samples may be required. Younger samples could attempt standard first-order false belief tasks (e.g. the Smarties test of Wimmer & Hartl, 1991), and the 'reading the mind in the eyes/face' test (Baron-Cohen et al., 1996) would provide a more context and language-free measure for a variety of age ranges.

Use of a wider range of social cognition tests may also cast some light on the less expected link between bullying and emotion understanding. In particular, a study is needed which distinguishes between emotion recognition, emotion understanding and empathy in children who bully. Such a study could utilize stories, self-report questionnaires of empathic concern (e.g. Bryant, 1982), and even physiological measures of arousal. Do those bullies with a good theory of mind show this in all kinds of mentalizing, or do they still show deficits in specific areas, in particular in theory of mind and false beliefs involving the moral emotions not included in this study (e.g. guilt, love, remorse, sympathy and shame)? Do they understand these emotions (at least better than their followers, who scored significantly lower on emotion score) but just not share them, in other words lack empathy? As noted earlier, children with conduct disorder most clearly showed their mentalizing ability in the domain of anti-social behaviour (Happé & Frith, 1996), raising the possibility that this group has an intact but skewed theory of mind, or a 'theory of nasty minds' (p. 395). This may be similar to Mealey's (1995) emphasis on 'cold cognition' in sociopathy: a theory of mind formulated purely in instrumental terms, without access to the empathic understanding that most people rely on. Blair et al. (1996) found evidence for a dissociation in psychopathy between mentalizing and empathic reaction.

It is possible, therefore, that a child who displays a heightened awareness of the feelings of others (i.e. high affective perspective-taking ability as demonstrated by the positive correlation in the present study between the Bully role score and the emotion score) but also demonstrates an inability or unwillingness to share those feelings (i.e. low empathic disposition) would be especially manipulative in his or her dealings with others (Hoffman, 1975; Staub, 1979). Randall (1997) notes (but fails to test empirically) that proactive aggressors are 'not easily upset emotionally ... their emotions do not interfere with their social cognition' (p. 29). In a small sample of clinic-referred children, Frick, O'Brien, Wootton & McBurnett (1994) identified the factor of 'selfish, callous, and remorseless use of others' – familiar behaviour to victims of bullying. Bullies have been reported to have higher levels of psychoticism (as measured by the Eysenck Personality Questionnaire) than groups of victims and controls (Rigby & Slee, 1993), and psychoticism does appear to be related to actual psychopathy (Hare, 1982). Longitudinal studies are needed in order to determine how many bullies actually go on to be classified as psychopaths, and also how these bullies differ from the less often studied successful or non-institutionalized psychopaths (Lynam, 1997).

Investigation of developmental trends like this, placing social cognition in bullying in a lifespan perspective, may be a fruitful avenue for research. First, what type of families might these socially skilled bullies come from? Contributory family factors in the development of social cognition could be integrated with existing knowledge of bullying and the family, possibly investigating the links between 'internal working models' (Bowlby, 1988) and social cognition in bullying. For example, the families of children who bully are often characterized by a lack of cohesion and an imbalance of power between the parents (Bowers, Smith & Binney, 1992). Is this style of relationship internalized in children, providing a model for a cold, manipulative way of thinking?

Second, where might these socially skilled bullies end up? Social cognition in adult bullying may also be of interest. Victims of bullying in the workplace often refer to managers who cunningly manipulate their workers, for example creating 'furtive alliances' and using 'entrapment' (inviting someone to commit themselves to a course of action that is already known by the abuser to be flawed; Thomas-Peter, 1997), and who also manage to hide their behaviour from their superiors, passing it off as an 'autocratic style'. Jacobson (1992) also links early bullying behaviour with domestic violence, referring to two distinct types: a hot-headed, excessively reactive type, and a cool, calculating and proactive type where the battering is part of a general subjugation of the partner. This latter type may be the adult version of a bully with good theory of mind skills.

One other area for further research within this lifespan perspective is the issue of the directionality of any link between bullying and theory of mind. While social cognition skills may well assist an individual in bullying and manipulating others, it would also seem possible that the experience of bullying itself may aid social cognitive development. Indeed, the strategic planning and execution of deceptive acts has been found to facilitate false-belief understanding in 3-year-olds (Hala & Chandler, 1996).

If certain types of bully are indeed found to have high level social cognition, this has implications for intervention strategies. These bullies, being cold, manipulative masters of a social situation, may resist traditional anti-bullying policies and curriculum work. For example, the 'No Blame' approach (Maines & Robinson, 1991; Robinson & Maines, 1997) relies heavily on empathy on the part of the bully. Considerable success has been reported using this method in terms of the reports of victims, but further research would be needed to determine if this success is greatest in the most empathic bullies, and whether the bully is also changed by the intervention. The empathic capacity of bullies is particularly important: bullies performed well on the stories assessing understanding of emotions, but if they do not actually share these emotions then intervention strategies may inadvertently hone the skills of an emotionally manipulative bully. In particular, the suggestion that young bullies should be trained in theory of mind abilities (Randall, 1996) should be treated with caution. Children with conduct problems are a notoriously heterogeneous group (Hinshaw, Lahey & Hart, 1993) and it is possible that no 'blanket' technique will be completely effective. The popular stereotype of bullies as lacking in intelligence and social skills may be guiding anti-bullying policy away from individuals who do not fit this picture, and confronting such individuals may depend on a much clearer understanding of the psychological weapons that some may use in causing distress to others.

Alternatively, the focus could be shifted towards the psychological defences that could be used by others: Bullies did not score significantly higher in terms of social cognition than Outsiders. Further research is needed to determine what prevents these children from becoming involved in bullying, and also how their skills could be used in prosocial ways to combat bullying. These children could be a useful resource in anti-bullying work, as could Defenders. The Participant Role approach could be used in combination with sociometry, identifying popular Defenders and Outsiders and encouraging them to play an active role in reducing bullying in the school. This could involve training them as peer mediators or counsellors

(Cowie & Sharp, 1996), or asking them to talk to Assistants and Reinforcers about bullying and the effects it may have. Targeting the social support of the Bully in this way may isolate them, and ultimately be more effective than attempting to change the more entrenched behaviour of the Bully or the Victim.

Given the low scores of Victims and the negative correlations found between Victim score and social cognition, one possibility for interventions to keep in mind is that a deficit in the social cognition skills of Victims contributes to their experience. Does this leave them more open to manipulation by others? Interventions could possibly use theory of mind training alongside assertiveness training to give victims added skills in assessing and responding to bullying, although clearly such a course of action would need to be carefully monitored and empathy also emphasized to avoid the potential problem of victims turning into bullies.

Further research could also investigate in more detail how Crick & Dodge's (1994) social skills model may apply to children who bully, without assuming any deficit. Bullies may perceive and interpret social cues very accurately (the first two stages), but may differ in goal selection, response strategy generation and response decisions, reflecting past experiences and strategies which have worked rather than demonstrating an 'error'. The difference may lie in their values, or the content or the cognitions, rather than the accuracy: aggressive children attach more value (or importance) to the rewarding outcomes of aggression and less value to the negative outcomes than do non-aggressive children (Boldizar, Perry & Perry, 1989). Further research is needed into this 'costs and benefits' analysis, and how this may be affected by both the cultural climate of the school and the peer group. Deviant beliefs and values may stem from a deviant network of peers (see Patterson, DeBaryshe & Ramsey, 1989), and the beliefs and values are then employed in the organization of views of relationships, and instigation of behaviours. Investigation into the interactions between beliefs, values and cognitions could incorporate social psychological research on conformity, prejudice and leadership, asking what individual and cultural expectations promote bullying behaviour. Askew (1989) has suggested that schools which value competitiveness may tacitly encourage bullying, and Olweus (1993) and Smith & Sharp (1994) have demonstrated the positive effects of a warm and participative school environment. This can presumably be extended to society as a whole: if some bullies are indeed skilled in 'psychological warfare', it may be necessary to change the battleground as well as the weapons used.

Acknowledgements

The authors are grateful to all the schools, teachers and pupils who participated in the study, to Francesca Happé, Simon Baron-Cohen and his co-authors for use of story materials, and to Jody Dearden for illustrating the emotion stories.

References

Ahmad, Y. & Smith, P.K. (1990) Behavioural measures: Bullying in schools. *Newsletter of Association for Child Psychology and Psychiatry,* **12**, 26–27.

Askew, S. (1989) Aggressive behaviour in boys: To what extent is it institutionalized? In D.P. Tattum & D.A. Lane (Eds), *Bullying in schools,* pp. 59–71. Stoke-on-Trent: Trentham Books.

Baron-Cohen, S. & Hammer, J. (1996) Is autism an extreme form of the male brain? *Advances in Infancy Research,* **11**, 193–217.

Baron-Cohen, S., Riviere, A., Cross, P., Fukushima, M., Bryant, C., Sotillo, M., Hadwin, J. & French, D. (1996) Reading the mind in the face: A cross-cultural and developmental study. *Visual Cognition,* **3**, 39–59.

Bjorkqvist, K., Lagerspetz, K.M.J. & Kaukiainen, A. (1992) Do girls manipulate and boys fight? Developmental trends in regard to direct and indirect aggression. *Aggressive Behaviour,* **18**, 117–127.

Bjorkqvist, K., Österman, K. & Kaukiainen, A. (1992) The development of direct and indirect aggressive strategies in males and females. In K. Bjorkqvist & P. Niemela (Eds), *Of mice and women: Aspects of female aggression,* pp. 51–64. San Diego, CA: Academic Press.

Blair, R.J.R., Sellars, C., Strickland, I., Clark, F., Williams, A.O., Smith, M. & Jones, L. (1996) Theory of mind in the psychopath. *Journal of Forensic Psychiatry,* **7**(1), 15–25.

Boldizar, J.P., Perry, D.G. & Perry, L.C. (1989) Outcome values and aggression. *Child Development,* **60**, 571–579.

Boulton, M.J. (1997) Teachers' views on bullying: Definitions, attitudes and ability to cope. *British Journal of Educational Psychology,* **67**, 223–233.

Boulton, M.J. & Smith, P.K. (1994). Bully/victim problems in middle-school children: Stability, self perceived competence, peer perceptions and peer acceptance. *British Journal of Developmental Psychology,* **12**, 315–329.

Bowers, L., Smith, P.K. & Binney, V. (1992) Cohesion and power in the families of children involved in bully/victim problems at school. *Journal of Family Therapy,* **14**, 371–387.

Bowlby, J. (1988) *A secure base: Clinical applications of attachment theory.* London: Routledge.

Bryant, B.K. (1982) An index of empathy for children and adolescents. *Child Development,* **53**, 413–425.

Cowie, H. & Sharp, S. (1996) *Peer counselling in school: A time to listen.* London: David Fulton.

Crick, N.R. & Dodge, K.A. (1994) A review and reformulation of social information-processing mechanisms in children's social adjustment. *Psychological Bulletin,* **115**, 74–101.

Crick, N.R. & Dodge, K.A. (1996) Social information processing mechanisms in reactive and proactive aggression. *Child Development,* **67**, 993–1002.

Crick, N.R. & Grotpeter, J.K. (1995) Relational aggression, gender, and social-psychological adjustment. *Child Development,* **66**, 710–722.

Dodge, K.A. (1991) The structure and function of reactive and proactive aggression. In D.J. Pepler & K.H. Rubin (Eds), *The development and treatment of childhood aggression*, pp. 201–218. Hillsdale, NJ: Lawrence Erlbaum.

Dodge, K.A., Pettit, G.S., McClaskey, C.L. & Brown, M.M. (1986) Social competence in children. *Monographs of the Society for Research in Child Development*, **51**(2), 1–85.

Dunn, L.M., Dunn, L.M., Whetton, C. & Pintilie, D. (1982) *British Picture Vocabulary Scale*. Windsor: NFER-NELSON.

Eslea, M.J. & Smith, P.K. (1998) The long-term effectiveness of anti-bullying work in primary schools. *Educational Research*, **40**, 203–218.

Feldman, E. & Dodge, K.A. (1987) Social information processing and sociometric status: Sex, age, and situational effects. *Journal of Abnormal Child Psychology*, **15**, 211–277.

Fletcher, P.C., Happé, F., Frith, U., Baker, S.C., Dolan, R.J., Frackowiak, R.S.J. & Frith, C.D. (1995) Other minds in the brain – a functional imaging study of theory of mind in story comprehension. *Cognition*, **57**(2), 109–128.

Frick, P.J., O'Brien, B.S., Wootton, J.M. & McBurnett, K. (1994) Psychopathy and conduct problems in children. *Journal of Abnormal Psychology*, **15**, 211–277.

Gibbins, C. & Craig, W. (1997) Mapping the path to aggression: Validation of a social cognitive model of childhood. Paper presented at the biennial meeting of the Society for Research in Child Development, Washington, DC, 3–6 April.

Guerra, N.G. & Slaby, R.G. (1989) Evaluative factors in social problem solving by aggressive boys. *Journal of Abnormal Child Psychology*, **17**, 177–289.

Hala, S. & Chandler, M. (1996) The role of strategic planning in accessing false-belief understanding. *Child Development*, **67**, 2948–2966.

Happé, F. (1994) An advanced test of theory of mind: Understanding of story characters' thoughts and feelings by able autistic, mentally handicapped, and normal children and adults. *Journal of Autism and Developmental Disorders*, **24**(2), 129–154.

Happé, F. & Frith, U. (1996) Theory of mind and social impairment in children with conduct disorder. *British Journal of Developmental Psychology*, **14**, 385–398.

Hare, R.D. (1982) Psychopathy and the personality dimensions of psychoticism, extraversion and neuroticism. *Personality and Individual Differences*, **3**, 35–42.

Hazler, R.J. (1996) *Breaking the cycle of violence: Interventions for bullying and victimization*. Washington, DC: Accelerated Development.

Hinshaw, S.P., Lahey, B.B. & Hart, E.L. (1993) Issues of taxonomy and comorbidity in the development of conduct disorder. *Development and Psychopathology*, **5**, 31–49.

Hoffman, M.L. (1975) Developmental synthesis of affect and cognition and its implication for altruistic motivation. *Developmental Psychology*, **11**, 607–622.

Jacobson, N.S. (1992) Behavioural couple therapy: A new beginning. *Behaviour Therapy*, **23**, 493–506.

Kaukiainen, A., Bjorkqvist, K., Lagerspetz, K., Österman, K., Salmivalli, C., Forsblom, S. & Ahlbom, A. (1999). The relationships between social intelligence, empathy, and three types of aggression. *Aggressive Behaviour*, **25**(2), 81–89.

Keating, C.F. & Heltman, K.R. (1994) Dominance and deception in children and adults: Are leaders the best misleaders? *Personality and Social Psychology Bulletin*, **20**, 312–321.

Lagerspetz, K.M.J., Bjorkqvist, K., Berts, M. & King, E. (1982) Group aggression among schoolchildren in three schools. *Scandinavian Journal of Psychology*, **23**, 45–52.

Lynam, D.R. (1997) Pursuing the psychopath: Capturing the fledgling psychopath in the nomological net. *Journal of Abnormal Psychology*, **106**(3), 425–438.

Maines, B. & Robinson, G. (1991) Don't beat the bullies! *Educational Psychology in Practice*, 7(3), 168–172.

Mealey, L. (1995). The sociobiology of sociopathy: An integrated evolutionary model. *Behavioural and Brain Sciences*, 18, 523–599.

Olweus, D. (1993) *Bullying – what we know and what we can do.* Oxford: Blackwell.

Patterson, G.R., DeBaryshe, B.D. & Ramsey, E. (1989) A developmental perspective on antisocial behavior. *American Psychologist*, 44, 329–335.

Pepler, D.J. & Craig, W.M. (1995) A peek behind the fence: Naturalistic observations of aggressive children with remote audiovisual recording. *Developmental Psychology*, 31(4), 548–553.

Premack, D. & Woodruff, G. (1978) Does the chimpanzee have a theory of mind? *Behavioural and Brain Sciences*, 1, 515–526.

Randall, P. (1996) Pre-school children: Experiences of being parented and the routes to bullying. In D. Tattum & G. Herbert (Eds), *Bullying: Home, school and community.* London: David Fulton.

Randall, P. (1997) *Adult bullying: Perpetrators and victims.* London: Routledge.

Rigby, K. & Slee, P. T. (1993) The relationship of Eysenck's personality factors and self esteem to bully–victim behaviour in Australian schoolboys. *Personality and Individual Differences*, 14(2), 371–373.

Rivers, I. & Smith, P.K. (1994) Types of bullying behaviour and their correlates. *Aggressive Behaviour*, 20, 359–368.

Robinson, G. & Maines, B. (1997) *Crying for help: The No Blame Approach to bullying.* Bristol: Lucky Duck Publishing.

Salmivalli, C., Lagerspetz, K., Bjorkqvist, K., Österman, K. & Kaukiainen, A. (1996) Bullying as a group process: Participant roles and their relations to social status within the group. *Aggressive Behaviour*, 22, 1–15.

Smith, P.K. & Sharp, S. (1994) *School bullying: Insights and perspectives.* London: Routledge.

Sparrow, S., Balla, D. & Cicchetti, D. (1984) *Vineland Adaptive Behaviour Scales (survey form).* Circle Pines, MN: American Guidance Services.

Staub, E. (1979) *Positive social behavior and morality: Socialization and development,* vol. 2. New York: Academic Press.

Steinberg, M.D. & Dodge, K.A. (1983) Attributional bias in aggressive adolescent boys and girls. *Journal of Social and Clinical Psychology*, 1, 312–321.

Sutton, J. & Smith, P.K. (1999) Bullying as a group process: An adaptation of the Participant Role Scale approach. *Aggressive Behaviour*, 25(2), 97–111.

Sutton, J., Smith, P.K. & Swettenham, J. (1999) Bullying and 'theory of mind': A critique of the 'social skills deficit' view of anti-social behaviour. *Social Development*, 8(1), 117–134.

Taylor, M. (1996) A theory of mind perspective on social cognitive development. In R. Gelman & T. Kit-Fong Au (Eds), *Perceptual and cognitive development,* pp. 283–329. London: Academic Press.

Thomas-Peter, B.A. (1997) Personal standards in professional relationships: Limiting interpersonal harassment. *Journal of Community and Applied Social Psychology*, 7, 233–239.

Whitney, I. & Smith, P.K. (1993) A survey of the nature and extent of bullying in junior/middle and secondary schools. *Educational Research*, 35, 3–25.

Wimmer, H. & Hartl, M. (1991) Against the Cartesian view on mind: Young children's difficulty with own false beliefs. *British Journal of Developmental Psychology*, 9, 125–138.

Small on chairs, big on inspiration

Running my finger down the list of third-year project supervisors and topics on the University of Sheffield noticeboard, I stopped at 'Bullying: Peter Smith'. That sounds interesting, I thought. It could easily have been so different. I like bullying (as a research topic), but if I had realised that once you've started down one research road the easiest thing is to plough straight on I might have chosen differently. I still imagine somehow stumbling across that sheet of paper now and finding that it went on to list research like that football fan observation study that gets the researchers grants to go to the World Cup. Lesson one: if you think there's any chance of you making a career out of psychology, choose your undergraduate project very carefully.

But there was a mob gathering behind me to make their choices, so I stopped at 'B', signed up and went to see Professor Peter Smith. This meeting was the seed for the paper you have just read, about five years before it was published. Peter was acknowledged as the national expert in the field, having just completed a large anti-bullying project. He had started to consider the 'theory of mind' skills of those involved in bullying; an area that had been studied in relation to aggression, but not bullying specifically. Your theory of mind (ToM) helps you to understand what another person is thinking, or what they are thinking about what you are thinking (second-order ToM). It is one part of social cognition: how we understand and respond to social situations.

I caught up with this literature and discussed it with Peter. We realised that while most studies discussed deficient or inferior social understanding in aggressive children, the more you think about the social nature of bullying the more sense it makes for bullies to actually have good social skills. Flipping the hypotheses like this certainly made our research more interesting over the years and gave it greater impact. If you can either adapt existing theories for a different field (as we did with aggression to bullying), or just turn what is already there on its head, the chances are that your research will then throw up unexpected results.

My third-year project served as a pilot study for 'Social cognition and bullying' (see Sutton, Smith & Swettenham, 1999a, 1999b). Moving down to Goldsmiths College for my PhD, Peter and I recruited John Swettenham as a second supervisor. John's expertise was theory of mind, and his input on the design of the social cognition stories was crucial. Draw people with a diverse range of abilities into your research team. Then spend time talking to them, preferably out of your usual research environment. It's amazing how many research ideas come from what seems like a fairly tangential chat over a pint. Other disciplines can also contribute, for example computer science or drama departments contributing to novel ways of assessing children's social understanding. Soon I was on to piloting the materials. Here I will explain the thinking behind each method, and what I learned about researching with children through using it.

Verbal ability

As my method of assessing ToM involved responding to written stories, I needed to measure this potential confounding variable. I chose the British Picture Vocabulary Scale, as a relatively quick and simple way to measure language understanding. I really resented this measure: I had no interest in language understanding *per se*, and found it as frustrating as the children did flicking through lots of easy pictures before getting to the four or five that actually seemed to discriminate between different abilities. I guess everyone finds this with measuring confounding variables: it's a necessary evil. I could have easily forgotten to include it and then been told by journal reviewers that my findings could be invalidated by differences in language ability between the groups.

Role in bullying

My priority was measuring bullying as a group process: I wasn't just interested in the bullies and the victims, I wanted to be able to compare the social cognition skills of those who helped the bully, those who stuck up for the victim, those who just stayed out of it. If I was measuring social cognition I might as well emphasise the social in the assessment of bullying, rather than just identifying bullies and victims and assuming that the rest were somehow 'controls'.

There are many methods of measuring bullying, and I considered them all: nomination by self, peers, teachers, or any combination of the three? Questionnaire, interview, observation? Would the measure be administered to a whole group or individually? The importance of assessing 'roles' rather than just identifying bullies and victims led me to Salmivalli's Participant Role Scale (PRS). But there was a problem. Piloting had shown that children of the age I wanted to study (7–10 years old, when second-order theory of mind was on the turn) had difficulties completing a lengthy questionnaire. I shortened it and administered it in individual sessions, using bits of paper with classmates' names on them that were sorted into various columns representing the different roles. Practically, this was rather time-consuming, and I think if I did it all over again I would consider having another go at simplifying that questionnaire.

This procedural change would also allow the information to be collected in one group session, reducing some of the ethical and practical concerns with individual 'interviews'. There is no doubt that children talk about the research process, and it's vital for both scientific and ethical reasons that you try to minimise the impact your presence has. I attempted to do this by asking teachers not to say I had anything to do with bullying. Unfortunately teachers did sometimes let it slip ('Jon's here to find out about bullying in the school', that kind of thing); in any case the ordering of the methods meant that the cat was out of the bag before the end of the study, and I was officially 'the bullying guy'.

I don't think that distress inevitably follows individual administration of the PRS, or similar methods asking young children about 'troubling' behaviour. Some children who bullied others were more than happy to admit to it (unfortunately aggression does still create a powerful reputation in many peer groups). Emphasising that I was asking about who helped out, who wasn't involved, etc. as well also helped. It was also crucial for me to attempt to gain their trust from the outset by emphasising that nobody else would get to hear what they had said. But when I packed up each day and went home, there was always a nagging thought that one of the kids was getting pressured into revealing who they had nominated.

If a child does show distress during the course of your research, it's important to be prepared for it. Several children told me that they were being bullied; some were clearly upset about this. I couldn't do much, but I could give them phone numbers of organisations trained to help, and offer to raise the issue in general terms with their class teacher (although respecting the confidentiality of the research situation by not naming the bully).

Assessment of social cognition

I originally intended to measure three types of social cognition in three types of situation: those where it seemed simple ToM or cognitive understanding was being assessed (e.g. double bluff), stories involving the display or understanding of emotion, and stories involving social conventions such as *faux pas*. It was not until data collection was complete that I started to think that the distinction I was really interested in was the 'cold cognition' one between cognitive and emotive understanding, and that such a distinction should be made on something other than my hunch. I gave the stories to 21 independent raters, and this led to the reclassification you see in the paper.

I went through several versions of the stories and illustrations in piloting, attempting to ensure that a correct answer really did demonstrate mental state or emotion understanding. I also tried to ensure that the scenarios were realistic, age-appropriate, and that there was an ethnic and gender mix of characters. If there is no 'standard' test available in the area you are researching, don't be afraid to make something up yourself.

Assessment of type of bullying and motivation to bully

Teacher questionnaires allowed some comparison with pupil views in terms of type and amount of bullying, and also gleaned some speculation on what was driving the bullying which the young children might have felt unable or unwilling to comment on. Added to these considerations was the fact that most teachers had so much to say about bullying that they were pleased to be actively involved in the study as well!

Of course I could have done with a finer analysis, such as distinguishing between emotion recognition, understanding and empathy. I could get more reliable or detailed information about types of bullying. But there's always another day, and when researching with children it's important not to overload them with too many measures in one study. Any longer than around 10 minutes at a time with each child and they will lose concentration, you will disrupt the teachers' work, and you will get bored and frustrated yourself. Choose or design your measures with this in mind: if you don't find them interesting, the chances are a young child won't.

If, like me, you are going to use several measures with the same child, you should also consider the order of presentation. You need to minimise the potential for bias, unconscious or otherwise. For example, knowing the child's role in bullying could have affected how I interacted with the children while assessing their social cognition. To reduce this risk I split the stories randomly into two sessions for each child, one conducted before the PRS and one after. The alternative would have been to finish with the PRS, but I felt that the potential for my knowledge of the child's performance on the stories affecting my interaction with them while discussing classmates' role in bullying was more serious, in both ethical and practical terms.

So a year or so into the PhD we were ready to start testing. We had a set of measures, and we had relatively simple hypotheses. The first two came directly from our previous work together and from our expectations of how the main two measures (PRS and social cognition stories) would interact. It would seem to make sense, according to our adaptation of the social skills deficit approach, that ringleader bullies should score higher than their victims and followers on the social cognition stories. Taking this one step further, our third hypothesis was that social cognition would be particularly related to indirect bullying, with its social and manipulative nature.

Data collection and analysis

The next step was to approach schools. I don't have a record of how many schools said no; I seem to remember it was about two or three, with at least one of them saying they didn't have any bullying in their school. If your research concerns anti-social behaviour, you may well find attitudes split between those glad to be seen to be doing something about a problem, and those denying there is one. Add to this the increasing pressures on the time of teachers, and I would predict it's going to get harder and harder to secure participation. I tried to do it by keeping the initial letter official-looking and very short (one side).

The letter suggested that the head teacher, Peter and I should meet to discuss the study further. (With hindsight I should have included the class teachers at this stage: often head teachers are more than happy to agree to things that won't actually directly involve them.) The key to a first meeting when you are researching in schools is to take handouts with you that explain the importance of the study through a very clear outline of the aims and measures. Also, consider what is in it for the schools, even if it's just a free book, or some general feedback about what you find (without identifying individuals). Another possibility is helping out in the class for a couple of days. This can create some kind of relationship with the children, and also give a little back to the teacher, seeing as you will be taking several hours of their time.

Fast-forward through many hours sat on small chairs reading 2,123 social cognition stories out loud, and all the data were in. This is when you wish your collaborative team included a stats genius. Always remember that a lack of stats knowledge not only stops you knowing how to perform the analyses, it also stops you even knowing what the right analyses are. You should be considering the analyses right from the experimental design stage.

The analysis threw up the odd surprise. We expected that any superior performance on the stories was most likely to be found with cognitive understanding: we thought that understanding of emotions might reduce bullying, through empathic concern. The study did act as a springboard for further research, but not necessarily through the findings. That social cognition debate has continued (see Sutton, Smith & Swettenham, 2001), but another strand unravelled simply through the experience of being in the schools and talking to the children. I was struck by how confident, popular and manipulative some of them were, and how bullying was just one of a range of strategies they used to look 'cool'. This led to some research on Machiavellianism and social competition (see Sutton & Keogh, 2000, 2001; Sutton, Reeves & Keogh, 2000). In particular I am now interested in the link between children's attitudes to schoolwork and their link with bullying: why is it less uncool to be a bully than it is to be a swot? This attitude seems particularly prevalent amongst boys, and I think if we get a handle on this we will be tackling several major social problems in one go. The thought hadn't occurred to me when I started the study: that's how research with children can surprise and inspire you.

References

Sutton, J. & Keogh, E. (2000) Social competition in school: Relationships with bullying, Machiavellianism and personality. *British Journal of Educational Psychology*, 70, 443–457.

Sutton, J. & Keogh, E. (2001) Components of Machiavellian beliefs in children: Relationships with personality. *Personality and Individual Differences*, 30, 137–148.

Sutton, J., Reeves, M. & Keogh, E. (2000) Disruptive behaviour, avoidance of responsibility and theory of mind. *British Journal of Developmental Psychology*, 18, 1–11.

Sutton, J., Smith, P.K. & Swettenham, J. (1999a) Bullying and 'Theory of Mind': a critique of the 'Social Skills Deficit' approach to anti-social behaviour. *Social Development*, 8, 117–127.

Sutton, J., Smith, P.K. & Swettenham, J. (1999b) Socially undesirable need not be incompetent: a response to Crick and Dodge. *Social Development*, 8, 132–134.

Sutton, J., Smith, P.K. & Swettenham, J. (2001) 'It's easy, it works, and it makes me feel good'? A response to Arsenio and Lemerise. *Social Development*, 10, 74–78.

5 Children's Experiences of Short-term Accommodation
JANE ALDGATE AND MARIE BRADLEY

This paper is an abridged extract from the book Aldgate, J. and Bradley, M. (1999) *Supporting Families through Short-term Fostering*, London: The Stationery Office.

Introduction

This study investigated the use of short-term accommodation to support families and help prevent breakdown in the long term. Short-term accommodation is a new provision of the Children Act 1989 characterised by being offered without any sanctions, in voluntary agreement with both parents and children, all of whom must be consulted before arrangements are made. In particular, a child's wishes and feelings must be considered if accommodation is being planned.

The areas and the organisation of service provision

Originally, the study was to be conducted in three areas that had a well-developed service of respite care prior to the introduction of the Children Act 1989. However, although all gave formal undertakings to participate in the study, one was unable to provide cases for the study. This was the result of reorganisation and a reluctance to continue to participate in the study. In another area, a major policy change away from a broad provision of family support services towards a concentration on disabled children and a concomitant concentration on child protection enquiries led to a sudden and dramatic end to the provision of general short-term accommodation. As a result the research was extended to two further study areas – providing four authorities to be called Midcity, River Town, Ferryport and Spire City.

The areas differed in terms of their geography and demography. Although it cannot be claimed that the four local authorities were representative of all authorities, between them they served very different geographical areas.

Midcity

The Midcity scheme covered part of a large city. The area the short-term accommodation scheme covered was one half of the city with a population of 273,000 with a wide range of ethnic and economic backgrounds. There are pockets of socio-economic deprivation located both in a number of outer city housing estates and in inner city terraces and high-rise flats.

River Town

River Town covered the central part of a county town, with a population of 134,300 in the area served by the scheme. The town is a mixture of afflu-ence, moderate wealth and poverty. The families served by the scheme lived mainly on council estates located on the periphery of the well-to-do areas of the town.

Ferryport

Ferryport included one-third of a large and busy seaport. The area served by the scheme has a population of 82,500 and represents a densely popu-lated urban area, with a dominance of council housing. The area has a significant proportion of families of African-Caribbean and mixed heritage origin. There are pockets of socio-economic deprivation.

Spire City

Spire City represents one half of a large, industrial city. The population of the area served by the scheme is 194,000. In this area, there is a minority ethnic population of 10%, comprising both black and Asian families.

The timing of the research: Special circumstances affecting the research locations

Since the study spanned the period leading up to and following on from the implementation of the Children Act 1989, the social services departments concerned were affected by this transition. There were understandable anxieties about the changes demanded by the new legislation and its phi-losophy. Social workers and their managers were anxious about imple-menting the changes. For the agencies involved in the study, the concerns about interpreting and using the Children Act properly were paramount.

The sample

There were 60 children included in the study. There was only one index child in each family even if other children were accommodated along with the index child. In all cases when more than one child was accommodated the eldest child was identified as the index child in order to facilitate interviews with children.

A case was defined when short-term accommodation had been offered and accepted by child and parent. The child's main carer was the adult subject although views of the other parent or any significant others present (for example, grandparents) were noted qualitatively.

The families of all children offered short-term accommodation from a specified date were approached by the research team until 60 cases had been recruited between the four authorities. Due to the difficulties in recruiting families in River Town and Spire City, as already outlined, these authorities contributed fewer cases. However, it was clear from later analysis of family characteristics that very similar families were using the service in the four areas. The 60 cases were distributed as shown in Table 5.1.

Any difference between the organisation of the service in the four authorities was taken into account by exploring the delivery and outcome of the service from the social work perspective.

Table 5.1 Case distribution between the four study local authorities (n = 60)

Local authority	Number of cases	Percentage
Midcity	31	52
River Town	8	13
Spire City	9	15
Ferryport	12	20

Recruiting families to the study

The process of recruiting families to the study had several stages. First, at the point where families had expected the offer of short-term accommodation, social workers gave families a pre-printed letter from the research team inviting them to participate in the project. This informed them about the study, assured them about independence from social services and confidentiality and sought their participation. If families indicated to social workers that they were willing to participate, workers sent the name and address of the family to the research team on a prepared pro forma. Alternatively, families could write to the research team themselves if they did not wish to make an instant commitment to participate and were provided with a pre-paid envelope for this purpose. The procedure was set up with the full co-operation of social workers and their agreement not to put families under pressure in any way.

If the parent agreed to participate, the research team sent a letter explaining the research and offering an appointment. Letters were sent with a pre-printed opt-out reply slip and a stamped addressed envelope to be used by parents who did not wish to participate. Letters were translated into five languages to reflect the cultural demography of the areas and some were sent in a language other than English on the advice of the families' social worker. In fact only five families of those approached refused to take part. A scrutiny of their background from files suggested that they were very similar to those who had opted into the study.

Thirdly, if parents did not opt out, the researcher visited the family at their own home. At the beginning of the initial interview parents' contributions were outlined and issues of confidentiality and anonymity discussed. The issues to be covered in interviews with children were carefully explained to parents and they were given a short outline of the areas to be covered with the children. They were also taken through the test materials. In addition, their informed consent to interviewing their child was established. Since children were to be interviewed on a second occasion, parents had time to consider this further. Parents' permission to talk to social workers and carers was also established, outlining the areas to be discussed.

Fourthly, a protocol was developed with the four agencies to deal with any revelations of possible child abuse. However, the research team was relieved to find it was not necessary to apply this in any case.

Piloting the study

An earlier study had informed the research team about the issues surrounding short-term accommodation which parents and social workers thought important in relation to service delivery. This helped to formulate ideas and hypotheses that would be tested out in the study. These ideas informed the development of the research instruments which were then piloted in a number of ways:

1 Draft interview schedules were tried out with six parents from two of the study authorities who had recently experienced short-term accommodation.
2 The adapted assessment and action schedules (see later) were piloted with a group of parents attending a family centre in one of the study locations. This was desirable because the schedules had originally been designed for looked-after children. At the beginning of this study, the extensive testing of the assessment and action schedules on a wider population had not been completed (see Ward, 1995).
3 Four social workers from agencies included in the earlier study but not in this one were consulted over both social work schedules and how best to access children.
4 Finally, materials for children were piloted in children's own family homes. The children's questionnaire was piloted with four children over

the age of 7 who had experienced overnight stays with child-minders in the belief that this respite experience was similar to the experiences of children accommodated short-term. Additionally, the games and toys used with very young children were piloted with three under-5s who had also been child-minded overnight.

The information gained from piloting the different research instruments helped shape the final version of interview schedules or tools used in the study.

Interviews

Interviews were conducted with parents, social workers, carers and children. When considering parents, the interview was carried out with the parent who considered him/herself more responsible for child care. Parents, social workers and children were interviewed at two points in time:

- when the offer of short-term accommodation had been made and had been accepted by the family; and
- at a re-testing after at least nine months had elapsed and the accommodation was ongoing, or sooner if the arrangements had ended earlier.

In the latter case this proved to be not less than seven months. It was felt that to leave some gap for reflection after the service had ended would be desirable in the shorter-term cases plus the fact that seven months would allow for changes to have been consolidated. In 97% of cases, children were accommodated for two or three days over the weekend. Only two children spent longer periods with carers, and none more than four days at a time. All interviews where arrangements had ended were conducted within three months of the ending. The span between first and second interview is shown in Table 5.2.

Carers were interviewed only once to coincide with the second interview with families and social workers. As with the parents, an index carer was identified as the one who considered him/herself most responsible for child care.

Table 5.2 Intervals between initial interview and final interview (n = 60)

Interval	Number of arrangements	Percentage
7 months	8	13
8 months	11	19
9 months	35	58
Over 9 months	6	10

Style and content of the interviews

The interviews were conducted informally following the guidance of Hammersley and Atkinson (1983). This style allows families to see the interview as an extension of normal conversation. The parents found this method facilitating and most were able to talk at length about their circumstances, their problems and the service.

In a proportion of cases early in the study, at least two members of the research team worked together interviewing the same family to develop a consistent pattern of interviewing and to prevent distortion (Glaser & Strauss, 1967).

One prominent issue was recognising the importance of being sensitive to cultural and linguistic issues in families of Asian origin. Accordingly, in these cases there was always a female member of the research team taking the lead. Additionally, in four cases, the services of locally based interpreters were used in interviewing parents whose first language was not English. The research team spent time with the interpreter before the interview, familiarising her with the research schedules. After the interview the interpreter and research team member spent time checking the accuracy and meaning of any qualitative comments.

After seeking permission, all interviews with parents, carers and children were tape-recorded. It was important to impress upon parents and children that they could have the tape recorder turned off at any time. After the interview was completed parents and children were given the opportunity to listen to as much of the tape as they wished. Many of the children were much amused by the sound of their voice: 'It was like being on the radio.'

Interviewing children: issues

As discussed earlier, parents gave their informed consent to participate in the study, having been given two opportunities to opt out. By contrast, the research team was aware that children agreed to be involved without really knowing what they were agreeing to. Young children would not be able to understand the implications of the research but did give agreement to take part in the study. In seeking children's assent the research team was aware that, while it is possible to match adults for social characteristics, the disparity of age when interviewing children cannot be overcome.

When seeking children's agreement, the research team emphasised the limits to confidentiality, discussed by Morrow and Richards (1996). Children were assured that information given to the research team would be kept confidential but at the same time it was made clear that they were free to share with their parents and others what had taken place. The research team was helped in interviews by the fact that members of the team had acquired many skills in talking to children through years of working professionally in social work with children.

There was awareness of the importance of talking to children in private. Children may conceal some of their feelings from parents because they do not wish to hurt them. Parents were aware that children might have a different perspective on the service and in all but one case parents were happy to arrange for the child to be seen in private.

The factors that influenced the interviews with children were similar to those with adults. It was important to establish a rapport, and in this the research was helped by the fact that most children were in the house while their parents were being interviewed. Thus they became familiar with the interviewer and also saw that the researcher was accepted by the parents. This had a normalising effect on the situation. Children were always seen on a second occasion and parents were urged to contact the research team if they or the children had any misgivings about the interview. In fact, there were no refusals.

Great effort was put into preparing for children's interviews using the skills of the research team to develop scene-setting explanations for children which took account of their cognitive development and linguistic ability.

Although an interview schedule could be used with older children, the research team developed a number of methods drawn from direct work with small children to gather information from young children. These included games, play materials and glove puppets. All of the children over 5 were interviewed, and three of the younger ones. The decision to interview children or to use play techniques was made in consultation with parents.

Throughout the interviews, researchers were very concerned not to lead children and to empower them not to feel inadequate if they could not answer a question. In addition, the team was highly sensitive to points when children were uneasy about answering a particular question and reassured them that it was perfectly acceptable not to do so. The team also gave children opportunities to end the interview at any point, a facility taken up by five children. On these occasions researchers empowered children to curtail the interview and negotiate its continuation at a later time. The careful approach to children helped to ensure a 100% response rate.

The children's experiences

Information was gained directly from the children, who were interviewed at the start of the intervention and again after six to nine months, depending on the length of individual arrangements. Age and cognitive ability limited who was interviewed; none the less, over two-thirds (41) of the children were able to participate fully. When children were re-interviewed, two children had been accommodated full-time during the study period; as a result findings on outcome are based on interviews with 39 children.

A starting point for the children's story was to explore their anxieties about being accommodated.

Children's anxieties about being accommodated

The children were interviewed when accommodation had been agreed but had not yet started. Some children spoke clearly about how they felt. Others said they were worried but could not articulate why. Overall, 17 of the 41 older children (41%) were worried about being accommodated. Nine were unsure whether they were worried or not and 15 (37%) were looking forward to going away without anxieties.

Those who could articulate their views said a major anxiety was about going somewhere strange:

> I was nervous a bit. I'd not stayed with strangers before and I was worried. But they seemed nice...and friendly. (Mark, aged 8)

The strangeness from children's point of view included anxieties about missing important TV programmes and worrying about strange food:

> What I worry about most is not seeing *Gladiators*. I always watch that on Saturday nights. My teacher doesn't like it – says it's too aggressive. I think it's great. They have to let me watch it. (John, aged 12)

> I hope my mum tells them I don't like onions and eggs. I really worry about that. They won't like me if I don't eat their food. (Sue, aged 10)

For others, there was the fear of a hidden agenda of rejection by parents:

> I was afraid that I wouldn't go home again. I don't know why I was...I was afraid. (Robin, aged 6)

Attachment is a two-way process and children were worried about the effect of their absence on siblings and parents, although some views also thinly disguised anxiety about their own separation:

> See, my mum, I look after her since my dad went. She needs me to feed the cat and go to the shops. I will miss Fluffy [cat]. I like playing with her. I hope she won't forget me. (Pam, aged 9)

A further source of anxiety was whether the carer family would treat them well:

> Will they be kind – not hit me or anything. I worry about that. (Neil, aged 9)

It was perhaps significant that eight of the 15 who felt positive knew the carers as child-minders before they were placed:

> I know Alice. She looks after me sometimes when my mum is working. I like going there. I will like staying longer. (Rosie, aged 12)

Consultation and involvement in decision-making

One way in which children's anxieties can be lessened is if they understand why the placement is necessary and have an opportunity to put forward their views about the arrangements. The value of considering children's thoughts and feelings to inform decisions needs to be explained to parents in a way which endorses their concern and responsibility for the child rather than undermines it. Moreover, the consultation of children can raise dilemmas for social workers. What is consultation? Does it need to be 'formal'? Does it require special skills? How can one be sure that the child understands? Who are the best people to carry out the consultation? Should this be delegated to parents, undertaken jointly with parents or, in order to ensure the requirement for recording is fulfilled, should a social worker always be present?

Children in the study were asked about consultation in terms of the information they had received and the opportunity they had been given to express their views about being accommodated. It was encouraging to find that the majority of older children (38 of 41) recalled being informed by someone about what was happening. Mostly, this was the parent but in a minority of cases children recalled talking to social workers.

But information-giving is only one aspect of consultation. When it came to having the opportunity to talk about how they felt and having an input into the decision-making, just over half the children (22) thought that this had happened, eight said it definitely had never happened while the remaining 11 (27%) were uncertain.

There was a distinct feeling from children's comments that there had been little opportunity to protest or change plans. Consultation was very much on the side of information-giving. By contrast, when children's views were compared with those of parents and social workers, it was clear that the adults thought children had been given the opportunity to air their views in rather more cases. Although differences between the views of the children and the adults were not statistically significant, it seemed likely from children's comments that they had felt more intimidated and coerced by any consultation than adults realised.

Involvement in planning meetings was more fruitful in terms of children's impact on the process. According to the adults, a minority of children (13 of the 41 children) had attended planning meetings. It was difficult to establish what constituted a meeting in children's minds. Some meetings had taken place at the child's home but these were registered by children as 'chats'. In children's minds, a meeting was only recognised as such when it took place outside the home. But in the nine cases where this did occur, both children and parents believed the meeting allowed the children to influence the shape of arrangements:

I didn't want to go every weekend. I said this to the social worker and my dad. They said OK – we'll make it every other weekend. (Dan, aged 11)

The findings do suggest that there needs to be clarification of the meaning of consultation with children. To separate out the component parts into information-giving, talking over anxieties and giving children the opportunity to influence plans is important. Each element needs a slightly different approach. To conflate the components into one session may not be helpful. Additionally, account needs to be taken of the natural power parents may wield over their children in any circumstances to get them to conform to the parents' agenda. Independent sessions with children either with social workers or, in some cases, if they are known, carers, may be more objective.

Although no child in the study complained about the abuse of power by adults, it is all too easy to see how consultation could degenerate into tokenism. If short-term accommodation is targeted at parents in the interests of preventing family breakdown, this needs to be made explicit to the children. Not being accommodated may not be an option. It is as much an abuse of power to set children up to make spurious choices as it is not to ask them for their views. The conclusion from this tentative exploration into new territory of practice can only be to think more honestly about the true nature of the balancing act which will necessarily need to be performed between the short-term needs of adults and children and the long-term interests of the family as a whole.

Whatever the shortcomings of the consultation process, it was clear that children did have views on the purpose of the short-term accommodation.

Children most frequently (41%) thought that the breaks were arranged to allow their parents some respite from the ongoing rigour of bringing them up. Indeed many children had some awareness that respite from them would help parents continue to look after the family, and that this was therefore a good thing:

> I think my mum needs a break and then she feels a lot better. It's quite nice for me, I like them [carers] and I know she's at home. (Mary, aged 14)

Where children thought that the arrangements were made primarily for their sake, very few viewed this as an indication that there was anything amiss with them. Much more frequently, children showed a 'down to earth' understanding of what the arrangements were about:

> There are a lot of us at home. It gets very busy. It will be nice to have someone to play with me. (Lisa, aged 10)

Some children simply accepted parents' views of the benefits of being with another family and wished to leave the matter there:

> Well I think my mum thought we could do with a break. They [carers] would be sort of like a friend, an aunty. Our family lives quite far off. Mum said it would be a bit of fun.

Eight children were not at all sure why they were going to be accommodated. All but one of these children were under 8 years:

No, I don't know. My mum knows, why not ask her? She'll tell you. (Katie, aged 7)

Younger children were even more muddled. For example, a 6-year-old-girl struggled in her understanding of why she was going to the carer family:

Well, I don't know…When I'm invited, I think.

What children expected from the service

As well as exploring children's understanding of the purpose of the intervention, at the beginning of the accommodation, children were asked to say whether or not the arrangements would be helpful and to elaborate on who might be helped.

Nearly two-thirds (27) of the children definitely thought the breaks would be helpful to their parents and occasionally also to them, a finding which supported their view of the purpose of accommodation:

Definitely it will help me and my mum and Chris. Oh, for sure. (Charlie, aged 11)

A further quarter (10) were not sure whether the breaks would help, and four felt they would not. It seemed hard for them to envisage how the breaks would help anyone.

The preparation stage

Preparation was confined to information-giving about the carers and preparatory visits to the carers' homes. In fact the two events were conflated in children's minds. Two-fifths of children (16) had the advantage of knowing the carer as a child-minder and therefore did not make a special visit before their first overnight stay. Nineteen children (46%) did visit specifically to prepare for their stay. Only three children did not have the opportunity to visit, because there was no time before the placement started. An additional three younger children were confused about whether or not they had visited the carers' home, although visits had been reported by parents. It may have been these children thought the pre-placement visit was part of the accommodation arrangements. Visits to the carer family's home were often recounted as the point when children began to feel more confident about having breaks away, and less anxious about what was going to befall them there. For those unfamiliar with the carers, the introductory visit cannot be overestimated. It seemed to allow them to judge for themselves what kind of care they would receive.

Preparatory visits undoubtedly did a great deal to reassure the children, but the anticipation of the changes involved remained unsettling for the children at the start of the short-term accommodation period. The anxiety over separation increased when children were worried about things at home, or uncertain about what was happening and why. Part of the preparation process is to help children talk about their worries and provide them with strategies for managing the transition to the new home. Several writers, including Fahlberg (1981), Jewett (1984), and Aldgate (1992), have commented on the significant part adults can play over this period. Accordingly, children were asked who might provide that support in terms of someone to talk to about the impending experience.

Given the emphasis on the service being there to support the family, it is disappointing that not more children felt they could talk the matter over with their parents. Of some concern are the seven children who reported that they did not know to whom they could turn if worried.

The findings suggest that there is room for emphasising the role of parents in supporting their children at this time. Parental desires for respite for themselves should not override parental responsibility. It was clear that the children who were able to speak to their parents gained considerable reassurance from so doing. Especially important to children was knowing that there was no hidden agenda of rejection.

Of considerable interest was the relationship between the accommodated children and their peer group. Earlier studies of children looked after have suggested that children may feel stigmatised by 'being sent away from home' or they may fear the envy of their friends for having a treat. Either way, children may be reluctant to tell their peers about the placement. At the early stage in arrangements, only 20% of children anticipated talking to friends about any worries about the visits. Two-thirds (66%) said they would not want their friends to know and certainly would not talk to them about their fears.

In discussion with some of the study social workers about these early findings, two social workers said that they were aware that children could encounter stigma from peers and had discussed the pros and contras of talking to friends in the preparation period. These workers thought it important for children to know how to deal with questions from friends and teachers at school – and that children needed to be helped to find a 'good cover story'. Such a view, while realistic, is sad in that it demonstrates that the Children's Act intention to eradicate the stigma of accommodation is far from being achieved on this front.

Settling into the carer's home

First, children were asked about the initial transition. Would the knowledge of the finite length of the placement alter the way they reacted to separation? To explore this area, albeit rather tentatively, children were asked how

Table 5.3   **Children's experiences of settling into carer's home (n = 41)**

Settling into carer's home	Number of cases	Percentage
No difficulty	12	29
Some difficulty	24	59
Great difficulty	5	12

they felt about the initial stay. More specifically, how children settled into the carer's home was seen as a possible indicator of how they coped with the initial transition (see Table 5.3).

Twelve children (29%), all of whom had previously known the carer as a child-minder, had no difficulty in settling on the first stay. Practically three-fifths of the children experienced some difficulty in settling into the carer's home and five children said they had great difficulty. A girl of 8 describes her early experience:

Just getting used to it took a while...just different, you know. I missed my mum, and Becky, and Nick...but...it's alright now.

And a boy of 9 found:

Well, it was strange. I didn't feel quite at home. Had to be really good, too. When I got used to it, they were just normal – d'you know what I mean?

The prevalence of homesickness

The other side of the coin to settling away from home is the degree of home-sickness felt by the children. In fact, there was no relationship between the two factors. Irrespective of how easily children settled in, the majority (85%) missed their family and home. In short, they felt homesick. Nor was there any change in the strength of feelings of homesickness according to age.

A child of 5 recalled:

I wished I could go home...but I couldn't and I just wanted to hide.

And another of 12 years commented:

I missed my mum and Jenny [best friend] and my bed and my CDs. It was all a bit funny. My mum said I had to behave well. It was a strain.

Homesickness is a normal part of separation feelings for both adults and children. The attachment to absent people and places is not uncommon but hitherto there has been little exploration of how children manage their feelings. Children in this study displayed a diversity of techniques. Nine children talked to someone about their distress, usually the carer mother:

> I used to go and talk to her [carer]…in the kitchen for a while…no, not about anything special really. She seemed to know how it was. (Neil, aged 8)

Three said they would think about home and family:

> I think about Mum and Dave and Henry and Teresa and then I feel alright. If I see them in my mind I know they are there. (Rosie, aged 12)

Three cried with the main carer:

> She gives me a cuddle – she says it's OK to cry. (Mark, aged 8)

But by far the largest group (21), just over half the children, dealt with their emotions privately:

> I missed everyone…Mum, and Dee and Sue and I miss Fluffy [the cat] and… Well, I used to go off for a while…to my room and think a bit, by myself. I always know I could go home if I wanted. (Pam, aged 9)

The fact that children of primary school age sought to cope with their feelings in private is of considerable interest and is rarely referred to in child care textbooks. It is an area which warrants further exploration and one which may need more highlighting in the training of carers.

For the children in this study, going home after their first stay away brought relief and happiness for well over half the children (25):

> I could watch the TV in peace and go to bed when I wanted. (Tom, aged 13)

A further 19 expressed no strong feelings either way:

> It was OK – didn't affect me much either way. I soon got used to it. (Don, aged 11)

Of concern were the eight children who recounted feelings of anxiety and uncertainty on returning home:

> My mum and dad fight all the time – it is different at Paul and Elaine's house. (Seth, aged 10)

Four worried that things had changed:

> When I hadn't been there…I expect it would be different. (Dave, aged 10)

Familiarity with a system generally brings with it a decrease in anxiety. For the study children, however, the difficulties in returning home continued. At the end of the series of short stays away, there was very little change in the children's views. Those who had felt at the start that going home after a visit could be a difficult time continued to feel this.

The findings are useful in highlighting salient aspects of preparing children for being looked after away from home. It is important to recognise that children feel homesick even if the stay away is a short and temporary one, and that good as well as painful experiences while away can contribute to difficulties or awkwardness between parent and child at the moment when they come together again. Because short-term accommodation does not remove children entirely from their homes, it is tempting to think that the effects of brief separations will be of a slighter intensity than those where separation is longer or the length is uncertain. The findings of this study suggest that adults need to be sensitive to individual children's reactions to any separation, however brief. At the same time, it must be stressed that generally, with appropriate support and sensitivity from adults, children managed their feelings and the comings and goings well.

Contact with family while away

In response to earlier research findings about the impact on children of loss of contact while they are being looked after (DHSS, 1985) the Children Act 1989 highlights the importance of children retaining links with their families while they are away from home (see DoH, 1991). Little is known about the relative merits of contact for children accommodated short-term. Consequently, this area was explored in this study.

Although there was a general understanding that parents would not actually visit during the breaks, except in special circumstances, there were no restrictions on indirect contact, for example by phone. However, given that only seven of the 60 families involved in the study had easy access to a telephone, it is not surprising that few children expected any contact between the carer home and their own home. As it turned out, this expectation was realistic. During the short-term accommodation period contact, always by phone, between the child's home and that of the carer occurred in only 12 of the 60 cases – equally divided between the under- and over-5s. No child (or parent) complained of feeling unable to be in contact during the visits. Three older children said they knew they could walk home if they wanted. Several of the under-8s remarked that their parents knew where they were. The specificity of the arrangements, and the knowledge that communication was possible between the two homes, seemed to be enough to make children feel secure.

To explore how children adapted to the carer's regime, they were asked, at both the start and the end of the period of short-term accommodation, about changes related to tangible everyday events such as bedtime, meals, seeing friends, pocket money and watching television. Overall, children experienced relatively few problems:

I watched less telly. Didn't miss it much, because we were playing. (Tommy, aged 9)

However, changes at the start of the placement in some routines held more significance than others. Just over half of the children (23) experienced a different bedtime regime. On the whole, this meant going to bed slightly earlier. For one or two, it meant not watching TV in bed. But for a handful (six) it meant not being able to seek comfort from parents in the night. Most children quickly adapted to this change:

> A bit different. Comfy and all that, but sometimes if I get frightened or I wake up…then I go through to my mum. I missed it … but anyway, I didn't get frightened or anything, so it wasn't bad … just different. (Lisa, aged 10)

Food also presented differences for 19 of the children. This was occasionally (in five cases) to do with what was on offer, but more often to do with the normal constraints of being a guest in someone's house:

> Oh, yes it was nice food…what I missed was that I couldn't just go to the cupboard and get something…biscuits, or crisps. Well, she'd say yes mostly. But I had to ask. (John, aged 12)

One disadvantage of the majority of the placements for the older children was that they disrupted normal weekend routines. This included going shopping locally and seeing relatives and friends:

> I missed going to the shop…like I usually do on a Saturday for my mum. (Rosie, aged 12)

Seven children did see their friends during the weekend but the majority did not expect to do so and accepted that being away from home brought a different routine. Their views suggested that, for many, the excitement of the placement outweighed any real disadvantage. Some of the over-10s also had faith that the relationships of home and peers would endure beyond the placement:

> I did different things, the people were different…good fun mostly. My own friends are there still. (Matthew, aged 14)

The children did not mention this as a disadvantage and none suggested that their regular friendships were affected by their periodic absences.

One issue held considerable significance for children – watching television. There were two areas of contention: missing favourite programmes because of alternative activities and not being allowed to stay up to watch particular programmes. This issue became more marked as the placement progressed. At the second interview stage there was a statistically significant increase in the numbers who felt customs over watching television were different from those at home ($p = < 0.05$, $df = 1$, Chi square). It is difficult to tell whether the direction of difference was positive or negative; indeed, children's comments suggested a variety of reactions:

No one liked to watch football. At home we have Sky TV. Me and my dad we watch football and sport all the time. I missed that a lot. (Mark, aged 12)

None of the differences perceived by the children was unsettling enough to affect the arrangements drastically, and nearly all were things with which the children quickly felt reasonably happy.

Relations with members of the carer family

The majority of children got on well with all members of their carer family. Although practically 70% of the children said they got on well with the mother, a further 27% were uncertain and 5% were not happy with the relationship. Ambivalence seemed mainly to relate to the fact that the carer mother would generally be responsible for setting and upholding family norms and rules:

Well, not sure about Mrs Harris. She was very strict. (Sophie, aged 9)

In addition, some children hinted that to develop a good relationship with the carer mother would have been disloyal to their own mother:

I liked being there but it wasn't like being with Mum. She said I could call her Mum. I didn't. I thought my mum wouldn't like it. (Dave, aged 10)

Good relationships with fathers seemed to relate to individual personalities rather than any comparison with children's relationship with their own fathers. There was no association between liking fathers and whether children came from a one- or two-parent family.

Good or poor relationships with the children in the household were characterised by the attitudes and attention of children to each other.

What children liked and disliked about carer family members

Children were asked to give their views on why they liked or disliked members of the carer family. These views fell into five categories. Children highlighted different characteristics when they talked about what they liked in different members of the carer family. There was a tendency to divide characteristics of mothers and fathers by gender.

Carer mothers were valued more for their attitudes than for any shared activities. For example, kindness was high on the agenda for practically half (48%) of the children, with an emphasis also on nurturing:

She was kind…treated me special, made me sandwiches and gave me Coca-Cola. (Don, aged 10)

Six children stressed being treated as 'special' by their carer mother. All came from families where there was a good deal of tension:

> What I liked was that she was kind...treated me special. (Sue, aged 10)

The attitude and attention of carer fathers was also valued but was focused more through shared activities:

> I helped him mend the car...learnt a lot. (Richard, aged 12)

Several children from households where fathers were unemployed commented that they did not like it when the carer father went to work, and one 6-year-old boy felt quite put out:

> Well, he did keep going off...I think he was going to work...every day, like!

Where there were other children in the home, playing together was the thing that children enjoyed most. Appreciation of other qualities, such as 'talking to' and being 'treated as special' was associated only with the presence of older carer children.

Throughout the exploration of the children's perceptions of their relationships with the carer family, the question of comparisons between their own home and that of the carers rarely arose. Although children appreciated small treats like popcorn at the cinema there was no sense of envy of carer households. Children were much more preoccupied by the attitudes of adults towards them. Although it can only be speculation, this may relate to the fact that cultural and economic differences between families are kept to a minimum and the fact that children did care about and value their own families.

The children found it far more difficult to identify features about their carer family which they did not like. Practically two-thirds could not identify any characteristic they disliked about their carer mother (65%), carer father (62%) or carer children (58%). It was impossible to develop any typology of dislikes because of the small numbers involved and the diversity of reasons given by individual children. Descriptions of what was disliked showed that criticisms of both carer mothers and fathers tended to the ordinary and largely represented part of the normal negotiations of boundaries between adults and children in many families. There was a minority of children who did not like their carer families, did not settle and wished continually that they were at home.

Perceptions of the value of the intervention

By the second interview, 78% of the children (31 of 40) believed the breaks had helped them personally while all but three thought that the breaks had been helpful to their parents. Children's answers about how the experience had helped them fell into four categories, defined by themselves:

1 They had had a good time (35%).
2 They felt happier (29%).
3 They had had a break from worries at home (20%).
4 The breaks had made things easier at home (16%).

What children would have changed

Two-thirds (26) of the children either did not suggest any changes to the arrangements they had experienced, or could not think of anything they would have liked to be different.

For those who did want things changed, this was usually in terms of the overall period of breaks. Nine out of the thirteen who wanted to change arrangements would have liked a longer series of breaks, while the remaining four wanted the opposite. These four children had not wanted to be accommodated in the first place and remained resentful about being sent away from home.

Conclusion

This study exemplifies the value of an approach to children's services that focuses on promoting and safeguarding children's welfare. It uses measurable outcomes to show that this kind of short-term fostering, when well targeted, can bring about changes in levels of family problems and help prevent family breakdown. The study also underlines the importance of traditional casework and demonstrates how social work is a family support service in its own right, which is valued by parents and children.

References

Aldgate, J. (1992) Work with children experiencing separation and loss. In J. Aldgate & J. Simmonds (Eds), *Direct Work with Children: A Guide for Social Work Practitioners.* 2nd ed. London: Batsford.

Department of Health (1991) *Patterns and Outcomes in Child Placement: Messages from Current Research and their Implications.* London: HMSO.

Department of Health and Social Security (1985) *Social Work Decisions in Child Care.* London: HMSO.

Fahlberg, V. (1981) *Helping Children When They Must Move.* London: British Agencies for Adoption and Fostering.

Glaser, B. & Strauss, A. (1967) *The Discovery of Grounded Theory*. New York: Aldine de Gruyter.

Hammersley, M. & Atkinson, P. (1983) *Ethnography: Principles in Practice*. London: Routledge.

Jewett, C. (1984) *Helping Children Cope with Separation and Loss*. London: BAAF.

Morrow, V. & Richards, M. (1996) The ethics of social research with children: an overview, *Children and Society*, **10**: 90–105.

Ward, H. (ed.) (1995) *Looking after Children: Research into Practice*. London: HMSO.

Starting points

I have long been a supporter of using foster care as a service to keep families together rather than a last resort when families have failed. My enthusiasm for this concept stems from my social work training in Scotland in the late 1960s where I was inspired by the work of foster families who helped families under stress stay together. So I was delighted when the Children Act 1989 in England and Wales changed legislation in order to break down barriers between children being in and out of care. Short-term foster care (now called accommodation to get away from the stigma of care) became the flagship of family support services. I was excited about this and wanted passionately to see whether or not the concept could work in practice. The Department of Health was setting up a research initiative on the implementation of the Children Act 1989 and invited me to draft an outline for a possible study on short-term accommodation. The outline led to a worked up proposal, and the proposal to the funded study which became one of 24 studies evaluating the Children Act 1989.

In this commentary I shall reflect on the whole study, rather than just on the extracts reproduced in this book.

Author collaboration

A timely chance encounter with Marie Bradley led to our collaboration. Together, Marie and I were a complementary team. I had experience of grant-funded research and a keen interest in the methodology and socio-legal background of the study. I also had undertaken many interviews with foster parents and birth parents in previous studies. Marie, by contrast, was very interested in children's development and the impact of loss and change on children. She was expert at interviewing children of all ages. We had a third member in the team, David Hawley, a newly retired, very senior social work manager. He had many years' experience of foster care practice and direct work with children and parents. David and I had previously undertaken a study on foster home breakdown.

I led on the study design, drawing on the practice wisdom of David and Marie in the framing of questions. They just knew what would work and the piloting proved them right. The whole team engaged in negotiating access to children and families but Marie and David took the lead on the interviewing although I joined one of them for about a quarter of the interviews to ensure I was in touch with the study. Marie took the lead on developing the coding frames for our quantitative data which Marie and I jointly analysed with help from a statistician. We all worked on developing the themes from our qualitative data. In the writing up, I drafted the scene setting and methods chapters while Marie wrote about the children, carers and families. I took the lead on the chapters on social work practice. We spent many long weekends and days writing the final draft together, consuming a great many cups of tea and bacon sandwiches. It really was a genuinely joint effort!

The research questions

Our research questions were driven by the policy agenda. The Department of Health wanted us to explore the implementation of the new service of short-term accommodation for families under stress. Our hypothesis was that the Children Act had provided an enhanced opportunity for foster care to be used to prevent family breakdown. The research questions were flooding in. How, in what circumstances, was this service best offered? What were the barriers to success? Had the Children Act made a difference to the way such a service was offered? What part did foster parents play in supporting or undermining the parental responsibility of the birth parents? Above all, what part did social work play in the success or failure of the service? We all agreed that a study of short-term fostering had to mirror the complexities of social work and fostering practice.

Choice of methodology

As the study aimed to evaluate the implementation of the Children Act 1989 we knew it had to look at the principles of practice contained in the Guidance and Regulations accompanying the Act. The most important principle for our study was that children should, wherever possible, be brought up by their own families and that services should be there to support families to do just that. There was also a mandate to work in partnership with parents in any service. Most importantly, in English and Welsh law, children's wishes and feelings were to be taken into account in any decisions that affected their lives. How were these principles being translated into the practice of the fostering service?

There was another layer of complexity. It was impossible to look at the service without understanding the social work role in the round. This meant not only looking at the legal requirements on social workers in carrying out their duties but also studying the processes and methods social workers used to work with parents, children and foster carers. These we felt should be grounded in social work theory and methods.

There were many ethical issues, particularly where the interviewing of children was concerned. We acted with utmost care in seeking to interview children, gaining permission from parents, ensuring children were never pressured to respond and agreeing that any interviews could be terminated by the children at any point. We were mindful of the sensitivities of child abuse. The research team had police checks and were credible to agencies. We set up protocols to ensure we knew what to do if we were unhappy about anything we had been told which might relate to the child's welfare. We therefore had link workers in each agency to whom we could turn if necessary. We had to ensure that children knew about this agenda. It is critical in this kind of applied research that the research team includes trained professionals. We were interviewing vulnerable children and families and researchers had to be able to deal with sensitive and challenging issues in a professional and ethical manner.

We thought long and hard about putting families at ease. We aimed to conduct the interviews in two stages, although this slipped because of time constraints. We made appointments to see families and always interviewed parents first. Then we saw the children. There was a tricky issue of whether to see children and parents alone or together. We felt that children might be inhibited with their parents present yet we did not want parents to feel we were gaining information behind their backs. Similarly, what would the children think about their parents being interviewed? The problem was solved by sharing the content of our questionnaires with parents and gaining their approval. We also told children and showed the older ones what we asked their parents. This transparency did much to build the confidence of the respondents and we felt reflected good social work practice. In the majority of cases we did see parents and children separately but each family made its own decision on this issue. We decided to pay parents and give children a small token (a pen or fancy pencil) although we did not tell families this would happen until after the first interviews.

We conducted two pilots. The first was a mapping exercise with eight sites offering short-term accommodation. We found these pragmatically by several routes:

- local knowledge;
- information from a national study mapping family support by Jane Aldgate and Jane Tunstill (1995);
- an advert in the trade press;
- the knowledge of the Social Services Inspectorate; and
- ringing up any social work friends who might know of services in their area.

This exercise was invaluable in telling us about the nature and duration of the service and helped to guide our decision about when to retest. The Department of Health was very concerned that this study should not simply describe the new service but should evaluate it as well. This influenced us to choose a longitudinal design that could revisit areas at a later point.

Finding out about the organisation of the service contributed to our decisions about when to follow up families. We agonised about when to place the cut-off point but took a pragmatic stance and opted for a month after the end in cases which had concluded within six months, and no longer than nine months in the rest. This was probably the most shaky part of our design but we tried to compensate for this by ensuring we evaluated the outcome from the perspectives of all concerned and triangulated the data.

We had an overt agenda to find research sites that were offering an established service with clear aims and objectives. In the end the choice of the four sites was a pragmatic one and we were very worried this would bias the samples but luckily found it did not. Children and parents were very similar across the four agencies in many respects. Having four agencies also added credibility to any generalisations we wanted to make at the end.

We conducted a pilot study in a family centre with parents and children of similar background to those with whom we would be conducting the research. The parents helped us shape the way questions were asked. We felt reassured that we seemed to be on the right lines and in fact we altered little.

Data decisions

We opted for a multi-methods approach, using quantitative and qualitative data. This enabled us to answer a range of questions. The quantitative data allowed us to:

- map the characteristics of families in each of the areas and compare for differences and similarities;
- identify patterns of service delivery, how long the service lasted, etc.;
- incorporate some standardised tests which could measure change over time;
- standardise analysis of attitudinal questions;
- triangulate the data and compare the views of different participants on the same issues.

We had some messy data in non-responses but the problems of handling these were minor. I put this down to the tenacity of David and Marie to make sure all questions were answered. We used the SPSS program to analyse the quantitative data and enlisted the help of a health statistician, Jane Barlow who advised us on the statistical tests appropriate to our data.

It was a very exciting part of the study when Jane came back with the statistics showing many of the associations we had hoped for. To interpret the meaning of the service for children, families, carers and social workers we needed the stories of the service as they were told by those involved. We spent a long time eyeballing responses, grouped them as patterns emerged and drew conclusions from these groupings. We involved others in this process to ensure that our judgements were sound and were reassured when our independent scrutineers came to similar conclusions. We were careful to choose from the range of respondents so the quotes would represent as many of our 60 children and families as possible. Using the multi-methods approach kept us focused and yet still enabled us to explore sensitive areas in depth.

We faced major challenges in the presentation of the work because there were so many areas of overlap. We decided to take apart the component parts and then bring them together by using the triangulation of data. To a large extent, the data led the presentation. We had looked at different areas – children, parents, social workers, carers – as well as comparing views on the same issues. Because this was a study on the implementation of the 1989 Children Act, the principles and guidance of the Act deliberately dominated the presentation.

Personal interactions

Doing this kind of research is unnerving because there is no cohort or a captive sample and you are completely dependent on the good will of agencies and workers to access respondents. There were periods when we had no families to interview and David continually had to remind agencies we were still there awaiting suitable cases. We had to be a bit more flexible in the timing of the first interview than we wanted. It was impossible to see all families within a week of the service beginning.

We were astounded at the enthusiasm of all the participants, who seemed to enjoy telling us their stories. We were more impressed than we expected to be with the resilience of families and with the expertise and commitment of foster carers and social workers. We were also surprised by how much the findings confirmed the theories. The homesickness of the children was much greater than we had expected and we were also surprised by the empathy between carers and families. Above all we were impressed with the children, particularly their attitudes towards their parents.

Writing up

The writing-up process was difficult because of the multi-layers of the study's design. At one point we felt overwhelmed by the large mass of data. Throughout the study we were guided by the wisdom of an advisory group appointed by the Department of Health and led by Dr Carolyn Davies. This included two expert child care researchers, Jane Rowe and Professor Roy Parker. It also included the civil servant, Geoff James, who had written the practice guidance for the Department of Health on short-term fostering. Though it was a bit daunting to have to reveal our processes in public the considerable trust between ourselves and the group enabled us to be honest about any problems. Our academic advisors inspired us towards a presentation that was creative and original and helped us keep our nerve at critical points.

There was no doubt that the writing up took forward the research questions in an organic way which had not originally been envisaged. There was a building block process to our writing. We started with the easy parts, drawing together the description of the families and the services, drafting the children's views and those of the parents and carers. This was very raw. We then built this draft into a framework of the law, policy, practice, theory and methods. This was really hard. The middle part on social work practice was rewritten many times. The problem was to ground the data simultaneously in social work theory, method and official practice guidance and these did not always align with each other.

Hindsight reflections

Would we have done anything differently? We found that, in spite of the piloting, our questionnaires were a bit too detailed and repetitive in parts. We could have refined them further but we were always anxious not to leave things out, so as to avoid regrets about missing data later. I think we were too cautious and could have been more focused. If we had not been so closely tied into evaluating the Children Act, we could have let children, families and carers lead the research agenda more. If we were doing the study now, this would be possible. Both government policy and methodology have moved forward on the participatory agenda.

This study was a trailblazer of studies that drew together policy, theory and practice within the context of the Children Act 1989 and provided a model for later studies in the series. It was really hard to make sense of the different layers but we felt we had helped take social work research a bit further along the methodological journey by trying to grasp the complexity. The study has been very well reviewed nationally and internationally. Its success has been a surprise because it is by no means perfect. Our samples were adapted to the messy world of social services. We would like to have compared our children with disabled children who receive a similar service. If anything, the study was limited by its length. We would have liked to follow up the families for a longer period but were constrained by funding. We would have liked a larger sample to reassure ourselves that what we found was truly representative of services across the country. Because we picked exemplars of good practice we did feel we presented the best rather than the range. On the other hand, this was all about seeing what worked and did not work in the context of 'textbook' social work practice.

The findings from this study and 23 others were drawn together by June Statham from the Thomas Coram Research Unit and myself into an overview (Department of Health, *The Children Act Now – Messages from Research*, TSO, London, 2001). Our study is one of a group on family support. It has been very reassuring to see our findings confirmed and supported by other studies. The study has generated interest from many local authorities and has informed the setting up of at least three schemes using short-term fostering to support families. It has been incorporated into an international book on measuring outcomes in child welfare.

Reference

Aldgate, J. & Tunstill, J. (1995) *Making Sense of Section 17: Implementing Services for Children in Need Within the 1989 Children Act*. London: HMSO.

Negotiating Autonomy: Children's
Use of Time and Space in Rural Bolivia
SAMANTHA PUNCH

This paper contains sections from two research papers by Samantha Punch: Punch, S. (2001) 'Negotiating autonomy: children's use of time and space in rural Bolivia', in Alanen, L. and Mayall, B. (Eds), *Conceptualising Child–Adult Relations*, London: Routledge Falmer, and Punch, S. (2001) 'Multiple methods and research relations with children in rural Bolivia', in Limb, M. and Dwyer, C. (Eds), *Qualitative Methodologies for Geographers*, London: Arnold.

Introduction: negotiating autonomy

The structures of adult society limit children's opportunities for asserting their autonomy. Children live in a world in which the parameters tend to be set by adults, especially in relation to children's use of time and space (Ennew, 1994). Therefore it is important to see how they negotiate their position within the constraints of that bounded world. It is necessary to explore children's competencies and strengths, as well as their constraints and limits, and their strategies for negotiating with adult society (see Harden & Scott, 1998).

Adult–child relations are based on unequal power relations between the generations but should not be seen in terms of independence versus dependence. Elements of exchange in reciprocal relations between adults and children should be considered (Morrow, 1994). Adults' and children's lives are interrelated at many different levels; adults are often not fully independent beings (Hockey & James, 1993). It is too simplistic to use the notion of dependency, whether of children on adults, or adults on children, to explain the often complex nature of the adult–child relationship. This chapter argues that adult–child relations should be explained in terms of interdependencies which are negotiated and renegotiated over time and space, and need to be understood in relation to the particular social and cultural context.

Finch and Mason (1993) explored the processes of negotiation of family relationships in adult life in the UK. Although their research is not about young children, it shows how people *work out* responsibilities and commitments in the absence of clear rules about precisely who should do what for whom: 'Family responsibilities thus become a matter for negotiation between individuals and not just a matter of following normative rules' (Finch & Mason, 1993: 12). In the Majority World,[1] where many children work, some parents are economically dependent on their children's contribution (Boyden et al., 1998; Schildkrout, 1981). For example, Boyden (1990) noted that in some countries children can be the main or sole income-earners in the household. It could be argued that in much of the Majority World, children's economic contribution to the household means that family relations of interdependence tend to be stronger (Punch, 2002a). The relationships of interdependence between children and adults, and between siblings, and how they manage the distribution of work for the household, is largely ignored in the literature on the household division of labour. However, the notion of interdependence does not simply account for the exact ways in which responsibilities are met by individual household members. Even though the cultural expectation in rural Bolivia is that children should have a strong sense of responsibility and obligation to their family, the ways these are fulfilled in practice are negotiable (see also Punch, 2000).

Mayall (2001: 114–128) relates negotiation to structure and agency debates (Giddens, 1990), where people struggle to gain a better deal in their relationships within different structures. She identifies the concept of a 'continuously re-negotiated contract as a feature of children's relationships with their parents', suggesting that 'children seek to acquire greater autonomy through re-siting the boundaries, challenging parental edicts, seizing control' (Mayall, 2001: 121). I would add that children's negotiation of a relative autonomy also occurs in their relationships with other children, especially siblings, and not just with their parents. Such negotiation varies according to the extent of interdependence between children and adults, between siblings, and between children.

Adults' power over children is not absolute and is subject to resistance (Hockey & James, 1993; Lukes, 1986; Reynolds, 1991; Waksler, 1991a, 1996). Children renegotiate adult-imposed boundaries and assert their autonomy, which can include decision-making, gaining control over one's use of time and space, taking the initiative to do something and taking action to shape one's own life. Thus autonomy is partial and relative, as no one lives in a social vacuum, and the ways in which one uses time and space, or makes choices, take place within social contexts involving other people, both children and adults. Autonomy is related to issues of power and control, which is why it has to be negotiated within social relationships, especially by children who are faced with unequal adult–child power relations.

Relatively few studies have focused on children's strategies of resisting adult power and control (Goddard & White, 1982). Waksler's research in the UK (1991b, 1996) indicated that children may lie, fake illness, have temper tantrums or act extra cute in order to cope with and control certain aspects of their lives. Reynolds' study of South African children (1991) referred to children's strategies of negotiating relationships in order to secure help for their future, and she also highlighted children's rebellion in defying adults' wishes, with reference to gambling, smoking and refusing to do certain tasks. However, it must also be recognised that children's reactions to adult power range 'from unquestioning acceptance to instances of resentful resistance'

(Mayall, 2001: 121). Within the two extremes of compliance and rejection, children's strategies emerge as they manage their responses to adult control. Children may not be fully independent, but they negotiate a relative autonomy within the constraints which limit their choices. In the present study I explored children's negotiation of autonomy in a rural community in Bolivia.

Methods and research relations

I used a range of qualitative methods, including informal and semi-structured interviews and semi-participant observation, with most members of a sample of eighteen households. Full participant observation with children is impossible for adults mainly because of their physical size (Fine & Sandstrom, 1988) and it has been suggested that a semi-participant observer role is more suitable (James et al., 1998). I spent three months carrying out classroom observation and task-based methods at the community school with children aged between 6 and 14. The school-based research consisted of children writing diaries, taking photographs, drawing pictures, completing worksheets and creating spider diagrams and activity tables (Punch, 2002b). These last two methods were adapted from Participatory Rural Appraisal techniques (see *PLA Notes*, 1996; Slocum et al., 1995). For example, the aim of the activity tables was to discover the range of activities and work that children do. They filled in a list of all the agricultural, animal-related and domestic tasks that they knew how to do, indicating whether they enjoyed doing that particular activity or not, and whether the activity was seasonal or year-round.

Building and negotiating research relations: being an adult and an outsider

A particular difficulty of conducting research with children of a different culture from the researcher's own is that a Minority World experience of childhood involves understanding childhood in a particular way. Minority World childhood is a time devoted to play and school, relatively free from 'adult responsibilities'. To understand rural childhoods in a Majority World country, preconceptions concerning personal experience needed to be minimised, along with notions of how childhoods are or should be (see Punch, 2002a). Nevertheless, studying childhoods within a different culture can in some ways be easier than studying the childhoods of one's own culture (Fetterman, 1989: 46).

Ethnography was the most appropriate research strategy. As a white, middle-class female brought up within an urban environment in the Minority World my background differed significantly from those whom I was studying.

Naturally my background has created biases which can never totally be abandoned and perhaps should not be (James, 1993: 8). Despite the cultural, social and economic differences between myself and the participants of the research, by living in the community for an extended period of time I could become closer to their lives and closer to an adequate understanding of their culture and lifestyle.

Ethnographic approaches accept that researchers may influence the research context (Hammersley & Atkinson, 1995). Reflexivity is a vital part of ethnographic research, as participation in the social world being studied requires constant reflection on the social processes and the personal characteristics and values of the researcher which inform the data generated as well as the subsequent interpretation and data analysis. It was important to maintain a record of observations, especially of the context and how the children reacted. How data are produced plays a vital part in interpretation (see Mason, 1996).

Geographical isolation meant that both the children and adult participants had experienced limited contact with outsiders. Many children had never seen a white European before meeting me. At the start of the research they reacted with stares and nervous giggles. Living in the community and taking part in some of the participants' daily activities meant I could form a relationship of trust vital for gathering data.

Building relationships

The researcher's relationship with participants must be acknowledged because researchers frequently worry about the appropriateness of their behaviour (Devereux, 1992: 43). Immersion in the local culture and the formation of closer relationships with research subjects can result in the researcher becoming so absorbed in their lifestyles that it can become difficult to detach oneself and observe as an outsider. A conscious effort must be made to record emerging ideas, difficulties and changing relationships with participants.

Forming relationships of trust can take a long time and varies with different people. Some people never lost their suspicions of me as the foreign visitor to their community. Various signs indicated when I began to be more accepted, such as when I was invited inside the house for the first time or when I was invited to eat a meal with household members rather than separately at the 'guest' table. Once, when a 4-year-old girl was sitting on my lap, a neighbour warned the mother of the household to take her from me or one day I would steal her. Fortunately my relationship was sufficiently good with that household for them to laugh off her suggestions.

My constant questioning would occasionally frustrate a few of the participants. I felt a need to 'give something back' as a token of appreciation for their time and patience (see also Francis, 1992). Caution had to be taken never to promise to do something that I would not be able to fulfil, since many rural people have experienced disillusion with outsiders whose promises to improve their lives never materialised. Throughout most of the fieldwork, I lived with two households: the families of Marianela (10 years) and Dionicio (12 years).[2] Neither family would accept payment for rent so I repaid their hospitality by bringing food or other gifts from my town visits.

My relationship with both the mothers, Felicia and Dolores, became stronger as fieldwork progressed. Their children also became important key informants.[3] It took longer to form relationships of mutual trust with the children than with the adults because of the unequal power relationship between an adult researcher and a child participant. I spent time with these children: accompanying them on their daily tasks, playing with them, walking to school, observing their work, their songs, their games, and how they negotiated their relationships with their parents and siblings. Caution had to be taken over revealing the hidden aspects of children's lives to adults. If something was told in confidence I had to be careful not to mention it to their parents or teachers. For example, once I saw two children going fishing and they told me that they were supposed to be looking after their mother's cows. They asked me not to say anything to their mother if I saw her. Consequently, when I saw their mother and she asked if I had seen the children, I chose to lie and say I had not.

Field relations were strengthened over time and as I learnt more about the lives of both the children and adults in the sample of eighteen households, they too learnt more about me. This shared knowledge enhanced a mutual, if unequal, relationship. Sometimes I felt I was manipulating our friendship in order to get good data (see also Punch, 1986). I found it increasingly hard to switch a very informal conversation to a more formal semi-structured interview situation. I wanted to carry out semi-structured interviews with the parents in order to cover the same kind of questions which I asked the children on their worksheets at school so that I could compare children's and parents' perceptions of rural childhoods. In order to compare their responses effectively, I had to write notes, which I felt sometimes disrupted the flow of a more informal interview which would be recorded afterwards.

Negotiation of the researcher's role

My research was conducted in the rural Bolivian village of Churquiales. Before going to Bolivia, I hoped to do some classroom observation in the Churquiales community school so that I would get to know many children and could observe them in a child-centred environment. I was concerned that my physical presence would disrupt the classes. After several weeks I asked if I could sit in on a few lessons. Despite my worries, the teachers were eager to have an extra pair of hands. I quickly assumed the role of teacher's assistant and found myself colouring in pictures, making decorations and sweeping the classroom floor. On my first morning, I was left in charge of the pupils while the teacher went home to finish preparing lunch and before long I was being left in charge of the pupils for whole mornings. When I suggested that I might prepare something for them to do, rather than rely on work set by the teacher, this was well received and I began devising research tasks (such as worksheets, drawings and diaries). This is an example of how ethnographic research relies upon opportunity and requires flexibility.

Over time some children wrote less and less in their daily diaries, but over half continued writing for more than two months. I collected the diaries each morning and sat at the back of the class reading them, which also proved to be an ideal opportunity for me to observe the class at the same time. The diaries provided a wealth of information about the everyday, routine aspects of children's lives.

I also prepared worksheets for the pupils on different aspects of their lives, some of which were closely related to issues explored in the other task-based methods. For example, questions on one worksheet about aspects of children's lives in the community complemented the drawings and photographs they had taken. Another worksheet was drawn up as a result of the activity table which children had completed. All the activities that they had mentioned were listed, and further columns were drawn up so that children could include who usually did that task in their household, who helped, who never did it, and at what age they learnt or could learn to do it.

I brought paper, coloured pens, pencils, exercise books and a camera to enable them to undertake different task-based activities. I always carried a range of materials so that I could replace teachers if they were absent. I spent time playing or talking with the children during break and lunch time. When I joined in their games both adults and children thought it was amusing, but some adults seemed to frown on such strange behaviour, as adults in Churquiales would almost never play with children.

Children often tried to provoke me to see how I would react. I tried to understand them on their terms, withholding judgement from an adult perspective. However, the role of assistant teacher tended to reinforce power inequalities between myself and the children – precisely what I had been trying to minimise (see also Morrow, 1999). A balance had to be struck between being their friend, a teacher, a teacher's assistant, an adult and a researcher. I had to switch between these different identities, but where possible I let the children decide what role they wanted me to play. Being an adult, but wanting to do the right things in children's eyes, can be problematic. My solution was to follow the children's lead wherever possible, letting them decide how they preferred to negotiate our relationship in different contexts. The most appropriate way for an adult researcher to behave with children is to try to understand the situation from their viewpoint, by listening to them, observing and reacting to their behaviour.

Combining methods

Rural children in particular tend to be shy with outsiders and not used to conversing with other people (except at school or at home). Semi-participant observation provides a way to get to know children better and build trust. It provides opportunities to carry out informal interviews and discuss issues as they occur. Semi-participation with the children meant learning by doing, thus reaching a greater understanding of children's activities. I could feel how heavy the water is that they have to carry, or how back-breaking it can be to harvest peas. I witnessed the special skills that children have, such as nimbly climbing up cliffs, finding their way in the dark, identifying individual animals and rounding them up. Active participation increased the depth of understanding through doing as well as observing.

I went with children on their daily chores, observing their daily lifestyle, which highlighted activities they took for granted, often not mentioned in interview. If I had only asked children about the work they do, many activities would have been omitted as they do not consider much of what they do to be 'work'. Observation was also useful for capturing the context of children's work and negotiations, as well as allowing for 'the recording of multiple task performance' (Reynolds, 1991: 76) when children carry out several activities at the same time. Also, there are most likely some differences between what people say they do and what they actually do in practice, which is why it was necessary to include observation methods.

One of the disadvantages of semi-participant observation is that it can only be carried out with limited numbers of children as it takes time to build rapport and a relationship of trust (Reynolds, 1986). It is difficult to compare the different sorts of data obtained since each situation is different and they are not easily comparable. Semi-participant observation relies heavily on flexibility and 'opportunistic moments' and is not easily planned. Consequently, I felt it was important to use semi-participant observation to complement the other methods I used, including the interviews and the written and visual methods. One benefit of using task-based research activities at the school was that many children could complete the tasks simultaneously, enabling me to obtain information more quickly and for a greater number of children than by using individual interviews or observation techniques (Boyden & Ennew, 1997: 107).

During the fieldwork period I visited all of the eighteen households regularly. The aim of repeated household visits was to monitor the household livelihood strategy, and carry out informal interviews about a variety of different topics. By regularly visiting the same sample households not only is a relationship of trust built up but accumulative interviewing (see Whatmore, 1991) allows for a detailed history of the household to be formed. Repeat interviews over time facilitate access to all household members, some of whom may be absent during initial visits. This permits a multi-perspective of the household lifestyle and contributes to a fuller picture of their present and past situation. Household visits were also used to carry out semi-structured interviews with fifteen parents and eight grandparents about their own childhood and about their children's lives.

The main disadvantages of household visits were that they were time-consuming and imposed on participants' time and privacy. The visits lasted from half an hour to a whole day. I tried to accompany household members on their tasks in order to carry out informal interviews whilst minimising disruption to their daily routine. I would talk to the women in the kitchen while helping to peel potatoes, or to various household members while helping to harvest or peel maize, or while going to round up the livestock.

Most of the recording of data was carried out immediately after observation or informal interview to keep the interactions as unobtrusive as possible (see also Boyden & Ennew, 1997: 149). During the semi-structured interviews notes were written to facilitate the more detailed writing up afterwards, which included observations of the interview setting and the reaction of the interviewee to the questions and to the researcher. Wherever possible, verbatim quotations were recorded for use in the presentation of data so as not to lose the richness of the participants' own language and choice of words. During semi-participant observation it was sometimes difficult to record exact quotations.

Since my first university degree was in Spanish and Latin American Studies, my fluency in the language enabled me to design the research tools in Spanish. Language competency was also essential for carrying out ethnographic research of this kind in the first place, since rapport and research relations could not have developed in the same way via an interpreter. Yet despite my fluency in Spanish, many local terms and farming vocabulary had to be rapidly learnt. I translated all the quotations but it was not always an easy task to capture the exact meaning in English. Consequently, my translation was sometimes flexible to incorporate the flavour of the local language, which was why I decided to keep the original words in the footnotes.

I chose not to use a tape recorder mainly because it was not a practical option since most of the informal interviews were carried out as I accompanied the respondents during errands or tasks. During semi-structured interviews I did not want to make the respondents feel more self-conscious, especially since they are not used to being interviewed and are unfamiliar with tape recorders. Consequently, I developed my own form of shorthand, scribbled notes to prompt my memory and learnt to write quickly while maintaining eye contact and the flow of conversation (Boyden & Ennew, 1997: 149).

Approximately every ten days I withdrew from the community to spend two days in the town of Tarija, to enable me to reflect on the data obtained and on my role as a researcher, to transfer field notes to a laptop computer and consider how my ideas were developing. Copies of detailed letters sent home regularly to family and friends were kept, describing the nature of field relationships, the cultural differences, the uncertainties, joys and dilemmas of life in the field. These have proved useful in reconstructing the changing nature of the fieldwork and the intellectual process involved.

Children in Churquiales

The study took place in the community of Churquiales, in the Camacho Valley of Tarija, the southernmost region of Bolivia. I visited a sample of eighteen households regularly in order to conduct semi-participant observation and semi-structured and informal interviews with all the household members. At the community school, I carried out classroom observation mainly with the eldest thirty-seven school children aged between 8 and 14 years. I also used a variety of task-based techniques at the school, including photographs (which the children themselves took), drawings, diaries and worksheets (see Punch, 2002b).

Churquiales has a population of 351 spread amongst 58 households, with approximately four children on average per household. The community is 55km from Tarija, the regional capital, a journey of about four hours on the local twice-weekly bus. Most of the families own two or three hectares of land, which they mainly use to cultivate potatoes, maize and a selection of fruit and vegetables. They also tend to own a small number of pigs, goats and chickens, as well as a few cows. Most of their agricultural and livestock production is for family consumption; any excess is sold in local and regional markets. The community has a small main square, where there are three small shops, a church, a medical post, a small concrete football pitch and the village primary school, and around the square there is a cluster of households. The other households are dispersed throughout the valley, up to about an hour and a half's walk away from the village square.

Most of the children in Churquiales face the same broad constraints of relative poverty and geographical isolation. The opportunities for waged employment are limited, and schooling is available only for the first six years of primary education. The community is comparatively isolated, having limited access to the mass media, as there is no electricity and no television, and communication networks are not extensive. The main form of transport is on foot and there are no cars. There are no pushchairs for young children, so they are tied by a shawl and carried on their mother's back. As soon as they can walk they are encouraged to get used to walking long distances and from as young as 3 years old they can be expected to walk several miles if necessary. Children cover a lot of ground every day as they walk between their home and school, go to the hillsides in search of animals or firewood, fetch water from the river and carry out regular errands for their parents to other households or to the shops in the community square.

Children spend most of their daily life outdoors, facilitated by the temperate climate. In contrast, the indoor space of their household is very limited. Each house usually consists of three mud huts with tiled roofs: a kitchen (cooking with firewood), a bedroom (where all the household members sleep together in three or four different beds, with sometimes two or three children to one bed) and a room to receive guests (and eat when it is raining). This contrasts with many children living in colder urban areas in the

Minority World, whose use of outdoor space is restricted and controlled, with most of their time being spent inside the house.

The following diary extract indicates a typical routine and daily movement for 10-year-old Maria in Churquiales:

> I got up at 5.30 in the morning and I went to get water from the river. Then I went to milk the goats. I brushed my hair and had my tea with bread. I changed my clothes and went to school. I read a book and afterwards we did language. We went out at breaktime and I played football with my friends. We came into the classroom and did more language. I went home and my mum gave me lunch. I went to get water and helped my mum make the tea. Then I went to bring in my cows and when I got back my mum gave me supper and I went to sleep at 9 at night.[4]

This extract describes a common school day: children get up early (usually between 5 and 6 a.m.), put on their old clothes and do a few tasks, usually while their mother is making them breakfast (although some children make their own). The tasks include fetching water and/or firewood, letting the animals out of their enclosures, feeding and/or milking them. They have breakfast, change into clean clothes for school, wash their faces, brush their hair and leave about 7.20 a.m., depending on how far they have to walk to arrive for an 8 a.m. start. When they arrive home from school about 2 p.m., their mother or elder sibling has lunch waiting for them (soup and a main dish).

In the afternoon, their household jobs vary according to the season and particular needs of the time and thus include: looking after and feeding animals, helping with agricultural tasks, fetching more water and firewood, looking after younger siblings, washing clothes and preparing food. If there is spare time children play or do their school homework. At approximately 5 p.m. they have their tea, which is similar to breakfast: a hot drink and a small snack. Then the animals have to be brought in to the paddocks for the night. This may involve travelling quite long distances to round up goats, sheep and cows from the mountainside. Donkeys and horses also have to be brought in and tied up for the night. Pigs are easier to manage as they do not usually roam far. Finally, at about 7–8 p.m. the children have supper, which is one dish, such as a soup or a stew, and tends to be the remains of lunch. Children go to bed shortly after supper, usually between 8 and 9 p.m. Since it gets dark quite quickly at about 6.30, the rest of the day is spent in candlelight, doing kitchen tasks such as supper preparation, or washing up.

To provide for the family's subsistence requirements, the households in Churquiales have high labour requirements in three main areas of work: agriculture, animal-related work and domestic work. In the countryside many jobs have to be done every day, such as caring for the animals, food preparation, and water and firewood collection. The household division of labour is according to sex, age, birth order and household composition (Punch, 2001). Children are expected to contribute to the maintenance of their household from an early age. Once children are about 5 years old parental expectations of their household work roles increase, and children are required to take on work responsibilities at home. As they acquire skills and competence their active participation in the maintenance of the household rapidly increases.

Bolivian children in rural areas perform many jobs without question or hesitation, readily accepting a task and taking pride in their contribution to the household. Children accept responsibility for some routine household tasks without having to be told to do them, e.g. daily water and firewood collection. Water collection is a child-specific task, usually performed by young children (i.e. age 3–4 years) as it is a relatively 'easy' job. They may begin by carrying very small quantities of water (in small jugs at first), but by the time they are 6 or 7 years old they can usually manage two 5-litre containers in one trip. Since children are assigned this job from a very early age and it has to be carried out at least once or twice every day, they know there is no point in trying to avoid doing something which is very clearly their responsibility. I observed that children frequently accepted responsibility for such tasks and initiated action to fulfil them rather than merely responding to adults' demands. Their sense of satisfaction for self-initiated task-completion often appeared to be greater than when they were asked to do something.

Children in rural Bolivia are not only expected to work and are given many responsibilities but they are also aware of the importance of their contribution and often fulfil their duties with pride. Parents encourage them to learn new skills by giving them opportunities to acquire competencies and be responsible. Parents do not expect to have to remind children constantly of their tasks and may threaten them with harsh physical punishment if their obligations are not completed. Children are encouraged to be independent: to get on with their jobs, to combine work and school, and to travel large distances within the community unaccompanied. In addition, children are also expected to maintain interdependent family relations by contributing to the survival of the household. Furthermore, parents teach their children to try to be relatively tough, for instance not to cry if they fall over and hurt themselves, not to sit on adults' laps or be carried on mothers' backs once they are over about 3 years old, and to be able to look after themselves and younger siblings when parents are away from the household.

Despite similar broad communal constraints and cultural expectations, children in different households face distinct limitations, shaped by the household wealth and composition. Different households offer varying opportunities according to parental attitudes towards discipline, work and school. Within households, children do not necessarily experience childhood in the same way, and such differences are a result of their age, sex, birth order and personal attributes. These factors combine to shape individual children's life experiences, and the opportunities and constraints with which they can negotiate. Within the restrictions that exist at a community, household and individual level, children negotiate ways to make the most of opportunities. They make choices within the limited range of possibilities available to them.

Within this social, economic, physical and cultural context, it is now interesting to explore the ways in which these Bolivian children actively negotiate the fulfilment of their work roles within rural households. Despite the threat of punishment if tasks are not completed, or the feelings of pride and responsibility gained when jobs are carried out, children find some of their work very tedious or arduous or would rather engage in their own pursuits than do all their household chores. Children also have their own agendas and preferences for their use of time and space.

Avoidance strategies

When I asked children in Churquiales whether they could refuse to do a particular job if told to do it by their parents, half the children said they could say no, and the other half said they were obliged to do the job (see Table 6.1). They explained various strategies they used to avoid doing an adult-imposed task that they did not want to perform. The most popular strategy was to send a younger brother or sister to do the task for them. Parents agreed that elder siblings were allowed to tell younger siblings what to do, regardless of their sex, and elder siblings could also punish younger siblings if they misbehaved. Sometimes younger children attempted to send an older sibling to do a job that had been assigned to them, but with a much lower likelihood of success.

Table 6.1   Children's avoidance and coping strategies

Child	Age	Avoid?	How?
Cira	9	yes	Tell my sister to do it
Benita	10	yes	Tell my sister to go and do it
Inés	11	yes	Tell my siblings to help me, and Ernesto helps me
Rosalía	11	no	I have to do it, or sometimes my sister does it
Luisa	12	yes	I send my brother and sister
Vicenta	13	no	Get my brother and sister to help me
Sabina	14	no	If they tell me to do something, I have to do it
Eduardo	11	yes	I have to do it
Julio	12	no	I escape
Dionicio	12	yes	I want to learn other jobs
Rafael	12	yes	I have to do it because they tell me to, I can't say no
Delfín	12	no	I can't say no, I have to do it
Santos	14	no	I can send my brothers
Yolanda	11	no	No
Alfredo	11	yes	I get my brother to do it, Sebastián

Half the children who began by saying that they could not refuse to do a task, extended their answer, indicating that sometimes they too used a particular strategy to avoid doing a job. The two main types of avoidance strategies which children use are delegation to a younger sibling, and escape: 'I can't say no, I have to do it. Or I do it with José (elder sibling), or I tell Hugo (younger sibling) to do it and he goes' (Delfín, 12 years).[5] Sabina explains her strategy: 'If they tell me to do something, I have to do it. When they tell me to do a job I don't want to do, I go off and visit my Uncle Carlos' (Sabina, 14 years).[6]

Escape can take several forms, such as pretending not to hear and wandering off quickly before the request can be repeated, or pretending to go and do the job, but then just going somewhere else to play instead. Alternatively, if children are really defiant, they may refuse outright and go off somewhere without taking any notice, but then they will have to face the consequences (usually some form of punishment) on return. Parents recognise that their children do not always do as they are told: 'They go off and play, and then they don't do it sometimes.'[7] Some parents get stricter, threaten them with punishment, or shout at them to help 'persuade' them to do the job anyway.

Coping strategies

When children are unable to use an avoidance strategy, they resort to a coping strategy in order to make a job more acceptable in their own terms, thereby making a tedious or arduous task more tolerable or enjoyable. One such coping strategy is for children to make their feelings known and openly state their dissatisfaction. Most parents say that their children often complain about doing certain jobs: 'My children say: "I'm not going to do it," and then they do go and do it all the same.'[8] Some children seem to enjoy protesting, but often give in and carry out the task. Their slight triumph is the complaining before doing the job, to make sure that the other person is aware of the sacrifice they are making by doing it, or of the effort involved, or of the valuable time it is taking up. Children also make symbolic protests to ensure that their complaints are registered with the parent, in the hope that they will not be given further tasks to do.

A favourite strategy which children use when they do not want to do a job, but see little chance of avoidance, is to persuade a sibling to help them. Having company means the job is less boring and can be completed more quickly. Alternatively they may chat or play while doing the task and it may take longer to complete. It also gives the child added satisfaction that he/she is not the only one having to do something while his/her siblings are doing nothing. Combining a job with play not only makes a job more enjoyable, but can also be a useful strategy to prolong a particular task and therefore delay the next one. For example, 10-year-old Sergio offers to cook pancakes because he enjoys eating them and spends plenty of time playing and making the dough into interesting animal shapes. His mother remarked that he tends to complain before doing a job and that he seems to enjoy moaning about his responsibilities: 'He likes to be begged to do things.'[9] She sees her children as being quite lazy, but does admit: 'When they want to do something, they do it well and quickly.'[10]

The likelihood of a child complying with parents' requests also depends on the child's personality. Some children are more obedient and willing to work than others. Others can be argumentative and rebellious. Parents often differentiated between their children, seeing some as keen workers and others as lazier. For example, Beatriz commented that one of her daughters 'complains a lot, she's very lazy and argumentative'.[11] Similarly, another mother explained: 'It also depends on whether the child is active when working, others are slower.'[12]

However, it also depends on whether the children really *want* to do something or not. For example, cleaning out and feeding the pigs is definitely not something that Sergio (10 years) enjoys doing, but another job – going on an errand to buy something from the local store in the main square – is a task he offers to do, before he is even asked. He knows that there he is likely to meet some friends and can stop to play marbles for a while before returning home. This coincides with Reynolds' (1991) findings that young people often use tasks to escape surveillance and meet friends.

Sometimes children deliberately take a long time to complete a task, or they stay and play for a while before going back to their household, because they know that if they rush back home the chances are they will be given something else to do. This strategy is especially easy to employ when they are sent to check up on animals, since they can pretend they had to spend time looking for an animal that had wandered off, when really they were playing. Parents are often aware of their children's strategies for combining work with play. Sergio's mother indicates that she knows that her son prolongs his return home on purpose: 'What takes Sergio a long time is in Churquiales [in the main square]. He stays and plays, he doesn't rush to come back.'[13]

Household negotiations

For children to be able to use coping and avoidance strategies successfully, they must be able to negotiate their position in the household. This section highlights some of the ways in which children in Churquiales can negotiate with parents and siblings in order to influence particular outcomes.

> Felicia said to her four children: 'Someone has to go and milk the goats. Who's going to go?' They all quickly responded 'Not me!' So she chose one of them: 'Marco, you go.'

Marco (14 years) responded: 'No, I'm not going to go, because yesterday I helped grandfather sow.' The children argued amongst themselves until finally Dionicio (12 years) reluctantly went off. He complained more than usual that day, because the day before it had rained and the river was good for fishing. The siblings had been assembling their rods to go and fish. Dionicio went quickly up the hillside, milked the goats and ran back to join his brothers and sister.[14]

One very common result of a child being told to do a job that they really would rather not do is a sibling argument and ensuing sibling or parent–child negotiation. For example, the appointed child suggests another should be told to do it, usually justifying why they themselves should not have to. This tends to provoke a sibling argument along the lines of 'But I did such and such' or, 'It's his/her turn'. One of the parents, or an elder sibling, usually has to intervene with suggestions of more jobs in order to divide the tasks between them. Sometimes the siblings themselves negotiate the outcome, often settling for going together so that 'No one gets out of it.' Children tend to have a strong sense of justice, wanting their siblings to fulfil their share of the household's responsibilities. This can be seen in 12-year-old Luisa's question to her mother: 'Has Carlos (8 years) been to get water yet? I've already been twice.'[15]

The following conversation is an example of child–parent negotiation in a household where the mother and eldest daughter share many of the domestic duties, and frequently have to negotiate who will do what and when:

Marianela: I'm not going to go.
Dolores: Now you have to go. Can't you take my place for just one day?
Marianela: No, I can't.
Dolores: But I always do it during the week.[16]

This conversation took place on a Saturday and refers to whether mother or daughter will take Ambrosio, the household's father, his lunch, which involves a half-hour walk each way. Dolores, the mother, usually does it during the week when Marianela (10 years) is at school, so feels that Marianela could at least do it at weekends. She tries to reason with and persuade her daughter that it is only fair that she do it for once. Yet Marianela is adamant, she has no desire to make the trip. In the end, her mother gave in and agreed to go on the condition that Marianela looked after Marcelo, her 2-year-old brother, and kept an eye on the animals. This example indicates how parents depend on their children to carry out certain tasks but they have to negotiate how they will be divided.

The following example illustrates another strategy children use to try to negotiate doing a different sort of job. They may say it is too difficult, or merely that they do not want to do that, or may offer to do something else instead:

Angélica (10 years) was looking after the pigs. Her mother said to her younger brother Simón (7 years):

'Go and take the donkeys to Uncle Serafín's house, or if not, Angélica should go.'
'Let her go,' said Simón.
'OK,' said his mum. 'But then you'll have to go and look after the pigs, because that's what she's doing at the moment.'[17]

This strategy does not always work: it depends on the urgency of the job and on the parent's willingness to change the job for another one.

Parents also used strategies to encourage their children to carry out household tasks. One particular strategy was to tell their children the tasks they themselves had to do at that moment, appealing to their sense of responsibility and justice so that the children also do their share. For example, when 12-year-old Dionicio complained about being sent to a neighbour's house to borrow some cooking oil, his mother became quite annoyed: 'It's as if I were the only one responsible for making sure there is food to eat. You're not too lazy to eat but you're too lazy to make sure there is some food' (Felicia, parent).[18] She persuaded her children to help by making them realise that she needed their help, she could not cope with the heavy workload alone.

Children's mechanisms for asserting their relative autonomy

The ways in which children respond to adult control over their lives varies in different contexts, in response to different individuals, and depending on the type and location of the task. Thus, children have a repertoire of strategies and the way they deploy them is opportunistic. Such strategies also vary, not according to sex, but according to the particular competencies, personality and birth order of individual children.

The Bolivian children's coping and avoidance strategies must be understood within this specific context: children are expected to work and are active contributors to the household from a very young age. Many of their strategies are facilitated by children's high level of mobility within their community: it is their extensive use of space away from adult surveillance that enables them to employ such coping mechanisms. Children's multiple strategies are not merely used in resistance to adults' power, but are part of a complex process in which they assert their agency, creating time and space for themselves despite restrictions from a variety of sources, including adults, other children and structural constraints.

This study of rural Bolivia shows that the transition from childhood to adulthood is not a simple linear progression from dependence and incompetence to independence and competence. This chapter has shown that children move in and out of relative independence and competence in relation to different people. It has argued that the notion of interdependence is a more appropriate way to understand relations between children and adults, and between children.

Household relationships are constantly being worked out and renegotiated through sibling negotiation and parent–child negotiation. Households are neither totally consensual units nor are they entirely sites of conflict (Cheal, 1989). Household relations include a mixture of co-operation and competition. On the one hand, households function as units of mutual support and solidarity, where moral obligations and expectations are fulfilled (Friedman, 1984). On the other hand, these are the result of long-term relationships built up over time and are subject to negotiation, tension and conflict (Finch, 1989; Finch & Mason, 1993; Katz, 1991). Intra-household relations are based on simultaneous relationships of dependence and independence. Individual household members are dependent on each other for different things at different times, yet they can also be independent individuals asserting a degree of autonomy, controlling their own use of time and space, and pursuing their own interests. Children use their resourcefulness to stretch adult-imposed boundaries to limits more acceptable to themselves.

Family expectations and obligations mean that most children have a strong sense of responsibility towards family members. Their sense of justice means that they try to ensure that all family members share the duties and responsibilities necessary to maintain the household. Families negotiate their intra-household responsibilities according to the different constraints and opportunities which exist, including household wealth, household composition, birth order, sex and age of siblings, and personal preferences of individual members. Children are competent at negotiating their role within the household, despite their inferior position in relation to more powerful adults.

Negotiation may include reaching compromises or balancing different interests, such as individual preferences and household needs. It may be co-operative or may involve conflict and tension. However, this chapter has shown that the ways in which these children create their own use of time and space do not all involve struggle. Sometimes children initiate their active participation in society, thereby asserting their relative autonomy of their own accord rather than merely reacting to others or to situations. This may occur, for example, when they take the initiative to fulfil their household responsibilities without being told to by their parents or siblings. Similarly, the children often accept being told to do things by their siblings or parents and do not attempt to assert their agency by offering any form of resistance. However, this should not be seen necessarily as passivity on their part, but can be quite the opposite. They may be making an autonomous decision to obey and contribute rather than resist. Since it has been shown in this chapter that children can resist, compromise and negotiate, they can equally choose to comply and accept. As we have seen, children in rural Bolivia are often proud of the contributions they make by participating actively in their household or community, and such contributions are sometimes the result of their own initiative. Therefore, it should be recognised that children, as competent social actors, may choose to respond to the requests or demands of others with a mixture of obedience, compliance, defiance and resistance. Equally they may act on their own initiative rather than just respond or comply.

Notes

1 I prefer to use the terms Majority World and Minority World to refer to the Developing and Developed World respectively. The Majority World has the most of the world's population and a greater land mass. Thus, it reflects the majority experience compared to the more privileged lifestyles of the Minority World. Although this unduly homogenises the 'Majority', the use of the terms Minority and Majority World may at least make the reader pause and reflect on the unequal relations between these two world areas.

2 All the names of the respondents as well as the community have been changed in order to protect their identity and maintain confidentiality.

3 'Key Informant' is used here as meaning respondents with whom close friendship was formed and much time was spent, and whose opinions were regularly sought (Boyden & Ennew, 1997: 124–5).

4 *Me levanté a las 5.30 de la mañana y me ido a traer agua del rio y despues fue a sacar leche de los chivos y me peinado y tomado mi te con pan y me camviado de ropa y me ido a la escuela y hey leido un libro y despues amos echo las lenguage y salido a recreo y amos jugado la pelota con mis compañeras. Amos entrado al curso y hey echo mas lenguage y me venido a mi casa y mi mamá me a dado a almorsar y me ido a traer agua y hey ayudado a mi mamá a cer te y me ido a traer mis vacas y venido mi mamá me a dado a cenar y me ido a dormir a las 9 de la noche* (Tuesday 15 October 1996).

Where quotations have been used from the children's diaries or worksheets, the original spelling has been left in order to capture the tone of the regional Spanish language.

5 *No puedo decir que no, tengo que hacer. O voy con José o a Hugo lo mando y él va* (Delfin, 12 years, November 1996).

6 *Si me mandan a hacer, tengo que hacer. Cuando me manda acer un trabajo yo no quiero acer me voy a mi tio Carlos* (Sabina, 14 years, November 1996).

7 *Se van a jugar y ya no hacen a veces* (Nélida, parent, December 1996).

8 *Mis hijos dicen – yo no voy a hacer, después igualito van y lo hacen* (Marcelina, parent, December 1996).

9 *Le gusta que lo rueguen para hacer las cosas* (Primitiva, parent, 5 August 1996).

10 *Cuando quieren hacer, hacen bien y rápido* (Primitiva, parent, 5 August 1996).

11 *Se queja mucho, es muy floja y malcriada* (Beatriz, parent, 17 September 1996).

12 *También depende del chico que sea activo para trabajar, otros son más despacio* (Felicia, parent, 17 May 1995).

13 *Lo que se demora el Sergio es en Churquiales. Se queda a jugar, no tiene apuro para venir* (Primitiva, parent, 5 September 1996).

14 *Alguien tiene que ir a sacar leche de los chivos. Quién va a ir?*
Marco, anda vos (Felicia, parent, 20 April 1995).
No, yo no voy a ir, porque ayer yo ayudé al abuelo a sembrar (Marco, 14 years, 20 April 1995).

15 *Carlos ya ha ido a traer agua? Yo ya he ido dos viajes* (Luisa, 12 years, 17 August 1996).

16 Marianela: *Yo no voy a ir.* Dolores: *Ya vos tienes que ir. Un dia-ito no me puedes reemplazar?*
Marianela: *No puedo.* Dolores: *Pero yo toda una semana* (19 August 1996).
17 *Anda llevar los burros donde tío Serafín, o si no que vaya la Angélica.*
Que vaya ella, dijo Simón.
Está bien, pero entonces vos tienes que ir a cuidar los cuchis porque ella está cuidan-dolos (Beatriz' household, 19 October 1996).
18 *Es como si yo fuera la única responsable para ver que haya comida. No tienen flojera para comer pero tienen flojera para ver que haya comida* (Felicia, parent, 6 September 1996).

References

Boyden, J. (1990) 'A Comparative Perspective on the Globalization of Childhood', in James, A. and Prout, A. (Eds), *Constructing and Reconstructing Childhood: Contemporary Issues in the Sociological Study of Childhood*, Basingstoke: Falmer Press.

Boyden, J. & Ennew, J. (Eds) (1997) *Children in Focus: A Manual for Experiential Learning in Participatory Research with Children.* Stockholm: Rädda Barnen.

Boyden, J., Ling, B. & Myers, W. (1998) *What Works for Working Children*, Stockholm: Rädda Barnen and UNICEF.

Cheal, D. (1989) 'Strategies of Resource Management in Household Economics: Moral Economy or Political Economy?' in Wilk, R. (ed.) *The Household Economy: Reconsidering the Domestic Mode of Production*, London: Westview Press.

Devereux, S. (1992) 'Observers are Worried: Learning the Language and Counting the People in Northeast Ghana', in Devereux, S. & Hoddinott, J. (Eds), *Fieldwork in Developing Countries*, London: Harvester Wheatsheaf, 43–56.

Ennew, J. (1994) 'Time for Children or Time for Adults', in Qvortrup, J., Bardy, M., Sgritta, G. & Wintersberger, H. (Eds), *Childhood Matters: Social Theory, Practice and Politics*, Aldershot: Avebury.

Fetterman, D. (1989) 'Ethnography: Step by Step,' *Applied Social Research Methods Series* 17, London: Sage.

Finch, J. (1989) *Family Obligations and Social Change*, Cambridge: Polity Press.

Finch, J. & Mason, J. (1993) *Negotiating Family Responsibilities*, London: Routledge.

Fine, G.A. & Sandstrom, K.L. (1988) 'Knowing Children: Participant Observation with Minors', *Qualitative Research Methods Series* 15. London: Sage.

Francis, E. (1992) 'Qualitative Research: Collecting Life Histories', in Devereux, S. & Hoddinott, J. (Eds), *Fieldwork in Developing Countries*, London: Harvester Wheatsheaf, 86–101.

Friedman, K. (1984) 'Households as Income-pooling Units', in Smith, J. et al. (Eds), *Households and the World Economy*, Beverly Hills: Sage.

Giddens, A. (1990) *Central Problems in Social Theory: Action, Structure and Contradiction in Social Analysis*, Berkeley and Los Angeles: University of California Press.

Goddard, V. & White, B. (1982) 'Child Workers and Capitalist Development', *Development and Change* 13(4): 465–477.

Hammersley, M. & Atkinson, P. (1995) *Ethnography: Principles in Practice*, London: Routledge.

Harden, J. & Scott, S. (1998) 'Risk Anxiety and the Social Construction of Childhood', paper presented at the International Sociological Association World Congress, Montreal, July.

Hockey, J. & James, A. (1993) *Growing Up and Growing Old: Ageing and Dependency in the Life Course*, London: Sage.

James, A. (1993) *Childhood Identities: Self and Social Relationships in the Experience of the Child*, Edinburgh: Edinburgh University Press.

James, A., Jenks, C. & Prout, A. (1998) *Theorising Childhood*, Cambridge: Polity Press.

Katz, E. (1991) 'Breaking the Myth of Harmony: Theoretical and Methodological Guidelines to the Study of Rural Third World Households', *Review of Radical Political Economics* **23** (3 & 4): 37–56.

Lukes, S. (1986) *Power*, Oxford: Blackwell.

Mason, J. (1996) *Qualitative Researching*, London: Sage.

Mayall, B. (2001) 'Understanding Childhoods: A London Study', in Alanen, L. & Mayall, B. (Eds), *Conceptualizing Child–Adult Relations*, London: Routledge Falmer.

Morrow, V. (1994) 'Responsible Children? Aspects of Children's Work and Employment outside School in Contemporary UK', in Mayall, B. (ed.) *Children's Childhoods: Observed and Experienced*, London: Falmer Press.

Morrow, V. (1999) 'It's cool, ...'cos you can't give us detentions and things, can you?!': Reflections on Research with Children', in Milner, P. & Carolin, B. (Eds), *Time to Listen to Children: Personal and Professional Communication*, London: Routledge, 203–215.

PLA Notes (1996) Special Issue: Children's Participation, *PLA Notes* **25**, London: International Institute for Environment and Development.

Punch, M. (1986) *The Politics and Ethics of Fieldwork*, London: Sage.

Punch, S. (2000) 'Children's Strategies for Creating Playspaces: Negotiating Independence in rural Bolivia', in Holloway, S. & Valentine, G. (Eds), *Children's Geographies: Living, Playing, Learning and Transforming Everyday Worlds*, London: Routledge, 48–62.

Punch, S. (2001) 'Household Division of Labour: Generation, Gender, Age, Birth Order and Sibling Composition', *Work, Employment & Society*, **15**(4): 803–823.

Punch, S. (2003) Childhoods in the Majority World: Miniature Adults or Tribal Children? *Sociology*, **37**(2): 277–295.

Punch, S. (2002a) 'Youth Transitions and Interdependent Adult–Child Relations in Rural Bolivia', *Journal of Rural Studies*, **18**(2): 123–133.

Punch, S. (2002b) 'Research with Children: The Same or Different from Research with Adults?' *Childhood*, 9(3): 321–341.

Reynolds, P. (1986) 'Through the Looking Glass. Participant Observation with Children in Southern Africa,' paper presented at a Workshop on the Ethnography of Childhood, King's College, Cambridge.

Reynolds, P. (1991) *Dance Civet Cat: Child Labour in the Zambezi Valley*, Athens, Ohio: Ohio University Press.

Schildkrout, E. (1981) 'The Employment of Children in Kano (Nigeria)', in Rodgers, G. & Standing, G. (Eds), *Child Work, Poverty and Underdevelopment*, Geneva: International Labour Organisation.

Slocum, R., Wichart, L., Rocheleau, D. & Thomas-Slayter, B. (Eds), (1995) *Power, Process and Participation: Tools for Change*, London: Intermediate Technology Publications.

Waksler, F. (1991a) 'The Hard Times of Childhood and Children's Strategies for Dealing with Them', in Waksler, F. (ed.) *Studying the Social Worlds of Children: Sociological Readings*, London: Falmer Press.

Waksler, F. (ed.) (1991b) *Studying the Social Worlds of Children: Sociological Readings*, London: Falmer Press.

Waksler, F. (1996) *The Little Trials of Childhood and Children's Strategies for Dealing with Them*, London: Falmer Press.

Whatmore, S. (1991) *Farming Women*, Cambridge: Polity Press.

Commentary: Samantha Punch

Scrambling through the ethnographic forest

Doing research provokes mixed emotions, it rewards and frustrates. Some days in Bolivia it gave me a real buzz but other days it reduced me almost to tears. When ideas slot together, I wonder what all the fuss is about, but when the data and my analysis both seem vague, I wonder if I will ever make any sense of it all.

I regard fieldwork as the fun part. Yet being in the field is far from free of ambivalent feelings. I remember feeling nervous before interviews, worrying constantly if I was asking the right questions, getting enough data, or if I was overlooking important details. I also learnt to recognise that sometimes I would not feel in the mood to observe and be observed in return. Would I be able to build rapport and maintain both the children's interest and mine? Usually my fears would emerge just before the interview or household visit or classroom observation, but once the interaction began I would switch into researcher mode. By the time it ended, my head would be spinning with ideas or reflections. An analogy would be going to an aerobics class: it is an effort beforehand though I enjoy it once I am there. The rewards of aerobics are cumulative over time. In some ways that is one of the keys to doing research: you have to stick at it; intellectual but also emotional stamina is required.

The writing-up stage is the hardest part of all. It is difficult to convince yourself to keep writing on days when inspiration has abandoned you. Motivation just to start writing can be the toughest hurdle and urges to clean the house one more time have to be overcome. Nevertheless, despite the frustrations, it is very satisfying once each small goal is achieved.

These divided emotions between feeling lost and getting nowhere on the one hand, as opposed to having clear vision and moving forward on the other, were magnified in my Bolivian research for two reasons. First, carrying out ethnographic research can be a more intensive experience particularly when it involves living in a remote community in a culture very different from one's own. Secondly, it was one of the first studies that I had conducted and in many ways the learning process of how to do research was just as important as the actual findings which emerged from the data. The research process provoked polarised feelings. It can be simultaneously exciting yet nerve-racking, fun yet hard work, rewarding yet overwhelming.

I began academic life as an undergraduate of Spanish and Latin American Studies. I spent a year in Bolivia to improve my Spanish and to attend a university in Santa Cruz. This seemed a more exotic option than going to Spain for the year. I chose to write my undergraduate dissertation on street children in La Paz, the largest city, and found out about their daily lives. Thus began my interest in childhood research. On finishing my degree, I was offered a post as research officer on a project funded by the European Union at the School of Geography at Leeds University: 'Farmer Strategies and Production Systems in Fragile Environments in Mountainous Areas of Latin America.'

The idea of studying rural Bolivian childhoods emerged after I had been working for several months on this two-year project. Though I talked with adults about maintaining household survival I was constantly witnessing children's active contribution. I decided to compare rural childhoods with the everyday worlds of urban street children, initially focusing on work activities since this differed from our western image of childhood as a time dedicated to play and school. Yet at this stage my ideas were vague and I began just to observe and find out all I could about the children's daily lives. I preferred to be flexible to try to take in as much of what was happening as possible rather than narrowing to a more specific topic. The downside of this approach is that I ended up collecting far much more data than I could really handle. I felt that everything was potentially relevant and this sometimes resulted in my feeling overwhelmed and lost in a mass of detail that had no central thread. I have since realised that this is not a unique experience amongst researchers.

The project helped me to decide to do a Ph.D. I spent the following year at Leeds University reviewing the relevant literature, analysing the data generated over the two years and redefining my research focus. This served as useful preparation for a second, more intensive fieldwork period of six months focusing on one community. I discovered that the daily lives of rural children were frequently neglected in the literature on Majority World childhoods. Studies tended to focus on urban childhoods and on child labour whilst overlooking other everyday aspects of Majority World childhood, e.g. play. Furthermore, in popular and media discourses children who work from an early age tend to be conceptualised as having 'abnormal' childhoods. I began to be interested in the extent to which the rural Bolivian children of my study conformed to this image of miniature adults deprived of childhood. Thus, other areas began to emerge as salient features of their lives – school, home and play – and these were the primary concern of the second phase of fieldwork. I chose Churquiales partly because it was in the middle of the three communities (which had been involved in the original EU-funded study) not just in a geographical sense but also socially and economically. However, the main reason why I chose it was because it was the friendliest community I had been in and the one in which I felt most comfortable and accepted.

Looking back over the letters I wrote home as a way of recording my experiences, I have been reminded of some of my first encounters in the field. The following is from my first letter home:

young people.'[30(p1)] This occurs in part by identifying characteristics of youth that influence their health and well-being. Major categories of variables addressed in the survey include the following: demographics, general health and well-being, family and peer relationships, school environments, exercise and leisure-time activities, diet, substance use, and sexual behavior.[30]

Injury

Reports describing medically treated injuries were collected in 12 of the 29 countries only: Belgium (Flemish sample), Canada, England, Estonia, Hungary, Israel, Lithuania, Poland, Republic of Ireland, Sweden, Switzerland, and the United States. Injury questions were derived from the 1988 child health supplement to the US National Health Interview Survey[32] and a previous version of the HBSC.[33] Injured youth were defined as those providing a response of one or more times to the question: 'During the past 12 months, how many times were you injured and had to be treated by a doctor or nurse?' Students then described their single most serious injury, if any. Supplementary questions asked about the nature of the injury (medical sequelae), injury type (e.g. sports or fighting related), treatment(s) administered, and number of days lost from school or other normal activities. Using a modified approach to the classification of severity,[34] severe injuries were operationally defined as those leading to one or more of the following: (1) one or more days missed from school or usual activities, (2) hospitalization overnight, (3) the use of casts or stitches, and/or (4) a surgical operation (these descriptors were only collected in 8 of the 12 countries).

Multiple risk behavior score

A list of health risk behaviors common to adolescents, as suggested by the literature, was compiled from the available questions in the HBSC. The following close-ended items were used (responses in parentheses were interpreted as the presence of the risk factor): smoking,[10,35] 'How often do you smoke tobacco at present?' (currently smoking from once a week to daily); drinking,[10,11,15,16,36–38] 'Have you ever had so much alcohol that you were really drunk?' (≥1 time); seat belts,[39,40] 'How often do you use a seat belt when you sit in a car?' (never, rarely, or sometimes); bullying,[41] 'How often have you taken part in bullying other students in school this term?' (more than once or twice); excess time with friends,[31] 'How many evenings per week do you usually spend out with your friends?' (5–7 evenings); alienation at home,[31] 'How easy is it for you to talk to your father/mother about things that really bother you?' (difficult or very difficult for all parents in the home); alienation at school,[31] 'I feel I belong at this school' (disagree or strongly disagree); truancy,[42] 'How many days did you skip classes or school this term?' (≥2 days); and an unusually poor diet,[37] 'How often do you eat or drink cola/sweets/potato chips or crisps?' (at least once a day for all 3).

Some of the preceding factors were selected as risk behaviors that could directly lead to injury. Others were selected as more generic indicators of a risk-taking lifestyle. Although there were several additional risk behaviors that optimally could have been included in the score (illicit drug use, nonuse of bicycle helmets, and unprotected sex), these were not assessed by most participating HBSC study countries. The 9 available risks were combined into an unweighted multiple risk behavior frequency score. Because of their low relative frequency, scores from 5 to 9 were collapsed subsequently into a single category, leaving 6 levels (0 to ≥5 behaviors).

Covariates

Factors selected as potential confounders were age (in years), sex, socioeconomic status (5 categorical responses to the following: 'How well-off do you think your family is?'), country of origin, and, because sports injuries are common among youth, hours of sports activity or exercise per week outside of normal school hours (0 to >7). This list was based on previous analyses[29] and exploratory analyses for colinearity within the international HBSC data set.

Statistical analyses

Analyses were initially conducted within individual countries for comparative purposes. Correlation analyses were used to examine the strengths of associations between individual risk factors contained in the multiple risk behavior score. Internal consistency analyses were performed by country, using Kuder-Richardson formula 20 (range, 0–1.0; with a score of >0.6 viewed, conservatively, as acceptable) and computer software (Statistical Product and Service Solutions; SPSS Inc., Chicago, IL). This was done to explore the reliability of the multiple risk behavior score and the individual high-risk behaviors used to construct the score.

The etiological analysis was conducted in two stages. First, unconditional logistic regression (the conventional form for unmatched data analyses) was used to examine each high-risk behavior (individually) as a potential risk factor for injury. Second, the same analytical technique was used to examine the strength of associations between the additive risk score and the occurrence of youth injury. For the individual risk behavior and additive score analyses, crude and adjusted odds ratios (ORs) and associated 95%

confidence intervals were calculated for each level of exposure compared with baseline (the referent level: multiple risk behavior score of 0).

Because consistent findings were obtained from the 12 countries, a combined logistic regression analysis was then performed using the overall sample. This involved calculation of adjusted ORs for each level of the multiple risk behavior score relative to baseline, controlling for the 5 covariates identified a priori, including country of origin. Stratified analyses were then performed to examine the consistency of the risk estimates by sex and age group. Restricted analyses were conducted to examine variations in risks for severe, nonsevere, sports, nonsports, and fighting-related injury.

All data management was performed using computer software (Excel 97; Microsoft, Redmond, Wash). The statistical analyses were conducted using computer software (Statistical Product and Service Solutions).

Results

A total of 50,691 youth in the 12 countries responded to the injury questions, and 49,461 completed records were considered in the final analysis. There were variations between countries in the types and numbers of health risk behaviors reported and the prevalence of medically treated and severe injuries (Table 7.1). Strong variations were observed between countries for the following behaviors: excess drinking, nonuse of seat belts, bullying, excess time spent with friends, an unhealthy diet, and truancy. There was considerably less variation between countries in the numbers of health risk behaviors reported by youth.

The internal reliability of the additive scale varied between countries (Kuder-Richardson formula 20 range, 0.50 [Estonia] 0.63 [Sweden]). The inspection of the corrected item-total correlation for the different risk behaviors showed rather modest correlations ($p < 0.50$).

Adjusted ORs that describe risks for injury associated with individual risk behaviors were all larger than unity (OR > 1.0) (Table 7.2). Risk estimates that were consistently higher were associated with smoking, drinking, and bullying; yet, even these ORs were modest. Within each country, risks for injury increased in accordance with the multiple risk behavior score (Table 7.3). Because all crude ORs calculated were within the bounds of the associated adjusted confidence intervals, only adjusted ORs are presented in Tables 7.2 and 7.3. These results suggest the presence of fairly strong associations between the additive risk score and the occurrence of injury.

A graphical summary of the combined analysis of data from the 12 countries (Figure 7.1) shows the overall gradient in risk for injury associated with the numbers of risk behaviors reported (P <0.001 for trend). The risk gradients were also observed among male and female subjects and within each of the 3 age groups. A stronger risk gradient was observed for severe vs nonsevere injuries, nonsports vs sports injuries, and injuries attributable to fighting (Figure 7.2).

Table 7.1   Frequency distribution of respondents reporting the presence of selected health risk behaviors and injuries

Variable	% of Respondents within countries*		
	Median	Minimum	Maximum
Health risk behavior type			
Smoking	18	12	20
Excess drinking	26	18	45
Nonuse of seat belts**	26	11	49
Perpetrator of bullying	14	4	34
Excess time spent with friends	16	5	28
Alienation			
At home	20	11	23
At school	16	11	29
Unhealthy diet	11	4	38
Truancy***	15	3	35
No. of behaviors			
0	24	18	50
1	27	24	29
2	20	11	23
3	13	7	17
4	8	4	10
≥5	7	4	10
Injury			
≥1 Medically treated injury	39	24	48
Severe injury****	16	9	28

*Percentages are based on the median and range of results for individual countries.
**Data not available for Switzerland.
***Definition varies for Switzerland.
****Data not available for 4 countries.

Comment

This international analysis of young people found that the risk for reported injuries increased in direct association with increasing frequency of reported risk behaviors. These gradients were observed in the combined multinational analysis; within young people from every country that collected these data (12 of 12 countries); in the restricted analyses of severe, nonsevere, sports, nonsports, and fighting-related injuries; and within all demographic strata defined by age and sex. The gradients were observed with and without adjustment for potential confounders, including indicators of socioeconomic status. Consistency across countries with different cultures suggests that this is a robust finding for affirming the relationship between risk-taking behavior and injuries.

There are several reasons why youth engage in risk behaviors. One reason is that risk-taking behavior represents a means by which independence can

Table 7.2 Logistic regression analysis examining associations between individual health risk behaviors and youth injury*

Health risk behavior	Belgium (Flemish sample) (n = 4361)	Canada (n = 6110)	England (n = 5288)	Estonia (n = 1624)	Hungary (n = 3238)	Israel (n = 3736)±	Lithuania (n = 3965)	Poland (n = 4606)	Republic of Ireland (n = 3914)	Sweden (n = 3329)	Switzerland (n = 4707)	United States (n = 4583)
Smoking	1.73 (1.45–2.07)	1.74 (1.51–1.99)	1.62 (1.39–1.89)	1.57 (1.14–2.16)	1.43 (1.18–1.74)	1.41 (1.16–1.71)	1.59 (1.31–1.93)	1.51 (1.26–1.82)	1.90 (1.61–2.26)	2.01 (1.62–2.50)	1.60 (1.36–1.88)	1.58 (1.35–1.84)
Excess drinking	1.73 (1.47–2.03)	1.88 (1.66–2.12)	1.57 (1.38–1.78)	1.49 (1.17–1.91)	1.61 (1.32–1.95)	1.53 (1.28–1.83)	1.53 (1.32–1.77)	1.40 (1.20–1.64)	1.89 (1.61–2.22)	2.01 (1.66–2.4)	1.88 (1.60–2.21)	1.55 (1.35–1.79)
Nonuse of seat belts	1.05 (0.91–1.21)	1.36 (1.16–1.59)	1.07 (0.94–1.22)	0.95 (0.76–1.20)	1.03 (0.87–1.20)	1.09 (0.95–1.24)	1.14 (0.99–1.32)	1.45 (1.24–1.69)	1.20 (1.04–1.38)	1.45 (1.15–1.82)	#	1.07 (0.93–1.24)
Perpetrator of bullying	1.17 (1.00–1.38)	1.69 (1.46–1.96)	1.29 (0.95–1.76)	1.10 (0.85–1.43)	1.38 (1.12–1.69)	1.59 (1.32–1.92)	1.37 (1.20–1.58)	1.53 (1.25–1.87)	1.99 (1.50–2.64)	2.09 (1.46–3.01)	1.31 (1.14–1.50)	1.43 (1.21–1.69)
Excess time spent with friends	1.22 (0.98–1.52)	1.29 (1.15–1.46)	1.25 (1.11–1.42)	1.22 (0.97–1.54)	1.25 (0.95–1.65)	1.29 (1.09–1.53)	1.68 (1.37–2.07)	1.41 (1.17–1.69)	1.37 (1.19–1.59)	1.55 (1.27–1.89)	1.28 (0.98–1.67)	1.11 (0.95–1.29)
Alienation at home	1.16 (0.98–1.37)	1.10 (0.97–1.25)	1.10 (0.93–1.30)	1.04 (0.81–1.33)	1.22 (0.97–1.54)	1.09 (0.91–1.29)	1.08 (0.91–1.28)	1.19 (0.98–1.44)	1.28 (1.09–1.49)	1.16 (0.93–1.43)	1.05 (0.91–1.22)	1.07 (0.93–1.24)
at school	1.26 (1.08–1.46)	1.19 (1.04–1.37)	1.35 (1.15–1.59)	1.55 (1.13–2.14)	1.14 (0.94–1.40)	1.13 (0.94–1.36)	1.10 (0.93–1.32)	1.43 (1.17–1.74)	1.28 (1.07–1.52)	1.74 (1.38–2.19)	1.08 (0.94–1.24)	1.30 (1.13–1.49)
Unhealthy diet	1.30 (1.00–1.70)	1.41 (1.17–1.70)	1.18 (1.05–1.33)	1.38 (0.98–1.95)	1.22 (0.98–1.52)	1.33 (1.14–1.55)	1.24 (0.99–1.55)	1.36 (1.15–1.62)	1.37 (1.20–1.57)	2.47 (1.68–3.61)	1.16 (0.92–1.46)	1.05 (0.91–1.22)
Truancy	1.59 (1.07–2.35)	1.70 (1.50–1.93)	1.34 (1.12–1.61)	1.98 (1.46–2.68)	1.55 (1.21–2.00)	1.03 (0.89–1.20)	1.56 (1.36–1.80)	1.64 (1.37–1.96)	1.83 (1.53–2.20)	2.77 (2.20–3.48)	1.50$ (1.27–1.77)	1.19 (1.03–1.37)

*Data are given as adjusted odds ratio (95% confidence interval). The odds ratios were simultaneously adjusted for age, sex, socioeconomic status, and physical activity.
±Weighted sample.
#Data not available.
$Definition of truancy varies.

Table 7.3   Adjusted logistic regression analysis for health behaviors and youth injury*

Health risk behavior	Belgium (Flemish sample) (n = 4361)	Canada (n = 6110)	England (n = 5288)	Estonia (n = 1624)	Hungary (n = 3238)	Israel (n = 3736)±	Lithuania (n = 3965)	Poland (n = 4606)	Republic of Ireland (n = 3914)	Sweden (n = 3329)	Switzerland (n = 4707)≠	United States (n = 4583)
0$	1.00	1.00	1.00	1.00	1.00	1.00	1.00	1.00	1.00	1.00	1.00	1.00
1	1.38	1.35	1.17	1.15	1.14	1.21	1.31	1.34	1.39	1.47	0.92	1.19
	(1.12–1.69)	(1.16–1.56)	(0.99–1.38)	(0.86–1.55)	(0.95–1.36)	(0.98–1.49)	(1.07–1.62)	(1.11–1.63)	(1.12–1.71)	(1.23–1.77)	(0.79–1.06)	(1.00–1.42)
2	1.42	1.58	1.47	1.02	1.38	1.50	1.68	1.68	1.63	1.68	1.42	1.31
	(1.15–1.77)	(1.34–1.85)	(1.23–1.75)	(0.74–1.42)	(1.12–1.71)	(1.21–1.86)	(1.36–2.07)	(1.36–2.08)	(1.31–2.02)	(1.31–2.15)	(1.19–1.69)	(1.09–1.57)
3	1.78	2.04	1.68	1.32	1.42	1.49	2.21	1.92	1.71	2.36	1.70	1.51
	(1.40–2.26)	(1.69–2.46)	(1.38–2.06)	(0.92–1.89)	(1.09–1.85)	(1.18–1.88)	(1.75–2.78)	(1.50–2.46)	(1.35–2.17)	(1.76–3.17)	(1.36–2.12)	(1.23–1.86)
4	1.75	2.18	2.03	1.82	1.80	1.80	2.38	2.21	2.69	3.49	1.62	1.47
	(1.31–2.34)	(1.76–2.71)	(1.61–2.54)	(1.20–2.76)	(1.28–2.53)	(1.36–2.38)	(1.81–3.11)	(1.65–2.96)	(2.04–3.55)	(2.43–5.01)	(1.23–2.14)	(1.16–1.85)
≥5	2.38	2.93	2.14	2.46	1.93	2.07	2.55	2.81	3.84	4.42	2.12	2.10
	(1.76–3.21)	(2.36–3.65)	(1.67–2.76)	(1.54–3.93)	(1.34–2.80)	(1.55–2.77)	(1.92–3.39)	(2.11–3.74)	(2.92–5.04)	(2.95–6.63)	(1.53–2.93)	(1.65–2.68)

*Data are given as adjusted odds ratio (95% confidence interval). The odds ratios were simultaneously adjusted for age, sex, socioeconomic status, and physical activity.
±Weighted sample.
≠Index based on the results of 8 health risk behaviors.
$Reference.

Figure 7.1   **Associations between numbers of health risk behaviors and youth injury: combined 12-country analyses. A, Overall. B, by sex. C, by age. The ORs are simultaneously adjusted for age, sex, socioeconomic status, physical activity, and country. OR indicates odds ratio; CI, confidence interval.**

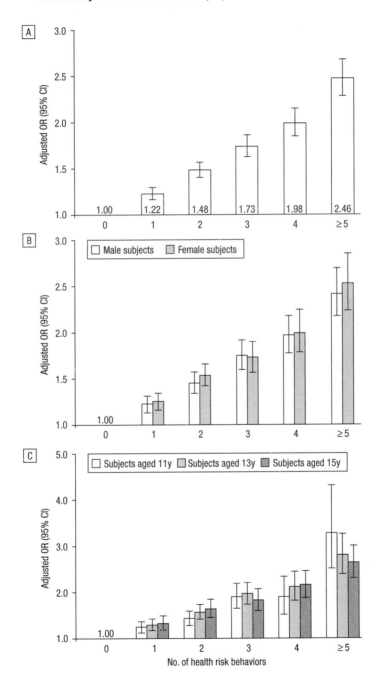

Figure 7.2 **Associations between numbers of health risk behaviors and youth injury: analyses restricted to specific injury types. A by injury severity. Data not available for 4 countries. B, by sports involvement. Data not available for 2 countries. C, fighting-related injuries. Data not available for 3 countries. The ORs are simultaneously adjusted for age, sex, socioeconomic status, physical activity, and country. OR indicates odds ratio; CI, confidence interval.**

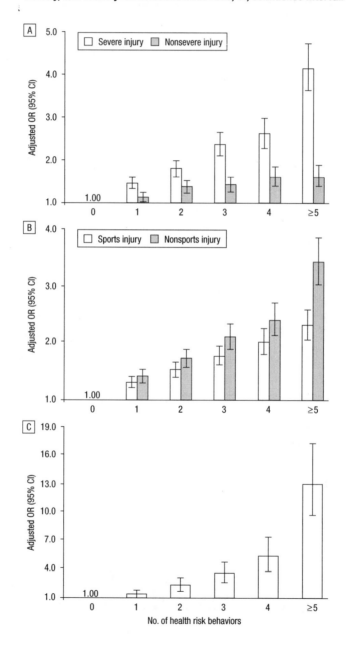

be asserted. The extent of this independence-seeking is influenced by individual personality and cultural norms that imperil or protect the growing child.[38,43] Personal behavior is influenced by peers, parents, the school, and the neighborhood in which adolescents reside.[44] Normative behavior may be related to protective concepts of social capital, including social networks, civic responsibility, perceptions of resources, and local identity.[45] The ability to predict health outcomes, such as injury from risk behavior alone, is tempered by these protective factors.[46]

Risk behavior may also be of social benefit to the growing adolescent. Experimentation is normal and reflects a willingness on the part of the adolescent to move away from dependence on family to a peer orientation. Problem Behavior Theory and Primary Socialization Theory[47] postulate that adolescent risk taking largely takes place within peer groups that provide a means of social support. Further understanding is required about the positive impacts of these social networks. The negative impacts of risk-taking lifestyles include elevated long-term risks for cardiovascular disease, cancer, and other debilitating illnesses. Our findings show that risk behaviors also have more immediate consequences in terms of injury, irrespective of the country and related cultural setting. Although associations were stronger for certain types of injury, the general association between numbers of behaviors and risk for injury was consistently positive.

Our analysis was unique in that we used a multiple risk behavior score to predict a negative health outcome: injury. While the dimensions and structure of adolescent risk-taking behavior still need to be identified, it may be fruitful to include additional risk behaviors, rather than fewer, in such indexes. Furthermore, behavioral risks may be grouped into categories, such as (a) active risk seeking: consumption of alcohol or tobacco or bullying; (b) passive safety and health risk seeking: lack of seat belt use or adherence to a nutritious diet; and (c) independence seeking and/or nonsupportive environments: alienation from parents or school, truancy, or excess time spent with friends. These groupings of risk behaviors need to be confirmed in other contexts using formal statistical techniques (such as factor analyses). Associations between the multiple risk index and other health outcomes, both positive and negative, require similar confirmation.

Our findings provide indirect support for the targeting of multiple forms of risk behavior simultaneously in health interventions. By themselves, individual risk behaviors may be only modestly associated with poor health outcomes because they may be mere markers for the development of a more involved behavioral complex. Our results suggest that, rather than the individual risk behaviors that are engaged in, what seems to be important is the total number of different risk behaviors that are experienced. The latter may be more important in the etiology of injury, especially if they eventually lead to overt risk-taking behaviors, such as physical abuse or impaired driving. A failure to address concurrent forms of risk behavior in interventions may lead to naive preventive strategies.

Common forms of bias warrant consideration as explanations for the observed associations. The population-based nature of the samples limited the extent to which selection bias could account for the gradients. The multivariate analysis simultaneously adjusted for the influence of some confounders, although it was limited to those that were measured and the self-reported manner in which they were assessed. It is possible that the results were enhanced because of the simultaneous conscientious over-reporting of risk behavior and injuries by some adolescents, a form of recall bias. Yet, the associations were strong and consistent multinationally, despite the fact that countries varied in social and cultural factors that might influence reporting inaccuracies. A further limitation is the focus on only one of possible multiple injuries reported by youth in the previous 12 months. This is most likely to bias the ORs and gradients toward unity,[29] meaning that the results presented are conservative.

The additive risk score used herein is admittedly at an early stage of development. The score itself and our approach to analysis were developed using conventional epidemiological methods and the rationale espoused by an existing behavioral model.[26] Formal factor analyses were not used during its construction, and the measures of reliability conducted suggest that there is room for improvement. Correlation between types of behavior contained in the score also might not be sufficiently high to fulfil criteria for reliability when compared with the psychometric theory and associated standards. The associations identified using our score were, however, consistent and robust. We would argue that the basic concept (if not the scale) has considerable potential for etiological research.

Conclusions

The associations between risk behavior and injury are intriguing, although it would be premature to suggest that they are causal. The observed associations were strong and statistically significant, followed a gradational pattern of risk, and were consistent with human theory that attests to their plausibility. The fact that similar associations were found across countries and cultures provides evidence in support of a common etiology to these injuries. Furthermore, the strong and consistent nature of these associations suggests that the additive risk score model of risk behavior, while admittedly at an early stage of development, has promise. Based on these findings, we conclude that the issue of multiple risk behavior, as assessed via an additive score, merits attention as an etiological construct. The latter may be useful in future injury control research and prevention efforts conducted among populations of young people.

Notes

1. Committee on Injury Prevention and Control, Institute of Medicine. *Reducing the Burden of Injury: Advancing Prevention and Treatment.* Washington, DC: National Academy of Sciences, 1999: 41–53.

2. Lescohier, I., Scavo Gallagher, S. Unintentional injury. In: DiClemente, R.J., Hansen, W.B., Ponton, L.E, Eds. *Handbook of Adolescent Health Risk Behavior.* New York: Plenum, 1996: 225–258.

3. Rivara, F.P., Grossman, D.C., Cummings, P. Injury prevention: first two parts. *New England Journal of Medicine.* 1987; **337**: 543–548.

4. Blum, R.W., McNeely, Q., Nonnemaker, J. Vulnerability, risk and protection. In: Fischhoff, B., Nightingale, E.O., Lannotta, J.G, Eds. *Adolescent Risk and Vulnerability.* Washington, DC: National Academy Press, 2001: 50–72.

5. Igra, V., Irwin, C.E. Theories of adolescent risk-taking behavior. In: DiClemente, R.J., Hansen, W.B., Ponton, L.E, Eds. *Handbook of Adolescent Health Risk Behavior.* New York, NY: Plenum, 1996: 35–53.

6. Zuckerman, M. *Beyond the Optimal Level of Arousal.* Hillsdale, NJ: Lawrence A. Erlbaum Associates, 1979.

7. Weinstein, N.D., Why it won't happen to me: perceptions of risk factors and susceptibility. *Health Psychology.* 1984, **3**: 431–457.

8. Connop, H.L., King, A.X., Boyce, W.E. *Youth Smoking and the Role of the Peer Group.* Toronto: Ontario Tobacco Research Unit, 1999. Working Paper Series 47.

9. Sussman, S., Dent, C.W., McAdams, L.A., Stacy, A.W., Burton, D., Flay, B.R. Group self-identification and adolescent cigarette smoking: a 1-year prospective study. *Journal of Abnormal Psychology.* 1994, **103**: 576–580.

10. Galambos, N.L., Tilton-Weaver, L.C. Multiple-risk behavior in adolescents and young adults. *Health Report.* 1998,**10**: 9–20.

11. Cherpitel, C.J. Alcohol, injury, and risk-taking behavior: data from a national sample. *Alcohol Clinical Experimental Research.* 1993, **17**: 762–766.

12. Cherpitel, C.J. Substance use, injury and risk-taking in the general population. *Alcohol Clinical Experimental Research.* 1999, **23**: 121–126.

13. Spirito, A., Rasile, D.A., Vinnick, L.A., Jelahian, E., Arrigan, M.E. Relationship between substance use and self-reported injuries among adolescents. *Journal of Adolescent Health.* 1997, **21**: 221–224.

14. Kalichman, S.C., Johnson, J.R., Adair, V., Rompa, D., Multhauf, K., Kelly, J.I.A. Sexual sensation seeking: scale development and predicting AIDS-risk behavior among homosexually active men. *Journal of Personality Assessment.* 1994, **62**: 385–397.

15. Windle, M., Miller-Tutzauer, C. Antecedents and correlates of alcohol, cocaine, and alcohol-cocaine abuse in early adulthood. *Journal of Drug Education.* 1991, **21**: 133-148.

16. Leistikow, B.N., Shipley, M.J. Might stopping smoking reduce injury death risks? A meta-analysis of randomized, controlled trials. *Preventative Medicine.* 1999, **28**: 255–259.

17. Baumert, P.W. Jr, Henderson, J.M., Thompson, N.J. Health risk behaviors of adolescent participants in organized sports. *Journal of Adolescent Health.* 1998, **22**: 460–465.

18. Patel, O.R., Luckstead, E.F. Sport participation, risk taking, and health risk behaviors. *Adolescent Medicine.* 2000, **11**: 141–155.

19. Dryfoos, J.G. *Adolescents at Risk*. London: Oxford University Press, 1990.

20 Dryfoos, J.G. Adolescents at risk: a summation of work in the field – programs and policies. *Journal of Adolescent Health*. 1991, **12**: 630–637.

21. Irwin, C.E. Jr, Millstein, S.G. Biopsychosocial correlates of risk-taking behaviors during adolescence: can the physician intervene? *Journal of Adolescent Health Care*. 1986, **7** (suppl.): 82S–96S.

22. Gabhainn, S.N., Frangois, Y. Substance use. In: Currie, C., Hurrelmann, K., Settertobulte, W., Smith, R., Todd, J, Eds. *Health and Health Behaviour Among Young People*. Copenhagen: World Health Organization Regional Office for Europe, 2000: 97–114. WHO Policy Series 1: Health Policy for Children and Adolescents.

23. Hibell, B., Andersson, B., Ahström, S., et al., Eds. *The ESPAD Report. Alcohol and Other Drugs Among Students in 30 European Countries*. Stockholm: Swedish Council for Information on Alcohol and Other Drugs, Pompidou Group at the Council of Europe, 2000.

24. DiClemente, R.J., Hansen, W.B., Ponton, L.E, Eds. *Handbook of Adolescent Health Risk Behavior*. New York: Plenum, 1996.

25. Hennessy, M. Adolescent syndromes of risk for HIV infection. *Evaluative Review*. 1994, **18**: 312–341.

26. Jessor, R. Risk behavior in adolescence: a psychological framework for understanding and action. *Journal of Adolescent Health*. 1991,**12**: 597–605.

27. Enquist, K., Edmundson, E., Parcel, G. Structure of health risk behavior among high school students. *Journal of Consultant Clinical Psychology*. 1995, **64**: 764–775.

28. Osgood, D., Johnston, I.L., O'Malley, P.M., Bachman, J.G. The generality of deviance in late adolescence: an eight year longitudinal study of a cohort of elementary school students. *American Sociology Review*. 2000, **53**: 81–93.

29. Pickett, W., Garner, M.J., Boyce, W.F., King, M.A. Gradients in risk for youth injury associated with multiple-risk behaviors: a study of 11,329 Canadian adolescents. *Social Science Medicine*. In press.

30. Currie, C.E. *Health Behavior in School-aged Children: Research Protocol for the 1997–98 Survey*. Edinburgh: World Health Organization Coordinating Center for the Study of Health Behavior in School-aged Children, 1998.

31. King, A.J.C., Boyce, W.F., King, M.A. *Trends in the Health of Canadian Youth*. Ottawa: Health Canada, 1999.

32. Scheidt, P.C., Harel, Y., Trumble, A.C., Jones, D.H., Overpeck, M.D., Bijur, P.E. The epidemiology of nonfatal injuries among US children and youth. *American Journal of Public Health*. 1995, **85**: 932–938.

33. King, A., Wold, B., Smith, C.T., Harel, Y. *The Health of Youth: A Cross-National Survey*. Copenhagen: World Health Organization, Regional Publications, 1996. European Series 69.

34. Overpeck, M.D., Kotch, J.B. The effect of US children's access to care on medical attention for injuries. *American Journal of Public Health*. 1995, **85**: 402–404.

35. Flisher, A.J., Ziervogel, C.F., Chalton, D.O., Leger, P.H., Robertson, B.A. Risk-taking behavior of Cape Peninsula high-school students, part III: cigarette smoking. *South African Medical Journal*. 1993, **83**: 477–479.

36. Slap, G.B., Chaudhuri, S., Vorters, D.I.F. Risk factors for injury during adolescence, *Journal of Adolescent Health*. 1991, **12**: 263–268.

37. Kann, L., Warren, C.W., Harris, W.A. et al. Youth risk behavior surveillance: United States, 1995. *Journal of the School of Health*. 1996, **66**: 365–377.

38. Brooks-Gunn, J., Graber, J.A. Puberty as a biological and social event: implications for research on pharmacology. *Journal of Adolescent Health*. 1994, **15**: 663-671.

39. Tenn, L., Dewis, M.E. An evaluation of Canadian peer-driven injury prevention programme for high-risk adolescents. *Journal of Advanced Nursing.* 1998, **23**: 329–337.

40. Christoffel, K.K., Donovan, M., Schofer, J., Wills, K., Lavigne, J.V for the Kids 'n' Cars Team. Psychosocial factors in childhood pedestrian injury: a matched case–control study. *Pediatrics.* 1996, **97**: 33–42.

41. Bijur, P.E., Stewart-Brown, S., Butler, N. Child behavior and accidental injury in 11,966 preschool children. *American Journal of Diseases of Children.* 1986, **140**: 487–492.

42. Pritchard, C., Cotton, A., Cox, M. Truancy and illegal drug use, and knowledge of HIV infection in 932 14–16-year-old adolescents. *Journal ofAdolescence.* 1992, **15**: 1–17.

43. Graber, A., Brooks-Gunn, J. Models of development: understanding risk in adolescence. *Suicide Life Threatening Behavior.* 1995, **25**: 18–25.

44. Millstein, S.G., Petersen, A.C., Nightingale, E.O., Eds. *Promotion of Health Behavior in Adolescence.* New York: Oxford University Press, 1993.

45. Kawachi, I., Kennedy, B.P., Lochner, K., Prothrow-Stith, D. Social capital, income inequality, and mortality. *American Journal of Public Health.* 1997, **87**: 1491–1498.

46. Jessor, R. Risk behavior in adolescence: a psychosocial framework for understanding and action. In: Rogers, D.E., Girizberg, E., Eds. *Adolescents at Risk: Medical and Social Perspectives.* Boulder, CO: Westview Press, 1992: 19–34.

47. Oetting, E.R., Donnermeyer, J.F. Primary socialization theory: the etiology of drug use and deviance, 1. *Substance Use and Misuse.* 1998, **33**: 995–1026.

Commentary: Will Pickett

I am an Associate Professor in the Faculty of Health Sciences at Queen's University; a small university located in a central province of Canada. Here, being a new associate professor means that you have been around long enough to be granted a permanent university position, but not long enough to be considered 'established.' I have spent most of my career trying to understand the causes and consequences of injuries. Along those lines, I have been involved in an international study of young people and their health. This study is called the Health Behaviour in School Aged Children Survey (or HBSC) and the latest count is that it involves researchers from 36 countries. The HBSC is conducted every 3–4 years according to an international protocol. It is coordinated from a central office in Edinburgh and is also affiliated with the World Health Organization and its European offices.

The authors

It is an unusual truth to admit but I haven't actually met many of my fellow co-authors in person. This paper was developed entirely via email. As I am writing this, I am sitting in a hotel room in Toulouse, France. I am excited, because tomorrow is the opening session of the semi-annual HBSC meeting. I will, for the first time, put a face to the name of many of these colleagues. My team of co-authors reflects considerable diversity and includes psychologists, social scientists, physicians, and biostatisticians working in universities and government departments. People at every stage of their careers are represented. The remarkable thing is that they come from so many different countries and backgrounds.

Starting points

My own personal history with this project began with a conversation that I had with Alan King, a very senior Canadian social researcher. Alan was particularly interested in the health risks that young people engage in. As part of the normal developmental process young people do things like smoke, drink, and take deliberate physical risks in order to become part of the social fabric of a group. This helps them to achieve a personal identity. Alan stressed that these behaviors would become exacerbated among children who felt alienated. As time went on, I came to realize that this view was influenced by thinking within the HBSC group.

Alan's charge to me as a new member of the HBSC was to determine whether these risky behaviors had any impact upon injuries. Injury is the leading cause of death among adolescents throughout much of the world, yet little is really understood about the factors that predispose young people to injury. With that in mind, we set out using a conventional epidemiological approach. Using Canadian data from the 1994 version of the HBSC, we examined each of a number of behaviors as 'risk factors' in some basic mathematical models. The results were unimpressive. We went on to publish a paper from this work, but we were left feeling rather dissatisfied with the whole affair.

A couple of years went by and another version of the HBSC survey (1998) came along. In the interim, I had been struck by the idea that there might be a more realistic way of examining these issues. Rather than the type of risk behavior being significant we wanted to test whether it was the number of things that youth were experimenting with. Some notable figures in the social science field had written about this concept.

Although there were several ways that you could model risk-taking behavior, the one that appealed to me was quite simple. First, we searched the literature and identified potential risk factors for youth injury. Second, we determined which of these risk factors were measured in the Canadian version of the 1998 HBSC survey. We then created a very simple additive scale that consisted of a count of these risk behaviors. The results of this initial Canadian analysis were exciting. Risks for injury went up in a linear fashion in association with increasing numbers of risk-taking behaviors. The relationships were strong, they were statistically significant, and they followed a lovely and consistent trend. The consistency was quite remarkable – this finding was there for both boys and girls, for all of the age groups, and it was present for every single form of injury examined. Perhaps Alan King's ideas were actually right all along, we just hadn't gone about testing them in an appropriate manner.

The natural next step for this work was to apply these concepts to youth in other countries. Twelve countries had collected injury information in 1998, and all 12 permitted us to use their international files to build our analysis. We were on our way to the international analysis reported in the paper.

Author collaboration

The HBSC is a rather formal research network that has been around for a while. There are rules to follow when you begin an international analysis.

You cannot just receive the data and start. You must inform the right people about your plans. There is even an international protocol that governs what to do here and it is not an easy process. Depending upon your intended analysis, this might involve getting permission from investigators in 35 countries. This is mainly done by email these days.

In this particular analysis, the first task was to write to everyone involved in the HBSC and ask if they wanted to take part in a paper. The central coordinating office in Edinburgh had created an email directory. I simply sent an outline of our proposed international analysis to every investigator. At the same time I asked if anyone objected to our use of their country's data for this manuscript. Potential collaborators were asked to write back suggesting how they could participate. Although I had heard that these arrangements sometimes fail, I was happy to receive an enthusiastic response. Approximately 15 people asked to be co-authors. Although we lost a few people along the way, most of these people persevered and contributed to the published manuscript.

Choice of methodology and data decisions

I am an epidemiologist and we tend to bring a certain approach to our work. We like health outcomes that fit into neat little packages. Binary (yes/no) outcomes that work with the sorts of mathematical models that we are used to are good. Very simple numeric scales are also nice. We are kind of intimidated by qualitative data that are difficult to assign numbers to, perhaps because we don't understand what to do with them.

I proposed the epidemiological analysis that is in the paper because it is fairly conventional, and frankly, I thought that we knew how to perform it. The basic idea was pretty simple – create a simple scale that consisted of counts of health risk behaviors and measure these against the presence or absence of reported injuries. There were, however, a number of tricky decision points.

The development of the scale caused a few dilemmas. First, we had to come up with an operational definition of a 'health risk behavior.' In the end, we established a fairly broad definition that encompassed direct risk taking, failure to take safety precautions, and perceived feelings of alienation. This rather loose definition was a natural source of controversy and debate; one that continued even after our paper was published.

Second, despite efforts to standardize the survey, not all countries in the HBSC had actually collected the same data. There are mandatory and optional topics addressed in the HBSC. Injury was an optional topic. We therefore needed to identify those countries that had injury data (there were 12) and then create a list of health risk behaviors that were common to them. Nine HBSC questions were suggested, although our list grew and shrank over time as people offered their opinions.

I personally underwent a revelation about the usual science behind scale development. Epidemiologists often put questionnaire items together into more complex scales, and then use these to predict the likelihood of health outcomes. However, there is a science behind this process, one that I didn't know a lot about. After we had run some preliminary analyses, one of our group proposed something called a 'reliability analysis.' This is simply a method to determine if your scale is legitimate. However, this suggestion came after we had constructed and circulated draft tables and were fairly far along in the process. We agreed to this with some trepidation and the result was that the scale didn't work very well by conventional reliability statistics. The good news was that I had learned a new technique for future work. The bad news was that attempts to refine our scale further weren't that successful, and we were left to acknowledge this as a limitation.

There were also some minor controversies within the research group. One of these surrounded the use of something called 'survey weights.' The international HBSC samples are meant to be representative samples where every person contributes an equal amount of information to the sample. However, it is more conventional in surveys to create weighted samples, a technique where observations from participants are multiplied by numbers called 'weights' in order to ensure that the sample population represents the population under study.

There appeared to be some politics and debate about the right thing to do here. Most countries supported the decision not to use weights because they wished to avoid the additional complexity that they introduce. Other countries didn't use weights but were worried that this resulted in biased samples. One country (Israel) found it necessary to use a weighting system in order to account for their unique demographic (they wanted to assure themselves that they could accurately describe students from both Israel and the Palestine Authority separately). Other countries (e.g. the United States) preferred to employ survey weights but didn't always in every situation. In the end we followed the HBSC 'non-weighted' directive with the exception of the Israeli data.

The appropriateness of our statistical modeling technique (logistic regression) was also questioned. The issue at hand was that the measures of association produced by logistic regression aren't that accurate in situations where the outcome under study is common. Injuries are certainly common enough among this population. Our risk estimates are likely to be biased due to this situation.

A final point of consideration was how best to present the data. The main points that we wanted to highlight were the linear increase in risks for injury, the consistency of this result crossnationally, and the fact that one could observe these trends in all groups of youth and for every type of injury examined. I like the use of illustrative figures in this situation, but tables could be used to say so much more (although they can be boring). In the end, we opted for the compromise that is presented in the paper. Kelly Simpson is responsible for all of these figures and tables, and I am grateful to her for her creativity and care.

Conclusions of the study

There are two important findings to take from our work. The first is the remarkable consistency of the risk taking and injury association. The second is the idea that the most important determinants of adolescent health may not be the actual health risk behaviors engaged in, but the number of things that kids are experimenting with. Clearly, there are large numbers of young people throughout the world who are experimenting with new behaviors. While this is an obvious part of human development, and these risks are not all 'bad,' they do have a profound influence on long-term health. What we didn't fully appreciate until this analysis was the immediate impact that these behaviors have on acute aspects of health.

We initially tried to argue that these relationships were causal, based upon conventional epidemiological criteria. These criteria include the strength and statistical significance of the associations, their consistency, their biological plausibility, and their 'temporality,' which refers to evidence that the cause (behaviors) preceded the effect (injuries). However, the cross-sectional nature of our survey was against us as one reviewer didn't think that our study had satisfied that last criterion. We therefore had to back off our arguments about causation. Causal or not, our hope is that these findings can be applied to the development of effective countermeasures.

The writing-up process

Writing up was challenging. There were four of us who led this. We started by dividing the paper up into sections with each of us taking responsibility for putting something on paper. It was then up to me to put these sections together. The first difficulty that I ran into was that each of us had a highly different style of writing. When they were put together, it read like something that was written by a committee. There was absolutely no flow to the article and it was my job to remedy this situation. It had to have an appropriate word length and style that would be acceptable to a biomedical journal. After several iterations, the four of us got to a version that we could all live with.

We then sent our draft out to our long list of potential co-authors. This is where the fun really began. It was early summer and our timing wasn't optimal. Some people were just going on holiday. Others must have had time on their hands, because they got right back to us but with long lists of suggestions for change. Still others never corresponded at first, and I think that as time went on they felt out of place about taking part as they had missed so much of the process. We never did hear from some of our original correspondents, which was disappointing but perhaps to be expected.

This process required great patience. What I initially thought would take a few weeks actually took close to 8 months. There came a point in time when we thought we might have to make some hard decisions. One of these was to send drafts to people and ask for feedback by a certain deadline. When the deadline came and went, we would write to individuals who had not responded and give them a gentle prod. I was a bit worried that people would think that I was being overly pushy. In the end, those I thought would be critics were supportive. They provided wonderful ideas and practical suggestions. In hindsight, being a bit strict with one's peers isn't necessarily a bad idea. Patience is certainly a virtue but there comes a time when you have to get on with things.

The final stage of writing up was the submission process. First, we had to make a final choice of journal. We decided to go with the *Archives of Pediatrics and Adolescent Medicine* because (1) it was a journal with a good reputation; (2) the subject matter fitted the journal's mandate; and (3) the new editor was a leading childhood injury researcher, and we felt that he might be sympathetic to our topic. It proved to be a wise choice, and the editor and the journal itself were highly efficient and professional. We had a positive decision within 3–4 weeks of submission, and were published within 6 months after minor revisions.

Hindsight and future directions

I am proud of our collective work on this manuscript and the attention that it received. Although at the time the paper was submitted I vowed I wouldn't get involved in something like this for a while, I am now anxious to try again. Projects like this can be frustrating yet enriching at the same time. The paper has led to a number of additional initiatives. Our group has created a second manuscript that evaluates the concept of 'population attributable risk' as applied to these behaviors. Members of the HBSC group are exploring the use of the additive risk model in other study situations. Personally, I have also become involved in manuscripts that are being led by other members of this team. All of this is interesting and gratifying.

8 The Mosaic Approach and Research with Young Children
ALISON CLARK

'In my cave listening to music. It's magic music from my magic radio.'

This was one response from 3-year-old Gary about his favourite place in the nursery. The statement was one of many insights given by a group of young children, under 5 years old about their views and experiences of everyday life in their early childhood institution. There is an increasing policy interest in listening to children and children's participation in decision-making. This is also a subject which continues to hold interest for researchers (Lewis & Lindsay, 2000; Christensen & James, 2000). Listening to young children, defined in this article as the under-5s, holds particular challenges for the research, policy and practice communities. Some of the major arenas for young children are early childhood institutions. These centres have become a feature of a growing number of children's lives in the UK. There have been few attempts to explore young children's perspectives on these institutions (Daycare Trust, 1998; Dupree et al., 2001).

This chapter explores the development of a methodological framework, the Mosaic approach, for listening to young children about the important details of their daily lives. I will look in particular at how this methodology has helped me to reflect on young children's experience of place.

Theoretical underpinnings of the Mosaic approach

There were three main theoretical starting points for this research approach, each based on notions of competency. Firstly, I acknowledged the importance of the ideas expressed in the emerging sociology of childhood. This supports the view of children as 'beings not becomings' (Qvortrup et al., 1994: 2). Childhood is seen as one of a number of structures within society: 'children have their own activities and their own time and their own space' (ibid.: 4). This proved to be a useful theoretical beginning for this study, acknowledging that children have important perspectives to contribute about their lives in an early childhood institution. This view of competency is in contrast to other research models which, as Qvortrup has pointed out, can often exclude the voices of children:

children often denied the right to speak for themselves either because they are held incompetent in making judgements or because they are thought of as unreliable witnesses about their own lives (Qvortrup et al., 1994: 2).

Instead, in the words of Langsted (1994: 42), this study viewed young children as 'experts in their own lives'.

Secondly, I looked to Participatory Appraisal to see how methodology developed to empower adults in communities in the Majority World could be applied to young children. The concept of 'voice' was important here. These tools have been designed to give 'voice' to those who are disempowered. In an international development context these methods acknowledge that local people are the ones best equipped to know about the lives lived in their own place. There has been some challenge as to whether these techniques have been used to bring about effective change (Cooke & Kothari, 2001). However, as a theoretical starting point this view of competency was of interest to the present study. It was the 'assumed competency' which led to the development of imaginative methods that enabled often illiterate adults to communicate their local knowledge. This same trigger has been the spur for developing the Mosaic approach with young children.

Thirdly, my background in early years education led me to consider notions of competency and young children, referring to pedagogical frameworks. The pre-schools of Reggio Emilia, a region in northern Italy, have influenced this study. The theoretical framework for these early childhood institutions, established by Loris Malaguzzi in the 1940s, is one of the competent child. Educators in Reggio refer to an image of the child as a 'rich child' who is strong, competent and active. This view is reflected in the architecture, the relationships, the routines and the pedagogy. Learning is seen as a collaborative process in which adults and children search for meanings together: 'We construct the meaning of school as a place which plays an active role in the children's search for meaning and our own search for meaning, shared meanings' (Rinaldi, 1999).

The study

The study took place between January 1999 and June 2000 at an early childhood institution which was part of a multi-agency childcare network or community campus (Wigfall & Moss, 2001). This exploratory study on listening to young children was part of a wider evaluation of the campus which includes an early childhood centre, a parents' centre and a homeless families project. The main focus of the study were two key groups within the early childhood centre: children aged 3–4 years in the kindergarten and children under 2 in the nursery. Pilot work was also carried out with refugee children attending the homeless families project. I will explore here the research carried out with a group of eight children in the kindergarten group. The children used the term 'nursery' to refer to their institution. I will therefore use 'nursery' in this way in the following account.

Developing the Mosaic approach

The focus for the development phase of this study was to find methodologies which played to young children's strengths rather than weaknesses. This ruled out certain traditional methods such as written interview schedules. I wanted to find ways of harnessing young children's creativity and physical engagement with their world. Such methods would acknowledge what Malaguzzi described as the 'hundred languages of children' (Edwards et al., 1998): the verbal and non-verbal ways in which young children communicate their feelings.

The approach developed as a multi-method model. It was important to include a range of methods in order to allow children with different abilities and interests to take part (Table 8.1). A multi-method approach also enabled traditional tools of observation and interviewing to contribute to the overall picture or 'mosaic'. There was also the opportunity for triangulation of the findings across the different methodologies.

Table 8.1   Tools used in the Mosaic approach

Method	Comments
Observation	Narrative accounts
Child conferencing	A short structured interview schedule conducted one to one or in a group
Using cameras	Children using single use cameras to take photographs of 'important things'
Tours	Tours of the site directed and recorded by the children
Map making	2D representations of the site using children's own photographs and drawings
Interviews	Informal interviews with staff and parents

The first tool used in the sequence was **observation**. I chose to use narrative accounts based on written descriptions of episodes of children's play. The use of learning stories in evaluation in the New Zealand early years programme, Te Whaariki, was an important influence here (Ministry of Education, 1996). I used two questions as the basis for my observations: 'Do you listen to me?' and 'What is it like for me to be here?'

This form of observation allowed me as the adult recorder to be the 'inexpert' who is there to listen and learn from the children. This form of participant ethnographic observation is similar to the technique used by Corsaro (1985, 1997) to reveal details of the lives of pre-school children. Observation is an important part of listening, but it still relies on an adult perspective on children's lives. I was also interested in pursuing participatory ways in which young children can convey their views and experiences.

Child conferencing provided a space for including formal conversations with children about their early childhood institution. This structured interview is based on a schedule developed by the Centre for Language in Primary Education in the 1980s. The questions I used were adapted from the interview schedule used by the head of the nursery. The fourteen open questions ask children why they come to their nursery, what they enjoy doing or dislike or find hard. Some questions focus on important people, places and activities. There is the opportunity for children to add other information they think the interviewer should know about their institution. I carried out the child conferencing with a group of children in the nursery twice over a four-month period. The children were able to listen to their previous responses, reflect on any changes and add new comments. However, not all the children were interested in talking in this formal way. I then adapted the child conferencing to be conducted 'on the move' so children could take me to places as they spoke.

Cameras provided a participatory tool through which the young children could communicate. Walker refers to the 'silent voice of the camera' (1993). A number of recent studies have incorporated the use of cameras with older children (e.g. Smith & Barker, 1999; 2002). This silent tool also appears to have potential for use with young children. I was interested in exploring their competency with using a camera, following the consultation carried out by the Daycare Trust (1998) where children photographed their 'favourite things'. I extended this approach to see if young children could provide a more in-depth view of life in the nursery using the 'voice' of the camera. I asked children to take photographs of what was important in the nursery. Single use cameras proved a useful tool for this age group as the children could be given freedom with the cameras without causing adult anxiety about expensive equipment. The children expressed pride in the photographs they had taken. Children who have seen adults taking photographs and pored over family albums know that photographs are valued in the 'adult world'. This is not always the case with children's own drawings and paintings. The cameras gave the children a powerful new language. They were given their own set of the photographs. The second set was used by the children to select photographs to make their own individual books about the nursery.

Tours and map making emerged from the use of the cameras. I was interested in finding ways of gathering young children's experiences which were best suited to their natural ways of communicating. This called out for an active approach. Tours are a participatory technique, similar to the idea of 'transect walks' which have been used in International Development programmes for people to convey their knowledge of their immediate surroundings (Hart, 1997). The physicality and mobility of this technique mean that it lends itself to being used by young children. Neighbourhood walks have also been used to involve children in environmental planning (Adams & Ingham, 1998). Langsted (1994) describes a similar approach in the BASUN Project, a comparative study of the daily lives of young children in five Nordic countries. Each 5-year-old took the researcher on a 'sightseeing trip of his/her daily life' (1994: 34).

Following Langsted's model, I used issues of time and space to help struc-ture the walking interview. Working with children individually, in pairs or threes, I asked the children to take me on a tour of their nursery, beginning with where they came in in the morning. The children then gave a running commentary on what happened next, who they met and which rooms they went into (or didn't have access to). Children were in charge of the tour and of how it was recorded. This involved the children taking photographs of important places and people and making sound recordings of the tours using a small tape recorder with clip mike and drawing.

Map making was developed as a way for the children to bring together the material they had gathered from the tours. Hart also describes the use of child-made maps:

> The method can provide valuable insight for others into children's everyday envi-ronment because it is based on the features they consider important, and hence can lead to good discussion about aspects of their lives that might not so easily emerge in words. (Hart, 1997: 165)

Children's photographs provided the bridge between the children's physical experiences of their environment and the two-dimensional nature of the map. The maps proved to be an interesting talking point for other children who had not been involved in the tours. Thus the mapping exer-cise led to more opportunities for talking and listening to a wider group of children about their nursery, through the visual language of the maps.

Interviews with staff and parents were developed as an important part of understanding young children's lives in this place. Accounts from those who know the personalities and daily routines of the individual children need to sit alongside the other participatory tools in the Mosaic approach in order to build a more detailed understanding of young children's expe-riences. The interview schedule was similar to the questions used in the child conferencing but the emphasis was on adults' perceptions of everyday experience rather than first-hand accounts from the children. These inter-views were particularly valuable when using the Mosaic approach with pre-verbal children.

Stages in the Mosaic approach

Stage One	Children and adults gathering documentation
Stage Two	Piecing together information for dialogue, reflection and interpretation

The focus in Stage One of the Mosaic approach is gathering information, led by the children using the tools described above. Each tool can be used in isolation. However, the strength of this approach is in the drawing together of the different methodologies through discussion. Stage Two focuses on this interpretation: staff and parents now listen to the children's own perspectives. This use of documentation has drawn on the process developed in the pre-schools of Reggio Emilia which Rinaldi (2001) has described as 'visible listening'. Listening is not limited to a two-way conversation between one adult and a child. Child conferencing is one of the pieces which provides this documentation but equal worth is given to children's photographs, narrative accounts from observations, recordings of tours, maps and recordings of role play. Discussions included both formal and informal exchanges between children and adults, planned and unplanned. One formal exchange of ideas, based on the documentation, took place between parents, the children and the researcher. This took the form of a planned meeting to explore the material gathered including children's responses to the child conferencing, the researchers' narrative accounts from observation, and children's photographs and maps.

A formal discussion was also held at a staff meeting, using documentation gathered by one 3-year-old as the basis for reflection and interpretation. Informal exchanges also took place between the children who had been directly involved in the study and other children in the nursery. This was mirrored by conversations with staff who had not taken part but who had become aware of the children's enthusiasm for the project.

In the following sections I will explore what the material gathered revealed about young children's experience of place.

A sense of place?

An important aspect of young children's lives is their physical engagement with their environment. The classic study by Hart (1979) into children's experience of place is relevant here. This was a two-year ethnographic study of the everyday experiences of locality conducted with children living in New England. His creative responses to recording children's intimate knowledge of their area has been of interest to me in this study. Hart discusses children's experience of place in terms of their place knowledge, place values and feelings and place use. In a similar way to Hart, I wanted to find out about children's knowledge and feelings about their everyday environment.

Constructing meanings: place use

The young children in this study defined the spaces according to their associations with people and past events, with objects, activities, routines and according to access.

People and events

During a child-led tour the children stop at a door and look in.

Researcher:	What's this room?
Clare:	It's the Parents' Room – where people have their leaving parties.
Researcher:	Can we go in here?
Clare:	Yep, we can go in there.

Clare, in this account, demonstrates how the meaning she gave to the Parents' Room was closely linked to her memories of past uses of the room for farewells. Other rooms were associated with the adults whom children regularly saw working in those spaces. The office was linked to the member of staff who was there when the children arrived in the morning and who was the first adult they met in the nursery each day. Two of the children had younger siblings in the nursery. The tours of important places and subsequent map making revealed the spaces where siblings 'lived' as significant parts of the nursery for the older children.

Objects

Children also associated rooms with certain objects or toys which they could play with in those spaces, as can be seen in the following excerpt from a child-led tour.

Gary:	There are some toys over there and books. Where are the toys gone? Here they are. Let's get them down. Can you get down the truck with the hook?

In this example, a layer of meaning was given to this room by the particular toy he liked playing with there. My observations had also shown that another inside space in the nursery was associated with the large soft toy dog which had been named by the children and lived in the carpeted area of the classroom.

Activities

There were specific spaces in the nursery in which children used the activities experienced there to describe them. One important space was the music room. This was a multi-purpose space which was the largest gathering point in the nursery. It had low windows allowing an open view of the courtyard and garden.

This room was described as the 'dancing room', 'the listening room' as well as the music room. Children included this room in their tours and took photographs of the room in use and when empty. This room was also associated with past uses. At one point it had been filled with small plastic balls, making it into a giant ball pool. This was remembered with affection. It served as an example of the complex layering of experiences which children could recall when revisiting a space.

Routines

Children also added meanings to spaces by the personal routines which took place there. The 'fruit place' was the phrase used by most of the group for the space in the conservatory where they had their mid-morning snack. The conservatory was a corridor space between the classrooms and the courtyard. It had several functions, including storage for children's coats and hats, as well as housing display areas and bookshelves. My observations had reinforced this space as an important one for the children. 'Fruit time' was a relaxed time when an adult would sit with the children, chatting and listening to the children whilst they prepared the fruit. In the following excerpt from a child-led tour the children are sitting in the Orange room during the tour.

> *Meryl:* We eat our dinners and then (ssh, I want to talk) I play in here. I eat my dinner. I get a knife and fork and when we've finished we having pudding and cake and custard and then we wash our hands and then we have a partner and then we play outside.

There was a wealth of detail given by children about place use in this way. Children's ability to talk about the meanings they gave to a place seemed to be enhanced by talking in that place. Hart also found working with older children that 'place expeditions' elicited far more details about children's experiences than traditional methods alone.

Access

Spaces also acquired significance according to whether the children had access to the space or not. Children remarked that the staffroom was a place they could not go into and were keen to photograph it on their tours. The kitchen was another space known to be out of bounds but signalled as important. Access was also controlled by adults according to age of child. The Orange room (described by Meryl earlier) was a place where 4-year-olds had their lunch. Each key group in the kindergarten section of the nursery had 3- and 4-year-olds together so these children would eat lunch separately according to age. Meryl had lunch in the Orange room but Gaby, being 3, had lunch in the conservatory. Gaby described on the tour how much she wanted to be old enough to go to the Orange room, saying 'I can't wait to get big.'

This example supports Sibley's view (1995) that children's experience of place is closely associated with issues of power. Adults' demarcation of place use by age led to a differentiation of experience for the children in the group.

Gaby's comment leads me on to the question of children's place feelings and values, which are at times difficult to separate from knowledge about place use.

Constructing meanings: place feelings and values

Hart describes children's experience of place feelings and values in terms of preferences and fears. I will use these categories to examine children's feelings about places in the nursery. The following excerpt is from a child conference about favourite places.

Researcher:	Where is your favourite place in the nursery?
Clare:	Outside and inside and having fruit time.
Laura:	On the bikes.
Gary:	Going in my cave, near the big dark trees [July]. In my cave listening to music. It's magic music from my magic radio [November].
John:	The garden. I roll in the green rollers.
Gaby:	Inside – the fruit place. We always do singing there.
Mark:	I live in here [classroom] so my mummy knows where I am. I like playing with the sharks.

Children's preferences ranged from personal spaces of imagination or safety to social places linked to activities as discussed above. Gary was unusual, at the age of 3, in being able to speak about his imaginary space. A traditional interview might however have left me baffled about this secret place. I took the decision to conduct the child conferencing with these boys on the move. It became a 'walking interview' (Langsted, 1994) or, as Hart describes it, a 'place expedition'. The boys took me outside and showed me the 'cave'. It was not a hidden corner as I had imagined but a curved bench on the grass in the play area. My observations had indicated that this was a public social place where children gathered with each other or with an adult. Gary's description shows the imaginative meanings children can give to familiar objects and illustrates Hart's descriptions of children's personal or phenomenal landscapes (Hart, 1979: 12–13).

Social spaces

Children identified several key sites in the nursery which were focal points for being with their peers and sometimes also with adults. The 'fruit place' was a shared space for children and adults to interact together, as discussed earlier. The curved bench in the garden was another meeting place. This indicates how the same object or space held different meanings for individuals within the group. Gary's 'cave' represented a significant social space for another child, Cary. She took a photograph of the bench and included it in her set of important photos. It represented for her the place where she used to sit with Molly, her key worker, who had recently left on maternity leave. The memories associated with the space still gave this part of the nursery meaning for Cary.

The large sandpit was a central feature of the outside play area and acted as a focus for social interaction. Children in the study took photographs of the sand and the toys and the features linked to the sandpit, a wooden bridge over the sand and a large canopy.

Another preferred social space was the climbing frame, tunnel and slide. This piece of play equipment featured in many of the children's photographs. Some children made carefully framed shots of the slide or the tunnel. Others chose this play equipment as a background against which to photo-graph friends. The photographs were then used as significant places on their maps.

Private spaces

Children in the study also valued places with a degree of privacy where they had the ability to regulate social interaction (Altman, 1975). There were few spaces indoors or outdoors where the children could exercise this control. One such space was behind the shed at the far corner of the garden. I had observed that some children would go to this corner to play before being asked to move away by an adult. It was one of the few places in the nursery where children were out of sight. It did not appear from my observations to be a space used exclusively by boys. However, in the group I was working with, it was Gary and John who identified this space as important. Gary selected the photographs he took of the shed to include on his map of the nursery.

The tunnel was another child-only space. It was also small enough for children to regulate who used this equipment. Several children in the group chose to take close-up photographs of the tunnel. Laura and Clare both included these photographs in their books of the nursery. The tunnel serves as another example of the multiple meanings given to places: the tunnel as private space as well as social space. The tunnel was also a raised space which was above the heads of the children. Corsaro (1985) discusses the importance of raised spaces for control. The height of the climbing frame and tunnel resulted in a useful vantage point for the children.

Individual landmarks

In addition to the shared spaces which held meaning for children in the group, this study also revealed a complex web of individual traces or landmarks (Weinstein, 1987; Trancik & Evans, 1995). These landmarks ranged from objects and photographs to people, which summed up what was important about the nursery for different children. Younger siblings acted as landmarks for two of the children in the group. The child-led tours indicated that their morning routine of taking their younger brother and sister to their place in the nursery was a significant part of the day. Gary and Meryl took photographs of their siblings including personal objects such as their siblings' mattresses, towels and pegs.

Photographs displayed around the building also acted as individual markers. The staff photographs near the entrance hall proved to be an interesting example. The photos were on a large display board which showed all the members of staff. Cary asked to have her own photograph taken on the tour and placed beside her previous key worker's photograph. This was the same child who associated the curved bench with previous conversations with this significant adult.

Photographs also provided links to past activities and events enjoyed by the children. A display of photographs taken on a recent outing to a train station was remarked on by Clare and she took a photograph of the display.

Children's own work also acted as personal landmarks around the nursery. Children leading me on the tour were quick to point out any of their work on the walls. They also stopped to show me their portfolios. These carefully presented folders held examples of their own work that the children had chosen with their key workers since joining the nursery. Children took photographs of memorable paintings and drawings in the portfolios. These personal details or 'traces' of the children's own work appeared to have great significance in developing place identity as well as self-identity: 'the history of who I am in this place'.

Place fears

The young children in my study were given direct as well as indirect opportunities to express negative feelings about places in the nursery. This can be seen in the following excerpt from a child conference.

Researcher:	Which part of the nursery don't you like?
Clare:	The staffroom, 'cos they have their lunch break.
Laura:	I don't like the boys.
Gary:	That building there and the bridge.
John:	Where 'x' did a poo.
Gaby:	Nowhere.

The direct question in the child conferencing led to a range of responses. Children interpreted this question in a broader way than I had anticipated. Children's negative feelings towards places included frustration. The tours and children's photographs had clarified the views expressed by some of the children in the child conferencing that the staffroom was out of bounds.

This underlined their interpretations of the nursery as a place where different hierarchies operated between adults and children.

One of the children in the group expressed what appeared to be fear rather than discomfort or frustration. These negative feelings were associated with a past incident involving another child whom he did not like. John mentioned this incident several times during the child conferencing. His key worker confirmed that he was aware that John had found this disturbing. It was like a negative marker which affected John's feelings about the space in the past and the present.

Discussion

The Mosaic approach offers a framework for listening to young children which reflects the complexities of their everyday lives. This complexity does not fit well with easily measured targets and standards. At the time of undertaking the study one approach to gathering the views of young users was by the use of stickers with 'smiley' faces and 'sad' faces to express preferences. This shorthand may be useful on occasions but there is a limit to such a simplified approach. Children are not in charge of the questions but only, in a limited way, of the answers. This seems to be an adaptation of a consumer model of gathering views designed for adults – a top down approach. The Mosaic approach is one attempt to turn this upside down and begin from young children's strengths – their local knowledge, their attention to detail and visual as well as verbal communication skills.

The use of participatory methods with young children has opened up more ways of communicating. This contradicts the myth that researchers and practitioners need to simplify their approaches with young children. This exploratory study has shown that there is a need to think differently and be flexible but not to oversimplify. I learned this lesson early on in the study when describing to the children how to use the cameras. I explained the procedure for using the viewfinder, the flash button and how to wind on the film. I added a comment about keeping the camera still 'otherwise you'll get a wobbly picture'. One of the girls then disappeared with her camera. When I caught up with her she was taking a photograph of the sandpit while moving the camera gently from side to side. When I asked her what she was doing she replied: 'I'm taking a wobbly photo.'

Participatory tools such as the cameras and the tours allowed the children to set more of the questions as well as provide answers. The issue of contact with siblings was one such question. The child conferencing did not reveal any details about this aspect of some of the children's lives in the nursery. It only became apparent when the children walked me to their siblings' rooms. The participatory nature of the tools meant that they acted as mediators between me as a researcher and the children as informants (Christensen & James, 2000: 162). I also found, like Christensen and James, that it was the *process* of using the various methodologies which increased my understanding of the children's lives.

The notion of 'interpretation' raises an interesting difference between some research and practice perspectives on listening to children. Within the research paradigm of the sociology of childhood there is an acknowledgement of need for interpretation to construct meanings. There is also a recognition that the research task is not limited to unearthing one 'true' meaning. This seems to differ from some understandings of children's participation where the task is seen as extracting children's views as untainted by adult 'interference' as possible. I have tried in the Mosaic approach to set up a platform where children are given many different opportunities to express their views and experiences and then to be part of the interpretation – this search for meanings. This seems to be of particular importance when working with young children who are in the process of establishing their identities and place identities. Throughout the study the children were involved in discussing, reflecting on and reassessing what it was like to be in their nursery. Tolfree & Woodhead (1999: 21) describe this process:

> It's not so much a matter of eliciting children's preformed ideas and opinions, it's much more a question of enabling them to explore the ways in which they perceive the world and communicate their ideas in a way that is meaningful to them.

This view of listening as part of an ongoing exploration of the world presents a challenge to policy makers. The outcomes will be open-ended and open to change. This calls for a redefinition of listening away from a one-off event to meet a prescribed target towards an acknowledgement of listening as an active process of communication involving hearing, interpreting and constructing meanings. One possible policy outcome for the Mosaic approach is in the conducting of childcare audits. These are reviews which are at present required to be conducted annually by Early Years and Childcare Partnerships. Research suggests that only a minority of audits have included the views of pre-school children (Clark et al., forthcoming).

Early years practitioners are in the best position to listen to the young children in their care. There is a danger in the target-driven climate of education that there is little time to notice young children's own agendas, feelings and experience. There may be a place for a framework such as the Mosaic approach to help practitioners concentrate on the small details of the children's lives around them. A new member of staff could work for example with a group of children using this approach as part of their induction. There may also be children within a group who could benefit from the opportunities for communication offered by the different tools. One of the shyest children in this study took great pleasure in taking me on a tour and in using the camera. Her key worker remarked on how keen she was to talk about her photographs.

There appears to be a practical application for using the Mosaic approach to change the environment. As discussed above, this study revealed a detailed picture of children's knowledge of place use and their place preferences and fears. Children could be involved in recording their feelings about an existing space. Older children in a setting (3- and 4-year-olds) could be involved in recording pre-verbal children's use of the space. This could inform future decisions about changes to the indoor and outdoor environment.

Conclusion

This small exploratory study set out to develop an imaginative framework for listening to young children. It has involved moving across disciplines and blending methods. The emphasis has been on the use of multiple methods, including the traditional tools of observation and interviewing but also investigating the use of participatory methods with children under 5. The suggestion from this study, subsequent training sessions and feedback, is that the Mosaic approach offers new possibilities for furthering our understanding of the complexities of the everyday lives of older as well as younger children.

Notes

This study was carried out with the advice and support of my colleague Peter Moss at the Thomas Coram Research Unit. The research was funded by the Joseph Rowntree Foundation in collaboration with Coram Family.

References

Adams, E. and Ingham, S. (1998) *Changing Places: children's participation in the environmental planning.* London: Children's Society.

Altman, I. (1975) *The Environment and Social Behavior.* Monterey, CA: Brooks/Cole.

Christensen, P. and James, A. (eds) (2000) *Research with Children.* London: Falmer Press.

Clark, A., McQuail, S. and Moss, P. (forthcoming) *State of the Art Review of Listening to Young Children.* London: Department for Education and Skills.

Cooke, B. and Kothari, U. (Eds) (2001) *Participation: the new tyranny?* London: Zed Books.

Corsaro, W. (1985) *Friendship and Peer Culture in the Early Years.* Norwood, NJ: Ablex.

Corsaro, W. (1997) *The Sociology of Childhood.* Thousand Oaks, CA: Pineforge Press.

Daycare Trust (1998) *Listening to Children. Young children's views on childcare: a guide for parents.* London: Daycare Trust.

Dupree, E., Bertram, T. and Pascal, C. (2001) 'Listening to children's perspectives of their early childhood settings'. Paper presented at EECERA Conference. Alkmaar, The Netherlands. 29th August – 1st September, 2001.

Edwards, C., Gandini, L. and Foreman, G. (Eds) (1998) *The Hundred Languages of Children: the Reggio Emilia approach to early childhood education*, 2nd edn. Norwood, NJ: Ablex.

Hart, R. (1979) *Children's Experience of Place*. New York: Irvington Publishers.

Hart, R. (1997) *Children's Participation*. London: UNICEF and Earthscan.

Langsted, O. (1994) 'Looking at quality from the child's perspective', in P. Moss and A. Pence, (Eds), *Valuing Quality in Early Childhood Services: new approaches to defining quality*. London: Paul Chapman.

Lewis, A. and Lindsay, G. (2000) (Eds), *Researching Children's Perspectives*. Buckingham: Open University Press.

Ministry of Education (1996) *Te Whaariki: early childhood curriculum*. Wellington: New Zealand Ministry of Education.

Qvortrup, J., Bardy, M., Sgritta, G. and Wintersberger, H. (eds) (1994) *Childhood Matters*. Vienna: European Centre.

Rinaldi, C. (1999) Paper presented in Reggio Emilia, Italy. April 1999.

Rinaldi, C. (2001) 'A pedagogy of listening: a perspective of listening from Reggio Emilia'. *Children in Europe*, **1**, 2–5.

Sibley, D. (1995) 'Families and domestic routines: constructing the boundaries of childhood', in S. Pile and N. Thrift (eds), *Mapping the Subject: geographies of cultural transformation*. London: Routledge.

Smith, F. and Barker, J. (1999) 'From Ninja Turtles to the Spice Girls: children's participation in the development of out of school play environments'. *Built Environment*, **25**(1), 35–46.

Smith, F. and Barker, J. (2002) 'Contested spaces'. *Childhood*, **7**(3), 315–333.

Tolfree, D. and Woodhead, M. (1999) 'Tapping a key resource'. *Early Childhood Matters*, **91**, 19–23.

Trancik, A. and Evans, G. (1995) 'Spaces fit for children: competency in the design of daycare center environments'. *Children's Environments*, **12**(3), 311–319.

Walker, R. (1993) 'Finding a voice for the researcher: using photographs in evaluation and research', in M. Schratz (ed.) *Qualitative Voices in Educational Research*. London: Falmer Press.

Weinstein, C. (1987) 'Designing pre-school classrooms to support development: research and reflection', in C. Weinstein and T. David (eds), *Spaces for Children: the built environment and child development*. New York: Plenum.

Wigfall, V. and Moss, P. (2001) *More Than the Sum of its Parts? A study of a multi-agency childcare network*. London: National Children's Bureau for the Joseph Rowntree Foundation.

Commentary: Alison Clark

Beginnings

My route into research began with teaching young children. I taught
4–7-year-olds, before a career break to have my own children. During this
time I became involved in research in a voluntary capacity, editing a booklet on *Carlisle for Families: a guide for the under-fives* on behalf of the
National Childbirth Trust. I followed this unorthodox beginning by working with a homeless families project. This combined practical advice work
with research on the access to schooling of children living in temporary
accommodation. My research career developed from this point. I gained
qualifications in research, ending in a MA in Social Justice and Education
at the Institute of Education, London alongside my ongoing project work in
the academic and voluntary sectors.

Gathering participant views has been a common thread running through
all of my research projects. This began with interviewing parents about
school-related issues. The emphasis has now moved to focus on children's
views. It is a question of ethics for me. Increasing our understanding of
society and education needs to involve the perspectives of all those
involved, regardless of their age, status or abilities. I jumped at the chance
to work on the project which led to the Mosaic approach. The funding had
already been secured from the Joseph Rowntree Foundation. The project
had been conceived as a collaboration between a voluntary sector organisation, Coram Family (known at the time as the Thomas Coram Foundation)
and the Thomas Coram Research Unit which is part of the Institute of
Education, London.

The project was designed to evaluate the Coram Community Campus,
a model of multi-agency working which included early years provision, a
parents' centre and a homeless families project. Access did not present a
problem as this had been designed as a collaborative venture. It was unusual
at the time for funding to include provision for a researcher to look at the
views and experiences of young children. This was designed to include a
development stage to allow new methods to be explored.

The initial research questions focused on how could young children's
(under-5) perspectives be gathered? The terminology 'views and experiences'
is deliberately broad. 'Views' alone suggested we were only interested in

opinions which could be stated. My colleague Peter Moss and I felt that our methodology needed to move beyond the spoken word if we were going to be able to capture the complexities of the everyday experiences of young children. I felt from the beginning of the project that there was a wealth of expertise in different disciplines which needed to be drawn together and applied in a new way. I refer in the chapter to the importance of the ideas developed in the sociology of childhood, in international development and in the theories of education expressed in the Reggio approach. These different strands fed into the 'melting pot'. The development of the Mosaic approach was an organic process. I began with an initial review of the literature, which at that time was limited. This was followed by days spent in the nursery observing the children, interspersed with more reading and discussions with early years practitioners and my colleagues. All three elements – observing, reading and discussing – were essential for the methodology to develop. It wasn't a question of locking myself away for six months and then, as in *Chitty Chitty Bang Bang,* opening the door and revealing the final product. The methodology developed as a reflexive process, adapted and amended as the project progressed.

The main group of eight children I worked with belonged to a 'key group' within the nursery. The children were divided into these small groups with one key worker. This key worker was my link in the nursery and an invaluable sounding board throughout the project. A total of twenty children were involved altogether, including children under 2 and a mixed-age group of children from the homeless families project on the site.

Methods

I decided early on that observation was going to be a key element. Observation has a central place in early years research and practice. This was of particular importance if the project was to succeed in including the experiences of pre-verbal children. I decided to use a narrative observation approach rather than a quantitative observation schedule as this seemed to convey more of the depth of experience that I wanted to reveal. I adapted the use of the interview schedule or child conferencing based on the experiences gained from the initial interviews with the children. The questions seemed useful as one source of data, but the child conferencing format seemed too rigid for some of the children in the group. This led me to experiment with conducting the interview on the move, which worked well.

The young children showed me the potential of cameras as a participatory research tool with 3- and 4-year-olds. The photographs I had seen taken by children in a study carried out by the Daycare Trust suggested that this was a useful medium to explore. I hadn't realised, however, how valuable disposable cameras would be for talking to children about their setting.

Children talked with me as they took the photographs and as they sorted the prints. My understanding of the value of the methodology began to grow as I observed the children's skill in handling the cameras.

The tours and map making were perhaps the most exciting tools to develop. These were the elements which seemed to be the most risky. I wasn't sure how the children would respond to my request to take me on a tour of their building and where they would lead me. This was the point in the research process when it became most participatory and inclusive. The children were quite happy with the idea that they knew far more about the place than I and that they could help me out. They were keen to take responsibility for the way in which the tour was recorded, to use the cameras again and carry the small tape recorder with a clip mike. The map making presented me with the greatest challenge in child development terms because the spatial awareness demanded in map making is not generally associated with 3- and 4-year-olds. It was a case of 'try it and see'. The children demonstrated that they were able to convey their spatial understanding, perhaps because of the physicality and immediacy of the tour and the use of their own photographs as central features of the maps.

Discussions with parents presented another leap of faith. What sense would they make of this approach? Would they support or contradict the areas which the children had shown to be important through their conversations, tours, maps and photographs? The parents who were interviewed were pleased to have new sources of information about their children's experiences of the nursery. Parents could help in the interpretation of some statements in view of their own understandings of their children's recent experiences and preferences.

Questions that arose

I have had the opportunity to discuss the Mosaic approach with colleagues at conferences and seminars during the research process and subsequently. Two of the areas of discussion have been the issues of validity and privacy. The question of validity is brought to the fore when gathering the perspectives of young children. How do we know if the material we gather is 'true'? What is 'truth' in this context? I was aware of the particular danger of young children telling me what they thought I wanted to know rather than sharing their feelings and experiences. This was one of the reasons why I chose to use a multi-method approach.

Firstly, employing a range of methods allows for triangulation of results. This happens at two levels: between the different tools used by the children and between the material gathered by the children and discussion with adults. Children's remarks in the child conference, for example, can be compared with photos taken of important places and then with comments made by parents and early years practitioners. Secondly, a multi-method approach allows several takes at gauging young children's views and experiences. This approach allows children to communicate in different ways, which reduces the chance that they will only deliver what they think the adult wants to hear.

Scandinavian colleagues were quick to point out questions relating to privacy in this research process. This dialogue arose out of a study tour I made to Denmark and Norway to explore methods of listening to and involving young children. Researchers expressed intrigue at why there was a growing interest in the UK in listening to young children. What was the purpose of this listening? Was it an invasion of children's privacy? Was it just a way of increasing the adult gaze on young children's lives? I was taken aback at first by these comments. I had developed an approach which deliberately set out to make young children's lives more visible. My response focused on the agency that the Mosaic approach gives young children. This methodology does lead to a more 'visible child' but this is a framework which intends children to play a central role in revealing their own priorities and interpreting meanings with adults. The status of children's knowledge about their own lives is raised through this approach. The responsibility however still rests with researchers and practitioners to use this knowledge appropriately. This led me to consider how the understandings gathered were to be used. Some insights remained at a private level between the children, their key worker and parents. I was, as a researcher, an intermediary in the process. I also needed to make judgements as to what were the wider public issues it was important to share. This I did in consultation with the children, parents and practitioners.

Writing up

One of the challenges of the writing-up process was how to bring together a complex range of material, including visual and verbal material. I saw my role as co-interpreter rather than sole interpreter. The Mosaic approach was designed to provide a framework for discussion and interpretation led by the children, in conjunction with myself as researcher and the adults who knew the children well. This is in keeping with the use of documentation in the pre-schools of Reggio Emilia where this negotiation of meanings is a central part of the learning process. However, this was a research project and I had the responsibility in this instance to make judgements and to draw conclusions. The final writing up involved a presentation of some of the key themes to the practitioners in the nursery, in order to share my interpretations and to hear their responses.

The dissemination process was a challenge. This exploratory project did not lend itself to a condensed executive summary, particularly in view of the visual data. This raises a general point: what are the best ways of bringing the results of qualitative research to the attention of policy makers, in such a way that the richness of the original research is not lost? If the views and experiences of young children are going to be brought to a wider policy audience then changes need to be made not only to research methodologies but also to expected modes of dissemination.

Future directions

Discussions with researchers and practitioners have led me to want to develop the Mosaic approach in several ways. I would like to introduce another tool to explore with children their perspectives on the future as well as the present. What would they like to change about a setting if they could? This raises methodological as well as ethical issues. What methods would be appropriate for young children to express their wishes? What problems would it raise? There is the concern that young children's experiences are limited by their age and therefore any thoughts about change would be based on insufficient knowledge.

This project has increased my interest in using the Mosaic approach as a participatory tool for exploring children's understandings of their indoor and outdoor environment. My belief is that there is a great deal to learn about young children's perspectives of the physical world, which if gathered and disseminated in appropriate ways, could surprise and inform the work of many experts in the field.

Making Progress? The Transition to Adulthood for Disabled Young People in Northern Ireland
MARINA MONTEITH

This paper is based on an unpublished methodological paper and a previously published paper: Monteith, M. (1999) 'Making progress? The transition to adulthood for disabled young people in Northern Ireland', in Iwaniec, D. and Hill, M. (Eds) *Current Issues in Child Care Research*. London: Jessica Kingsley Publishers.

Introduction

This chapter explores the transition to adulthood for young people with disabilities and describes the findings of a two-year study carried out in Northern Ireland by the Centre for Child Care Research (Monteith & Sneddon, 1999). It examines also how transition planning can assist success-ful progress to adulthood.

The transition to adulthood for young people covers a period of life from the early teens through to the mid-twenties. Adulthood is defined legally in terms of a range of rights obtained between the ages of 14 and 21 years. Definitions of adulthood, however, are complicated, with boundaries between childhood and adulthood being blurred. There are further changes brought about by new social groups and relationships.

Young people with disabilities may have additional barriers to face in order to achieve adult status. Many social groups (e.g. youth clubs, leisure organisations) do not actively promote inclusion. In addition, the depen-dent care relationships built up with adults throughout childhood may make it more difficult for disabled young people to develop autonomy and independence.

Developing a conceptual framework

McGinty and Fish (1992) viewed the transition to adulthood as both '... a phase in time and a process of personal growth and development'. Young people with disabilities should have equal opportunities with others of their generation. The conceptual framework for understanding their transition should be the same as for all young people, and not based on a model of existing services and resources, so that their needs can be identified, assessed and appropriate resources targeted to service delivery.

McGinty and Fish (1992) identified three main stages of transition, and pointed out that these may occur at different times for different individuals. The three stages were:

1 the final years of school;
2 further education and job training;
3 the early years of employment and independent living.

Conceptual frameworks identified in the literature are outlined briefly below.

The OECD/CERI study (OECD, 1986) provided a useful framework of transitional goals, each representing an aspect of adult life. These were:

1 employment or other valued activity;
2 independent living and personal autonomy;
3 social interaction and community participation, including leisure and recreation;
4 adult roles within the family, including marriage and parenthood.

The transition to adulthood can be viewed as a number of interconnected elements based on normative expectations (Morrow & Richards, 1996; Barnardo's, 1996; Jones & Wallace, 1992). Morrow and Richards (1996) reviewed a wide range of literature and found that young people were often economically dependent on their families at least until their mid-twenties as a result of the economic and social policy changes over the last two decades, which had restricted consumer behaviour. Young people, although becoming sexually active at an earlier age were delaying parenthood until their late twenties or early thirties. McGinty and Fish (1992) suggested that, although the transitional goals were different aspects of adult life, they should be tackled through one 'coherent individual transition plan', requiring collaboration and co-ordination between the many different agencies involved in working with young people with disabilities.

The various models of youth transitions consist of similar components which are interrelated. The progress towards adulthood and the experiences of a young person can be understood further by consideration of a career route proposed by Bullock et al. (1998). Bullock et al. (1998) present the idea of two dimensions to such young people's lives, firstly a life route and secondly a process. The life route involves those decisions made by the young person (and his or her family) which have an impact on life chances. The concept of life route includes all areas of a person's life from birth and incorporates individual personality. The young person's life route interacts with the second dimension, process, which involves the decisions made by professionals and/or courts which also affect life chances. Process includes health, social services, education, child guidance and the legal system. Perhaps a third dimension in addition to Bullock's 'life route' and 'process' is that of environment, including social and physical barriers. These three dimensions of a young person's life combine to form the pathway to adulthood (see Figure 9.1).

Figure 9.1 Conceptual model of transition to adulthood

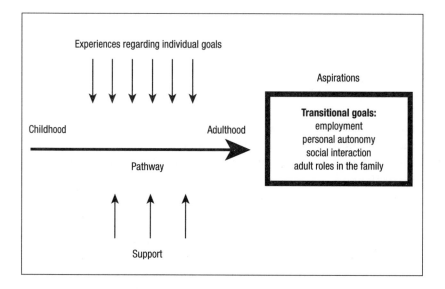

A combination of the framework of transitional goals (OECD, 1986; McGinty & Fish, 1992; Hirst & Baldwin, 1994) and the idea of a pathway to adulthood provided a conceptual model for this research (Monteith & Sneddon, 1999). This study examined the views and experiences of disabled young people and/or their parents. Their experiences were mapped in terms of these transitional goals, the choices made, progress towards achieving adulthood, and the formal support received including transition planning and social work services. Before presenting the findings the chapter briefly reviews relevant legislation and previous studies.

Legal framework in Northern Ireland

Within Northern Ireland, there is a range of key social welfare legislation including the Children (NI) Order 1995, the Disabled Persons (NI) Act 1989, the Chronically Sick and Disabled Persons (NI) Act 1978, the

Disability Discrimination Act 1995, and the Health and Personal Social Services (NI) Orders 1991 and 1994. Additional legislation pertinent to the transition to adulthood for young people with disabilities includes the Education and Libraries (NI) Order 1986, and the Education (NI) Order 1996. Table 9.1 indicates the equivalent legislation in Scotland, England and Wales.

Table 9.1   Comparison of legal frameworks within the United Kingdom

Northern Ireland	Scotland	England and Wales
Children (NI) Order 1995	Children (Scotland) Act 1995	Children Act 1989
Disabled Persons (NI) Act 1989	Disabled Persons (Scotland) Act 1986	Disabled Persons (Services, Consultation and Representation) Act 1986
Chronically Sick and Disabled Persons (NI) Act 1978	Chronically Sick and Disabled Persons (Scotland) Act 1972	Chronically Sick and Disabled Persons Act 1970
Education and Libraries (NI) Orders 1986 &1987		Education Act 1981
Education (NI) Order 1996	Education (Scotland) Act 1996	Education Act 1993
Disability Discrimination Act 1995	Disability Discrimination Act 1995	Disability Discrimination Act 1995
Health and Personal Social Services (NI) Orders 1991 and 1994	National Health Service and Community Care Act 1990	National Health Service and Community Care Act 1990

It is evident that a whole range of legislation can be relevant to young people with disabilities, and this can be confusing for young people and their carers as well as for professionals involved in the delivery of social care services. For example, young people with disabilities could have their social care needs assessed under 'children in need' and be provided with appropriate family support services under the Children (NI) Order. They could also be assessed under the Disabled Persons (NI) Act 1989 for a range of personal social services, or have a statement of special education needs made under the Education (NI) Order 1996. The Children (NI) Order did not replace assessments for disabled people under other legislation (e.g. Chronically Sick and Disabled Persons (NI) Act 1978, Disabled Persons (NI) Act 1989, Education (NI) Order 1996) but instead empowered Health and Social Services Trusts to combine assessments under the Order with those under other legislation, and facilitates interagency working to this end. The confusion created by the range of legislation of relevance to disabled young people is mirrored by the fragmentation of service delivery for them, with many agencies involved in providing a whole range of services. Each of these organisations has its own priorities, cultures, definitions and assessment procedures which can lead to a piecemeal approach to the provision of services for these young people and their parents or carers.

Disabled young people and the transition to adulthood

Empirical studies in the 1980s suggested that disabled young people often experience significant transition difficulties. These include a high degree of social isolation which tends to worsen after leaving school, a higher incidence of psychological problems compared to non-disabled peers, a lack of self-confidence, low self-esteem and difficulty finding or keeping a job (Brimblecombe, 1987; Walker, 1982; Anderson & Clarke, 1982). Clarke and Hirst (1989), in a follow-up study ten years after Anderson and Clarke's research, found that few of the young people had made the transition to a more independent adult life. These disabled young people were less likely to have had a paid job, to have set up household on their own, to have married or to have become a parent, compared to other young people in the general population. They seemed to have experienced either a lengthened, or a limited, transition to adulthood.

Walker (1982) found that young disabled people were less likely to have experienced paid employment, and were more likely to experience unemployment than other young people. In addition, disabled school leavers had very low aspirations for employment compared with their non-disabled peers. Those disabled young people who had found employment were less likely to be in skilled or professional jobs, compared to other young people. A number of researchers have indicated that there is a need for changes in attitudes to enable ordinary life experiences, independent living and employment (Parker, 1984; Hirst, 1984).

These studies were confined to particular localities, disabilities or services which young people used. In the light of this, Hirst and Baldwin (1994) developed a major study that aimed to provide coherent research on the transition to adulthood for disabled young people. Interviews with a large sample of young people themselves were conducted, covering all the teenage years and including all types and degrees of disability. They included a comparison sample of non-disabled peers. Hirst and Baldwin's study provides a comprehensive picture of disabled young people's experiences of this crucial phase in their life.

Contrary to the earlier findings, Hirst and Baldwin found that substantial numbers of disabled young people were moving towards adulthood without major disruption or widespread anxiety or unhappiness. They showed that many had achieved some degree of independence and enjoyed social activities appropriate for their age. Many had a positive image of themselves and had some feeling of control over their own lives. They concluded that the lives and circumstances of disabled young people can fall within the same range as other young people.

Hirst and Baldwin (1994) did report some significant differences in the experiences of young people. They found that disabled young people were less likely to be in paid work than their non-disabled peers. Disabled young people were often less prepared for, and less likely to be, living independently of their parents and were more dependent on their families for social networks. Although most disabled young people had positive views about themselves, they were more likely than other young people to have low self-esteem and have a limited sense of control over their life. Feelings of low self-esteem and helplessness were even more likely for disabled young people who had attended segregated (special) schools. Non-disabled peers were more likely to have closer friendships, more frequent contacts and a wider circle of friends in comparison to disabled young people, who were less socially active.

Hirst and Baldwin (1994) found that young people with severe and multiple disabilities experienced most difficulty in the transition to adulthood. These young people had limited social lives and friendships, had less of a sense of control over their lives, had lower self-esteem, and only a few had obtained employment training or paid work. Hirst and Baldwin found that severely disabled young people were more likely to experience inequalities in both support and opportunities.

The circumstances, experiences and aspirations of disabled young people in Northern Ireland

This section presents some of the methods and findings from a two-year study (1997–9) carried out by the Centre for Child Care Research regarding the circumstances, experiences and aspirations of disabled young people in Northern Ireland (Monteith & Sneddon, 1999). The study included 76 young people with a range of disabilities (physical, sensory and/or learning) and aged between 16 and 21 years.

Research advisory group

A research advisory group was set up at the beginning to support the project. This group included policy makers and practitioners from both the voluntary and statutory sectors and two disabled people. The role of this group was to advise and support the group throughout the design phase, fieldwork and analysis stage. The group fulfilled this role effectively.

Developing the instruments

The research aimed to include young people with learning disabilities, as disability professionals were of the opinion that these young people were often excluded from mainstream research on disability. This presented its own difficulties in terms of developing appropriate research instruments. Semi-structured interviews were chosen as the data collection method as they provided flexibility and yet retained some degree of standardisation (Hutchinson & Wilson, 1992). It is important to recognise the tension between standardisation and flexibility (Parahoo, 1997). As the researcher strives for more flexibility the degree of standardisation decreases. In this way, semi-structured interviews which are more flexible in their approach, with more freedom to probe, are more qualitative and focused. While reliability may have been somewhat reduced through loss of standardisation, the credibility and accuracy of the study were increased by ensuring that the young person understood the question asked.

Reflexivity is an important but difficult concept in qualitative research and involves the process where researchers reflect on their own preconceptions, values and beliefs and how they might affect the research. I worked with a group of disabled young people at the design stage to explore their views on issues involved in their transition to adulthood. These discussions proved very beneficial to the research and an additional gain was insight into the practicalities of communicating with young people with learning disabilities. It was important to include young people with all types of disabilities, and additional consideration has to be given to communicating with young people with learning disabilities. Flynn (1986) suggested that the ability of young people with learning disabilities to participate in research depended on the type of questioning. Straight yes/no questions were often subject to acquiescence, tending to elicit affirmative answers, and thus invalidated the responses. She cited Wyngaarden (1981) who recommended that open-ended questions which were simply phrased were used, with the interviewer having freedom to reword questions, while Sigelman et al. (1982) found that multiple choice questions were a useful alternative to yes/no questions. Flynn (1986) also suggested avoiding questions relating to time and frequency as these pose particular problems. Mattison (1970) suggested that interviews should be taped to reduce the levels of anxiety associated with detailed note taking in interviews.

Sampling

The study aimed to include young people across Northern Ireland with a range of disabilities (physical, learning and/or sensory), aged between 16 and 21 years. A multistage sampling method was used. Firstly, one Health and Social Services Trust was selected from each Board area, ensuring a mix of urban and rural areas, religious and geographical representation. Secondly, young disabled people aged between 16 and 21 years were identified in each Trust area. A variation on snowball sampling was used where key individuals in a range of statutory, voluntary and community organisations identified young people with disabilities known to them and approached them on our behalf regarding their possible participation in the study. This involved briefing these key personnel in detail about the project. Snowball sampling is particularly useful in situations such as this where a sampling frame does not exist (Parahoo, 1997). In this way a list of young people who were willing to participate in the project was identified. A total of 76 young people took part in the interviews which were conducted between March and June 1998. The young people involved in the study represented an even mix of both genders, a good spread across all of the ages involved and a wide range of types of disability.

Data collection

Semi-structured interviews use interview schedules rather than topic guides and have elements of both qualitative and quantitative research (Parahoo, 1997). In this study the freedom to reword questions and to move away if necessary from the original question format was greater than that given in some studies using semi-structured interviewing. Greater freedom was a necessity to enable interviewers to rephrase questions and develop discussions with young people with learning disabilities. Where possible, the researchers tried to maintain a standardised approach and yet be adaptable to the context of the interview and the young person's needs.

Semi-structured interviews were conducted using interview schedules which included components adapted from the work of Hirst and Baldwin (1994) and Flynn and Hirst (1992). The interview schedules used in this study consisted of two parts. Part 1 collected mainly socio-demographic background information and lasted about 15 minutes. It consisted of a number of fixed, pre-coded questions that recorded what the young person was currently doing during the day, household details, income details, and whether the young person had contact with a social worker. Part 1 could be completed by the young person him/herself, by the young person assisted by a parent or another person nominated by the young person, or by the parent/carer only. In 32 cases the young person alone completed the Part 1 interview, while a further 27 completed it with some help from a parent, and in 17 instances the parent/carer completed it for the young person.

Part 2 of the interview schedule consisted of a mix of closed and open-ended questions. The aim was to conduct Part 2 with the young person him/herself where possible. There were six sections covering current weekly activities, preparation for leaving school, leisure activities and social life, experience of social work services, home life, and aspirations. Within each of these sections there were a number of open-ended questions and some pre-coded questions with probes provided where necessary.

Interviewers started with the set questions, which could then be adapted or rephrased if the young person was having difficulty understanding the question. Questions were kept short and straightforward in an attempt to involve young people with learning disabilities in the research. It was felt that the length of the interview (40–50 minutes) was too long for some of these young people. For this reason, a shorter version of the questionnaire was designed which the interviewer could use where young people had more severe learning disabilities. In this way it was hoped that young people with learning disabilities would be included in the research design, rather than included by using a separate instrument, as was the case in the studies by Hirst and Baldwin (1994) and Flynn and Hirst (1992). The latter was actually a specially designed study for young people with learning disabilities, to parallel the main study conducted by Hirst and Baldwin (1994).

A total of 49 disabled young people completed the full Part 2 interview, while a further 18 completed the shorter version. If a young person completed a shorter Part 2 interview, some additional information was obtained from the parent or carer. Information obtained from the parent rather than the young person was clearly identified in the analysis. Nine young people with communication difficulties were unable to take part in the interview and information was obtained by proxy from a parent or carer in these cases. Interviews were carried out with a total of 67 disabled young people including those with learning disabilities, and of these there were 49 full interviews and 18 shortened interviews. Only 9 young people who had severe learning and/or communication difficulties were unable to participate themselves in the study, but were included by proxy as it was important to get some perspective on their lives at this time of transition.

Three researchers completed the interviews. To ensure that each interviewer had a similar understanding of the interview schedule and its use a detailed briefing took place prior to interviewing and regular debriefing sessions were held throughout the interviewing period to share experiences and thoughts on the use of the interview schedule. This was particularly important where the schedule was being used much more flexibly to aid the inclusion of young people with learning disabilities. Guidance notes were also provided to act as memory joggers to the interviewers when 'in the field' and researchers were referred to Poland's strategies for ensuring high quality tape recording (1995: 304). The agreement of the participants was obtained for tape recording.

Ethical issues

The issue of informed consent was of particular concern. Great efforts were made to ensure that the young people understood what the research involved and that they could refuse to participate or could withdraw at any time. This posed particular difficulties with young people with learning disabilities in ensuring that their consent was 'informed' and that they understood what they were actually agreeing to. Parents of the young people acted as 'expert advisors' here by helping the researchers explain the research to the young people and helping them understand their right to refuse/give consent.

Transcription and analysis

The transcription of the tapes was a major task involving over 300 hours' work. The demographic information collected by the Part 1 interview and some of the closed questions on Part 2 were analysed using the computer software packages SPSS for Windows (statistics package). The computer package, NUD*IST (non-numerical, unstructured data: indexing, searching and theorising), was used to aid the analysis of qualitative data.

Gaining employment

Obtaining work provides economic independence and is a key goal in making the transition to adulthood. Jobskills Training Programmes, work placements, NVQs, vocational training, and further/higher education may all play a part in providing young people with adequate skills for future employment.

The study found that disabled young people participated in a range of daytime occupations, with 43 young people attending some form of educational institution, either on a full-time (18) or part-time basis (25). Similar numbers attended school (18) and further education colleges (19), while a few students attended residential schools (3) or further education residential colleges (2). Many young people (21) were undertaking a youth training programme (Jobskills) and this usually combined work placements with part-time study for vocational qualifications at a local college. Forty-five of the 76 young people were currently studying for a qualification, with 23 studying for National Vocational Qualifications (NVQs). Six respondents were studying for A Levels and a further 6 for GCSEs. Small numbers of young people were reported to be studying for other qualifications such as certificates from day centres, or other vocational qualifications from technical colleges (GNVQs, or BTEC Higher Certificates/Diplomas).

Although only one person stated that they had no formal activity during week days and many young people were occupied with vocational training and/or work placements, only two young people had actually obtained a job which did not involve a work placement. One of these young people was employed on an ACE scheme and earned below the minimum wage level for this age group (£3 per hour) which was being implemented in April 1999. The number of young people aged between 19 and 21 years who had moved from the vocational training system to actual employment was low. As might have been expected, many young people aged between 16 and 18 years participated in vocational training and work placement schemes, but it might have been hoped that higher numbers would have progressed to employment. In comparison to Hirst and Baldwin's study (1994), achievement of adult status in terms of employment has yet to be realised for most young disabled people in Northern Ireland. In contrast, 15 per cent of disabled young people aged 16–22 years in Great Britain were in employment, with this increasing to 33 per cent for those aged 19 or 20 years.

Many young people in this study were occupied with school or a combination of job placements and college; some had very limited or no weekday occupations. One young person reported no formal activity while a further four had no current activity but were going to commence job training or a job placement soon. One young person attended a day centre full time, while part-time attendance at a day centre was the sole weekday occupation for six young people. Five others combined attendance at a day centre with participation in vocational education, job training or work placements.

Independent living and personal autonomy

Developing independent living skills and gaining personal autonomy is another transitional goal. As young people grow up they begin to develop some degree of independence. To gain insight into this area, the following were examined: the sources of income; the extent to which the disabled young people managed their own money and made their own purchases; if they had a house key; and whether they saw their GP or social worker alone.

The findings revealed that most of the disabled young people were reliant on benefits and training allowances as their main source of income (see Table 9.2). Some young people also received income from either their parents (12) or other relatives (6). Only seven people reported an income received through a regular job, although five of these were spare-time jobs involving small amounts of money.

Table 9.2   Source of income*

Source of income	Number
Disability living allowance	51
Severe disability allowance	29
Income support	28
Training scheme/placement	22
Parents	12
Regular job (including spare-time jobs)	7
Other relatives	6
Invalidity benefit	2
Student grant	1

*Some young people had more than one source of income.

The majority of young people (65) in the sample said that they had some money to spend each week. Parents and benefits were the main sources of income for many young people. A few had money from earnings or from a training allowance. Money was mainly spent on clothes, food, sweets, going out, magazines/books or CDs. Almost two-thirds of the young people said that they bought their own clothes, while parents (mostly the mother) purchased clothes for the remaining one-third. One young person said his grandparents bought his clothes. Of those who said they bought their own clothes, 38 said they had help to do so. This help came mainly from parents (27), siblings (5), friends (8), and other relatives (2).

Forty-nine young people were asked if any of their money went towards rent, housekeeping, food and other bills. Twenty-nine young people did contribute to household bills, although 13 did not specify an amount. Twelve said they paid amounts ranging from £10 to £25 per week, while one person said they paid for telephone calls.

Three-quarters of the sample of disabled young people put some of their money in a savings account. Twenty-two deposited the money in their account themselves, while parents made the deposits for 32 others. Young people were, however, more likely to get their money out by themselves (35), with only 10 saying that their parents took out the money for them. It would seem that many young people did have access to money of their own, and some were able to make purchases and manage their money by themselves.

Eighteen out of the total sample of 76 young people said that they went to see their GP alone. Of the 18 young people who had seen a social worker in the last year, eight had done so on their own. Nine were accompanied by their parents, while one young person sometimes saw the social worker by herself and sometimes with a parent. Half of the young people said that they would make an appointment themselves.

Forty-four of the 76 young people had their own house key, while a further 13 had access to a key (e.g. it was left with a neighbour or hidden in an outhouse/garage), making a total of 75 per cent of young people having either access to a key or having their own key to their home. A slightly higher proportion of young people in rural areas had their own key or access to a key (82%) compared to those living in urban areas (72%). Larger urban areas differed from smaller ones, with young people living in cities (76%) more likely to have access to a key or have their own key than young people living in towns (67%).

Young people with multiple disabilities (54%) were much less likely to have access to a house key, or have their own, than other young people. All young people with physical disabilities only, and 85 per cent of those with sensory disabilities only, had a house key or access to one, compared with two-thirds (68%) of those with learning disabilities only. Thirteen young people who did not have their own house key said that they would like one. Over half (7) of these were young people with multiple disabilities.

Social life and community involvement

The research examined the friendships of young people with disabilities and their participation in social and/or leisure activities. The sample of young people seemed to have a wide range of leisure and social activities. Table 9.3 indicates the range of activities that young people said they

Table 9.3 Number of young people taking part in leisure/social activities at home*

Activity	Young people's responses (N = 67)	Responses by proxy through parent (N = 9)	Total number of young people (N = 76)
Taking part in outdoor games (at home)	59	8	67 (88%)
Watching TV or video	55	7	62 (82%)
Listening to records, tapes, CDs	29	3	32 (42%)
Using home computer/ video game	22	1	23 (30%)
Listening to the radio	16	4	20 (26%)
Reading books	13	2	15 (20%)
Taking part in indoor games	11	2	13 (17%)
Doing a hobby/creative art/craft	10	2	12 (16%)
Looking after pets/animals	5	0	5 (7%)
Gardening	1	2	3 (4%)
Other	15	4	19 (25%)

*Some young people engaged in several activities.

undertook at home, the most popular involving taking part in outdoor games, watching TV or videos, and listening to records, tapes or CDs. Sports, visiting friends and going shopping were the most frequently mentioned activities outside the home (Table 9.4). Almost half (37) the young people belonged to a club, group or society. Some of these were groups for disabled young people, such as Gateway clubs and Sportsability, but many were mainstream organised activities including youth clubs, church clubs, sports clubs, Girl Guides/Boys' Brigade, or the Phab clubs aimed at facilitating interaction between young disabled and non-disabled people.

Nine out of 10 young people said that they had friends their own age, and all young people reported having at least one friend. Friends were made through school/college, work or job placement, or through clubs/societies. Some young people also had friends at a day centre. Three-quarters of young people said that they saw their friends in their spare time, outside of college, work or day centre hours. Friends were equally likely to visit the young person's home, or to be visited by the young person. In addition to friends, a quarter of the sample said that they had a boyfriend/girlfriend. It would seem that many young people had an active social life and took part in several social and leisure activities.

Adult roles in the family

McGinty and Fish (1992) argued strongly that any conceptual framework adopted for transition should 'embrace family roles…as legitimate objectives

Table 9.4   Number of young people taking part in leisure/social activities outside the home*

Activity	Young people's responses (N = 67)	Responses by proxy through parent (N = 9)	Total number of young people (%) (N = 76)
Taking part in sports activities	37	1	38 (50%)
Visiting friends/relatives	29	4	33 (43%)
Going shopping	21	5	26 (34%)
Going to pub/café/ restaurant	17	3	20 (26%)
Going to cinema/theatre	19	1	20 (26%)
Going to disco/party/ dancing	17	2	19 (25%)
Going to social/youth club	10	3	13 (17%)
Going for a walk	5	3	8 (10%)
Watching sport/games/ racing (live – not TV)	6	1	7 (9%)
Going for a drive	6	0	6 (8%)
Going to church/chapel	2	0	2 (3%)
Going to concert/folk club/bands	1	0	1 (1%)
Playing slot machines	1	1	1 (1%)

*Some young people engaged in several activities.

for young people with disabilities' (p. 16). Young people with disabilities have the right to the same aspirations as other young people, including consideration of getting married and/or having children. This study examined young people's roles within their household, including developing household skills, carrying out routine household tasks, and aspirations for the future, including living arrangements and views on marriage.

Sixty-seven young people were asked if they helped around the home with a variety of tasks. In addition, a further nine responses were obtained from parents where interviewers had difficulty communicating with some young people with learning disabilities.

Young people seemed more likely to complete certain tasks such as washing up, making their bed, cleaning their room and doing the shopping, than getting meals ready or washing or ironing their own clothes (Table 9.5). Many young people, however, were involved in the whole range of tasks. Most of those helping reported that they did so all of the time or sometimes. Only a few said that they did not help very often. Thus many young people were developing responsible roles within their households.

Nearly all young people still lived at home and they were asked whether they would like to leave home in the future. Some young people were not asked this question as they had difficulties understanding time periods. Of those asked, 43 thought that at some stage they would like to leave home. The stage in their life, however, that they said they would like to leave

Table 9.5 Number of young people who help with housework at home

Household task	Young people's responses (N = 67)	Responses by proxy through parent (N = 9)	Total number of young people (N = 76)
Washing up	54	3	57 (75%)
Making own bed	51	4	55 (72%)
Washing/ironing own clothes	28	1	29 (38%)
Getting meals ready	31	1	32 (42%)
Cleaning own room	56	2	58 (76%)
Shopping	41	4	45 (59%)

home varied greatly. Twenty-nine young people stated an age when they might do so, ranging from 18 to 50 years. Similarly, questions were asked about getting married at some time in the future, and 38 thought that they would like to. Of these, 24 thought that they actually would get married at some time. Table 9.6 indicates the age at which young people would like to either leave home or get married. It would seem that most expected to leave home some time before getting married.

Table 9.6 Age when young person thought they might like to leave the parental home/get married

Age (years)	Leave parental home (n)	Get married (n)
Under 20	8	1
Early 20s	15	2
25	–	8
Late 20s	3	11
30	1	5
30 something	–	1
50	1	–
When I get a job	–	1
As soon as possible	1	–

Fifteen young people said that they would need some help in order to live on their own. Half the young people said they would ask their parents for help. Other sources of aid included carers, friends, other relatives and social workers. Access to accommodation was a major issue for several young people, who felt that adaptations would be necessary for them to live somewhere else.

The findings suggest that young people with disabilities have similar aspirations to those of any young people, ranging from winning the lottery to the more practical, such as having a good job or a nice house. The most frequently occurring wishes were to get a job (23), to have their own home (20), to get married (14), to have a boyfriend/girlfriend (6), to be happy

(12), and to a have children (10). About a quarter of the sample wished for their dream of winning the lottery or being rich and/or being famous. Some of the young people's wishes are listed in their own words below.

'I want a boyfriend...and a house key...'

'I'd love to have a job that I love to do with a reasonable salary, and probably get married...if I wasn't deaf, if I could hear – maybe if there was a new device that came out and I can hear.'

'...that I'd have a good job, that I'd have children hopefully and settle down.'

'I'll be here all day – come back in half an hour ... to be a popular famous singer ...get rid of my gambling problem – to arrest it – write that down, to arrest it... to meet the right person and to settle down and get married and have children... to find a pot of gold at the end of the rainbow [laughing].'

'Three wishes...get married...to represent Northern Ireland in the Bowling World Cup and...to have kids of my own.'

'Stay single – what else – get better at snooker – what else – have no more operations.'

'To have a full time job with good money...to live in my own house with a partner and...maybe have children when I'm older maybe.'

'Loads of money...to have children. I want children. And get married as well. To have a nice boyfriend or be married.'

'Get rid of the epilepsy...be able to drive a car...pass all my NVQs...the main one is I just want rid of my epilepsy.'

'To meet friends...go and sometimes play football.'

Several other researchers (Armstrong & Davies, 1995; Shepperdson, 1995) have noted considerable change over the last decade in the aspirations of disabled school leavers regarding access to further education and occupational choices. Many more young people with disabilities are now seeking further education places and have clear ideas about future occupations. Obtaining viable employment plays an important role if a young person is to develop some degree of independence and to make a successful transition to adult life. The research to date shows that, although disabled young people no longer have low aspirations for their future, they are less likely than their non-disabled peers to have access to employment and the associated financial independence.

The role of formal social support, and in particular transition planning, plays a crucial part in the extent to which many disabled young people will achieve adult status successfully. The findings of this study suggested a lack of cohesion and integration in transition planning. The research found little evidence of collaboration between education establishments and social services. While over half (40) young people had talked to someone in school (usually a teacher or careers advisor) about preparing to leave school and 28 out of the 76 young people had an assessment of their needs carried out by a social worker, very few had actually had a transition plan drawn up. A number of young people complained that there was too much emphasis on careers information, such as colleges, courses and qualifications, and not enough advice on independent living, day-to-day issues and specialised advice in relation to their disability.

From the young person's viewpoint, a cohesive, collaborative arrangement for transition planning, as intended by the Children (NI) Order 1995, was not evident. It would seem from these young people's experiences that planning is piecemeal, with different agencies having some input, resulting in an overall lack of co-ordination and direction. Interviews with the young people (or their parents) seemed to indicate a limited social work resource available to them, with a lack of clarity about the role of the social worker. Most young people found their social worker easy to talk to, approachable and helpful.

Conclusions

The Northern Ireland study supported previous research findings that disabled young people have the same range of aspirations and expectations for their future as other young people. However, while some disabled young people deal successfully with this important phase of their lives, other young people experience some degree of difficulty, in particular in terms of gaining employment. Financial independence is difficult for young people to achieve if they are solely dependent for income on benefits and training allowances and this in turn impacts on other aspects of the transition to adulthood, including living independently.

In order to overcome the fragmentation of provision, the range of professionals and agencies involved in meeting statutory obligations and providing services to young people with disabilities need to work together. A framework for transition planning needs to be developed which facilitates collaboration between agencies, enables shared assessment arrangements, allows the exchange of information between agencies and professionals, and recognises the young person's own views and right to make choices. Transition planning needs to include regular assessment, review and planning including educational, vocational and personal preparation for adult life. The mechanism developed to facilitate such collaboration needs to address issues of the availability and sharing of information between professionals and agencies and across the phases of transition, and needs to involve young people and their parents or carers.

The transition planning process under the Education (NI) Order 1996 identifies a framework that could be adopted as a mechanism to enable collaborative and interagency working. Disabled young people who do not have a statement, need to be included in the process of transition planning to assist their progress towards adulthood. Potential problems and possible solutions or options need to be identified. Transition planning should take place at a strategic level as well to ensure that these mechanisms are properly in place and that appropriate funding and budgets are allocated to this important area of work. Children's Service Plans can play a vital role here in the planning of appropriate services for disabled young people and the identification of key partners for this collaborative work. Transition planning will only be effective through the commitment of everyone involved. A particular difficulty lies in the resources available to interagency collaboration, as this in itself requires some financing to sustain.

If agencies are to assist disabled young people in their progression to adulthood a collaborative framework of transition needs to be put in place, supported by joint working agreements between agencies which also address the issue of access to necessary budgets for service delivery. This will involve developing shared values, agreeing a structure for working together, understanding each other's roles in the transition process, committing resources, developing joint planning arrangements and sharing good practice and information. There is a clear need for a key person, perhaps nominated by an interagency working group, to take a lead role in liaising with the various agencies and professionals and working closely with the young person and his/her parents. Initiatives elsewhere such as the Kurator system in Denmark may provide important models of good practice for such a development.

References

Anderson, E.M. and Clarke, L. (1982) *Disability in Adolescence*. London, Methuen.

Armstrong, D. and Davies, F. (1995) The transition from school to adulthood: Aspirations and careers advice for young adults with learning and adjustment difficulties. *British Journal of Special Education*, **22,** no. 2: 70–75.

Barnardo's (1996) *Transition to Adulthood*. Essex: Barnardo's.

Brimblecombe, F.S.W. (1987) The Needs of Handicapped Young Adults. Exeter: Institute of Child Health, University of Exeter.

Bullock, R., Little, M. and Millham, S. (1998) *Secure Treatment Outcomes: The Care Careers of Very Difficult Adolescents*. Aldershot: Ashgate.

Children (NI) Order 1995. Belfast, HMSO.

Chronically Sick and Disabled Persons (NI) Act 1978. Belfast, HMSO.

Clarke, A. and Hirst, M. (1989) Disability in adulthood: Ten year follow-up of young people with disabilities. *Disability Handicap and Society*, **4**: 271–281.

Disabled Persons (NI) Act 1989. Belfast, HMSO.

Disability Discrimination Act 1995. Belfast, HMSO.

Education and Libraries (NI) Order 1986. Belfast, HMSO.

Education (NI) Order 1996. Belfast, HMSO.

Flynn, M. (1986) Adults with mental handicap as consumers: Issues and guidelines for interviewing. *Journal of Mental Deficiency Research*, **30**: 369–377.

Flynn, M. and Hirst, M. (1992) *This Year, Next Year, Sometime...? Learning Disability and Adulthood.* London and York: National Development Team and Social Policy Research Unit.

Health and Personal Social Services (NI) Orders 1991. Belfast, HMSO.

Health and Personal Social Services (NI) Orders 1994. Belfast, HMSO.

Hirst, M.A. (1984) *Moving On: Transfer of Young People with Disabilities to Adult Services.* York, Social Policy Research Unit, University of York.

Hirst, M. and Baldwin, S. (1994) *Unequal Opportunities: Growing Up Disabled.* London: HMSO.

Hutchinson, S. and Wilson, S.H. (1992) Validity threats in scheduled semi-structured research interviews. *Nursing Research*, **41** (2): 117–119.

Jones, G. and Wallace, C. (1992) *Youth Family and Citizenship.* Milton Keynes: Open University Press.

Mattison, J. (1970) *Marriage and Mental Handicap.* London: Duckworth.

McGinty, J. and Fish, J. (1992) *Learning Support for Young People: Transition: Leaving School for Further Education and Work.* Buckingham: Open University Press.

Monteith, M. and Sneddon, H. (1999) *The Circumstances, Experiences, and Aspirations of Young People with Disabilities Making the Transition to Adulthood.* Belfast: Centre for Child Care Research.

Morrow, V. and Richards, M. (1996) *Transitions to Adulthood: A Family Matter.* York, York Publishing Services (for Joseph Rowntree Foundation).

OECD (1986) *Young People with Handicaps: The Road to Adulthood.* Paris: Centre for Education Research and Innovation (CERI), Organisation for Economic Co-operation and Development (OECD).

Parahoo, K. (1997) *Nursing Research: Principles, Process and Issues.* London: Macmillan.

Parker, G. (1984) *Into Work: A Review of the Literature about Disabled Young Adults' Preparation for and Movement into Employment.* York, Social Policy Research Unit, University of York.

Poland, B. (1995) Transcription quality as an aspect of rigor in qualitative research. *Qualitative Inquiry*, **1**, no. 3: 290–310.

Shepperdson, B. (1995) Changes in options for school leavers with Down's Syndrome. *Care in Place*, **2**, no. 1: 22–28.

Sigelman, K.C., Budd, E.C., Spanhel, C.L. and Shoenock, C.J. (1982) When in doubt say yes: Acquiescence in interviews with mentally retarded persons. *Mental Retardation*, **19**: 53–8.

Walker, A. (1982) *Unqualified and Unemployed: Handicapped Young People and The Labour Market.* London: Macmillan Press.

Wyngaarden, M. (1981) Interviewing mentally retarded persons: Issues and strategies. In R.H. Bruininks, C.E. Meyers, B.B. Sigford and K.C. Lakin (eds) *Deinstitutionalization and Community Adjustment of Mentally Retarded People.* Washington, DC: American Association on Mental Deficiency.

Commentary: Marina Monteith

Background

In 1995 I accepted a post as Research Fellow at Queen's University, Belfast in a new child care research centre funded by a partnership of the four Health and Social Services Boards, the DHSS (NI) and Queen's University. The area of child care research was new to me although I had worked in the NHS and in public sector housing research for several years. You may ask, why move from housing to child care research? but in Northern Ireland there are few long term research opportunities within the academic field and this new centre with five years' funding provided just that opportunity. Interestingly, the other Research Fellows appointed also came from non-child-care backgrounds, indicating a shortage of research expertise in this area at that time in Northern Ireland.

The project on the Transition to Adulthood for Disabled Young People in Northern Ireland was one of the first projects completed within this new centre. The DHSS (NI) and the four HSS Boards were particularly interested in the area of childhood disability as very little was known about this area of child care services and these children and young people tended to be 'buried' in official statistics about disabled people of all ages generally. This coincided with the implementation of the 1995 Children (NI) Order and the recognition that disabled children were children first and foremost and with the realisation that there was a need for HSS Trusts and Boards in Northern Ireland to refocus their thinking in terms of service provision for disabled children and young people. So, a major research project was funded with two strands, firstly a study examining the implementation of the 1995 Children (NI) Order for disabled children generally (Monteith et al., 1997; Monteith & Cousins, 1999) and a more focused investigation of the transition to adulthood for disabled young people (Monteith & Sneddon, 1999; Monteith, 2000). This commentary focuses on the second study in the project which lasted two years, from 1997 to 1999.

The brief I was given was to conduct research examining how young people with disabilities were making the transition to adulthood. The research questions were formed after consultation with our funders and with key stakeholders (practitioners and policy makers, voluntary organisations) and an initial trawl of the literature. There was recognition within social services in Northern Ireland that very little was known about disabled young people and how they fared moving on from childhood and from school. Few resources were targeted to this area though it was a key stage in these young people's lives. The research was funded to explore their experiences, their needs and what support they currently received. The aim of the research was to inform key policy makers and practitioners in Northern Ireland and to raise awareness of the needs of disabled young people.

Legislative and policy context and theoretical framework

I had previously worked as a data analyst in human resource planning and pay research in a regional health authority in the NHS and therefore was familiar with equality legislation, but that was as far as my knowledge went. I started this new research project on a steep learning curve, rapidly immersing myself in child care and disability issues. In addition, the new Children (NI) Order was about to be implemented so everything was changing and there was a wealth of disability legislation to be grappled with. At this stage I found the setting up of a Research Advisory Group a great help as I was able to talk through my understanding of key issues and obtain insight from key people in the field.

The Research Advisory Group (RAG) consisted of representatives from the statutory sector (DHSS/SSI, HSS Trusts and NI Statistics and Research Agency) and the voluntary sector (MENCAP, Save the Children Fund, Disability Action) as well as two disabled people (one of whom was a young person). The group helped me unravel the complexity of organisational structures in the provision of services (as disabled young people could fall into a number of different programmes of care) and the different legislation applicable to young people. At the beginning there was some friction between the voluntary and statutory representatives which led to delays. Some of the voluntary sector representatives voiced concerns that there was a considerable lack of funding for services for disabled children. Moreover they alleged that the statutory sector did not understand these children's needs. Statutory sector representatives defended their position, arguing that they were doing the best they could with the resources available. After the first few meetings this settled down into a cohesive group with the aim of assisting the project as it developed.

From the literature I discovered that most theoretical frameworks were based on young people generally and not disabled young people. Reading about the social model of disability made me aware of the importance of the context of the young people's experiences. As a result I combined the idea of a framework of transitional goals and a pathway to adulthood (Bullock et al., 1998) within a social model of disability to provide a conceptual model for the project.

Access

Access to the target population necessitated going through the Trust, i.e. a third-party gatekeeper. We relied on this third party to contact the young people to explain the nature of the research and encourage participation in the study. In addition to contacts made via Trusts, attempts were made via the voluntary sector, schools and colleges to identify additional young people resident in the Health and Social Services Trust area who were not 'known' to the Trust. A lot of time was invested in explaining the research to the third parties in order that they gave appropriate information to the young people. Leaflets, accompanying letters and consent forms were designed and distributed to young people with disabilities via these third parties. A difficulty associated with the involvement of third parties was that researchers were unable to compare Trust records with those of other organisations contacting disabled young people about the research project. It was impossible, therefore, to identify how many people were contacted in total, as some young people with disabilities known to a number of organisations could have been contacted several times. Then we proceeded to talk with the young people themselves (and/or their parents in some cases) to discuss the project and to check that they did want to participate. At this stage a small number of young people decided not to participate further. Due to the gatekeeping process we could not properly address the issue of informed consent until this point. This meant that the period of time spent identifying, contacting and receiving consent from young people (and their parents where necessary) was prolonged.

Making access arrangements without the involvement of the third parties was not possible as there was no central database of disabled young people. To avoid bias and achieve a representative sample we included a wide range of organisations. In the end I think we did achieve a representative sample but many of the organisations were protective of the disabled young people and insisted they talked to them first and got their agreement to take part before arranging any access. I would have preferred to have been able to make direct approaches to the young people myself. An alternative approach might have been to attempt to get gatekeepers to organise a 'gathering' of disabled young people where I could go along and talk directly to them about the project, thus overcoming any dependence on the gatekeepers' enthusiasm for the research.

Data analysis

As anyone who has completed qualitative research will know, the analysis of 76 qualitative interviews is an immense organisational task. I made a decision early on in the project to investigate qualitative analytical packages to see if they could help in the task. NUD*IST, a tool I was unfamiliar with, was purchased and at this stage of the project I found I was again plunged back on to that steep learning curve. NUD*IST enabled me to make an initial attempt at data reduction by identifying main themes .

Data reduction is an important stage in any project whether it is a quantitative data set or a qualitative one. In quantitative research statistical techniques are used to 'reduce' the mass of data to meaningful pieces of information. In qualitative research data are reduced through abstracting the data and attempting to draw meaning from the bulk of the transcriptions. This means reading and re-reading the transcripts looking for common themes and ideas, instances of similarity and of difference. The NUD*IST coding and indexing system is a way of helping you manage the abstraction of data so that you can extract information in support of your theories about the data.

Concluding reflections

Reflecting on the study, given my previous lack of experience in child care and disability issues, I am quite proud of this research. However, there are things I would do differently if I had to do it again.

One of the biggest issues was ensuring that there had been 'informed consent' at an early stage and that the young people had an understanding of what the research was about. Staff at MENCAP provided much needed advice on developing a second version of our information leaflet about the project for young people with learning disabilities, but again I think given more resources for the project, more time could have been spent on this.

Another issue for the research was that disabled children and young people in Northern Ireland were not used to being asked their opinions or views by strangers. At the time of the research, the inclusion of their views in formal processes such as statementing or the provision or inspection of services was unusual. Participation and sharing their views was something new and thus several young people were not very forthcoming. Interviews often involved time spent on rapport building and encouragement, and many interviews took much longer than originally anticipated. I would recommend that any similar project should anticipate a significant period of 'development time' to build rapport with potential interviewees.

At both the design stage and the writing-up stage a key person involved in the study was a disabled young girl who was a member of the research advisory group. Her advice and insight throughout the project were very valuable. She helped me rework questions and advised on what were important issues for young disabled people growing up. The Research Advisory Group was helpful with access issues, context issues, and comments on the final report before publication.

If funding were available, I would like to revisit these young people in their mid-twenties and see how they have progressed. I have developed a strong interest in disability research and have since worked on a Barnardo's study related to childhood disability and public services involving interviews with 23 disabled children aged between 5 and 15 years and their parents (Monteith et al., 2002).

References

Bullock, R., Little, M. and Millham, S. (1998) *Secure Treatment Outcomes: The Care Careers of Very Difficult Adolescents*. Aldershot: Ashgate.

Children (NI) Order 1995. Belfast, HMSO.

Monteith, M. (2000). Making progress? The transition to adulthood for disabled young people in Northern Ireland. In D. Iwaniec and M. Hill (Eds) *Current Issues in Child Care Research*. London: Jessica Kingsley Publishers.

Monteith, M. and Cousins, W. (1999) Children and Young People with Disabilities in Northern Ireland: Part II Report. *Social Services Developments and the Impact of the Children (NI) Order*. Belfast: Centre for Child Care Research.

Monteith, M. and Sneddon, H. (1999) *The Circumstances, Experiences, and Aspirations of Young People with Disabilities Making the Transition to Adulthood*. Belfast: Centre for Child Care Research.

Monteith, M., McCrystal, P. and Iwaniec, D. (1997) *Children and Young People with Disabilities in Northern Ireland. Part 1: An Overview of Needs and Services*. Belfast: ICCR.

Monteith, M., McLaughlin, E., Milner, S. and Hamilton, L. (2002) *Is Anyone Listening? Childhood Disability and Public Services in Northern Ireland*. Belfast: Barnardo's.

10 Improving Pedestrian Road Safety among Adolescents: An Application of the Theory of Planned Behaviour
DAPHNE EVANS AND PAUL NORMAN

This paper has been abridged from: Evans, D. and Norman, P. (2002) 'Improving pedestrian road safety among adolescents: an application of the Theory of Planned Behaviour', in Rutter, D. and Quine, L. (Eds), *Changing Health Behaviour*, Buckingham: Open University Press. In addition, a section has been inserted from: Rutter, D. and Quine, L. (2002) 'Social cognition models and changing health behaviours', in Rutter, D. and Quine, L. (Eds) *Changing Health Behaviour*, Buckingham Open University Press, pp. 11–12.

Abstract

This chapter considers the utility of the Theory of Planned Behaviour (TPB) for informing the development of interventions to increase road safety awareness among adolescent pedestrians. During adolescence it is likely that motivational and behavioural factors play an important role in accident involvement. A survey of over 1,800 school children (Evans, 1999) employed the TPB to examine the motivational determinants of potentially hazardous road-crossing decisions. On the basis of the results of this survey, a school drama group (n = 13) was invited to devise and develop a short theatre intervention to increase road safety awareness among adolescent pedestrians. The theatre piece was then performed to a group of school children (n = 88) who completed TPB questionnaires two weeks before the performance and again directly afterwards. A control group (n = 141) completed the questionnaires on two occasions separated by two weeks. After watching the theatre piece, the school children reported more negative behavioural and normative beliefs. In contrast, the beliefs of the control group remained stable over time. In addition, pupils in the drama group, who completed TPB questionnaires before and after developing the theatre piece, reported more negative intentions and lower perceptions of control about crossing the road in a potentially hazardous manner at the end of the project. The results are discussed in relation to the potential of school-based theatre interventions to increase road safety awareness and the need to engage recipients of the intervention actively so that they process the road safety information being presented systematically.

Improving pedestrian road safety among adolescents

Incidence and characteristics of pedestrian accidents

In 1998, over 17,000 children were killed or injured in pedestrian accidents (Department of the Environment, Transport and the Regions, 1999), which represent 'the single, biggest accidental killer of children and adolescents in Britain' (Avery & Jackson, 1993). Ward et al. (1994) report that 10–15-year-olds have the highest casualty rates per 100,000 of the population per 100 million pedestrian kilometres walked and per 100 million roads crossed; one child in fifteen is injured in a road traffic accident before his or her sixteenth birthday (Jones, 1990). Accident statistics have reduced in recent years, although the absolute number of pedestrian casualties among children remains high. It is likely that this reduction is not due to road safety education but rather to decreased pedestrian exposure. Roberts (1993) reports that child pedestrian casualty rates have fallen as car ownership has increased; as children are increasingly being transported to school by car their exposure to risk is decreasing. This is related to socio-economic status as car ownership is lower among lower income families; perhaps accounting for the finding that children from the lowest socio-economic group are four times more likely to die through pedestrian injury than those from the highest socio-economic group (Christie, 1995). Children from lower socio-economic backgrounds play in the street more frequently, further increasing pedestrian risk.

Tight (1996) revealed a number of common features in child pedestrian casualties. First, child pedestrian accidents typically peak between 8 and 9 a.m. and again between 3 and 6 p.m., coinciding with journeys to and from school (Tight, 1987), supporting Grayson's (1975) observation that 50 per cent of accidents occur between 4 and 5 p.m. in term time. Second, the majority of the accidents occur on urban roads (Southwell et al., 1990) and within a quarter of a mile of the child's home (Grayson, 1975). Third, boys are twice as likely as girls to be involved in a pedestrian accident (Pless et al., 1989), perhaps because they are more likely to play in the road. Fourth, involvement in pedestrian accidents peaks around 12 years of age; coinciding with entry into secondary education, perhaps a time when children are often afforded greater freedom of movement (Lynam & Harland, 1992). Finally, a number of studies have found that the majority of accidents occur when the child is intent on crossing the road (Grayson, 1975; Southwell et al., 1990). These studies demonstrate that children engage in three risky pre-crossing activities. First, failing to stop at the kerb. Second, failing to check that the road is clear. Third, running and paying little attention to the traffic environment. Children demonstrate perceptual/cognitive errors when crossing the road, e.g. misjudgements of speed and/or distance (Tight et al., 1990).

Previous research on pedestrian accidents

Studies of the causes of accident involvement among children have focused on the development of perceptual skills and 'risk-taking' behaviour. Young children do not have the perceptual or cognitive skills that are required to cross the road safely (Avery & Jackson, 1993; Demetre & Gaffin, 1994). Whitebread and Neilson (1996) found that young children had little or no understanding of what constitutes a safe place to cross and were poor at making judgements about crossing in sight of oncoming traffic. However, they concluded that the majority of adolescents had acquired the skills necessary to cross the road safely. It can be inferred that, among adolescents, it is not the failure to acquire adequate road-crossing skills but the failure to employ these skills that may determine accident involvement (Tight et al., 1990).

Antisocial behaviour and/or delinquency and children's proneness to accidents, including road traffic accidents, can be linked (Bijur & Stewart-Brown, 1986; Wadsworth, 1987; Junger et al., 1995; Thuen & Bendixen, 1996; Pless et al., 1989; West & Farr, 1989). Some individuals may have a predisposition that influences their behaviour and makes them more prone to accidents. Zuckerman et al. (1978) argue for the existence of such a sensation-seeking personality trait. In addition, children identified as having conduct behaviour problems and attending special clinics have also been found to have elevated sensation-seeking scores (Russo et al., 1993). Nevertheless, as West et al. (1999) suggest, there are likely to be further motivational factors that account for the increased proneness of adolescents to pedestrian accidents.

Road safety education

Road safety education is often provided to children from an early age, e.g. in the UK there are 'Children's Traffic Clubs', which children may join on their third birthday. Where the scheme is used wholeheartedly, it has been found to be an effective introduction to road safety education for pre-school children. Many local authorities adopt 'Further Ahead' for 5–11-year-olds, a package developed by the Royal Society for the Prevention of Accidents to be used in conjunction with the National Curriculum. However, the provision of road safety education in schools is not uniform. Moreover, learning road safety in a classroom environment may lead to the material being learned more as theoretical concepts than as practical skills.

Thus there has been a recent trend towards the development of practical pedestrian skills training for young children (Thomson et al., 1996).

Road safety education among 11–15-year-olds in secondary schools is sparse. Singh and Spear (1989) found that only a minority of secondary schools have any road safety education provision. It is likely that road safety education for this age group will need to focus on different factors from those selected at primary school. The vast majority of these children have acquired the cognitive/perceptual skills to cross the road safely. It may be the failure to deploy these skills that contributes to the high rate of pedestrian casualties among adolescents. Intervention that focuses on the motivational determinants of unsafe road-crossing behaviour may be more successful.

Theoretical perspective: The Theory of Planned Behaviour

The Theory of Planned Behaviour

The Theory of Planned Behaviour (TPB) was expanded from the Theory of Reasoned Action (TRA: Fishbein & Ajzen, 1975; Ajzen & Fishbein, 1980) (see Figure 10.1). TPB/TRA theorises about how attitude, subjective norm and behaviour intentions combine to predict behaviour. TRA suggests that the best predictor of behaviour is the person's intention to perform the behaviour (for example 'I intend to do X'). Intention summarises the individual's motivation to behave in a particular way and indicates how hard the person is willing to try and how much time and effort they are prepared to expend in order to perform the behaviour (Ajzen, 1991: 199). Intention is determined by two factors: attitude towards the behaviour and subjective norm or perceived social pressure to perform (or not perform) the behaviour. Attitude is the product of a set of salient beliefs about the consequences of performing the behaviour (for example, 'Wearing a safety helmet would protect my head if I had an accident'), each weighted by an evaluation of the importance of each of the consequences (for example, 'Protecting my head if I had an accident is good/bad'). Subjective norm is determined by the person's normative beliefs about perceived social pressure from significant others (for example, 'My parents think I should wear a safety helmet') weighted by the person's motivation to comply with those others ('Generally I want to do what my parents think that I should do').

The TRA was intended to be applied to the prediction of purely volitional behaviours but, as Ajzen (1988) later argued, many behaviours are not under complete volitional control. He therefore expanded the TRA by adding the concept of perceived behavioural control, which refers to people's appraisals of their ability to perform the behaviour. According to Ajzen (1988), perceived behavioural control should predict behavioural intention and, when people's perceptions of control accurately reflect their control over behaviour, it should predict actual performance of the behaviour

Figure 10.1   The Theories of Reasoned Action and Planned Behaviour (TPB components shown shaded in grey)

(From: Rutter, D. and Quine, L. (2002): Social cognition models and changing health behaviours. In D. Rutter and L. Quine, *Changing Health Behaviour: Intervention and Research with Social Cognition Models*. Buckingham: Open University Press, p. 12)

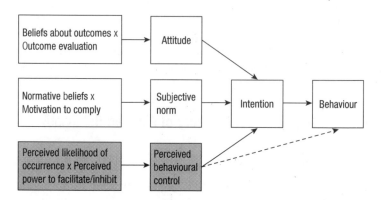

too. Perceived behavioural control is underpinned by control beliefs about perceptions of obstacles, impediments, skills, resources and opportunities that may inhibit or facilitate performance of the behaviour. These may be external (for example availability of time or money) or internal (for example ability, skills). Both the TRA and TPB have attracted enormous attention from social psychologists interested in identifying beliefs underpinning health behaviours that may be amenable to change.

Intervening through the TPB

The majority of child pedestrian accidents occur when the child is going to or from school (Tight, 1996) and is intent on crossing the road (Southwell et al., 1990). In addition, most pedestrian accidents occur when the child attempts to cross the road away from a designated crossing point (Avery & Jackson, 1993). Thus, a clearer understanding of the motivational determinants of 'risky' decisions is likely to aid the development of road safety interventions aimed at the 11–15-year-old age group.

The Theory of Planned Behaviour (Ajzen, 1988, 1991) has been applied successfully to a range of social and health behaviours (see Conner & Sparks, 1996; Armitage & Conner, 1998). Meta-analyses reveal that the TPB typically explains between 40 and 50 per cent of the variance in behavioural intention (Sutton, 1998). TPB provides a simple model of the proximal determinants of individuals' decisions (that is, intentions). Some researchers have argued that the predictive power of the model might be improved by the inclusion of additional variables. Three such variables may be relevant in the present context. First, a distinction can be made between subjective norms (that is, the perception of social pressure to perform a behaviour) and personal or moral norms (that is, the individual's perception of the moral correctness or incorrectness of performing the behaviour) (Ajzen, 1991; Manstead, 2000). Moral norms that take account of 'personal feelings of responsibility to perform, or refuse to perform, a certain behavior' (Ajzen, 1991: 199) may be a further, independent, form of normative pressure. Armitage and Conner (1998), in their review of the TPB, report that the addition of moral norms typically produces a small, but significant, increment in the amount of variance explained in intention. Second, anticipated feelings associated with the performance of the behaviour may also be an important determinant of an individual's decision to perform a behaviour (Triandis, 1977). Recent research has focused on the influence of anticipated regret. Individuals who anticipate feeling regret after performing a behaviour are less likely to intend to perform the behaviour (for example Richard et al., 1996). However, in the present context, individuals may also expect to experience positive emotions following 'risky' road-crossing behaviours. Third, self-identity (that is, the labels individuals use to describe themselves) may also predict intentions to perform a behaviour (Biddle et al., 1987; Charng et al., 1988). For example, Sparks and Shepherd (1992) found that individuals who saw themselves as 'green consumers' were more likely to intend to consume organic vegetables. This effect was over and above the influence of the TPB variables. In the present context, the extent to which individuals see themselves as 'safe pedestrians' may influence their road-crossing behaviour.

The TRA and the TPB have been applied to a range of road safety behaviours. For example, the TRA has been used to predict seat-belt use (Wittenbraker et al., 1983; Budd et al., 1984; Martin & Newman, 1990; Stasson & Fishbein, 1990; Thuen & Rise, 1994) and the use of car seats and restraints for children (Gielen et al., 1984), as well as motorcycling behaviour (Rutter et al., 1995). The TPB has been applied to three main road user groups: drivers, cyclists and pedestrians. Parker et al. (1992) used the TPB to examine drivers' intentions to commit driving violations. Drivers were presented with scenarios depicting a number of common driving violations (that is, drink-driving, speeding, close following, risky overtaking) followed by items measuring the main TPB constructs. The TPB was able to explain between 23 and 47 per cent of the variance in intentions, with attitude, subjective norm and perceived behavioural control all emerging as significant independent predictors. More recently, Parker et al. (1995) tested an extended version of the TPB to examine intentions to commit motorway driving violations (for example overtaking on the inside). Again, all three components of the TPB were predictive of intentions, explaining between 34 and 37 per cent of the variance. However, the additional variables of moral norms and anticipated affect made significant contributions to the prediction of intentions to commit violations over and above the influence of the TPB variables. Considering cyclists, two studies have successfully applied the TPB to safety helmet use among school children (Sissons Joshi et al., 1994; Quine et al., 1998). For example, Quine et al. (1998) found that the TPB was able to explain 34 per cent of the variance in intentions to wear a safety helmet and 43 per cent of the variance in reported safety helmet use at one-month follow-up among a sample of 11–18-year-old schoolboys. Subjective norm and perceived behavioural control were the strongest predictors of intention, with intention and perceived behavioural control predicting actual safety helmet use. Evans and Norman (1998) used a similar methodology to that used by Parker et al. (1992, 1995) to examine adult pedestrians' road-crossing decisions in response to three potentially hazardous road-crossing scenarios (for example crossing a busy dual carriageway). The TPB was able to explain between 37 and 49 per cent of the variance in pedestrians' intentions to cross the road in the manner depicted in the scenarios. In addition, a measure of self-identity led to small but significant increments in the amounts of variance explained in intention for two of the three scenarios.

Considering adolescents' road-crossing decisions, Evans (1999) completed a survey of over 1,800 secondary school children in South Wales. Respondents were presented with two potentially hazardous road-crossing scenarios (that is, crossing a busy road, crossing from behind a bus) followed by items measuring the main TPB constructs and the additional variables of moral norms, anticipated affect and self-identity. The TPB was able to explain between 21 and 27 per cent of the variance in intentions to cross the road in the manner depicted in the two scenarios, with all three components emerging as significant predictors. The additional variables produced significant increments in the amounts of variance explained, although only anticipated affect and self-identity emerged as significant predictors. In both scenarios, attitude and self-identity were the most powerful predictors of road-crossing intentions. More detailed analysis of beliefs that crossing the road in the manner depicted would be easier and would get children home more quickly were strongly correlated with intentions. For normative beliefs, the views of friends were found to have the strongest impact on intentions for both scenarios. These findings suggest three main avenues that interventions designed to encourage safer road-crossing behaviour among adolescents may explore. First, they should focus on the belief that crossing the road in a potentially dangerous manner necessarily leads to easier and quicker journeys. Second, given the importance of self-identity as a predictor, interventions should aim to increase adolescents' views of themselves as 'safe pedestrians' and encourage a more 'thoughtful' approach to road crossing. Third, interventions should take advantage of the powerful influence of friends and peers among this age group to change attitudes and behaviour.

Theatre and drama interventions

One potentially useful way of presenting a road safety message is through the use of a theatre intervention. Adolescents watch a play, usually performed by a professional theatre company, that has been designed to focus on road safety issues. Theatre interventions are likely to engage the audience and present material in ways that are easy to understand (Petty & Cacioppo, 1986). Powney et al. (1995) have suggested that theatre interventions in schools have a number of advantages over other more traditional modes of presentation. In particular, they may be a useful method for dealing with sensitive social issues and are likely to have a greater 'impact', which may motivate students to consider the issues presented and thereby change their attitudes and behaviour.

Evaluation studies of theatre interventions in schools have produced mixed results. Gliksman et al. (1984) assessed the impact of a theatrical performance focusing on alcohol use on the knowledge, attitudes and behaviour of Canadian high school students. It was found that the performance had a significant impact on attitudes and behaviour, although this impact was no greater than that of a more traditional lesson plan intervention. Powney et al. (1995) evaluated the impact of a theatre tour focusing on drink-driving, in five schools in Scotland and Wales. The study compared three interventions. The first was a performance by a professional theatre group of a play, detailing a true story, of two sisters in an alcohol-related fatal road accident. The second was a presentation by a road safety officer based on a television documentary on drink-driving. The third was a teacher presentation of a road safety video. Following each of the presentations, the students engaged in discussion groups to explore in more detail the issues raised. The results indicated that, following the presentations, students had better knowledge and more negative attitudes towards drink-driving. However, no differences were found between the intervention groups in knowledge or attitudes, although students watching the theatre presentation reported that they found it more enjoyable, harder hitting, and more informative than the other presentations.

Evans (1999) reported that the views of friends have a strong influence on adolescents' road-crossing intentions. Thus the impact of theatre interventions may be increased by using peers to design and perform the intervention. Such an argument is consistent with research by Telch et al. (1990), who evaluated a peer-led smoking prevention programme in which peer teachers led a number of sessions to help younger students to develop strategies to resist social pressures to smoke cigarettes. Significant differences were found between the intervention and control groups at nine-month follow-up. Peer-led interventions may be effective for a number of reasons. First, the level of understanding between same-age participants is better. Second, there are no language barriers, because participants use and understand the same colloquial words and expressions. Third, participants are likely to be more receptive and responsive to suggestions from their peers. Thus, a road safety theatre intervention that is developed and performed by similar-aged students may have the requisite characteristics to motivate and enable recipients to reconsider their attitudes towards pedestrian road safety.

Whatever the impact on the theatre audience, it is likely that those responsible for developing and producing the intervention will have their views about pedestrian road safety challenged. A distinction can be made between theatre interventions, in which participants watch a theatre production, and drama interventions, in which participants work together over a period of time to produce a drama piece. The use of drama may have several benefits, including the ability to encourage exploration and illumination (O'Neill et al., 1989). Thus, participation in drama interventions may encourage the systematic processing of information that is likely to lead to changes in attitudes and behaviour (Heppner et al., 1995). Studies have found that participation in drama interventions can lead to increased knowledge about AIDS (Dalrymple & Du Toit, 1993), increased seat-belt use (Lehman & Scott, 1990) and improved interpersonal cognitive problem solving (Johnston et al. 1985).

The intervention

Development of the drama used in the theatre intervention study took place in sessions over a six-week period. In the first session, pupils were asked to complete a TPB questionnaire on road crossing (see later) and the topic of road safety was introduced. The pupils were informed of the broad aims of the project (that is, research into the road-crossing behaviour of 11–15-year-olds). Pupils were supplied with figures on the number of young people killed or injured in pedestrian road accidents each year. Finally, a summary of the results from the survey of adolescents' road safety attitudes (Evans, 1999) was presented, which emphasized the importance of attitudes, self-identity and friends' beliefs on road-crossing decisions. With the help of their drama teacher, the group was then invited to produce a 15-minute play based on the information given. It was emphasized that the information should be interpreted in their own style, using whatever topical information they thought might reinforce the road safety message. Before the second session, the pupils were asked to observe their own and their peers' road-crossing behaviour. In the next session, these observations were discussed in light of what the group might already know about safe road crossing (that is, the Green Cross Code) and the information presented in the first session. The group then developed their drama piece over the next few weeks and finally performed it in front of invited audiences.

Participants and procedure

Theatre intervention

Two schools agreed to take part in the study, and the pupils from Year 7 (11–12 years old) in each school were allocated to either the 'theatre' condition or the control condition. Each school was visited twice. During the first visit the first author introduced the broad aims of the research and the pupils completed the TPB questionnaire. In the second visit to the theatre condition school, pupils in Year 7 ($n = 88$) saw a live performance of the intervention developed by the drama group and then completed the TPB for a second time. In the control condition school, pupils in the same year ($n = 141$) completed the TPB for a second time before watching a live performance of the intervention.

Drama intervention

Thirteen pupils in a Year 11 (15–16 years old) drama group were invited to participate in the development and production of a road safety intervention over six weeks. Pupils completed TPB questionnaires at the start of the project and again at the end.

Questionnaire

The questionnaire described a potentially dangerous road-crossing behaviour. The scenario was written in the second person singular in order to encourage respondents to imagine themselves in it. The scenario was as follows:

> You are on your way home from school. It is cold, so you are hurrying home. About half-way from home, you have to cross a busy road – there is a crossing further down the road, but that will take you a lot longer to get home because you will then have to walk back up the other side. You cannot see any vehicles coming so you run across the road.

The respondents were asked to answer questions about the scenario based on the TPB. All items were followed by seven-point response scales, with descriptive labels to aid comprehension and understanding. *Behavioural intention* was measured using two items. Respondents were asked to indicate how likely it was that they would run across the road, first if they were the person in the description, and second, if they came across a similar situation themselves in the next few weeks (scored -3 to $+3$). The mean of the two items was used as a measure of behavioural intention. This measure was found to have satisfactory internal reliability at Time 1 and Time 2 (alphas = 0.79, 0.80). Respondents' *attitude* towards crossing the road as depicted in the scenario was measured using four semantic differential scales (e.g. 'Running across the road, as described, would be... bad/good') (scored -3 to $+3$). The mean of the four items was used as a measure of attitude (alphas = 0.84, 0.88). *Subjective norm* was measured using a single item ('Most people who are important to me would think that I should run across the road') (scored -3 to $+3$). Three items were used to measure *perceived behavioural control*, but subsequent analyses revealed that they did not form a reliable scale. As a result, only one item, asking how difficult or easy it would be to cross the road, was used as a measure of perceived behavioural control ('If I were the person in this description, I think running across the road would be...difficult/easy') (scored -3 to $+3$).

A number of additional variables were measured in the questionnaire. *Moral norms* were measured using two items. Respondents were asked to indicate the extent to which they felt they ought not to cross the road as described in the scenario (for example 'I shouldn't really run across the road') (scored -3 to $+3$). The mean of the two items was used as a measure of moral norms and was found to have satisfactory internal reliability at both time points (alphas = 0.67, 0.61). *Anticipated affect* was measured using two items that focused on respondents' feelings about running across the road (for example 'Running across the road would make me feel big') (scored -3 to $+3$). The mean of the two items was used as a measure of anticipated affect (alphas = 0.77, 0.75). Finally, in order to measure *self-identity*, respondents were asked two more general questions about their view of themselves as safe pedestrians (for example 'I like to think of myself as a careful pedestrian') (scored -3 to $+3$). The mean of the two items was used as a measure of self-identity (alphas = 0.72, 0.80).

In addition to the direct measures outlined above, the questionnaire also measured behavioural beliefs and normative beliefs about the behaviour depicted in the scenario. The modal salient beliefs for the scenario were generated through pilot interviews with 61 children, following the recommendations of Ajzen and Fishbein (1980). Control beliefs were not measured, as the pilot interviews revealed a large overlap with the modal salient behavioural beliefs. Four *behavioural beliefs* were used in the questionnaire. Belief strength (for example 'Running across the road, as described, could get me run over') was assessed using a response scale ranging from 'Very unlikely' (-3) to 'Very likely' ($+3$). For each belief statement there was a corresponding outcome evaluation (for example 'Getting run over would be ... very bad/very good') (scored -3 to $+3$). The products of the pairs of items were averaged to provide a summary measure of behavioural beliefs. Four referents were used to measure *normative beliefs*. Respondents were asked to indicate whether each referent would approve of them crossing the road in the manner depicted (for example 'My friends would think I should run across the road') (scored -3 to $+3$) and the extent to which they were motivated to comply with their views (for example 'I generally like to cross the road in a way that my friends think I should') (scored -3 to $+3$). The products of the pairs of items were averaged to provide a summary measure of normative beliefs.

Results

Theatre intervention

A MANOVA was performed to examine the effect of the experimental conditions (theatre/control) over time (Time 1/Time 2) on the dependent variables. Overall, the main effect of condition was found to be non-significant ($F = 1.83$, $df = 9,186$, NS). However, the main effect of time ($F = 3.19$, $df = 9,186$, $p < 0.01$) and the condition x time interaction ($F = 2.79$, $df = 9,186$, $p < 0.01$) were both found to be significant. The F values from the univariate analyses for the main effects of condition and time and the condition x time interaction are presented in Table 10.1, and the means of each variable for each condition over time are presented in Table 10.2. As shown in Table 10.1, significant univariate effects were found for only two variables, behavioural beliefs and normative beliefs. For behavioural beliefs, the main effects of condition and time, as well as the interaction between condition and time, were all found to be significant. Inspection of the means in Table 10.2 reveals that respondents in the theatre condition had more negative behavioural belief scores than those in the control condition, and that over time behavioural belief scores became more negative. Post-hoc analysis of the interaction revealed that while the behavioural belief scores of the control condition remained relatively stable between Time 1 and Time 2 ($t = 0.27$, $df = 140$, NS), the scores of the theatre condition became more negative over time ($t = 3.69$, $df = 54$, $p < 0.01$). As a result, while there was no difference between the two conditions at Time 1 ($t = 0.60$, $df = 194$, NS), at Time 2 respondents in the theatre condition had more negative behavioural beliefs than those in the control condition ($t = 3.48$, $df = 194$, $p < 0.01$).

Table 10.1   Theatre intervention: Univariate ANOVA summary table (F values)

Variable	Condition	Time	Condition x time
Intention	1.60	3.53	1.78
Attitude	1.38	0.01	0.02
Subjective norm	0.63	0.69	2.64
Perceived behavioural control	1.06	0.38	0.14
Moral norms	0.02	0.04	2.15
Anticipated affect	0.01	1.64	1.49
Self-identity	0.48	1.14	1.95
Behavioural beliefs	6.89*	9.07**	7.40*
Normative beliefs	3.17	7.15**	8.38**

$*p < 0.05$ $**p < 0.01$

Considering normative beliefs, the main effect of time and the condition x time interaction were found to be significant. Inspection of the means in Table 10.2 reveals that between Time 1 and Time 2 scores on this measure became more negative. Post-hoc analysis of the interaction revealed that while the normative belief scores of the control condition remained relatively stable between Time 1 and Time 2 ($t = 0.20$, $df = 140$, NS), the scores of the theatre condition became more negative over time ($t = 3.47$, $df = 54$, $p < 0.01$). However, post-hoc analysis of the interaction also revealed that the two conditions were not equivalent at Time 1, in that respondents in the

Table 10.2　Theatre intervention: Means of the variables under consideration by condition (control/theatre) and time

Variable	Time 1		Time 2	
	Control	Theatre	Control	Theatre
Intention	−0.75	−1.22	−0.68	−0.81
Attitude	−1.86	−2.02	−1.84	−2.02
Subjective norm	−2.46	−2.11	−2.13	−2.22
Perceived behavioural control	−0.87	−1.06	−0.71	−1.02
Moral norms	1.48	1.27	1.28	1.43
Anticipated affect	−1.70	−1.55	−1.37	−1.53
Self-identity	1.38	1.34	1.35	1.37
Behavioural beliefs	−2.26	−2.49	−2.33	−3.85
Normative beliefs	−2.26	−0.61	−2.20	−2.25

theatre condition had less negative normative beliefs than those in the control condition ($t = 3.45$, $df = 194$, $p < 0.01$). As a result of the reduction in normative belief scores between Time 1 and Time 2 in the theatre condition, the two conditions did not differ at Time 2 ($t = 0.08$, $df = 194$, NS).

Drama intervention

The responses of the children involved in the development of the drama piece to the evaluation questionnaire at the start and end of the project were analysed using Wilcoxon signed-ranks tests. As can be seen from Table 10.3, both intention and perceived behavioural control showed significant reductions over time. Thus, at the end of the project, the children were less likely than at the beginning to intend to run across the road as described in the scenario and were less likely to believe that doing so would be easy.

Table 10.3　Drama intervention: Means of the variables under consideration over time (Wilcoxon's Z-values)

Variable	Time 1	Time 2	Z-value
Intention	1.15	−0.31	2.62**
Attitude	−1.57	−1.52	0.25
Subjective norm	−2.69	−2.46	0.80
Perceived behavioural control	0.58	−0.08	2.27*
Moral norms	1.31	1.31	0.25
Anticipated affect	−1.73	−1.73	0.51
Self-identity	0.88	1.08	0.42
Behavioural beliefs	−1.85	−1.73	0.31
Normative beliefs	−0.25	0.48	0.86

$*p < 0.05$ $**p < 0.01$

Discussion: implications for theory, policy and practice

This study sought to evaluate the impact of a TPB-based theatre intervention on adolescents' pedestrian road safety attitudes. The results of the study indicated that the intervention had only a modest effect on the attitudes of the children who watched the intervention. None of the direct measures of the TPB constructs or the additional variables under consideration were found to have changed as a result of the intervention in comparison with the control condition. Significant effects were found for behavioural beliefs and normative beliefs, in that the beliefs of children who watched the theatre intervention became more negative over time while the beliefs of children in the control group remained stable. The children were also likely to believe that running across the road (in the scenario) would lead to positive outcomes and less likely to believe that it would attract social approval.

The intervention was designed to capture the recipients' attention and encourage active processing of content. Yet the results indicate that the intervention had a relatively modest impact on attitudes. Given that the theatre intervention was compared only with a no-intervention control condition, we cannot be sure that its impact on behavioural and normative beliefs was any greater than that of more traditional road safety, education lessons. Powney et al. (1995) likewise reported that a theatre intervention on drink-driving attitudes was no more effective than a presentation led by a road safety officer or teacher, and similar results have been reported by Gliksman et al. (1984) in relation to alcohol use.

There are a number of possible reasons for these results. First, the intervention was very brief, lasting only 15 minutes. Perhaps more intensive intervention to produce stronger changes in road safety attitudes and behaviour should be designed; e.g. further follow-up discussion groups could explore the issues raised by the intervention in more detail (Powney et al., 1995). Second, the school children completed the second TPB questionnaire directly after watching the intervention. Perhaps there should have been more time for them to consider and process the intervention contents. Third, school children may enjoy theatre interventions but this does not necessarily lead to a differential impact over other road safety education methods (Powney et al., 1995). Fourth, the theatre intervention by similarly aged peers may increase the salience of the message, but the influence of peers on attitudes and behaviour may be limited to close friends and associates (Blyth et al., 1982).

Watching a theatre intervention may, in itself, not be sufficient to encourage the systematic processing of information that is crucial for changes in attitudes and behaviour (Petty & Cacioppo, 1986); it may be a passive, rather than an active experience. Follow-up sessions aimed at exploring the intervention may be required. Powney et al. (1995) note, in their evaluation of theatre interventions in schools, that follow-up work is often not carried out, because of timetable pressures from examined subjects.

An alternative approach is to use the development of the theatre piece as an intervention in itself. We found that the school drama class who developed the intervention as a class project were responsive to the message they portrayed. At the end of the project the pupils were less likely to report that they would run across the road as depicted in the scenario and less likely to believe that doing so would be easy. While the small sample size and the lack of a control group mean that the findings should be treated with caution they are, nevertheless, encouraging. Intention and perceived behavioural control are the two proximal determinants of behaviour in the TPB; research by Parker (1997) has found that respondents' indications of their intentions in response to road safety scenarios are related to their actual observed behaviour.

Drama encourages thinking over impulsiveness (O'Neill et al., 1989; Heppner et al., 1995). Assisting children to develop thinking skills can help to reduce impulsive or careless behaviour (Hyman, 1994). This is important as a number of researchers have concluded that careless or reckless behaviour is a major cause of involvement in road traffic accidents (Elander et al., 1993; West et al., 1999). An advantage to drama interventions is that they can be incorporated into the school timetable, promoting a detailed consideration of road safety issues. Nevertheless, it still needs to be shown that the use of a drama intervention to encourage safer road safety attitudes and behaviour is more effective than other more traditional methods.

We have attempted to highlight TPB's utility for identifying the motivational determinants of adolescents' road-crossing decisions. The TPB model can be used as a framework for developing a road safety intervention to target beliefs related to making unsafe road-crossing decisions. While the TPB can identify which beliefs to target, it does not outline how to change these beliefs. Persuasion and attitude change that emphasize the importance of encouraging recipients to process the content of all intervention systematically should be considered (Petty & Cacioppo, 1986; Eagly & Chaiken, 1993). Previous work suggests that theatre interventions may be a suitable medium for presenting road safety education to adolescents. The results of the present study indicate that peer-led drama had a relatively modest impact on attitudes. To be effective, follow-up discussion groups may be required. An alternative approach is to view the development of the theatre piece as an intervention in its own right, which may encourage participants to process road safety information systematically. Participation in a drama intervention was found to have an impact both on intentions and on perceptions of control. However, these initial findings will need to be replicated in future studies, with larger sample sizes and appropriate control groups. This may confirm the potential of the TPB as a framework for developing effective road safety interventions to change attitudes and behaviour, and in turn may help to reduce the number of pedestrian road traffic casualties among adolescents.

References

Ajzen, I. (1988) *Attitudes, Personality and Behavior.* Milton Keynes: Open University Press.

Ajzen, I. (1991) The Theory of Planned Behavior, *Organizational Behavior and Human Decision Processes*, **50**: 179–211.

Ajzen, I. and Fishbein, M. (Eds) (1980) *Understanding Attitudes and Predicting Social Behavior.* Englewood Cliffs, NJ: Prentice-Hall.

Armitage, C. and Conner, M. (1998) Extending the theory of planned behavior: a review and avenues for further research, *Journal of Applied Social Psychology*, **28**: 1429–64.

Avery, J.G. and Jackson, R. (1993) *Children and their Accidents.* London: Arnold.

Biddle, B., Bank, B. and Slavings, R. (1987) Norms, preferences, identities and retention decisions, *Social Psychology Quarterly*, **50**: 322–37.

Bijur, P.E. and Stewart-Brown, S. (1986) Child behavior and accidental injury in 11,966 pre-school children, *American Journal of Diseases of Children*, **40**: 487–93.

Blyth, D., Hill, J. and Thiel, K. (1982) Early adolescents' significant others: grade and gender differences in perceived relationships with familial and non-familial adults and young people, *Journal of Youth and Adolescence*, **11**: 425–50.

Budd, R.J., North, D. and Spencer, C. (1984) Understanding seat-belt use: a test of Bentler and Speckart's extension of the 'theory of reasoned action', *European Journal of Social Psychology*, **14**: 69–78.

Charng, H.W., Piliavin, J.A. and Callero, P.L. (1988) Role identity and reasoned action in the prediction of repeated behavior, *Social Psychology Quarterly*, **51**: 303–17.

Christie, N. (1995) *Social, Economic and Environmental Factors in Child Pedestrian Accidents: A Research Review*, TRRI, report no. 116. London: Department of Transport.

Conner, M. and Sparks, P. (1996) The theory of planned behaviour and health behaviours, in M. Conner and P. Norman (Eds) *Predicting Health Behaviour: Research and Practice with Social Cognition Models.* Buckingham: Open University Press.

Dalrymple, L. and Du Toit, M.K. (1993) The evaluation of a drama approach to AIDS education, *Educational Psychology*, **13**: 147–54.

Demetre, J.D. and Gaffin, S. (1994) The salience of occluding vehicles to child pedestrians, *British Journal of Educational Psychology*, **64**: 243–51.

Department of the Environment, Transport and the Regions (DETR) (1999) *Road Accidents Great Britain: The Casualty Report.* London: The Stationery Office.

Eagly, A.H. and Chaiken, S. (1993) *The Psychology of Attitudes.* New York: Harcourt Brace Jovanovich.

Elander, J., West, R. and French, D. (1993) Behavioural correlates of individual differences in road traffic crash risk: an examination of methods and findings, *Psychological Bulletin*, **113**: 279–94.

Evans, D. (1999) Understanding and changing road safety awareness in adolescents. PhD thesis, University of Wales Swansea.

Evans, D. and Norman, P. (1998) Understanding pedestrians' road crossing decisions: an application of the theory of planned behaviour, *Health Education Research*, **13**: 481–9.

Fishbein, M. and Ajzen, I. (1975) *Belief, Attitude, Intervention and Behavior: An Introduction to Theory and Research.* Reading, MA: Addison-Wesley.

Gielen, A.C., Erikson, M.P., Daltroy, L.H. and Rost, K. (1984) Factors associated with the use of child restraint devices, *Health Education Quarterly*, **11**(2): 195–206.

Gliksman, L., Douglas, R.R. and Smythe, C. (1984) The impact of a high school alcohol education program utilizing a live theatrical performance: a comparative study, *Journal of Drug Education*, **13**: 229–48.

Grayson, G.B. (1975) *Observations of Pedestrians at Four Sites*, Department of the Environment report no. 670. Crowthorne: Transport and Road Research Laboratory.

Heppner, M.J., Humphrey, C.F., Hillenbrand-Gunn, T.L. and DeBord, K.A. (1995) The differential effects of rape prevention programming on attitudes, behavior, and knowledge, *Journal of Counselling Psychology*, **42**: 508–18.

Hyman, M.H. (1994) Impulsive behaviour: a case for helping children 'think' about change, *Educational Psychology in Practice*, **10**: 141–8.

Johnston, J.C., Healey, K.N. and Tracey-Magid, D. (1985) Drama and interpersonal problem solving: a dynamic interplay for adolescent groups, *Child Care Quarterly*, **14**: 238–47.

Jones, D. (1990) *Child Casualties in Road Accidents*. London: Department of Transport.

Junger, M., Terlouw, G. and van der Heijden, P. (1995) Crime, accidents and social control, *Criminal Behaviour and Mental Health*, **5**: 386–410.

Lehman, G.R. and Scott, G.E. (1990) Participative education for children: an effective approach to increase safety belt use, *Journal of Applied Behavior Analysis*, **23**: 219–25.

Lynam, D. and Harland, D. (1992) *Child Pedestrian Safety in the UK*. Berlin: VT1/FERSI Conference.

Manstead, A.S.R. (2000) The role of moral norm in the attitude–behavior relationship, in D.J. Terry and M.A. Hogg (eds) *Attitudes, Behavior and Social Context: The Role of Norms and Group Membership*. Mahwah, NJ: Lawrence Erlbaum.

Martin, G.L. and Newman, I.M. (1990) Women as motivators in the use of safety belts, *Health Values, Health Behavior, Education and Promotion*, **14**: 37–47.

O'Neill, G., Lamber, A., Linnell, R. and Warr-Wood, J. (1989) *Drama Guidelines*. London: Heinemann.

Parker, C. (1997) The relationship between speeding attitudes and speeding behaviour, in G. Grayson (ed.) *Behavioural Research in Road Safety VII*. Crowthorne: Transport and Road Research Laboratory.

Parker, D., Manstead, A.S.R., Stradling, S.G., Reason, J.T. and Baxter, J.S. (1992) Intention to commit driving violations: an application of the theory of planned behaviour, *Journal of Applied Psychology*, **77**: 94–101.

Parker, D., Manstead, A.S.R. and Stradling, S.G. (1995) Extending the theory of planned behaviour: the role of personal norm, *British Journal of Social Psychology*, **34**: 127–37.

Petty, R.E. and Cacioppo, I.T. (1986) *Communication and Persuasion: Central and Peripheral Routes to Attitude Change*. New York: Springer.

Pless, I.B., Peckham, C.S. and Power, C. (1989) Predicting traffic injuries in childhood: a cohort analysis, *Journal of Pediatrics*, **115**: 932–8.

Powney, J., Glissov, P. and Hall, S. (1995) *The Use of Theatre Tours in Road Safety Education: Drinking, Driving and Young People*, SCRE research report no. 66. Edinburgh: Scottish Council for Research in Education.

Quine, L., Rutter, D.R. and Arnold, L. (1998) Predicting and understanding safety helmet use among schoolboy cyclists: a comparison of the Theory of Planned Behaviour and the Health Belief Model, *Psychology and Health*, **13**: 251–69.

Richard, R., van der Pligt, J. and de Vries, N. (1996) Anticipated affect and behavioral choice, *Basic and Applied Social Psychology*, **18**: 111–29.

Roberts, I. (1993) Why have child pedestrian death rates fallen? *British Medical Journal*, **306**: 1737–9.

Russo, M.F., Stokes, G.S., Lahey, B.B. et al. (1993) A sensation seeking scale for children: further refinement and psychometric development, *Journal of Psychopathology and Behavioral Assessment*, **15**: 69–86.

Rutter, D.R., Quine, L. and Chesham, D.J. (1995) Predicting safe riding behaviour and accidents: demography, beliefs, and behaviour in motorcycling safety, *Psychology and Health*, **10**: 369–86.

Singh, A. and Spear, M. (1989) *Traffic Education: A Survey of Current Provision and Practice in Secondary Schools*, TRRI, report no. CR115. Crowthorne: Transport and Road Research Laboratory.

Sissons Joshi, M., Beckett, K. and Macfarlane, A. (1994) Cycle helmet wearing in teenagers: do health beliefs influence behaviour? *Archives of Disease in Childhood*, **71**: 536–9.

Southwell, M.T., Carsten, O.M.J. and Tight, M.R. (1990) *Contributory Factors in Urban Road Accidents*. University of Leeds: Institute for Transport Studies.

Sparks, P. and Shepherd, R. (1992) Self-identity and the theory of planned behavior: assessing the role of identification with green consumerism, *Social Psychology Quarterly*, **55**: 388–99.

Stasson, M. and Fishbein, M. (1990) The relationship between perceived risk and preventive action: a within-subjects analysis of perceived driving risk and intentions to wear seatbelts, *Journal of Applied Social Psychology*, **20**: 1541–57.

Sutton, S. (1998) Predicting and explaining intentions and behavior: how well are we doing? *Journal of Applied Social Psychology*, **28**(15): 1317–38.

Telch, M.J., Miller, L.M., Killen, J.D., Cooke, S. and Maccoby, N. (1990) Long-term follow-up of a pilot project on smoking prevention with adolescents, *Journal of Behavioral Medicine*, **5**: 1–8.

Thomson, J.A., Tolmie, A., Foot, H.C. and McLaren, B. (1996) *Child Development and the Aims of Road Safety Education*, Department of Transport Road Safety Research Report no. 1. London: Department of Transport.

Thuen, F. and Bendixen, M. (1996) The relationship between antisocial behaviour and injury-related behaviour among young Norwegian adolescents, *Health Education Research*, **9**: 215–23.

Thuen, F. and Rise, J. (1994) Young adolescents' intention to use seatbelts: the role of attitudinal and normative beliefs, *Health Education Research*, **9**(2): 215–23.

Tight, M.R. (1987) Accident involvement and exposure to risk for children as pedestrians on urban roads. PhD thesis, University of London.

Tight, M.R. (1996) A review of road safety research on children as pedestrians: how far can we go towards improving their safety? *ATSS Research*, **20**: 69–74.

Tight, M.R., Carsten, O.M.J., Kirby, H.R., Southwell, M.T. and Leake, G.R. (1990) Urban road traffic accidents: an in-depth study. Paper presented at the Public Transport Research and Computing Eighteenth Summer Annual Meeting, Seminar G, University of Sussex, Brighton, September.

Triandis, H.C. (1977) *Interpersonal Behavior*. Monterey, CA: Brooks/Cole.

Wadsworth, M. (1987) Delinquency prediction and its uses: the experience of a 21 year follow-up study, *International Journal of Mental Health*, **7**: 43–62.

Ward, H., Cave, B.L., Morrison, A., Allsop, R. and Evans, A. (1994) *Pedestrian Activity and Accident Risk*. Basingstoke: AA Foundation for Road Safety Research.

West, M.A. and Farr, J.L. (1989) Innovation at work: psychological perspectives, *Social Behaviour,* 4: 15–30.

West, W., Train, H., Junger, M., West, A. and Pickering, A. (1999) Accidents and problem behaviour, *The Psychologist,* **12**: 395–7.

Whitebread, D. and Neilson, K. (1996) *Cognitive and Metacognitive Processes Underlying the Development of Children's Pedestrian Skills,* Department of Transport report no. S2/141 Child Development, London: HMSO.

Wittenbraker, J., Gibbs, B.L. and Kahle, L.R. (1983) Seat belt attitudes, habits and behaviours: an adaptive amendment to the Fishbein Model, *Journal of Applied Social Psychology,* **13**(5): 406–21.

Zuckerman, M., Eysenck, S. and Eysenck, H.J. (1978) Sensation seeking in England and America: cross-cultural, age and sex comparisons, *Journal of Consulting and Clinical Psychology,* **46**: 139–49.

Commentary: Daphne Evans

The idea for the road safety research project for young people began when I was a mature undergraduate student reading Psychology. It was one of those 'AH-HA' experiences that began as a personal challenge and, eventually, led to the research project described in the previous article.

The 'AH' experience occurred whilst carrying out a mini-project designed to familiarise students with 'observational' techniques. In the exercise we had to observe and report on a real life setting, in this case, road-crossing behaviour. During this 'observing' exercise, I was concerned to discover how ambivalent people were regarding their own (and often their children's) safety whilst crossing the road. Our observations suggested that irrespective of the dangers and the safety measures built for their protection, people took the shortest route possible.

The 'HA' experience occurred whilst I was attending lectures in Social Psychology. Through the observational study I became particularly interested in Ajzen's Theory of Planned Behaviour (TPB). This theory argues that the stronger a person's intention to carry out a behaviour, the greater the likelihood of it occurring. I decided that my third year research project would examine adult road-crossing behaviour using the TPB to try to find out which, if any, particular component of this model was influencing their behaviour.

I discussed my ideas with the Social Psychology lecturer, Paul Norman who, though initially sceptical, was won over by my enthusiasm! Together, we devised a survey questionnaire, providing descriptions of common potentially hazardous road-crossing scenarios, followed by a number of questions relating to the behaviour and the components of the TPB. Dianne Parker at Manchester had used this type of questionnaire when she examined 'driver' behaviour. We felt that a similar questionnaire aimed at pedestrians would be helpful for providing evidence of the utility of the model. The study was successful and we published the results (Evans & Norman, 1998).

The idea for the young pedestrian research took root during this time. I discovered that the highest pedestrian casualty figures for death and serious injury were to children/young people in the 10–15-year-old age group. I discussed the possibility of a further research project for a PhD with Paul. We proposed to examine adolescent road-crossing behaviour using the TPB model. The plan was to use the findings to develop an intervention that might influence and/or change their road-crossing behaviour. Ultimately, if it worked, there would be a reduction in child pedestrian casualties. At that time, in my enthusiasm for the project, it all seemed so clear, so simple!

A number of issues arose at this stage. How were we going to reach this age group? Would they complete such a questionnaire? More importantly, would they complete it properly and honestly?

I approached head teachers in all 22 comprehensives within the local authority, inviting them to participate in the research. The county had schools in a variety of socio-economic areas and thus we would be able to sample young people from a broad spectrum. Since the statistics showed that young people in the age group 11–15 years were most at risk, pupils in their first, second and third year of secondary education (Years 7, 8 and 9) would be our target group.

I visited local youth clubs to discuss the project with the young people to check that the draft questionnaire would be understandable to them. A return to the literature found other researchers using TPB in relation to young people and this suggested other variables that we might include in the questionnaire. We also needed to identify the people who were important to the young people to examine how influential they might be in the circumstances outlined. Would young people be willing to participate and to complete the questionnaire honestly and in the right spirit? I asked the young people how much they knew about road safety – they clearly knew the theory, e.g. how to cross the road safely. I also told the group about the accident statistics and why, as a result of work I had done with adult pedestrians previously, I was now carrying out research with their age group to try to find a means of reducing these accident figures. The general feeling was that it was a good idea and that young people would be likely to help.

These discussions led to us shortening the questionnaire. This was for two reasons. First, we planned to have the questionnaires completed during a class period and this would give us a maximum of 40 minutes. Second, the repetitious nature of the questions meant that young people would be unlikely to finish completing the questionnaire.

Sixteen schools finally agreed to participate. I attended the year group's assembly and explained the purpose of the project. Following this, the young people dispersed to their classrooms where the class teacher handed out the questionnaires. I asked class teachers not to 'embellish' what I had said in the assembly as a means of reinforcing the road safety message as I particularly wanted the pupils to respond honestly, rather than 'how they felt they ought to'. In addition, responses to the questionnaires were anonymous. This portion of the project was exacting and time-consuming, but the support I received from the pupils and the schools was excellent.

I also made very useful links with road safety professionals in many areas, including the Department of Transport. I should perhaps add here that I was unable to get a grant for living costs for this research project, apart from my university department agreeing to waive my fees for the three years. I was fortunate too, that the Road Safety Section of the local authority agreed to cover the cost of printing the questionnaires.

Over 1,800 questionnaires were completed, each generating 79 items of data per questionnaire, around 150,000 pieces of information. Entering of all these data was quite a challenge! Analysis of these data provided us with a great deal of information. For example, we found that the younger age group, i.e. 11–13, whilst heavily influenced by their peers when in a group, were still mindful of the opinions of their parents; but, from the age of around 14 years, young people's beliefs appear to become very similar to that of adults.

We found that the young people knew about road safety, e.g. how and where to cross the road, but this knowledge was not 'transferred' into real life situations. In other words, the problem was apparently a cognitive one. Thus our intervention had to generate something that would encourage the transfer of knowledge into real life situations.

TPB had helped to tease out possible variables that may influence intentions but the model could do little to provide a means of changing that behaviour. Paul and I discussed the next move. We reached the conclusion that the intervention would need to encourage some 'cognitive activity' to raise real awareness of the problem. The literature and our research suggested that some processing of road safety 'messages' is relatively simple and unlikely to alter opinion (we called this 'heuristic processing'). Deeper, more systematic processing is required to change or at least consider change. Thus, we needed to develop an intervention that encouraged systematic processing.

Past experience helped to suggest a way forward. I had belonged to a drama group and also helped in a youth drama group. I remembered how those young people had developed as a result of their acting experience. Could the medium of drama help in this case? Fortunately, drama was within the school curriculum. We sought the support of a drama teacher to encourage and guide pupils to develop a short play about road safety. This would be shown to other pupils in the school (and others). The response of the audience could be compared with that of those taking part in the drama. The essential element in this intervention was, we believed, not the end item – the product – but the *process* involved in developing and polishing the play to performance level.

I met with the pupils who were to become the actors on several occasions to discuss the project. I explained how research had demonstrated the importance of peer influence in decision-making, hence the need for their help. I wanted them to make a short play about road safety that would appeal to their age group. I also asked them to use as few props as possible, so that people would really listen to the message rather than look at the costumes, etc. It would be useful if the theme was topical, of interest to young people – I, as an older adult, was not likely to be very aware of what appealed to their age group.

Subsequently, I informed them about accident statistics and driver behaviour. We, the drama teacher, the pupils and I, discussed a number of scenarios. Pupils' initial contributions featured a lot of blood and dying. We suggested that maybe this was a little too dramatic and that it would be more effective to feature the antecedents and *hints* of consequences of an accident. Another very useful aid was to suggest observing their friends and other pupils crossing the road. For them, this was an illuminating experience – highlighting the very real difference between their knowledge of road safety and the reality that they observed!

The young people worked very hard and their performance was exceptionally polished. I also arranged for them to perform the play to an invited audience of local councillors, road safety professionals, head teachers from other schools and politicians (even the Secretary of State for Wales at the time – he did not come, but sent a representative). The upshot of this performance was an invitation to perform again at the launch of the Welsh Road Safety Campaign, which the group did with great aplomb and there was even an invitation to go on tour!

Data analysis showed that the actors were affected by the intervention, becoming far more negative about the scenarios described. Furthermore, in discussions following their performance, every pupil indicated that the process of developing and performing the play had a major positive effect on their own road-crossing behaviour. The young people reported being far more aware of events around them not only as pedestrians but also as car passengers. In developing the intervention, they had to actively process (more systematic processing) the information they already knew, along with the new information I had given them. Moreover, in order to be able to put together the play and perform it to their peers they had to reinterpret the information and this involved further information processing.

It is not suggested that the intervention changed their behaviour, but we were successful in raising their 'reality' awareness of road-crossing dangers. Regarding pupils who watched the performance we found modest but encouraging effects. I observed the audience during the performance. The children became totally absorbed in the events that unfolded and their response was quite literally rapturous at the end. Had there been the opportunity to develop post-performance discussions with the audience I believe it might have encouraged greater cognitive processing.

I was enthusiastic but naive when I began the project. I learned a great deal about road safety. I learned about how the effects of our actions can provide clues and ideas for any number of areas in psychology as well as research methodologies. I also learned the value of incorporating previous 'life' experience into the research process. I had hoped that the findings might reach a wider audience, e.g. in schools, as our intervention showed that road safety could be quite simply enhanced. I would have liked to continue the research using more rigorous methodologies but unfortunately funding has not been forthcoming. Yet interest in the project continues via publications and I regularly receive requests for further information from around the UK.

References

Evans, D. and Norman, P. (1998) Understanding pedestrians' road crossing decisions: an application of the theory of planned behaviour, *Health Education Research*, **13**: 481–9.

11 Young Black People leaving Care
LYNDA INCE

This paper is based on: Ince, L. (1999) 'Preparing young black people for leaving care', in Barn, R. (ed.) *Working with Black Children and Adolescents in Need*, London: British Association for Adoption and Fostering, and Ince, L. (1998) *Making it Alone*, London: British Association for Adoption and Fostering.

Introduction

The preparation of young black people leaving care is a neglected area in child care research. There are gaps in knowledge and understanding as to what is needed in preparation work with young black people. In relation to leaving care, the Children Act 1989 (Department of Health, 1989) gives guidance to local authorities with strong messages regarding the need to prepare young people for independence. Macdonald (1991) notes that the Children Act 1989 recognises the importance of race, culture, religion and language as applying to all sections of the Act. This chapter focuses on the relationship between race, culture and identity as contributory factors in the ability of young people to cope successfully after discharge from the care system. It is derived from a study exploring various levels of preparation and outcomes for ten young black care leavers (Ince, 1998).

Themes in the literature

There were few research studies concerning young people leaving care until the mid- to late 1970s when some descriptive studies were published (Godek, 1976; Mulvey, 1977; Kahan, 1979). These early studies highlighted the vulnerability of young people leaving residential institutions and substitute families. They revealed that young people leaving care were not a homogeneous group, and their pre-care and in-care experiences differed depending on background, culture and ethnicity. Many young people faced disruption in their placements, experiencing multiple moves, instability and inconsistency in their care. Links with family and community often tended to be severed, particularly for those who were 'looked after' for longer periods. This frequently resulted in stress associated with feelings of rejection and loss and a distinct lack of knowledge about their heritage. This was particularly true for young black people who were brought up in predominantly white settings. Of central importance was the disturbing finding that young people received little or no preparation for leaving care and independent living after care.

The second wave of research, in the 1980s, particularly that of Stein and Carey (1986), brought to light the harrowing experiences of young people leaving the care system. In 1984 a Parliamentary Committee considered that local authorities had a general statutory obligation both to prepare those in care for leaving and to provide after care services. In the 1980s, the campaigning work of the National Association for Young People in Care (NAYPIC) became widely associated with the views of young people in care and leaving care, and First Key, a national voluntary organisation for advising young people, was also set up. The third significant development was the debate regarding the status given to leaving care and preparation for young people. Research studies conducted in the mid- to late 1980s by Fisher et al. (1989), the Department of Health (1985) and Berridge and Cleaver (1987) were all important landmarks and informed the Children Act 1989, giving young people a higher profile and promoting good practice in terms of the duties and responsibilities of the local authority.

Poverty and high unemployment are consistent themes in the literature. Burgess (1981) showed that young people tended to occupy the lowest paid positions in semi-skilled and unskilled work. A study commissioned by the London Borough Regional Planning Committee into local authority policy and practice on leaving care, conducted by Bonnerjea (1990), found that local authorities were not fulfilling their responsibilities to young people leaving care. The After Care Consortium report by the National Children's Bureau (1994) found that only 76 per cent of local authorities (21) had policies and procedures on leaving care. Of the 21 local authorities with some provision, one local authority stated that procedures were in place and were always followed; 13 stated that procedures were mostly followed; six said that procedures were sometimes followed; and one stated that procedures were hardly ever followed. Eight per cent of authorities had no policy or procedures and 16 per cent did not respond.

Black young people leaving care

Literature relating specifically to young black people leaving care is relatively sparse. The First Key study (1987), funded and produced by the Commission for Racial Equality (CRE) provided information derived from three London boroughs and a number of preparation for independence units. Data were gathered regarding the circumstances of young black people with experience of the care system. The study reported disparity between the three boroughs in the way they made or did not make adequate provision for young black people leaving care. A study by Biehal et al. (1995) which included 25 young people of black and mixed heritage background in their sample of 183, found that black children of mixed heritage were proportionally the highest group being 'looked after'. A significant and important finding was that black children were two and a half times more likely than white children to come into care earlier and remain in care longer. However, very little was said about the impact of this finding on leaving care and after care outcomes.

Black and In Care, an organisation formed to raise the profile of and give a voice to black young people in care, held a series of workshops in 1984. The conference concluded that:

- residential units were staffed mainly by white people;
- there were insignificant numbers of black staff in management positions;
- there was overt and covert racism within the care system;
- the effects of the loss of racial identity were very strong and remained with the young black people long after care had ended.

Consequences for young black people

In 1990, Centrepoint's publication, *A National Scandal*, reported on youth homelessness and claimed that young black people were at a greater disadvantage than their white peers and suffered from 'direct and indirect discrimination'. According to the report this was 'demonstrated throughout the UK by landlords who would not let to young black people, and by bureaucratic systems which shut them out. Young black people also face discrimination in employment and on Youth Training Schemes, which has a knock-on effect on their access to housing'.

Morgan and Taylor (1987) observed that an additional problem for black care leavers was their lack of a strong racial identity, which could lead to isolation and loneliness, coupled with a lack of information about organisations that are likely to offer help. A further problem cited by Pennie (1987) was that black young people leaving care were more likely to have experienced contact with the juvenile justice system, which could substantially diminish their chances of gaining employment. This accords with the views of Centrepoint, stressing that young people leaving custody experienced severe problems in finding employment and accommodation. In terms of preparation for leaving care, Carton (1990) evaluated a programme set up to prepare adolescents for life after foster care. She stated that: 'Black foster parents can be a valuable source of such knowledge to agencies, and they are in a key position to advocate for services needed by youths approaching discharge from care'.

The above view was supported by research conducted by the National Foster Care Association (NFCA). Their survey, reported in *After Care – Making the Most of Foster Care* by Fry (1992), found that young black people were more likely to be homeless in proportion to their percentage in the population. This research cited direct and indirect racism within the public sector as a major cause of discrimination in the housing sector. Fry adhered to the view that financial and other supports, including training opportunities, should be given to black foster carers to enable them to 'support vulnerable young people as they leave care and afterwards'.

Race, culture and identity

The term 'race' has many meanings and has historically been used to denote or categorise people into specific groups. In general the term is often used interchangeably with colour, heredity and nationality. For the purposes of this study I offer the definition used by Barker and Moran (1991) who describe 'race' as:

> a social concept by which groups and individuals differentiate other groups from themselves. Physical appearance and cultural indicators are the key criteria of such labelling processes.

The social concept of 'race' emphasises that physical appearance and culture are key signs for labelling. Colour is one of the significant factors in the process of categorisation because it makes distinctions and is a sign of group membership, as are characteristics based on physical and cultural differences. 'Race' has also been used to determine levels of ability in terms of superiority and inferiority; skin colour has been cited as a prime factor in determining difference. Thus, the concept of 'race' has been embedded within a theoretical framework that seeks to reinforce value-laden notions of difference and categorisation. For the purposes of this study, the importance of 'race' focuses on labelling of people with black skins who live in a predominantly white society and who are adversely affected by the outcome of racism. Barker and Moran (1991) stated that for black citizens, skin colour will always place them in a different category to other minority ethnic groups who are white.

For black children in care the debate is concerned with how cultural transmission is possible when measures have not been taken to sustain racial and cultural identity. This is a point made by Ely and Denny (1987), who said that all children in care have a need to sustain their cultural identity, but this is more profound for black children who are surrounded exclusively by white images. They argued that the wish of social workers to work with minority ethnic groups must be accompanied by a deeper understanding than 'the usual casework theory or general social work training'. It must include an understanding of 'shared group history of migration, and the struggle to sustain existence and identity'.

Cheetham (1981) noted that black children in care did not have the tendency to become fluent in two cultures, but became children 'who have lost the capacity to identify, feel and communicate readily with members of their community of origin'. The black perspective within social work puts forward a strong argument for 'race' and culture to be guiding principles in the placement of children for adoption and fostering.

Implications for black young people leaving care

Black children in care are at risk of losing their racial identity and their ability to connect with their own community after leaving care. A particular difficulty for black young people who are placed for adoption or in long-term foster care is that their placement might come under pressure during the adolescent years. It is at these times that loss of racial identity is most striking. The research of McRoy et al. (1984), examining racial identity, indicated that the children who had a positive identity were those who were encouraged to value their 'race' and who were given positive feedback on their appearance. Some correlation was also found between positive racial identity and the environments within which the respondents lived. However, where the adoptive parents placed more emphasis on factors such as 'human identity, intelligence or hobbies' and discouraged the child from focusing on racial issues, there was a corresponding reluctance for these children to refer to themselves 'as belonging to a particular racial group'. What they found was that a high proportion of the families adopted a 'colour-blind approach to racial differences between the child and the family'. Significantly they all lived in predominantly white areas, and the children attended predominantly white schools. Racial differences were not discussed and the children viewed themselves as better than other black children.

Aims of the study

The study aimed to do the following:

- understand the personal experiences of a small group of young black people who had been in local authority care;
- examine what relationships, if any, may exist between their ethnicity and their care experience; and,
- present the findings of this research with a view to improving provision for young black people in local authority accommodation.

The research sites

The study was conducted in two local authorities in England; for the purpose of retaining confidentiality, these are referred to as Departments A and B. I worked in Department A and experienced limited problems in gaining access to local teams. The young people from black and minority ethnic groups were identifiable, since information on ethnicity was recorded in accordance with the department's policy.

Access to Department B was negotiated at a fairly early stage in the research process, and was granted largely due to the researcher's prior links with a senior manager who readily gave permission for the research to take place. A request was made for allocated social workers to make initial approaches and explain the purposes of the study to the young people, thereby presenting them with enough information to enable them to make an informed choice about whether or not to participate. Following this, arrangements were made to meet the young people to describe the process of the research to them.

All of the young people, with the exception of two, willingly gave their consent to participate in the study.

Methodology

In selecting a method the major considerations were to:

- determine how this would help to develop a reliable research tool;
- determine how the data could be gathered and analysed in the most effective way, allowing the subjects to speak for themselves and bringing to the fore all the nuances associated with their experiences;
- limit the extent to which the researcher could introduce her own opinions and beliefs.

There was a need to choose a method that would give primacy to the accounts given and preserve them in the form that they were communicated. Individual in-depth interviews were considered to best fulfil these characteristics. A qualitative approach was adopted that enabled young people to talk without constraint or inhibition.

A pilot study was undertaken with two young people. This helped to shape the questions and categories for the interview schedule and identified two additional methods to be included. The first of these was the use of documentation as additional source material. Notes taken from these records were integrated within the text of the analysis to strengthen points made by the young people but without taking precedence over the original words of the young people themselves. Viewing these casework files was useful in creating an awareness of the young people's problems, the significance of their experience and depicting salient issues that arose from them. It also revealed to what extent 'race' and 'culture' had been recognised and integrated into the casework process. The second interviews were with two senior members of staff in the local authorities concerned. These individuals gave information and commented on departmental policies regarding black children within local authority care. Only general themes and observations of what was communicated were recorded in the findings of the study.

Sampling was based on information supplied by the two local authority departments concerned and first approaches were made by social workers and then the researcher. This probability sample was stratified on race, gender, age and length of time in care. It consisted of ten young black people who had either left care or who were in the process of doing so. All of the study sample had been placed in long-term care in the early 1970s; six were female and four were male.

A semi-structured questionnaire was developed for individual in-depth interviews. This covered four areas: Care experience, Family, Preparation for leaving care and Race and Culture. Under each category there were questions which acted as probes to facilitate the young people to talk freely.

We drew on some of the insights gained from Glaser and Strauss (1968) in their grounded theory to analyse our data. These data were subjected to rigorous scrutiny, leading to the development of categories or concepts and their dimensions. Theoretical memos were written in conjunction with the data collections, so that the researcher's thoughts about the connections between the categories could be identified. It is through this process that the data became more conceptually abstract and this led to the construction of a theoretical hypothesis. In this study three types of coding were used in the analysis of the data: open coding, axial coding and selective coding. Memo writing and theoretical commentaries were also included.

Open coding was the process whereby each line of the interview data was broken down, examined, compared, categorised and subjected to a rigorous line by line analysis. Each discrete incident was given a name to represent a phenomenon (Strauss & Corbin, 1990). For example the word 'care' led to a basic category of caring and non-caring. From this framework it was possible to code sentences or paragraphs that conveyed the meaning of 'care'. An important part of the coding was asking questions of the data in order to lead to precise questions being asked in subsequent interviews. *In vivo* codes (words that describe behaviour or actions) were also used, e.g. the words 'I was put into care' as opposed to 'I went into care' tell us something about control and powerlessness. *In vivo* codes were taken directly from the language used by participants and were incorporated into the analysis.

Axial coding concerns the connections and relationships that are made between categories. In this study, axial coding concentrated on relationships between behaviours, the strategies adopted to manage behaviour and the consequences of those strategies. This was achieved through a procedure of asking questions about conditions, context, action/interaction, strategies and consequences.

Selective coding was used to highlight developing themes from the story-lines. In this process a core category was first selected and then systematic-ally related to other categories, e.g. the single category of 'powerlessness' to others such as 'rejection', 'timing', 'identity stripping', etc. Relationships between categories were noted and conceptions were formulated about what was being studied. These were integrated within the data to make a connection between the concepts and producing the theory.

An example of how codes were constructed is given below:

Data	Code	Category
I thought I was white		
They cut off my hair ⇨	Identity ⇨	Identity stripping
I was scared of black people		

Memos were written as the data were coded and these helped make connections and give direction about what needed to be followed up in subsequent interviews. Memo writing formed a continuous part of the analysis and led to inductive and deductive thinking related to the cate-gories and the relationships between them.

The findings

A summary case history was compiled for each young person and illustra-tive trajectories produced on flow chart models. An example of a case history follows, with the trajectory reproduced on p. 219.

Name:	David
Age at interview:	19
Time in care:	18 years
Care leaving age:	18
Present status:	Convicted prisoner

Despite facing a long prison sentence and an uncertain future, David is surprisingly relaxed and willing to talk openly about his life in care. Yet the care path that led him to prison is one filled with abuse, rejection and violence. David's connection with the care system was cemented almost from birth. At the age of one month he came to the local authority's attention when his father abused him. Although the subject of a Place of Safety Order under the Children and Young Persons Act 1969, he was still returned to his parents, a white English mother and African-Caribbean father.

By the age of six months he had been taken into care following serious neglect by his mother. He and his sister were then adopted by a white couple living in an all-white suburb where they had no contact with black people. David was subsequently physically abused by his adoptive parents, which led to his return to the care system. While in a residential home, he was abused by a staff member. No support was forthcoming. Instead he was moved from one residential placement to another.

With each move, David became more rootless, disturbed and aggressive. Over time he became virtually unmanageable. His care records show clear signs of psychological trauma stemming from his early abusive experiences. Attempts to manage his challenging behaviour through placements in Community Homes with education and socio-therapeutic units failed. Labelled as maladjusted, he was expelled from junior school. From this point on he never gained a significant foothold in education.

David's racial identity was only addressed when he was 14 years old. That was when he requested to be sent to a black-run residential project for young black people. Somehow, he managed to develop a significant relationship with a black couple who became his informal support and he responded to them positively.

Contact with his birth family was virtually non-existent. He was, in his view, well and truly institutionalised. When he left care he was unable to cope. The only real family he had was his sister who had also been abused by the adoptive parents. She became an underage mother and had regular contact with the police. At the time of interview, David had limited contact with her.

No formal attempt was made to appropriately prepare David for leaving care. But he had had the benefit of living, albeit briefly, in a preparation unit at a children's home. Afterwards he went to live with a family as a lodger, an arrangement that soon broke down. His next home was a self-contained flat with a resident landlord, but he was unable to cope with independent living.

His survival in the community was short lived as he was arrested and detained in custody and is now serving a long-term prison sentence. He says that the only way he can live is in an institution. That is all he knows.

Eurocentric care

Prolonged and extensive periods in care exposed all of the young people to a white Eurocentric model of care, with adverse implications for reintegration with their family and community. This was a key variable in their perceptions of themselves and their ability to cope after leaving care. Restricted contact with parents, relatives, black friends and the wider black community diminished the extent to which opportunities were presented for cultural exchange and conscious awareness of being black.

The duration of their stay in the care system had serious repercussions. These only became evident at the stage of leaving care and when the young people had an opportunity to reflect on and review their life experiences. Leaving care is simultaneously associated with the transition to adulthood, moving from relative dependence to independence, and developing and exploring their sexuality, and these factors may lead to young people experiencing turmoil. Given support, this sense of turmoil can be overcome but

Figure 11.2   Flow chart trajectory for David

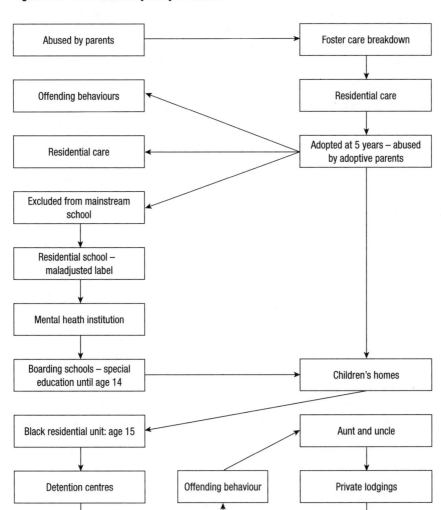

for young people who are 'looked after' the turmoil may last longer, particularly for those who have lived in residential institutions.

The young people in foster care had an advantage in that they were less fearful and had some ideas, however minimal, of how to survive, after care. They also felt reassured that the placement would be open to them after leaving care. Clearly where this resource is made available to young people, it can significantly reduce feelings of loneliness and isolation. This made a marked difference to self-confidence and the ability to become independent and self-motivating. Nevertheless, the serious nature of the task that confronted them was not understood until they had left care and support systems were no longer available to them.

Disengagement from black family community

Systematic denial of contact with those most likely to transfer cultural values was a recurrent theme in the stories that were recounted. The role of the family in transferring meanings, values, folkways, symbols and tradition was lost to those young people who were separated from their family of origin and community. This effectively dislocated the young people from any understanding of themselves and gave the opportunity for negative value systems and confusion over racial identity to develop. The role of culture and its importance to young black people growing up in Britain was not well understood, and was always undermined as unimportant and without value. This led to suppression and denial of the importance of 'race'.

The young people had no personal attributes or strategies to resist the many states of powerlessness and oppression that were experienced. Lack of strong identification with family and relatives deprived them of opportunities to learn how to cook, how to care for their hair and skin, how to enjoy black art and history, and indeed how to feel proud about themselves. Those who entered the care system when they were older did not experience this problem. The study found that during the early years of reception into care there was little or no knowledge of the needs of black children. Assumptions were made that it was better to place children in white families than to leave them in residential care. Attempts to find black carers were extremely limited. Poor policy and practice had a deep impact upon the lives of black young people even after they had left the care system. Many of them still had vivid memories of what had occurred and how it had affected their present day abilities to cope.

Identity stripping

This was a process defined as a method whereby racial and cultural needs were not met; racial identity was 'stripped' through neglect, which did more to serve the interests of professionals and white carers than the young people. This emerged as an important aspect of the care trajectory. Its impact on leaving care meant that many of the young people did not see themselves as black and felt ashamed of their colour. Transracial placements and environments where there were no reflections of black people reinforced identity stripping.

The research findings showed a failure amongst professionals and carers within fieldwork teams, residential and foster care settings to recognise and instil a positive representation of black reality. This occurred because of the absence of positive images of the young people's racial origins and was a theme throughout their care experience. It was to be replicated over and over again. Many of the young people noted that no one had ever sat down with them and discussed their 'race' as a factor influencing their care experience. Lack of knowledge and understanding of the importance of 'race' and culture contributed to lack of promotion of the positive aspects of this part of the young people's identity. Consequently it was never actively discussed. One young person said:

> No one ever said anything to me about my race.

Another said:

> I've been in care for as long as I can remember, so it don't make no difference.

The inability on the part of staff and carers to discuss matters of 'race' led the participants of this study to develop ambivalent feelings and lack of understanding about themselves. This resulted in the conclusion: 'I am white' or 'I am me'. One young man said:

> I didn't understand the difference between colour. I thought there were no differences. I thought they were my mother and father. I thought that I was white.

To be brought up in care contributed to over-identification with white values and under-identification with their own 'race', leading the respondents to separate themselves from other black people, at times being afraid of them. One young woman summed up this feeling by saying:

> There was me going around thinking I was white, and then I realised I was not white…I was scared of black people to be honest. I was scared of them, but now I know they are the same as everyone else.

The lack of attention given to the racial/cultural aspects of their lives in care rendered these black young people incapable of relating to black people. The loss of family and relatives reinforced loneliness and isolation in what one young person termed 'the big wide world'.

Overt/covert racism

All of the young people reported acts of racism of varying degrees from fieldwork staff, residential staff, carers, peers and within the education system. In all of these instances the young people described the care system as 'uncaring'. Uncaring was a word used by most of them to describe an activity that had a significant effect on preparation for leaving care and their perception of how others had devalued their existence.

Accounts were given of many incidents of unfair treatment, racism, oppression and discrimination within the care system that had long-term effects on their psychological development. A central theme in 'non caring' was the neglect of racial and cultural needs:

> You get stricter punishments than other people and things like that. Other people done the same things, but some people just treat you differently.

> They would say we want to treat everyone equal, but we were not the same at the end of the day. I had to start caring for myself when I was young, they didn't care for me.

> Like if a member of staff was against you, you don't click, they would make life hard for you. They always say we care, but you know they don't really. There was a lot of that, it does hurt, it's not very nice.

In the absence of positive black role models, all of the study sample reconstructed their internal worlds to idealise the people who were in many ways their oppressors by wanting to be white themselves or seeing themselves as individuals, but not *black* individuals. This was a way of making sense of their experiences and normalising inconsistencies. In so doing they moved along a continuum throughout the care process, fearful of challenging racism and always internalising negative concepts of themselves and others like themselves. An example of this is given in the following quote in which one young person used pejorative descriptions to express his views. These views replicated those of his carers, who had a history of fostering Nigerian children through private fostering arrangements. The distinctions that are made stem from internalised negative attitudes, but are also a paternalistic response to those who are perceived as helpless and deserving of pity and charity. He described these views as 'white' views and attributed them to where he had lived and the way he had been 'brought up'.

> I've been brought up with white people, so I've missed a lot of cultural things. When I see coloured children on the telly in Ethiopia, I feel something. But when I see coloured people in London, and the way they act, I think some people got an attitude problem. I think, oh what the hell are they doing? I've got a lot of white views.

Analysis of the data revealed that such thinking prohibited the young people from understanding the nature of the black experience in Britain, and they absorbed negative racist views from those around them. The dilemma was the price that had to be paid for the transformation from black to 'white'.

Disruption in care

Movement and disruption were dominant features in the lives of some of the young people who had had several moves whilst in care. Barn et al.

(1997) found that African-Caribbean children spent lengthy periods in care, and that there was a strong correlation between length of stay in care and placement disruption (Barn, 1993). This study found that placement disruption led to a sense of rootlessness and instability, accompanied by an inability to achieve stability after leaving care.

The young people had also linked this to rejection regarding the way in which parents, professionals and carers had controlled them. This led them to feel a sense of powerlessness and an inability to write their own life script; they described feelings of rootlessness that they internalised as normal events. After leaving care, the feelings of rejection, separation and loss impinged heavily on their own ability to maintain stability and the problems remained unresolved.

Those who had achieved a stable foster placement or who had remained in their family until their teen years expressed more optimism about their ability to remain in their accommodation. Those who were in foster care or with relatives were also less troubled by instability since they were reassured that they could return to the family.

Educational needs

Nine of the sample identified problems both at junior and secondary school. One said that she was helped only because there was a black teacher in her secondary school. Four were permanently excluded from school. Exclusion for long periods undoubtedly affected the young people's ability to achieve and to acquire a positive self-image. One young man came into care when he was one month old. He was excluded at age nine and drifted into crime. By the time of this research he was serving a long custodial sentence. Three males and two females in the study also had encounters with the police and left school without any qualifications.

Inadequate education had a direct impact on the ability of the study sample to find employment after leaving care or to engage in further education. Failure in education also means an inability to become economically independent.

Life skills

The young people in the sample varied in the degree of help they had in acquiring practical life skills; only two had some help in independent units. Two others had gained some skills from being in foster care. By and large the young people felt unequipped and with limited skills. In some instances the idea of 'making it alone' was a burden. Responses from social workers showed that help received by the young people depended on the efforts of individual social workers. In such instances the young people described such acts as 'caring'. The general response, however, was that there was a lack of instruction or preparation for the transition to adulthood.

No one has come and talked to me and said you're leaving care on this day and this is happening. I know nothing, nothing at all about it.

and

I wasn't shown how to live my life.

Several years after leaving care one young person admitted:

I've only just in the last two years started literally to sit down with pen and pad to work my money out, whereas if I was prepared for that before, maybe I wouldn't be in as much money problems as I am now.

The young people in this study spoke of their loneliness, boredom, poverty, and feelings of rejection and stigmatisation by the wider society. They were also concerned about managing money, caring for children, how to keep the house tidy, and generally how to survive. One young person said that he wanted help in knowing how to 'keep out of trouble with the law'.

Implications for practice

The preparation for leaving care that young black people require should be based on a critical analysis of how 'race' and culture impinge on the leaving care experience. Such an analysis shows that while it is important to provide training in life skills, more attention needs to be given to the individual and institutional acts of racism which can have long-term emotional and psychological effects on young black people.

For all black children and young people more support networks are required to sustain them through the care system. This means consciously building bridges across to the black community to encourage a more proactive role in recruiting black carers, volunteers and 'social aunts and uncles'.

The implications for practice have far-reaching consequences. Some specific aspects for consideration are:

- more attention given to providing placements that reflect the needs of black children and those which can offer positive role models;
- representation of black people at all levels of decision making within social services departments;
- more attention paid to the educational needs of black children;
- a need for advocates and independent visitors to act as representatives for young black people;
- facilities to enable young people to test out living independently, make mistakes and be given support to do so;
- skilled work on identity and helping young people to feel safe in exploring their racial origins and feeling a sense of pride;

- addressing issues of racial harassment and abusive experiences both in the care and education systems;
- restriction of placement of black children in geographical areas that are predominantly white.

The Children Act has replaced the term 'in care' with 'being looked after' but it will not significantly change the context of young people's experience unless there are major shifts in conceptual understanding. Such shifts will provide new impetus to provide good and positive black role models, and basic life skills from entry into care until the day they leave care.

References

Barker, R. and Moran, M. (1991) *Workbook Prejudice and Abuse*, Buckingham: Open University Press.

Barn, R. (1993) *Black Children in the Public Care System*, London: BAAF/Batsford.

Barn, R., Sinclair, R. and Ferdinand, D. (1997) *Acting on Principle*, London: BAAF.

Berridge, D. and Cleaver, H. (1987) *Foster Home Breakdown*, Oxford: Blackwell.

Biehal, N., Clayden, J., Stein, M. and Wade, J. (1995) *Moving On*, London: HMSO.

Black and in Care (1984) *Black and in Care: Conference Report*, London: Children's Legal Centre.

Bonnerjea, L. (1990) *Leaving Care in London*, London: London Borough Regional Planning Committee.

Burgess, C. (1981) *In Care and into Work*, London: Tavistock.

Carton, A. (1990) *Building on the Strengths of Black Foster Families*, Washington DC: Child Welfare.

Centrepoint (1990) *A National Scandal: Survey of Published Information on Young People Leaving Care*, Washington DC: League of America.

Cheetham, J. (ed.) (1981) *Social and Community Work in a Multi-Racial Society*, Columbia, NY: Harper and Row.

Department of Health (1985) *Children in Care in England and Wales*, London: HMSO.

Department of Health (1989) *The Children Act 1989*, London: HMSO.

Ely, P. and Denny, D. (1987) *Social Work in a Multi-Racial Society*, Aldershot: Gower.

First Key (1987) *A Study of Young Black People Leaving Care*, London: CRE.

Fisher, M., Marsh, P., Phillips, D. and Sainsbury, E. (1989) *In and Out of Care*, London: Batsford.

Fry, E. (1992) *After Care – Making the Most of Foster Care*, London: National Foster Care Association.

Glaser, B. and Strauss, A. (1968) *The Discovery of Grounded Theory*, London: Weidenfeld and Nicolson.

Godek, S. (1976) *Leaving Care*, Basildon: Barnardo's Social Work Papers 2.

Ince, L. (1998) *Making it Alone*, London: BAAF.

Kahan, B. (1979) *Growing Up in Care*, Oxford: Basil Blackwell.

Macdonald, S. (1991) *All Equal Under the Act*, London: Race Equality Unit.

McRoy, R., Zurcher, L., Lauderdale, L. and Anderson, R. (1984) The identity of transracial adoptees, *Social Casework* **651**: 34–39.

Morgan, C. and Taylor, A. (1987) A study of young black people leaving home, *Social Sciences Research* **16** (1): 10–12.

Mulvey, T. (1977) After care who cares? A study of young people who have left care at the statutory leaving age of 18. Unpublished MA thesis. University of Essex.

National Children's Bureau (1994) Report presented at the After Care Consortium Conference.

Pennie, P. (1987) Black children need the richness of black family life. *Social Work Today*, 2nd February, 1987.

Stein, M. and Carey, K. (1986) *Leaving Care*, London: HMSO.

Strauss, B. and Corbin, J. (1990) *Basics of Qualitative Research: Grounded Theory, Procedures and Techniques*, London: Sage.

Commentary: Lynda Ince

Author note: The working definition of the term 'black' was used in this research to refer to young people of African and African Caribbean descent.

In reflecting on what was the driving force for my research among young black people, I am aware that it was a long-standing interest in black children in the care system and my need to embark on a journey of exploration. In many respects this journey dates back to 1982 when I first came into contact with black children who were in the care of local authorities. I was a newly qualified social worker who had a special post of working with fellow professionals and colleagues to increase their awareness of the needs within black communities. I found that white professionals lacked knowledge about black children and their families, and had a tendency to respond to them in controlling ways neglecting to consider their strengths. The children and young people that were allocated to me tended to be in public care for considerable periods of time. I wondered what the causes were for this. It was this sense of enquiry that led me eventually to conduct my study on the experiences of young black people. The interest in this area was largely based on my observations of professional practice and the hunch that very often black children were not being served well by the care system: acts of racism and discrimination distorted their care experience, perceptions of themselves and their interaction with people, which in turn reflected badly on their own identities.

During these early years after qualifying, I was requested to conduct a small-scale study among professionals for the social services department where I worked. I found that there were few ethnically sensitive (or competent) services that were designed to meet the needs of black and minority ethnic children. The responses from individual social workers and managers varied from being interested and acknowledging and identifying problems to uninterest and feelings that the needs of black children were no different from the needs of white children. However this small but unsophisticated study demonstrated that 'race' and culture were important factors that should have had an influential bearing on the types of services that were offered. Services were not culturally sensitive to the needs of black children, neither was the practice of professionals culturally competent. The findings from this small-scale study were ignored; verbal reporting brought about little change. No action was taken and the study disappeared into the annual of the institution without recognition.

I attended a Black and In Care conference in London in 1984. It was the first conference ever held in this country organised by young black people. For the first time they spoke passionately about their experiences in the care system. They called for a number of changes to improve their lives whilst in public care. They made reference to the lack of positive role models within their care settings, and the negative impact that being in care had on their lives. Inspired by this conference I decided to carry out some research in this area. However, I could not find any in-depth reference to young black people: either the samples were very small or they were excluded from studies that became the focus for changes in child care legislation, policy and practice. In all of the literature on leaving care I could only find one study in this country that had focused on black children and this had been completed by the national organisation called First Key (1987). Since that study progress had been almost non-existent.

I was also influenced by the developing debate on transracial placements (i.e. the placement of black children in white families and white institutions; it was almost never used to mean white children placed with black families).

Methodology

The choice of methodology was guided by my wish to understand and explicate experiences. I chose to conduct a qualitative study since this methodology offered the opportunity of conducting individual, but in-depth interviews with young people and would encourage the respondents to be reflective and to tell their stories. At the same time I hoped that this methodology would have the effect of drawing attention to lived experiences by enabling us to hear the credible voices of those who had undergone the care experience. I wanted to explore and explicate the experiences of these young people based on an Afrocentric frame of reference. This proved to be a source of much tension. I wanted to get my M.Phil. and felt constrained to fit into a white frame of reference in order to get the qualification and for the research to be accepted as credible. The accepted paradigm was Eurocentric. To adopt an Afrocentric theoretical model I would have needed support from a black supervisor with experience in this field. None was available. Studying in an institution where there was no access to black scholars or thinkers operating in an African worldview was a fundamental constraint on pursing an alternative paradigm. Most unhappily, I found I was having to conform to a Eurocentric paradigm in order to complete my work and get it accepted.

In gaining access to the sites and the young people I promised to keep their identities confidential and to pay due regard to respect and anonymity. The young people gave informed consent to participation in the study and particularly to allowing me to tape-record their interviews. This entailed giving young people intelligible information about the process and the contract they would enter into with myself as the researcher. It also involved taking into account the power dynamics within each interview and how this was likely to affect the young people. As a black researcher I am sure that I was able to gain information that might have otherwise remained hidden and this was achieved through creating an environment and setting in which there was trust and credibility.

Ownership of the research was also an important consideration. I was aware that mainstream research had done little to benefit the black community, most of it being negative and controversial. It was important to find a method that would not simply encourage research for its own sake, but would be of value to those being researched.

Data decisions

The collection of the data was determined by the study design. I opted to conduct individual in-depth interviews with ten young people of African, African-Caribbean and dual heritage backgrounds who had been placed in care under a legal order and who had remained in care for more than two years. The interviews were tape-recorded and subsequently transcribed verbatim. I constructed an interview schedule that had few questions, but indicated general areas that I wanted to explore. I entered the interviews wanting the young people to talk and not to be unduly influenced by my views or opinions. I gave them ample opportunity to think and I allowed silences to be part of the process. At the end of one interview a young person said that she had found the process very helpful in talking about painful life events that she had never really expressed to anyone. She asked if I wanted to talk to her friend. This is called 'snowball sampling'. Her offer to expose this process to her friend indicated that she had trusted me and felt that her friend would have a story to tell. The young person she recommended provided key information and many of her quotes were used in the analysis of the data. I also opted to complete a documentary analysis on the young people's file records and this helped me to build up a picture of their care trajectories.

Data analysis: making sense of the findings

The analysis of data began with a meticulous line-by-line examination of the words that had been used by the participants to describe their experiences. Central to the analysis was the system for coding the data and as the analysis developed these were linked to conditions, contexts, interactions and consequences or outcomes and results of actions. This became a very sophisticated technique for constantly comparing the interviews and interpreting the data. I searched the data for recurring themes and made connections by literally drawing diagrams to assist in carefully reconstructing events. By using this vivid demonstration, I could show very clearly the context in which actions had occurred. For example I used boxes and arrows to indicate movement from one placement setting to another. This had the effect of showing disjointed care trajectories, and lack of stability whilst in care. The length of the care experiences was highlighted, showing the intensity and the duration of the experience. This enabled me to make a strong link between movement in care and poor outcomes in preparation for leaving care.

An important aspect of the research was how I eventually arrived at the quotes that were used to substantiate the findings. Throughout the process of analysis I kept a careful record in the form of what are known as 'memos'. These are reflective summaries that helped me interpret the data and put it back together in a relational way. The quotes were used in such a way as to substantiate the findings based on the analysis of the data and contributed to a sense of grounding the findings within the data. In each category quotes were chosen that substantiated the category. Below is a brief example of how this was achieved.

Causal condition	Phenomena	Dimensions
'I was put into care'	Loss – separation family, community	Specific dimensions of loss – pain, intensity, duration, location
	impact on identity	trajectory, history.

The next stage of this activity was to analyse context, intervening conditions and consequences. Thus in the above example of being 'Put into care' the context in which this occurred influenced the conditions and eventually provided the evidence for outcomes.

This way of viewing and interacting with the data became a very complex activity but also a model for grounding the data within the experiences of the participants and thus developing a theoretical framework for explicating what was being communicated in a consistent way. Quotes were chosen to support a particular idea that was occurring with frequency. Another example of this was the category 'Identity stripping'. Words that related to identity and gave a sense of stripping were clustered together and became very powerful when the quotes were used to demonstrate how identity was stripped away and the circumstances in which it frequently occurred. The quote 'My hair was chopped off because they couldn't manage it' was an indication that the texture of the hair could not be managed by white carers and therefore they cut it off, but the significance of this action was profound since it represented part of the child's identity and had an emotional and internal impact on her self-esteem.

Overall the analysis was by far the most difficult process, because it called forth many emotions in me, ranging from anger to sadness and very frequently tears. I felt that the young people had suffered many terrible injustices and that the care system had made little or no reparation to them as citizens with rights.

Writing up the study

This was a long, agonising, arduous, but sensitive and rewarding process. As the research was initially for an M.Phil. dissertation, I had to achieve academic rigour and remain conscious that I must meet certain criteria. The findings confirmed my original belief that racism and discrimination were a major factor in how services were being delivered and that 'race', ethnicity and culture were factors seldom taken into account. Lack of understanding of black families, the climate and ecological factors impacting on family life had never been considered as part of assessment. Yet the responses of the young black people showed that these were having detrimental outcomes at the stage of their leaving care. Indeed the writing-up stage proved to be a cathartic process.

When I came to writing the book, it took two years to get it published. The process of editing was a difficult one. I had to retrace my steps, and reduce the work considerably, but at the same time retain the most poignant aspects of the study along with the most pertinent quotes to highlight each theoretical claim that was made. I also had to rewrite it in a style that would suit general readership.

The most beneficial aspect of the book has been the knowledge that I was making a useful contribution to young black people and helping their voices to be heard. I recall handing the book *Making it Alone* to one of the young people from the study. Her response was:

At last we have a voice: for years I wanted someone to listen

For her, it seemed like a dream come true and I was humbled by that experience and the depth of what the young people had shared with me.

This research has led me to conduct further studies towards a PhD into kinship care and its role in preparing adolescents who cannot live at home with their birth parents but whose relatives and kinship network provide care that diverts them from the care system. Unlike my experiences when undertaking the M.Phil., I have been able to pursue this study from an Afrocentric perspective. Perhaps this says something about power relations and the perceived 'weightiness' of research at different levels. When you've proved yourself at one level, more doors are open to you.

Developments in legislation

Since I conducted this research and published its findings, there have been some developments of note. The Children (Leaving) Care Act 2000 has been implemented. This new legislation is driven by research and by the voices of young people who have spoken about their experiences and inability to survive after leaving care. As far as young black people are concerned, it was disappointing that this legislation did not move beyond what was contained in the Children Act 1989 but only re-emphasised the need for professionals to have regard for a child's 'race', culture, religion and language.

The Department of Health has recognised the need for gathering information on services to black children and their families. The publication *Excellence not Excuses* (2000) found that whilst local authorities reported having equal opportunities policies these were not implemented. Further it found that black families often had problems in accessing services. Recruiting black staff and promoting them to senior positions continues to be a problem for most local authorities. Importantly, it found little evidence of planning for the long term care of children from minority ethnic groups and that placement needs were difficult to meet. This finding accords with the observations of early black commentators, that through lack of recruitment of black carers, local authorities find it difficult, if not impossible, to meet the true needs of black children in their care.

The Race Relations Amendment Act (2000) should help local authorities to avoid racism and discrimination at all levels of organisational practice and service delivery and to promote racial equality. This should improve the life chances of black children in future generations.

References

Department of Health (1989) *The Children Act*. London: HMSO.
Department of Health (2000) *The Children (Leaving) Care Act*. London: HMSO.
Department of Health (2000) *Excellence not Excuses*. London: HMSO.
First Key (1987) *A Study of Young Black People Leaving Care*. London: CRE.
Race Relations Amendment Act (2000) London: HMSO.

12 Flexible Identities: Exploring Race and Gender Issues amongst a Group of Immigrant Pupils in an Inner-city Comprehensive School
NAZ RASSOOL

This paper has been abridged from: Rassool, N. (1999) 'Flexible identities: exploring race and gender issues amongst a group of immigrant pupils in an inner-city comprehensive school', *British Journal of Sociology and Education*, 20(1): 23–36.

Historical discourses

Racial discourse in Britain has historically focused on the image of immigrant = alien = problem to be managed through immigration control, on the one hand, and social welfare intervention programmes on the other. Within general educational discourse, pupils from ethnic minority immigrant groups and, particularly, Afro-Caribbeans, have been regarded, historically, as underachieving. This has been ascribed to, *inter alia*, language deficits/differences, cultural differences, family practices and problems of adjustment to British society (NFER, 1966; Home Office, 1981). These homogenized views, grounded in cultural determinism and the social pathology of immigrant lives, have, at least since the 1960s, provided a potent means by which their social and educational experiences have been defined.

Yet these dominant social meanings contrast sharply with the reality of many pupils' lives. While for some Britain is their country of adoption, for many others Britain is their country of birth. That is to say, Britain is the context in which their individual, group and social consciousnesses – their concept of 'self', their subjectivities, their cultural and social identities – have been shaped in relation to their experiences within their communities and in wider society.

The study

The idea for this study developed within the context of previous research that explored black feminist identities in contemporary British society, which focused on the complexities, contradictions and ambiguity in which they exist as well as their transformative power (Rassool, 1995, 1997a). The issues raised within that context, combined with the awareness that the children born of those who immigrated during the 1960s are now moving into adulthood to carve out their own personal, professional, social and political spaces, led me to further questions regarding the ways in which children from ethnic minority groups identify culturally and educationally within British society. For example, are there differences in the perceptions of first- and second-generation immigrants' social and educational experiences, and if so, what are they? In which ways do they encounter racism and what strategies do they employ in order to survive and redefine themselves? Do they experience cultural/religious conflict and if so, what is the nature of this conflict, and what strategies do they employ in order to cope? Are the variables of ethnic identity and cultural differences important to the ways in which they live their lives? If so, how? What are the main influences on their lives with regard to their education and social development? How do they experience schooling? What roles and positions do they envisage for themselves as adults in British/European society? In relation to this, what are their aspirations, expectations; their dreams and desires – and how do they envisage themselves fulfilling these? How do these relate to existing social realities? What are the social constraints on these students fulfilling their educational, individual and social potential?

Elmwood comprehensive school

Elmwood is a mixed comprehensive school within a culturally diverse area on the borders of inner London. At least 50% of the students are from ethnic minority groups. Of these, the majority are children of second-generation immigrant families. There are also children of first-generation immigrant families and, more recently, the school has had a significant intake of children from Somali refugee families. The governing body comprises mostly members from the different ethnic minority groups within the community. Facilitating equality of opportunity, valuing the diverse cultures and creating the best learning opportunities for the pupils in the school are seen as central to the school's aims. There has been friction between pupils from second-generation immigrant families and the Somali pupils. The latter group are predominantly Muslim, and have a more traditional approach to religion – a factor which has marked them out as 'different' to the rest of the school population. In order to address this issue, the school had earlier in the year celebrated a 'One World' Day, which involved parents and other members of the community in the organization of the day's proceedings. This has now been incorporated into the school's development plan and will be an annual feature in the school calendar. In addition, a Women's Action Forum, organized by women from the wider community, regularly meets within the school.

Methodology

In collaboration with the Head of Year (HOY), who has responsibility for pastoral care provision in Year 10, the research project became incorporated into the action plan of the year group's Personal, Social and Moral Education programme, and was introduced in tutorial time during the last week of the summer term. Pupils would then be evaluating their achievements and attainments in preparation for further target-setting in their records of achievement at the start of Year 11, when they would sit their General Certificate in Secondary Education (GCSE) examination. Thus it involved all Year 10 tutors, and was coordinated by the HOY. Involving the teachers directly in the research process related to a large extent to the sensitive nature of the work involved. Doing research in deeply personal areas of people's lives can make them feel vulnerable and disempowered; it can also be a traumatic experience in which painful, sublimated and, often, forgotten emotions can be reopened and rekindled (Rassool, 1997a). This requires sensitivity among those doing the research and in this instance it was felt that the well-established relationship of trust that already existed between the teachers and pupils would overcome many of the potential difficulties. It also related to the fact that the school had identified this area as a pastoral development priority and it was, therefore, imperative for teachers to become sensitized to the experiences, needs, and the views of the pupils.

The task

The teaching activity comprised four stages: Stage One involved the whole year group charting, individually, their life histories, their 'River of Life', which could be represented in any way that they chose. The 'Rivers of Life' activity provided the context in which the individual could construct the 'narrative of the self' (Giddens, 1991), building a biography in terms of the shaping of 'past-present' (Bhabha, 1994), giving an account of their personal and cultural histories. This stage focused on having an opportunity to reflect on their lives, harnessing their personal knowledges and organizing these into a coherent whole. In addition to drawing on their subjective perceptions, pupils could also draw on a range of discursive knowledges, including their experiences and understanding of the different social world that they inhabit.

Stage Two involved the whole year group in sharing their 'Rivers of Life' within their tutor groups, in which they were allowed to ask positive questions. The underlying intention was to treat the pupils as 'subjects of their experiences rather than as objects of research' (Chase & Bell, 1994, p. 64). By treating them as 'knowers' and agents of personal change, it was hoped to transform the research process into a constructive learning experience in which all those who participate could become more self-aware of personal strengths and needs, and also become aware of, and sensitive to, the experience, needs and strengths of others. At Stage Three, the HOY asked for six volunteers from her year group to participate in individual interviews that were to be tape-recorded.

Pedagogically, the research approach adopted digressed from established norms, in that the teachers would become the listeners and learners, learning to know the pupils as people. In such a learner–teacher relationship, knowledge hierarchies, the fixedness of normative knowledges are challenged; knowledge is produced in the process of interaction, emerges from and is owned by the pupil. Within this framework pedagogy is not something that is done 'to' the pupils; 'it is a complex interaction of at least three agencies – the teacher, the learner and the knowledge they produce together' (Morley, 1998, p. 16). However, this is not to argue that the power position of the teachers had been changed completely. As teacher-researchers, they still maintained control over how long the interview would last, who could speak and for how long. External constraints also defined the context of interaction; for example, the set of questions that framed the interview and discussion had been determined by the researcher.

Overall, and in a more critical sense, the set of activities could provide an insight into the 'categories that students use to construct meaning and to locate themselves in history' (Aronowitz & Giroux, 1991, p. 107). It could also, potentially, provide them with the possibility of learning to reflect upon and understand their socially displaced identities within the broader context of politics, ideology and history – and to reposition themselves as change agents in relation to the dominant definitions that define their lives.

Conceptualizing 'Black' British identities

Afro-Caribbeans represent the first major group of immigrants to arrive from former colonies in the aftermath of mass immigration policies in the 1950s when, during a period of economic boom, workers were recruited to staff the service industries. The identities and subjectivities of this group of people have been shaped very powerfully by the social dislocation effected by slavery, and subsequently, the experience of colonialism followed by immigration settlement in the UK.

Other significant migrations included those from Southern Europe, Cyprus, the Indian sub-continent as well as the Hong Kong Chinese, working predominantly in the catering industry. Again, colonialism played a key role in the shaping of these groups' cultural identities. This was followed during the late 1960s by the arrival of large groups of second- and even third-generation 'Asians' from East Africa. Among these were refugees who had been expelled by the Ugandan regime. Here, colonialism and immigration settlement in their first country of adoption were followed by enforced social displacement to what had previously been their colonial mother country. This migration to the UK was followed by immigrants from the Indian sub-continent and also by Vietnamese refugees. More recently, during the 1970s and 1980s, significant numbers of refugees fleeing poverty, war and political instability arrived from countries as varied as South America, Bangladesh, Lebanon, Bosnia, Somalia, Eritrea and Zaire.

For many of these people, and particularly those from former colonies, their cultural identities have not developed in a 'straight unbroken line, from some fixed origin' (Hall, 1993, p. 395). Rather, they are marked by discontinuity, differences and social displacement. Hall (1993, p. 394) high-lights the complex way in which cultural identities evolve, in his argument that:

> Cultural identities come from somewhere, have histories. But, like everything else which is historical, they undergo constant transformation. Far from being eternally fixed in some essentialist past, they are subject to the continuous 'play' of history, culture and power...cultural identity is a matter of 'becoming' as well as of 'being'. It belongs to the future as much as to the past.

Subjectivities thus forged in an ongoing dialogue between past and present (Bhabha, 1994) are contingent; they are always in the process of becoming. In terms of this, 'black', 'immigrant', 'ethnic minority', 'migrant' or 'refugee' identities cannot be viewed as fixed states of 'being'; they are continually being shaped within and through everyday interactions with the social world. These multiple identities further intersect with social class, gender and generational variables.

Flexible identities

At least three of the pupils interviewed had been born in Britain to parents who, although they would be classified as being 'Asian' in Britain, nevertheless came from different geographical regions, each with its own cultural tradition: Arun's mother was born in India while his father was born in Kenya; Kassim's mother was born in Delhi while his father was from the Punjab; Maria was born in Colombia and emigrated to Britain with her mother, who subsequently married an Afro-Caribbean. These multi-faceted cultural narratives clearly interrupt the binary of a simplistic 'past-present', the representation of the continuity and stability of a 'uniform' tradition, and the possibility for the imagining of a singular 'homeland'. In addition to the mapping of a rich cultural tapestry, it also provides examples of discontinuity, disruption and displacement across time and space. Arun's identity, for example, is marked by the experience of colonialism (British Colonial India) which in turn intersects with that of transportation (indentured labour to the colonies) and then again with enforced social dislocation (expulsion from Kenya), and immigration settlement in the previous 'mother country'. Kassim's identity is marked by regional differences in terms of both customs and traditions, and the forging of a new identity in Britain. While integrating into British society, Maria also seeks to identify with the Afro-Caribbean culture of her stepfather, who is a formative influence in her life.

The complexity of experiences described here serves to illustrate the fact that immigrant groups in Britain are marked by historical and cultural differences from each other, in addition to those that mark them as different from the host culture. Furthermore, different reasons and circumstances underpin their emigration, migration or flight from their countries of origin. Invariably, these experiences have become internalized and interwoven into the text of everyday social life within their country of adoption, and consequently influence both individual and group subjectivities, expectations and aspirations.

Conceptualizing flexible identities

Rather than being something radically new and specific to the project of 'postmodernity' redefining identities has been part of human experience for as long as people have migrated from one region to another, from one country to another, from one continent to another. The process of adaptation involves a reworking of the norms, behaviours, beliefs and values of the culture of origin. This invariably results in the hybridization of cultures over a period of time, which brings its own sets of contradictions, ambiguities and conflict for individuals and groups experiencing that change.

For both Arun and Kassim, the unifying factor is provided by religion, which constitutes the cultural basis of their family life. But far from viewing it as a rigid identity variable, Kassim appears to have synthesized the religious-traditional into his own personal identity, remarking that 'I have traditional views as well as modern…I'm in-between'. Again, this 'in-between-ness' disrupts the signification of him as a culturally homogeneous 'Asian' in dominant discourse. Arun, on the other hand, identifies very strongly with being a Hindu who practises vegetarianism as a religious principle. Manjit, a female participant, has worked with the religious aspect of her identity in a more conscious manner, stating that:

> I do value my background [Sikh] because it is part of who I am, where I come from…my parents…it's where they come from so it's definitely a part of me…but the so-called family values and tradition…some of it is OK but some of it is too backward…so you've got to give a little and take a little. I've taken a bit of my parents' background and I'm changing it a little bit because of the influences where I live…I don't think it's the religion that is constraining, I think it's more the tradition, for example, arranged marriages.

Here, then, we have an example of conscious hybridization as part of the way of adapting to new influences within a different cultural terrain. For her, cultural hybridity forms part of the sense of 'self-identification'. The latter term refers to 'the cognitive re-appropriation of the categories of racialized and genderized subjugation, and the process of encoding these with empowering meanings as part of the struggle to maintain control over [her] everyday life' (Rassool, 1997a, p. 191). Drawing on her 'knowledge-ability' (Giddens, 1984), Manjit and, to some extent, Kassim were able to engage in the construction of a discursive narrative of the self in which culture is made malleable as part of the act of social survival – and in the process, carving out a new cultural space to inhabit. This gives some credence to the view that, transferred across space and time, cultural identities inevitably become transmuted and therefore gain in complexity. At the same time, as is evident in her allusion to arranged marriages, hybridized cultures existing as minority groups within a broader dominant culture always exist in conflict, contradiction and ambiguity.

Cultural hybridity, as part of the project of redefinition, can be seen, to a large extent, as a reactive, self-defining strategy forged within a context circumscribed by unequal power relations between dominant and subordinate minority cultures in the framework of the metropolitan nation-state. As such, it is always partial and provisional; it does not necessarily signify assimilation. Rather, it works to redefine difference in dialogue with structures that serve to reproduce existing relations, and in so doing, to rework these into a project of possibility. This system of engagement, of course, differs fundamentally from the notion of cultural hybridity that inheres in the concept of cosmopolitanism. Within the framework discussed here, cultural hybridity is created by the struggle of those often living at the outer edge of society, for survival, social belonging and self-definition. 'Self-definition' places emphasis on the affective process through which gendered and racialized subjects engage in an ongoing process of critique, evaluation, negotiation, self-affirmation and validation of themselves, in relation to their experiences in everyday life. The notion of cultural hybridity referred to here evolves within a context of unequal social relations, of privileged voices, of dominant cultural forms and practices. As such, it constitutes an important contesting variable. Cosmopolitanism, on the other hand, represents a chic lifestyle choice exercised by a small international elite group.

Fracturing national certainties

Cultural hybridization is, nevertheless, a two-way process of change. Migration space and time bring together dissonant narratives. New sets of social relations are events that fracture previous certainties (Rassool, 1997b). It brings chaos to the hegemony of 'culturally stable nations'. Minority cultures challenge the homogeneity of national cultures from within by changing expected behaviours and experiences of and within everyday life (Massey, 1994). Moreover in time 'they create their own cultural space within which they can express their need to suffuse society with a plurality of dissenting political voices, articulating demands, [that] often conflict with, or challenge the hegemony of ethnic nationalism' (Rassool, 1997a, p. 189). On the one hand, this often gives rise to a reactive 'anti-immigrant' racist regime, as was the case with the rise of the National Front and the British National Party in the 1970s in Britain. On the other hand, it also stimulates the emergence of new identities actively engaged in counter-struggle, ultimately redefining the parameters of social action. In the case of Britain, we can refer to the development of, *inter alia*, the Organization of Women of Asian and African Descent (OWAAD) which operated nationally to combat racial, sexist and class discrimination during the 1970s, the formation of the Southall Black Sisters Group and the Anti-Nazi League that emerged to combat racism during the late 1970s. With regard to OWAAD and the Southall Black Sisters, Brah (1996, p. 107) suggests that:

> The devaluation of black cultures by the onslaught of racism meant that for some women the priority was to 'reclaim' these cultural sites and to situate themselves 'as women' within them...Other women argued that, while affirmation of cultural identity was indeed crucial, it was equally important to address cultural practices in their oppressive forms.

The latter refers particularly to the problem of male violence, forced marriages, circumcision and the suppression of issues related to homosexuality within some communities. Again, a dynamic and complex process of social change is indicated: while these were new modes and forms of political organization which emerged to refract the imagined worlds of culturally cohesive nations, they were also consciously aimed at fracturing historically derived patriarchal oppressive religious-cultural practices.

Countering gendered identities

The girls participating in the study have learned to self-identify as women living in a different culture, and all have found it a liberating experience. According to Maria, when she returned for a visit to Colombia,

> although I enjoyed it, I did not like the way girls are treated...just staying home, cleaning and cooking. They were not allowed to go out...when I used to go out they used to call me a tomboy or [say] that I was not a 'proper' girl, they thought I was very different.

Socialized gendered subjectivities, then, are not the preserve only of 'Asian' culture. Manjit's family had been traumatized after her older sister ran away from home because of an arranged marriage. Since that time, her family has changed its approach and, as a result, seeking a future life partner is more of a collaborative affair in which the girls also have a say. She is not opposed in principle to the idea of having an arranged marriage, as long as her views are taken into account in making the choice. For Azra, her family's willingness for her to participate fully in a broad social life has meant that she has relative control over what she wears and does, not an option that she would have in Pakistan, 'I would have to cover myself up, not wear any jewellery or make up and stay at home every day cooking...Here I'm not that restricted.' Again, this highlights the extent to which her parents have modified and adapted to the norms of Western society.

Heimat and Heimweh

In response to feeling excluded from mainstream society, many second-generation immigrant youths often revert to traditional cultural practices as part of the psychological and geographical pilgrimage to the 'homeland'. According to Maira (1996), this shift stems from many layers of experience, many of them imbued with emotional significance, that give rise to wishes to learn more about family history or to feel a sense of belonging. In Azra's case, after a difficult period in middle school, she visited Pakistan, 'I got to meet my relatives for the first time and learned about my background.' She felt that this was important: it helped to place her in a wider context of cultural and familial origin, to 'learn more about my parents' past and why certain things are important to them'.

For many second-generation youths, returning to their cultural and religious roots has formed an important part of disidentifying with the dominant culture, a means of rejecting the culture of those who reject and marginalize them as 'other'. Thus, it is a consciously reactive response to societal racism and social exclusion. On the other hand, some use religion as a self-defining process during moments of personal difficulty. Azra, for example, resorted to religion during a period of adolescent crisis:

> then I discovered my religion, I went to *madressa* [muslim religious classes] after school, I prayed every day and that made me think about responsibility and about the future...religion has made me more sensible, makes me think more about the future and...stop mucking about.

Rather than retrogressively, simplistically adopting religion, she uses it reflexively as a self-identifying variable. This contrasts somewhat with generalizations regarding the inherently oppressive nature of the Muslim religion, especially as it relates to women. It may not always be something that is imposed on women, sometimes they may choose to enter that world as a space for reflection, for a period of time. Indeed, Azra explained that although her parents are religious, they do not impose their traditional views on her: 'I can wear what I like, my parents are OK. My parents don't want me to look different to other people, they want me to be part of this [British] community as well.' Again, this points to a conscious hybridization as part of the process of adapting to new or different social mores. There are expectations within the 'host society', to blend in, to belong by the parents. This is being reworked by Azra as a means of defining herself as part of growing up. This contrasts somewhat with the stereotype of the authoritarian and conservative 'Asian' family, which is seen as existing in a constant state of inter-generational conflict.

The emphasis on religion as an identity variable in the 'Asian' community contrasts with the experience of Maria, who, although she defines her family as being Christian, stated that the issue of religion does not influence greatly the way in which she identifies herself in Britain, 'because I'm in a Christian country'. Seemingly then, religion represents a stronger identity variable for those with religious-cultural roots outside the Christian/Judaic tradition, which constitutes a defining principle of Western 'civilized' society.

Community, racism, culture and belonging

Living in a culturally diverse community produced a sense of security and belonging for all those interviewed. This was expressed in certain ways. Kassim argued that the multicultural community that he lived in

> plays a big part in what I am, because if I lived in another area such as Acton or Northolt [less culturally mixed areas] I would not be like I am...I would feel different. I feel comfortable about my culture and my religion and I have many friends...I hang out...we go to bhangra disco...I can do normal things that interest me.

This provides a good example of the evolution of new hybridized forms of culture, playing an important role in introducing aspects of the different cultures that frame the pupils' lives while, simultaneously, serving as a powerful means of disidentifying with mainstream youth 'pop' culture. Kassim's reference to the fact that his experience of everyday life would have been different in a less culturally diverse community is an example of the extent to which ethnic minority groups have internalized the ubiquity of societal racism and highlights his tacit knowledge of the realities of everyday life as an immigrant in Britain – the ever present possibility of being excluded on the basis of his skin colour or 'ethnicity' – of not 'belonging'. Living in a culturally diverse area means that he is confident about expressing himself in terms of his religion and culture.

For Azra's family, it was a conscious decision to live in the borough because 'it is a multicultural community'. For her, Elmwood provides insulation against the wider world which she perceives and has experienced as being racist: 'I feel uncomfortable with white people...not in Elmwood but outside. I feel very scared in case something happens...I don't want to leave Elmwood.' Having had similar experiences to Maria she views the problem in a different way. She argues that 'living in Elmwood you find you're quite isolated from everything else that is happening. Because it's multicultural you learn a lot from each other...but when you go out [of Elmwood], it is much more different.' In contrast to Azra, she would like to leave the area to travel and 'hopes [to] learn more about England'. It could be argued that Azra's lack of confidence in the world outside Elmwood relates to the comfort that the warm, insulating environment of a 'ghettoized' culture (which developed in response to the racism that exists in society as a whole) can bring, while not preparing her for participating more in everyday life or addressing the realities of societal racism.

To the question of how the pupils define themselves culturally, Arun described himself as a member of the 'Asian community', and Azra describes her family as 'Pakistanis in England'; others felt that they would describe themselves as British citizens but 'non-British' culturally. There was strong feeling among the group about the fact that the pejorative term 'Paki' is used as an insult against all 'Asian' people, and about racism within their own communities, some of whom use 'the white stereotype to place people into boxes...to let out frustration, and because of conflict between groups'. These forms of inverted racism and other forms of internalized oppression highlight the fact that the black British experience is fundamentally different and, moreover, that it is riven with inner contradictions, 'racial' tensions and inter-ethnic group discrimination.

Maria clearly sees herself as being 'different' to the 'Asian' students. At the same time she has reworked her understanding of living as a member of a broader community and has managed to develop an informed and mature perspective on societal racism. She argued that:

> if I had lived in another area, I might have been racist, but because I live in Elmwood, you learn that although people live in different cultures, as people, they are basically the same. I think that I've learned a lot of things...that the world is only that big...and racist people do not know much about the world.

Maria felt very strongly about the fact that she had experienced racism from one of her teachers who had referred to Colombia as 'a country full of crime and drugs...and that children of drug dealers are dumb'. This highlights the ubiquity of racist cultural/national stereotypes that still prevail and illustrates the casual way in which children are exposed to it on an everyday basis, sometimes by those who teach them. What strategies do children have to combat such personal violations? Maria's response to this cultural stereotype was to study hard – obtaining an A Star in Spanish at GCSE level, one year ahead of her year group. As such, she used this racist encounter as a self-defining principle. After a difficult period initially, because she did not speak English, she decided to change her views:

> I want to prove that I can do things, that I can be someone...I just decided that Elmwood is full of people from different communities and that they were all struggling to show other people that they're not stupid just because they come from another country...and I felt the same. I think that living in Elmwood has helped me a lot...if I'd lived in another area, I would have continued to blame the other [white] culture, instead of working with myself.

Again, it shows evidence of reflexivity, to redefine herself as a person in the face of the racist practices that seek to silence and make invisible those who are culturally/ethnically defined as the 'other'.

Although their perspectives differed, all those interviewed were united in the belief that they learned and benefited from living in a multicultural community. Yet for all of them, there is still an 'other' world out there which is potentially hostile, unwelcoming and exclusionary. Nevertheless, they all have high ambitions relating to the professions they want to pursue (e.g. architect, medical doctor), and see education as providing them with the opportunity to participate effectively in the wider world. Similarly, all found their families highly supportive of their studies without putting too much pressure on them. Manjit, for example, recounted her dad telling her early on that 'life is very short and you have to go out and make it for yourself'. The need to 'get on' with their lives featured very strongly in the discussions with the students in the interview sample. The strong support that 'black' parents give to their children's education has been well documented (Stone, 1981; Mirza, 1992). The dissatisfaction among parents about the lack of equity, social justice and quality meted out in the education system has led to a sustained rise in supplementary educational provision among black immigrant groups. Mirza found that black parents attach a high value to education and subscribe very powerfully to the meritocratic ideal; they strongly identify with credentialism. This is borne out in the high expectations and aspirations that these families and their children have with regard to education. Again, the belief in education as a means of access to power and empowerment has been a rich and recurring theme among immigrant communities throughout the world. It provides an important means of self-identification, of reworking the 'self' in relation to the realities of the social worlds that they inhabit.

Conclusion

This paper has focused on the individual speaking subject, and has described each of them in turn in terms of their own articulations of the social world. Thus, it has positioned students as real, coherent participants engaged in a constant negotiation of meaning in the social world. Underlying this was the view that the conscious positioning of social actors in relation to the social world, and encouraging the questioning of constructed norms and inequalities, would allow them to produce theories about the world in which they live – and, ultimately, to act on them (Rassool, 1998). The limited nature of the study leaves questions about how successfully this was achieved. In placing the individual speaking subject at the centre of my analysis, I wanted to concentrate on the children themselves – to hear them speak their lives in their own voices. I wanted them to have the opportunity, in an educational context, to articulate their understandings of how they perceive the social world, and operate in the multiple worlds that they inhabit. Central to this methodological approach is the view derived from oral historians, who argue that 'people are not stamped into place by history and culture, but patch together a place for themselves...[and that] in personal statements we see the power of the individual to compose the terms of [her] life' (Modell, 1983, p. 11). Placing emphasis on cognitive awareness, personal knowledge and reflexivity, I wanted to explore also the range of strategies that they use to chart their own lives, to negotiate a space which would later, as adults, help them to occupy a place as active citizens within British/European society. In making them aware of themselves as thinking people able to reflect on their lives and social experience, it was hoped to examine the ways in which they make their internalized oppressions transparent through the processes of self-definition and self-identification.

Starting from the particular and the everyday provided the opportunity to 'critically appropriate the voices of those who had been silenced and to help move the voices of those who have been located within narratives that are monolithic and totalizing – beyond indifference – to emancipatory practice' (Giroux, 1992, p. 76). Thus, the study formed part of a broader project grounded in critical pedagogy; in this instance, providing pupils with the opportunity to explore their 'border lives' (Bhabha, 1994), and helping them to develop critical and reflexive self-awareness. It is hoped that participating in the activities contributed, albeit in a limited way, to their awareness of themselves as young people growing up in Britain. Although they acknowledged difficulties where these existed, all expressed positive feelings about their cultures. They felt confident about who they were and had a vision of how they would like to develop as adults. All have drawn significantly on their cultures, community and family for support in their development. Other than Maria, this was also the case with religion. They all possess a rich language and cultural repertoire and are flexible in their ability to switch and make adjustments suited to the context in which they find themselves. They could articulate complex feelings and experiences with clarity and displayed a developed sense of understanding of the multiple social worlds that they inhabit. Although they have all experienced some form of racist prejudice, they have developed different strategies to deal with it when it arises. They are dynamic and positive and, despite the fears expressed by Azra, all are focused on the task of becoming integrated members of the society in which they live. Brah (1996, p. 47), describing politicized black identities, argues that in the case of the second generation:

> they lay claim to the localities in which they live as their 'home'. And, however much they may be constructed as 'outsiders', they contest these psychological and geographical spaces from the position of 'insiders'. Even when they describe themselves as 'Asian', this is not a reaching back to some 'primordial Asian' identity. What they are speaking of is a modality of 'British Asian-ness'. These home-grown Asian-British identities inaugurate a fundamental *generational* change.

Using the 'Rivers of Life' activity and focus group discussion provided useful opportunities to explore complexities. The activities were integrally linked with a conscious evaluation of the past and a projection towards allowing the participants to chart the building blocks that are in place towards a self-actual. In this sense, the concept of identity became that of 'self-identification'. They are not a homogeneous group culturally, nor do they live their lives according to cultural stereotypes; there have been major generational transformations. The interviews have illustrated Brah's (1996) view that although inter-generational differences do occur they do not necessarily represent conflict. Indeed, the parents of most of these pupils have been instrumental in supporting the process of change and adaptation. The pupils feel that they belong in Britain and want to participate as citizens; they have learned the skills of living what Bhabha (1994) refers to as 'border lives'. Clearly the issues of cultural hybridization, adaptation and redefinition need to be taken into account as part of the wider aim of maximizing the educational potential of children in 'ethnic minority' groups. Moreover, this highlights the need for education, especially in the later secondary school years, to take on board the issue of providing pupils with the necessary tools to operate in a world that, to a significant extent, is still exclusionary. The difficulties they face do not relate to their living between 'two cultures', or to 'identity', as is often presumed. The interviews have shown that they are quite comfortable with their multiple and multi-faceted identities; that often, despite daily experiences of racism, they are able to work reflexively in constituting themselves as fully integrated people in British society. This bears out the argument that oppressive or exclusionary meanings, structured in a variety of discourses, including political, are not necessarily assimilated in an unproblematic way by those who have been objectified. Rather, the major problems that they will have to face later in life are the specific ones that, potentially, may render them 'invisible', disempowered, disillusioned and unfulfilled. One of the issues pertinent to them as young people growing up in Britain is the fact that the problem of representation of black people generally remains more than 30 years after the first major arrival of 'black' immigrants. These people are, on the whole, largely absent – and where they do feature, it is often in negative and stereotypical roles, or 'novelty'/token positions. These pupils need evidence of positive and dynamic role models in public life that they can identify with to give them a sense of what is possible and what they can approximate. At a basic level, they need the means to cope with the systemic aspects of racism that are reflected in organizational cultures, and with the structural barriers that exclude them from full and equal participation in everyday life. Here we can see the endemic racism of organizational cultures and its impact on recruitment, training and mentoring, retention and promotion possibilities, the power of gatekeepers, job ghettoization, career entrapment and pay differentials (Davidson, 1997). Together, these systemic variables constitute the 'concrete' ceiling that may prevent such pupils ultimately from fulfilling their hopes, dreams and desires as citizens within society.

References

Aronowitz, S. and Giroux, H. (1991) *Postmodern Education: Politics, Culture and Social Criticism.* Oxford, MN: University of Minnesota Press.

Bhabha, H. (1994) *The Location of Culture.* London: Routledge.

Brah, A. (1996) *Cartographies of Diaspora: Contesting Identities.* London: Routledge.

Chase, S.E. and Bell, S.L. (1994) Interpreting the complexity of women's subjectivity. In: E.M. McMahan and K. Lacy Rogers (Eds) *Interactive Oral History Interviewing,* pp. 63–82. Hove: Lawrence Erlbaum Associates.

Davidson, M.J. (1997) *The Black and Ethnic Minority Woman Manager: Cracking the Concrete Ceiling.* London: Paul Chapman.

Giddens, A. (1984) *The Constitution of Society.* Cambridge: Polity Press.

Giddens, A. (1991) *Modernity and Self-identity: Sex and Society in the Late Modern Age.* Cambridge: Polity Press.

Giroux, H. (1992) *Border Crossings: Cultural Workers and the Politics of Education.* London: Routledge.

Hall, S. (1993) Cultural identity and diaspora. In: P. Williams and L. Chrisman (Eds) *Colonial Discourse and Post-Colonial Theory,* pp. 392–403. New York: Harvester Wheatsheaf.

Home Office (1981) *West Indian Children in our Schools.* Interim Report of the Committee of Inquiry into the Education of Children from Ethnic Minority Groups. Chairman: Anthony Rampton, OBE. London: HMSO.

Maira, S. (1996) *Making Room for a Hybrid Space: Reconsidering Second-Generation Ethnic Identity.* http://webgenesis.com/rapture/worldbeat/india/hybrid_space. html.

Massey, D. (1994) *Space, Place and Gender.* Cambridge: Polity Press.

Mirza, H.S. (1992) *Young, Female and Black.* London: Routledge.

Modell, J. (1983) Stories and strategies: the use of personal statements, *International Journal of Oral History,* **4**(1), pp. 4–11.

Morley, L.M. (1998) All you need is love: feminist pedagogy for empowerment and emotional labour in the academy, *International Journal of Inclusive Education,* **2**(1), pp. 15–27.

National Foundation for Educational Research (NFER) (1966) *Coloured Immigrant Children: A Survey of Research Studies and Literature on their Educational Problems and Potential in Britain,* Slough: NFER.

Rassool, N. (1995) Black women as the 'other' in the academy. In: L. Morley and V. Walsh (Eds) *Feminist Academics: Creative Agents for Change,* pp. 22–41. Basingstoke: Taylor & Francis.

Rassool, N. (1997a) Fractured or flexible identities? Life histories of 'black' diasporic women in Britain. In: H.S. Mirza (Ed.) *Black Feminism: A Reader,* pp. 187–201. London: Routledge.

Rassool, N. (1997b) Postmodernity, cultural pluralism and the nation-state: problems of language rights, human rights, identity and power, *Language Sciences,* **20**(1), pp. 89–99.

Rassool, N. (1998) *Literacy for Sustainable Development in the Age of Information.* Clevedon: Multilingual Matters.

Stone, M. (1981) *The Education of the Black Child. The Myth of Multicultural Education.* London: Fontana Press.

Commentary: Naz Rassool

Starting points

My background was a significant factor in channelling me towards doing research on the construction of black 'identities' in the UK and, in this instance, identity formation in education. I was born in South Africa and grew up under the Apartheid regime's policies of *eiesoortigheid* or 'ethnic purity' that delimited the life experiences of various population groups whose identity, officially, was defined in terms of their 'ethnic' origins. This ordering constituted a political, cultural, social and economic hierarchy in which whites of various ethnic origins were positioned at the apex, and African population groups were located at the base. An acute sense of 'Otherness' permeated almost all aspects of everyday life, as people were required to label themselves as 'white/non-white' in order to partake of their differentially allocated civic entitlements such as housing, voting, etc. Thus my earliest sense of identity evolved within a social context defined by a rigid process of 'racial' classification that was monitored under the gaze of both the police and the state security apparatus. I grew up with a keen awareness, at least subconsciously, of structured 'Otherness', and of the mutability of the concept of identity. That is to say, it can be imposed or socially constructed, and it can also be self-defined; it is therefore subject to change and manipulation.

During the early 1970s I transmigrated to the UK where I encountered more subtle, yet more potent forms of exclusion – as against those I experienced in South Africa, where racism was blatant and the social exclusion of black people formed the basis of social policy. Exclusion in the UK arose out of a more indirect cultural racism that permeated practices and processes in social institutions. This contributed to systemic discrimination against immigrant groups largely from former colonies, particularly the Caribbean, India/Pakistan/Bangladesh, Uganda and Kenya. Different categories of racial description prevailed – non-white people were either 'West Indian', 'Asian', or 'African' despite the fact that the Caribbean Islands constitute an archipelago, and Africa and Asia represent vast continents inhabited by diverse groups of people all having different histories. These categories of description therefore constituted homogenizing labels. Derogatory terms such as 'coon', 'Paki' and 'wog' were common referents in popular discourse, especially in television sitcoms and stand-up comic routines. This was a major culture shock to me, coming from a 'racially' stratified society with notions of a free world outside. I did not quite realize the extent of racism outside the boundaries of Apartheid South Africa. What was even more disconcerting was the extent to which immigrant children in the classes that I taught had internalized these racist categories and were using them as terms of abuse against one another. I became aware that schooling for many of these pupils was an experience full of conflict with its origins in a lack of identity in relation to the dominant culture. Within British society at the time the concept of identity was closely tied in with an ethnocentric cultural 'belonging'. 'Britishness' was defined in terms of an ethnically homogeneous norm, that is, a white cultural heritage and tradition. Immigrant groups became the *de facto* 'Other'.

Over the years as I came to terms with the evolution of my own identity, I became interested in how black immigrant groups identified themselves within this context. How they made sense of their lives, the strategies that they adopted in order to survive, and the ways in which they inserted themselves into mainstream life. I had a personal interest in examining identity formation in relation to my own fractured past.

Research questions

This particular research built on two previous case studies in which I explored the construction of black women's identities in contemporary British society. The main findings of both these studies were first, that black people are not static subjects, that they are actively engaged in shaping their own lives. Second, black identities are not linear constructions but richly textured cultural tapestries that continue to evolve within the context of everyday life. Building on these findings this research aimed to gain insight into how immigrant pupils relate to life in modern Britain. This refers to:

- how they identify as citizens and as students;
- how interactions and events in their everyday lives shape them;
- how, in turn, they construct the process of schooling, and the society in which they live;
- the nature of the cultural choices that they make as an integral part of their survival;
- the dilemmas that these choices often present, how meanings are negotiated and the compromises that immigrant children need to make in order to belong;
- their dreams and aspirations as future adults within this society.

The research thus developed around several questions centred on aspects of identity formation in education.

Early thinking processes

Whilst these were very interesting and potentially exciting areas to look into, the fact that I intended to work with a group of young people between the ages of 14 and 15 raised several practical and ethical issues. First, I was concerned that the issues to be explored were of a very personal nature, that the pupils were in a critical phase of their development when the world can be quite a confusing place, and when great uncertainty often surrounds identity, relationships and belonging. I was aware that these issues had to be handled in a sensitive manner. Second, it was important that the pupils should not be exploited emotionally. The research therefore had to be sensitively done yet be thorough in its investigation of the different aspects of identity formation. These ethical issues were paramount in deciding whether the proposed research was a viable undertaking – and these concerns persisted throughout the research process. Third, I was concerned that I would not be able to find a large enough group of pupils willing to discuss their personal experiences and their views – and, moreover, that they would not be able to engage at a level that would answer some of the research questions. The choice of school would therefore be of major importance as would be my relationship with the teachers. At this stage I did not quite realize the extent to which I would depend on them for the success of the project.

The most effective way of collecting data was also a central consideration. I was aware of the many pressures under which teachers were working in schools, and that intrusion into their teaching context as well as the extra demands placed on them by academic researchers added further stress. It would be important to find a means of conducting the research in order to cause minimal disruption to teachers' routines and classroom life. It would help significantly, for example, if the research could link with ongoing activities within the year group and, more importantly, link with the school development plan. After much deliberation the idea came to mind that if positioned within the pastoral care programme the research could potentially contribute to pupils' personal development and also support some of the school's development aims. The problem was to find appropriate activities.

Fourth, there were the questions of what criteria to use in choosing the school, and what would be the best way to approach this. The main criterion was that the school should represent a wide range of cultures from different generations. I chose an inner-city school within the London area where I had an excellent relationship, developed over many years, with the Head of Year responsible for the pastoral needs of Year 10 pupils. The reason for this was that the sensitive nature of the research required careful coordination and the full support of the pastoral team. The school had an excellent reputation for its policies on inclusion, as well as working closely and sensitively with its diverse communities.

The question now was how best to frame the research theoretically, and to find the most effective way of addressing the research questions. It seemed that exploration of the construction of 'black' British identities incorporating the concepts of cultural hybridity, social change, gendered and racialized identities, systemic racism, religion, culture, knowledgeability, and individual reflexivity would provide a useful theoretical framework.

Choice of methodology

Since I was interested in accessing pupils' perceptions of their actions, behaviours, interactions, experiences and choices a qualitative approach was deemed appropriate. The exploratory nature of the project indicated that a small in-depth study would be more suitable than a broad overview involving large numbers of participants. In order to explore the multifaceted nature of pupils' identity formation, and considering the personal nature of the information that they were asked, it would be important for me to get to know them well enough to trust me. The options were that I could choose to work with them in their tutor groups or select a group with whom I could work over a period of time. I was concerned that what I intended to do might be construed as prying into their lives. I wanted them to maintain their self-respect at all times. I also wanted as much of the information to come from them in a situation that, although structured, they would not find intimidating. After discussing the different options with the Head of Year we decided to devise a programme of activities that could fit into the current Personal, Social and Moral Education programme. Instead of me as an outsider working separately with a group of pupils, we decided that it would be more effective if we could involve the whole year group in the research. In doing this tutors would become part of the research by introducing activities (that I would devise) to their tutor groups, and provide support. In turn tutors would benefit by learning to know their pupils on a different level, and it would also develop their skills as teacher-researchers. Ultimately a small group to be interviewed would be arrived at by asking for volunteers following the main classroom-based activities. The bulk of the data collection would be done by the teachers – with me observing each class for part of each lesson, and the final interviews being conducted by the Head of Year and myself.

In order to generate common understandings of the purpose and process of the research, I had to do two one-hour-long workshops with the staff involved. This revolved mainly around the aims of the research, ethical issues, and the purpose of doing the activities with the pupils. I remained concerned, however, that I was outside the actual research process to a significant extent, and that the quality of the data might be affected as a result since the teachers were not experienced researchers. Other ethical issues revolved around obtaining both pupils' and parental permission – was this necessary if the exercise formed part of their teaching programme? Since the ultimate purpose was to answer the research questions, it was imperative that all the normal ethical issues associated with working with human subjects – and especially children – applied.

Data decisions

What would count as data was a major consideration, especially since much depended on a teaching activity. As my main aim was to get to know the pupils in considerable detail, I needed to build up a biography of each pupil. If this was constructed by the pupils it could provide insight into different aspects of their identity formation, allowing them to reflect on their past lives, the events and experiences that have influenced them, the various strategies that they have adopted to define themselves, and to set goals for the future. I decided that the 'Rivers of Life' activity, if carefully structured, would provide a useful mechanism with which to build up a composite picture of each individual's development trajectory, including their development goals for the future. These potentially would provide useful information on how they perceive themselves as individuals, as learners, as children of their parents, as members of communities, as citizens in everyday life. It could also be particularly useful in identifying key mechanisms in their development as well as the constraints that they have had to overcome. Hopefully it would develop pupils' self-awareness of their strengths and weaknesses.

The diagrammatically represented 'Rivers of Life' constituted a major data source but would only be useful with commentary on their construction. Sharing their life histories with the rest of the group would therefore provide rich data whilst at the same time also developing their ability to articulate their own experiences, their awareness of the experiences of others, and more importantly, sensitivity towards others' life experiences. Tutors were asked to tape-record this sharing activity and provide the name of each contributor.

The interviews that followed would enable issues to be explored at a deeper level, allowing the pupils to give more opinions and to adopt a reflective perspective on themselves in relation to their parents, their culture, their teachers and society.

I was confident that the study had a strong theoretical base, and that it was informed by previous research within the area. However, the fact that much of the research itself was being managed and executed by the teachers was a rather novel approach. Whilst I was more secure in the knowledge that the pupils would be treated in a sensitive manner, I was still concerned about whether I would obtain enough data to answer the research questions.

Hindsight reflections

Although it delivered very useful insights, I was nevertheless disappointed with the data collected in the 'Rivers of Life' activity as the tape-recording of the feedback sessions did not take place in all the classes, and the fact that the pupils were not identified meant that I could not follow through their stories in the interviews. Ideally these should have been videotaped. The interview data were very interesting although if doing a similar project in future, I would opt to conduct the interviews myself. I would prefer also to have a group discussion with a whole class, which would be videotaped. A discussion would allow for more interaction, and perhaps richer data.

I was excited that the concept of 'black' identities that emerged in the study bore out some of the findings of my earlier studies in the area. It showed complexity and a high level of engagement by the pupils in constructing their identities and, to a large extent, engaging reflexively in defining their place within contemporary British society. How much the exercise enabled teachers to get to know their pupils was evident in some of the comments they made to me in subsequent conversations. Again, this aspect could have been discussed and explored further. Should the teachers have been involved in the way that they were? I still think that it was the best means of dealing sensitively with the pupils. The teaching approach was deemed to have been successful by the teachers, and it has now been incorporated into a getting-to-know-you exercise and goal-setting at the start of Year 7.

My next project will again use personal narrative as a means to explore 'black identities' in relation to career trajectories.

13

Gender Play: Girls and Boys in School
BARRIE THORNE

This is an abridged extract from the book: Thorne, B. (1993) *Gender Play: Girls and Boys in School*, New Brunswick, NJ: Rutgers University Press.

When I first entered the Oceanside fourth–fifth-grade classroom as a note-taking visitor, I thought of myself as an ethnographer with an interest in gender and the social life of children. Beyond that, I had not given much reflection to what I was bringing to the research. But I slowly came to realise that within the ethnographer, many selves were at play. Responding to our shared positions as adult women and as teachers, I easily identified with Miss Bailey and the other school staff. Being around so many children also stirred my more maternal emotions and perspectives. Occasionally I felt much like the fourth-and-fifth-grader I used to be, and the force of this took me by surprise. This jangling chorus of selves gave me insight into the complexity of being an adult trying to learn from kids. Hearing first one, then another, of these different selves, or types of consciousness, helped shape what I discovered and how I put my ideas together.

Like Westerners doing fieldwork in colonised Third World cultures, or academics studying the urban poor, when adults research children they 'study down,' seeking an understanding across lines of difference and inequality. When the research is within their own culture, the 'studying down' comes swathed in a sense of familiarity. Despite their structural privilege, Western ethnographers who enter a radically different culture find themselves in the humbling stance of a novice. But it is hard to think of one's self as a novice when studying those who are defined as learners of one's own culture. To learn *from* children, adults have to challenge the deep assumption that they already know what children are 'like,' both because, as former children, adults have been there, and because, as adults, they regard children as less complete versions of themselves. When adults seek to learn about and from children, the challenge is to take the closely familiar and to render it strange.

When I started observing in the Oceanside School, I set out to learn about gender in the context of kids' interactions with one another. I began to accompany fourth- and fifth-graders in their daily round of activities by stationing myself in the back of Miss Bailey's classroom, sitting in the scaled-down chairs and standing and walking around the edges, trying to grasp different vantage points. I was clearly not a full participant; I didn't have a regular desk, and I watched and took notes, rather than doing the classroom work. As the kids lined up, I watched, and then I walked alongside, often talking with them, as they moved between the classroom, lunchroom, music room, and library. At noontime I sat and ate with the fourth- and fifth-graders at their too crowded cafeteria tables, and I left with them when they headed for noontime recess on the playground. Wanting to understand their social divisions and the varied perspectives they entailed, I alternated the company I kept, eating with different groups and moving among the various turfs and activities of the playground.

In Ashton, the Michigan school, I also followed the kids' cycle of activities, but I stuck less closely to one classroom and its students. I observed in a kindergarten and in a second-grade classroom, and I spent a lot of time in the lunchroom and on the playground mapping all the groups and trying to get an overview of the school and its organisation.

Looking back on my presence in both schools, I see how much I claimed the free-lancing privilege of an adult visitor. I could, and did, come and go, shift groups, choose and alter my daily routines.

I entered students' interactions to varying degrees. In teaching settings like classrooms and the Oceanside music room and auditorium, I felt most like an observer. In the lunchrooms I joined more fully in kids' interactions by eating, conversing, and sometimes trading food with them. On the playgrounds I usually roamed and watched from the margins of ongoing activities, although I often talked with kids and sometimes joined groups of girls playing jump rope and games like 'statue buyer.' I was continually struck by kids' forms of physicality and by the structures of authority that separate them from adults.

Kids' physicality and imagination

Watching kids day after day, especially on the playground, I was struck by their quick movements and high levels of energy, the rapidity with which they formed and reformed groups and activities. Public schools are unusually crowded environments, which intensifies the sense of chaos; the playgrounds were often thick with moving bodies.

After I had observed for several months, I saw much more order in the chaos, and I developed strategies for recording rapidly shifting and episodic activity. For example, when I entered the playground, I went on an initial tour, making an inventory of groups and activities. Then I focused on specific groups or individuals, sometimes following them from one activity to another, or from formation to dispersal. I tried to spend time in all the playground niches.

I was struck not only by kids' rapid movements but also by their continual engagement with one another's bodies – poking, pushing, tripping, grabbing a hat or scarf, pinning from behind. Since adults in our culture experience such gestures as invasions of personal space, I initially interpreted these engagements as more antagonistic than, I realised over time, the kids seemed to experience or intend. Trying to sort out playful from serious intent alerted me to the nuances of kids' meanings and to my personal readiness to look for trouble, a readiness magnified by my outlooks as a teacher and a mother.

I came to relish kids' playful use of their bodies, their little experiments in motion and sound, such as moving around the classroom with exaggerated hobbling or a swaggering hula, bouncing in a chair as if riding a horse, clucking like hens or crowing like roosters, returning to a desk by jerking, making engine noises, and screeching like the brakes of a car. They wrote on their bodies with pencil and pen and transformed hands into game boards by writing 'push here' across their palms. They held contests to see who could push their eyeballs farthest back and show the most white, or hold their eyes crossed for the longest time. Sometimes these performances were private, at other times, constructed with dramatic flair and a call for an audience.

Getting around adult authority

I entered the field through adult gatekeepers. A friend introduced me to Miss Bailey, the fourth–fifth-grade Oceanside teacher, and she, in turn, agreed to let me observe in her classroom, as did Mr Welch, the school principal, who asked only that I not 'disrupt' and that I report back my findings. My more formal entry into Ashton School, via district Title IX office, seemed to make the Ashton principal a little nervous. But Mrs Smith, the kindergarten teacher, and Mrs Johnson, the second-grade teacher, seemed at ease when I was in their classrooms, and I had ample latitude to define my presence to the students of both schools.

In both schools I asked kids as well as staff to call me by my first name, and I called the staff by their first names when we spoke directly with one another. But when I talked with kids, and that's where I did most of my talking as well as watching, I joined them in using titles to refer to the teachers and principals.

I went through the school days with a small spiral notebook in hand, jotting descriptions that I later expanded into fieldnotes. One girl who asked if I was 'taking down names' voiced what seemed to be their major fear: that I was recording 'bad' behaviour and that my record would get them into trouble. I assured them again and again that I would not use their real names and that I would not report anything to the teachers, principal, or aides. But of course what I wrote was not under their control, and, like all fieldworkers, I lived with ambiguous ethics. I guarded the information from local exposure, but intended it, with identities disguised, for a much larger audience. I was the sole judge of what was or was not reported and how to alter identifying information.

Although the teachers made few formal demands that drew me into their orbits of authority, they sometimes turned to me for a kind of adult companionship in the classrooms. While the students were seated, I usually stood and roamed the back, while the teacher often stood in front. That arrangement spatially aligned me with the teacher, and it was easy for our adult eyes to meet, literally above the heads of the kids. When something amusing or annoying happened, the teacher would sometimes catch my eye and smile or shake her head in a moment of collusive, non-verbal, and private adult commentary. During those moments, I felt a mild sense of betrayal for moving into allegiance with adult vantage points and structures of authority.

The underground economy of food and objects

From my position in the back of Miss Bailey's classroom, which gives a very different perspective than the front, I could see what went on when desk-tops were raised, presumably on official business. Some kids had customised their desks by taping drawings or dangling objects from the inside top. In addition to official school artefacts like books, papers, rulers, pencils, and crayons, the desks contained stashes of food, toys, cosmetics, and other objects brought from market and home. These transitional objects, most of them small and pocketable, bridge different spheres of life. Although schools maintain far less control than prisons, students have little choice about being present, and members of a smaller, more powerful group (the staff) regulate their use of time, space, and resources. Like prison inmates or hospital patients, students develop creative ways of coping with their relative lack of power and defending themselves against the more unpleasant aspects of institutional living.

Some of the objects that kids stash and trade, like 'pencil pals' (rubbery creatures designed to stick on the end of pencils), rabbit feet, special erasers, and silver paper, could be found in the desks of both boys and girls. Other objects divided more by gender. Boys brought in little toy cars and trucks, magnets, and compasses; and girls stashed tubes of lip gloss, nail polish, barrettes, necklaces, little stuffed animals, and doll furniture. Patterns of trade marked circles of friendship that almost never included both girls and boys. The exception was a flat pink and yellow terry cloth pillow that Kathryn, the most popular girl in Miss Bailey's class, brought in to cushion her desk chair. Invested with the manna of Kathryn's popularity, the pillow travelled around the entire room; girls and boys sat on it and tossed it around in a spirit more of honouring than teasing.

Ashton School felt like a much harsher environment than Oceanside School, in part because of the difference in weather (California was spared the cold winter of Michigan), but also because Ashton had strict rules against kids bringing objects from home. Even when it was raining, Ashton students were not allowed to carry umbrellas onto the playground, and if aides spotted any personal toys or objects, they immediately confiscated them. As a result, the school had an impoverished underground economy. (School staff might describe this differently, as eliminating distractions and maintaining order.) I saw a few sneaky sharings of food, lip gloss, and, on one occasion, a plastic whistle, but nothing like the flourishing semi-clandestine system of exchange at Oceanside School.

When kids invited me to participate in their secret exchanges, I felt pulled between my loyalty to them and my identification with and dependence on the teacher. During a social studies lesson, the fourth–fifth-grade students were supposed to be drawing pictures of early California missions. As Miss Bailey helped someone in another part of the room, I wandered to a corner where Jeremy, Don, and Bill leaned over and loudly whispered behind their raised desktops. Jeremy asked Don, 'What's your middle name?' Don replied, 'Top secret.' Bill chimed in, 'Pork chop.' Don, who was taking pins from a box in his desk and sticking them through an eraser, responded, 'Pork chop! I have two nicknames, Dog and Halfbrain.' Jeremy reached for some pins from Don's desk and fashioned an X on his pencil eraser. Bill played with an orange toy car, making 'zoom' noises as he scooted it into Jeremy's open desk. Jeremy took out an almost-finished bag of potato chips, held it out to Don, and shook a few into his hands. Bill held out his hand, but Jeremy ignored the gesture. 'Give me one,' Bill said. 'No, you're too fat; you should be on a diet.' 'I am on a diet,' Bill said as Jeremy shook a few chips into his hands. 'Give Barrie some,' Bill said. Jeremy turned (I was sitting behind him) and asked, 'Do you want some?' 'Yes,' I said and held out my hand as he shook a few chips into it. All of this forbidden activity went on behind the screen of the open desktops. Jeremy grinned, and I grinned back, feeling conspiratorial as I quietly munched the chips.

I had an observational feast on a day when there was a substitute teacher who 'couldn't keep control,' in the words of a disgusted bilingual aide who came for several hours each day. The kids made lots of noise and ran boisterously about; a group of them talked loudly about who had beat up whom in the third grade, and who could now beat up whom. They brought out objects that were usually kept relatively under cover – a skateboard magazine, a rubber finger with a long nail, bags of nuts and potato chips – and openly passed them around. As the kids walked out the door for lunch, Jessie, one of the girls who joined in the talk about fighting, got into an angry fistfight with Allen. This was the one fight where I intervened; the substitute teacher and I jointly worked to separate their flailing bodies. In the lunchroom Jessie retreated to sit with a group of girls, and talk about the fight went on for the rest of the day. After lunch a row of girls sat on the radiator and threw an eraser at several boys, who threw it back in an improvised game of catch. Another group went to the blackboard and drew hearts encircling different boy – girl paired names.

Tugs of memory, and the child within

After a few days of observing, I had figured out that Kathryn was the most popular girl in the classroom. Her cute face, stylish curly brown hair, nice clothes, and general poise and friendliness were easy to notice, and she received a lot of deference from both girls and boys. After a few weeks at Oceanside, I realised that my fieldnotes were obsessed with documenting Kathryn's popularity. 'The rich get richer,' I thought to myself as I sorted out yet another occasion when Kathryn got extra attention and resources. Then I realised the envy behind my note-taking and analysis and recalled that many years ago when I was a fourth-and-fifth-grader of middling social status, I had also carefully watched the popular girl, using a kind of applied sociology to figure out my place in a charged social network.

Rita, another girl in the present who evoked strong memories from my own past childhood, was from a family with thirteen children and an over-worked single-parent father. I wrote in my fieldnotes:

> Rita's hair was quite dirty, greasy at the roots, and it smelled. There was dirt on her cheek, and her hands were smudged. She wore the same clothes she had on yesterday: a too small, short blue nylon sweater with white buttons and dirt on the back, and green cotton pants that didn't zip right. Leaning over and catching the scent of her hair, I thought of Edith Schulz, whom we all avoided, in the fifth grade. I remember Edith, whose parents were immigrants from Germany, wearing a cotton sleeveless blouse and dirndl skirt in the dead of winter. The smell, the incongruous clothing – the signs, I now see, of poverty – set her apart, like Rita; both were treated like pariahs.

In such moments of remembering I felt in touch with my child self. I moved from the external vantage points of an observer, an adult authority, and a 'least adult' trying to understand kids' interactions in a more open and lateral way, to feeling more deeply inside their worlds. This experience occurred only when I was with girls. With boys, my strongest moments of identification came not through regression to feeling like one of them, but from more maternal feelings. Sometimes a particular boy would remind me of my son, and I would feel a wave of empathy and affection. But I generally felt more detached and less emotionally bound up with the boys.

I felt closer to the girls not only through memories of my own past, but also because I knew more about their gender-typed interactions. I had once played games like jump rope and statue buyer, but I had never ridden a skateboard and had barely tried sports like basketball and soccer. Paradoxically, however, I sometimes felt I could see boys' interactions and activities more clearly than those of girls; I came with fresher eyes and a more detached perspective. I found it harder to articulate and analyse the social relations of girls, perhaps because of my closer identification, but also, I believe, because our categories for understanding have been developed more out of the lives of boys and men than girls and women.

Instead of obsessing over Kathryn and avoiding Rita, I tried to understand their different social positions and experiences, and those of other girls and boys. This emphasis on multiple standpoints and meanings came to inform my understanding of gender.

Schools and bodies

Like Valerie Walkerdine (1986), I have been struck by the gap between the physicality and sexuality of childhood and the 'sanitised and idealised images of innocence and safety' found in much of the research on schools. Keenly aware of physical size, kids tease the unusually large ('Ricardo's a blubber butt', 'fat Carol'), stand face to face or back to back and use a flattened hand to compare heights, and compete to see who is tallest. They sometimes rib those who wear braces ('railroad tracks') or glasses ('four eyes').

A dramatic period of bodily change starts, for a few, in third or fourth grade and expands over the course of fifth and sixth grades, generally con-solidating in middle school or junior high. The names for this transition – 'pubescence,' 'sexual maturation,' 'entering adolescence' – feel awkward and unpleasant, expressing a prevalent attitude toward this socially defined period of life.

Diverse shapes and sizes

There was great variation in size and shape especially among the fourth – fifth, and sixth-graders. A few, nearly all of them girls, had the full height and bodily development of adults; others were so short and small, they could be mistaken for second-graders. And when fifth- and sixth-grade girls and boys lined up separately, girls were, on the average, notably taller and bigger than boys, reversing the adult pattern of sexual dimorphism.

Popular beliefs suggest direct biological causation – the hormones rage and *then* girls get interested in cosmetics and dating. But adolescence is not a given of biology. Like other age categories, adolescence is deeply cultural; collective beliefs and practices organise and give meaning to bodily changes, and they redefine the contours of gender. In our culture we have few if any rituals to mark passage from 'child' to 'adolescent,' and the transition is sur-rounded by negotiation and ambiguity.

The experiences of 'early developers'

Soon after I began doing fieldwork in the Oceanside School, I noticed a tall, heavyset Latina with full breasts and rounded hips – she had the figure of a woman and the face of a child – standing in line outside a fourth-grade classroom. Several members of the school staff pointed her out to me and, with cluck-clucking voices, noted that 'she's only nine years old'. A week later her family moved, and she left the school. The staff talked in the same mildly amazed and disapproving way about Lenore, a white, tall, and 'well-developed' (their euphemism for 'big breasted') fourth-grader who wore short tight sweaters and often chased and flirted with boys. One of the staff told me, 'Lenore isn't getting adult guidance; she should wear a loose fitting smock or something.' Adults felt uneasy around girls who 'had their development,' especially big breasts, way ahead of their peers.

Kids also gossiped about girls with big breasts, like an Ashton white third-grader whom other kids call 'cow.' After an episode of teasing, the girl came crying to her teacher, who counselled, 'Just tell them your body has a reason.'

Early developing boys also stand out; their greater height and musculature visibly set them apart from other boys. But, in contrast with early developing girls who, especially if they have large breasts, are treated almost as if they are physically handicapped, early developing boys reap social advantages. John and Nick, the tallest boys in Miss Bailey's classroom, were also the most popular; other kids spoke admiringly of their athletic prowess and sheer size ('We call John the Empire State Building,' Rosie told me in a praising way). In contrast, kids occasionally teased Don and Scott about their short stature, tousling their hair and repeatedly pinning their arms from behind. The two boys used various strategies, like joking and squirming away, to get out of these physically subordinating positions. Kevin was also short, but he did not receive these ritual reminders, perhaps because he was unusually skilled in athletics and a member of the group of boys with the highest status.

My observations echo the findings of survey research on the consequences of different rates of physical maturation. Several longitudinal studies (see Gross & Duke, 1986) have found that early maturing girls tend to have less prestige with their peers and to be less satisfied with their bodies than are other girls of the same chronological age. On the other hand, boys who enter puberty early tend to have higher self-esteem and prestige, and a more positive body image, than other boys of the same age. Early maturing boys tend, more often than other boys, to become outstanding athletes and student leaders, although some early maturing boys, perhaps because they form friendships with older boys, may be more likely to get involved in truancy and minor forms of delinquency. By junior high or middle school, some physically small and weak boys may be labelled 'wimps' and 'fags'; social hierarchies have a loose relationship to somatic type (Canaan, 1987).

The striking difference in the experiences of early developing girls and boys points to key features of our sex/gender system and the dynamics of male dominance. Height is valued in boys, but for girls the judgement is relative because they are 'supposed' to be shorter than boys. Since the average girl physically matures two years before the average boy, a fourth- or fifth-grade girl who has begun the growth spurt of puberty towers over most of the boys in her class. Furthermore, while boys' growth tends to be more muscular, a form that is positively regarded in males, 'pubescing' girls tend to put on body fat; their physicality often violates the cultural ideal of the thin female, as well as the ideal of being shorter than boys.

On several occasions during my fieldwork, kids conveyed a sense that a world in which females are taller than males is out of kilter. During a school assembly when a group of Oceanside fourth-graders had paused in the middle of a square dance, a boy stood straight and moved his flattened hand back and forth toward his taller female partner. 'Whew,' he said, publicly displaying amazement at the disparity in size. On the playground two tall sixth-grade girls who were watching a group of boys playing on skateboards engaged in a wistful verbal exchange: 'I wish there were more guys who were taller'; 'I wish there were more *good* guys.' On the other hand, girls sometimes enjoyed their bigger size, like Nancy, the Oceanside fifth-grader who, in a moment of anger, was able to physically overpower Matt, who was much smaller. But the talk afterward, about a girl beating up a boy, suggested this was not the way things are supposed to be.

The literature on gender differences in experiences of early pubescence discusses the fact that height and musculature are valued in males, while height and greater body fat violate standards of appearance for girls (Petersen, 1988). But the authors tiptoe around an obvious point: height and breasts (which have overt sexual connotations) are the most visible early changes of puberty, and only girls grow breasts. The breaking and lowering of boys' voices and the emergence of facial hair are also public phenomena, but these transitions happen well after elementary school. Other physical changes of early puberty – menstruation, the development of ejaculate sperm (wet dreams), the growth of underarm and pubic hair, the expansion of genitals – are much more private, except in locker rooms, a scene of junior high trepidation over issues of differential development.

Third-, fourth- and fifth-grade girls with 'figures' (big breasts and rounded hips) are treated as deviant and even polluting because they violate the cultural ordering of age categories. In our culture we draw sharp divisions between 'child' and 'adult,' defining the child as relatively asexual (although the media sexualise children of younger and younger ages) and the adult as sexual. 'Teen,' a third, transitional category, is also sexualised. Charged with sexual meaning, fully developed breasts seem uncomfortably out of place on the body of individuals who are still defined as children. A sense of pollution derives, as Mary Douglas (1966) has argued, from the violation of basic lines of social structure.

Kids' talk about their changing bodies

The physical events of puberty – a girl's first menstruation, the budding breasts, a boy's wet dreams, the emergence of pubic and underarm hair – are intensely private and often surrounded by feelings of secrecy and shame. Moments of public revelation may be dramatic, couched in humour, teasing, and experiences of embarrassment. Kids sometimes shame early developing girls, whose breasts cannot be hidden from view. But even those whose development is paced with the majority remember moments when their personal bodily changes became the stuff of public commentary.

Some of this commentary, like bra snapping, takes ritual form. Once in a classroom and several times on the playground I saw a girl or boy reach over and pull on the elastic back of a bra, letting it go with a loud snap followed by laughter.

Kids are often curious about one another's bodily changes, which they may transform into public news. When I attended summer camp between sixth and seventh grades, two girls sneaked into everyone else's suitcases and then announced who had or had not packed sanitary napkins. Melanie, a sixth-grade Ashton girl, told me that other girls kept asking her if her period had come. 'It hasn't, but even if it did, I wouldn't tell them; it's none of their business.'

Girls may more readily share their private vulnerabilities, but boys also discuss matters of the body in same gender contexts, with, some evidence suggests, emphasis on genital sexuality. Gary Fine (1980) has described vivid, often bragging talk about sex among boys on Little League teams who used words like 'blow job,' 'header,' and 'pusslick.'

John Gagnon and William Simon (1973) have suggested that adolescent boys and girls emphasise two different strands of sexuality. Boys more often learn about sexual acts before they pick up the rhetoric of romantic love and commitment. The sequence for girls is more often the reverse: they emphasise the emotional and romantic before the explicitly sexual. Same gender groups carry and circulate these meanings, and when heterosexual dating ensues, males and females teach each other about what they want and expect, a process that does not always go smoothly.

Lest the contrastive difference be taken too far, however, I would add examples of elementary school girls engaging in sexually explicit talk. An Oceanside staff member overheard a group of sixth-grade girls discussing 'blow jobs,' and Margaret Blume, who also observed on the Oceanside playground, reported that she saw one girl ask another, who was passing by, 'Mona, do you like Jeff?' 'Jeff who?' Mona responded. 'Jeff hard-on.'

The official agenda: sex education

While kids talk about and deal with bodily changes in both same and mixed gender contexts, school staff generally ignore these topics unless circumstances press them to respond. The adult staff at both schools mostly ignored bra snapping and snippets of folklore with sexual content, although they sometimes punished kids for saying 'dirty words.' Several times I heard the staff privately discuss the pubescing bodies of students, but in the course of my fieldwork I saw only one official acknowledgement of sexually maturing bodies: the menstruation movie. Annually shown to Oceanside fifth-graders near the end of the school year, the film was the first step in the school system's sex education curriculum; the next step was a film about the facts of sexual reproduction, shown to sixth-graders. Nervous constraints related to the subject matter and to the community and state controversy over sex education that surrounded the event: only fifth-graders could attend, and a parent or guardian had to sign a prior note of permission. As she set up the projector, Miss Bailey joked to me, 'You can be a witness if they try to take my teaching credential away.'

In previous years the movie was shown only to girls, but afterwards boys had repeatedly asked girls what the film was about and even offered to pay money for copies of the booklet the girls received at the end. The staff decided that in the future, boys should also see the film. The movie was preceded by rustles of anticipation. Jeremy came over and asked me, 'You gonna see the film?' 'What's it about?' I asked. 'Sex education for fifth-graders,' he replied. The two Oceanside fifth-grades crowded into Miss Bailey's classroom, the girls choosing seats on one side of the room, and the boys on the other; Jessie sat with the boys, at the edge by the girls. Miss Bailey asked the students to vote on how they wanted to divide for questions after the movie – into their two classes, or with all the boys in one group and all the girls in another. Four boys raised their hands for the former, and the rest of the students voted for gender separation.

After the movie Mrs Sorenson, the other fifth-grade teacher, led the girls to her classroom for a discussion, and I followed; the boys stayed with Miss Bailey. The ensuing half-hour went very slowly; when various girls turned around to look at the clock, they expressed what I was also feeling. Mrs Sorenson opened by telling the girls that she was not supposed to volunteer information but only answer questions raised by students. (This nervous gesture left a hanging sense of deep secrets that would not be revealed.) There was a long pause with giggles, but no questions. Mrs Sorenson talked about the importance of 'keeping clean' (thereby implying that something quite dirty was involved). Still no questions. She then talked about how 'everyone is different; some flow longer, some cramp; some get pimples'. No questions? No questions? She looked around.

Finally Helen spoke up, 'Why didn't the girls see it alone? Some boys were serious, but some laughed and everything.' Mrs Sorenson responded, 'Why do you think they laughed? They were nervous about it too; boys go through changes at that age too.' Julia loudly added, 'Their sperms.' Nancy giggled and quietly repeated to Sherry, 'Their sperms.'

As I participated in this uncomfortable event, I wondered how many girls had already started menstruating and how the official messages related to their varied experiences, anxieties, knowledge, and conversations with friends and family. In spite of the matter-of-fact upbeat tone of the movie, several themes reverberated: menstruation is a secret, emotionally loaded, and shame-filled topic; adults and kids don't feel very comfortable discussing these matters; these issues are charged with tension, awkwardness, and mistrust between girls and boys. Mrs Sorenson twice put Jessie on the spot in what I felt was a punitive mode, in effect reminding her that although she hung out with boys and preferred their activities, her body was marked by sexual difference. Julia's observation that she couldn't marry her best friend showed insight, although she would not have recognised this language, into the mismatch between the heterosexual imperative and the fact that boys and girls are rarely close friends. Finally, the fact that official sex education begins with such a central emphasis on girls reinforces their definition in terms of sexuality.

Uneven transitions to teen culture

Cosmetic culture

Cosmetics have powerful symbolic status in the gendered marking of age grades. When young children 'dress up,' they often use makeup; preschool girls, and sometimes boys, use red felt pens and crayons to paint their lips and nails. By fourth and fifth grades some girls own their own cosmetics, which they often freely share. Most adults disapprove of elementary school girls using makeup, and some schools have formal rules against the wearing of lipstick or eye shadow; the forbidden nature of makeup, of course, may heighten its allure.

One day when Miss Bailey was explaining antonyms, I noticed Nancy reach into a small leather purse and pull out a clear plastic container with pink contents. Holding her hands beneath her desk, she screwed off the lid and held it out; Rosie reached over and put her finger in, smelled the dab of pink and, lowering her head, quickly rubbed it around her lips. Nancy smoothed some around her lips. Then Jessica got a dab and rubbed it around her mouth. Seeing that Miss Bailey was beginning to notice, Nancy screwed on the lid and tucked it back in her purse.

Elementary school girls may favour lip gloss because its shiny trace is less detectable than bright lipstick. Some brands, designed for younger girls, feature the smells and flavours of commercialised childhood. In the Ashton lunchroom a third-grade girl showed me a tube of lip gloss packaged to look like a pink Crayola; she flashed it under my nose, saying, 'Smell it; strawberry. I got chocolate too.' Another version that circulated in Miss Bailey's class came in a tube and had a strong grape smell: 'Lip Smackers, Bonne Bell' was printed on the side.

At these ages there is still ambiguity about whether the use of cosmetics is 'pretend' or 'real', a vacillating line that assumed interesting proportions on Hallowe'en. Ashton School had an annual Hallowe'en parade; students brought in costumes and, after lunch, changed for the event. Before the parade was due to begin, I went into the girls' bathroom and discovered a group of sixth-graders in the throes of preparation. Two girls, each holding an elaborate makeup kit with many colours of eye shadow and rouge, had cornered the mirror above the sinks. One, a short white girl with small breasts, had changed into a black leotard cat costume with a tail and a cap with perky ears. The other, a black girl, wore a long white dress with ribbons threaded through it, high heels with open backs, and an aluminium foil crown kept in place by a row of bobby pins. Side by side they leaned over the two sinks and into the mirror applying eyeliner, eye shadow, mascara, lipstick, and rouge. They wielded various tools – sponges, Q-tips, tubes, and wands – with expert gestures. I was struck by how much more these girls knew than I did about the world of cosmetics.

Other girls watched with admiring faces. One of them, a white girl, wiggled into a long printed nylon dress and then took a small makeup kit out of her brown paper bag, turned to me in hesitating manner, and asked, 'Would you put this on me?' 'Can't you do it?' I asked. 'I don't know how, I'm scared.' She first handed me a wand of mascara. 'Pretty or garish?' I asked. 'Pretty,' she said, so I did my best, getting some on her skin. Then she gave me a small sponge of pale eye shadow to apply, and then a tube of lipstick. Another white girl who wore bobby socks and a flared felt skirt decorated with a cut-out poodle said to a girl near her, 'I've never worn makeup before. I have to put on gobs.' She went to the mirror and worked on eyeliner, smeared it, and then asked my help in getting it off. 'It looks dark under my eye. I need some blush!' she exclaimed, coming up with a cosmetic solution.

Other girls, dressed as clowns and a vampire, used makeup in a slapstick mode. Two white girls dressed as men, one in a suit, coat, and tie and a false moustache, and another in faded blue jeans and a flannel shirt with a false beard and moustache fastened from her ears. There were crossings of race and ethnic lines, as well as of the gender line. An African-American girl wore a Wonder Woman costume, including a mask with pinkish skin. Wilma, who wore an elaborate feathered Native American costume, was, in fact, Ojibwa. 'She's dressed like an Indian; she is an Indian,' two different girls explained to me in appreciative tones. Wilma later told me her mother made the costume at the Indian Centre and that it was 'a boy costume; a girl's would have beads not feathers.'

The boys also wore garb that crossed boundaries between real and fantasy (monsters, ghosts, robots, superheroes), historical eras (pirates, hobos), ages (professional football players), body sizes (with pillows to add bulk), but not between genders. In Hallowe'ens over the years I've noticed that boys don't costume up as females until they are in junior high. However, boy vampires did wear lipstick, which they applied in outlandish fashion and called 'blood.'

Hallowe'en exemplifies what anthropologists call a 'ritual of reversal,' when rules are loosened and one can dress and behave in usually forbidden ways – females as male, younger as older, humans as monsters. Among the youngest girls, cosmetics are full-blown pretend; the second-graders all asked adults to help with their lipstick or mascara. But as girls get older, the line between child and adult, between innocent and knowing, becomes increasingly ambiguous. Some of the sixth-grade girls demonstrated the skills of cosmeticised women, which brought admiration from other girls. Others were amateurs, and one confessed that the unfamiliar challenge of applying one's own makeup was scary.

'Goin' with'

By fifth and especially sixth grades the rituals of 'goin' with' become a central activity. Although pairs are the focus, 'goin' with' is a group activity that bridges moments of teasing to the construction of more lasting and self-proclaimed couples. On the day when a substitute teacher tried in vain to bring order to Miss Bailey's classroom, the kids spent some of their time launching couples on the blackboard. Mike drew a heart, and inside he wrote, 'Rita + Bert' (Rita and Bert were both on the social margins, and the gesture compounded their humiliation). Kevin erased 'Rita' and replaced it with 'Kathryn,' the name of the most popular girl, thereby insulting Kathryn by linking her with a stigmatised boy. Then Rita erased 'Kathryn' and wrote 'Allen + Bert,' venturing a homophobic insult, perhaps to deflect attention from the insult she had received. Allen quickly ran up and erased it. Picking up on a couple who were widely said to be 'goin' with' each other, Freddy wrote 'Nick + Judy', and the heart-circled inscription remained on the board.

Much effort goes into calibrating publicly named couples with actual, but hidden patterns of desire; a mutually acknowledged fit distinguishes fully-fledged 'goin' with' relationships from those that are teasingly ventured. Sometimes an individual who 'likes' another will directly inquire to see if the feeling is reciprocated. Joan, an Ashton fifth-grader, told me, 'Wally sent me a note asking me to go with him. I said yes, and now we talk on the phone.' David, another fifth-grader, explained, 'I hired a messenger, a friend; he asked Pam if she'd go with me, and she said yes.' Sometimes 'goin' with' requests are turned down. Early in the year in Miss Bailey's classroom, Bill sent Tracy a note asking, 'Will you go with me? yes – no –.' She checked 'no' and silently sent it back.

Third parties play a busy role in discovering and circulating news about who 'likes' whom and declaring a 'goin' with' pair when they find a match. Both Ashton and Oceanside kids would come up to one another on the playground with queries like 'Craig likes you; do you like him?' 'Do you like Jane?' When there was 'liking' affirmation from both parties, the news travelled widely. At Oceanside there was a wave of gossip about Judy going with Nick, a pairing that three different kids went out of their way to report to me. I asked one of the gossipers if the pair went on dates. 'Nick asked her to the movies, but her mom wouldn't let her go' was the reply, from a girl who wasn't a close friend of either party.

Tracy and Allen, another Oceanside couple who started going together in May, were the focus of much gossip and teasing. One day in the classroom

Jessie loudly asked Allen, 'Having fun with Tracy?' Then she added, 'Tomorrow Allen and Tracy are going to get married.' Sheila ran over to the boys' side of the classroom and whispered and laughed with them, gesturing toward Tracy. Tracy looked a little embarrassed, and Allen slumped in a chair by the back table. As they lined up for recess, Kevin told Allen, 'We won't bug you any more.' But then Sheila came over and said, 'Kevin's best man.' Tracy grabbed Sheila's sleeve and urgently whispered, 'Why is it such a big deal?'

Although that teasing episode bothered her, Tracy took pride in her romantic relationship with Allen. A week later she came up to me and announced, 'Did you know I'm goin' with Allen?' 'Did you go on a date?' I asked. 'One, last Sunday; we went to the movies.' 'Was it fun?' 'Yeah, except RJ tried to spoil it; he's Sheila's old boyfriend. He poured ice on Allen.' Jessica, who was standing next to us, started to tease, 'I'm gonna tell Allen.' Tracy retorted matter-of-factly, 'He doesn't care. At first they really teased him till Miss Bailey said if they bugged us any more she'd send them to the principal.'

Most of the elementary school 'goin' with' relationships I learned about were fairly distant. Various couples sent notes, talked on the phone, exchanged gifts on birthdays and holidays, and sat, danced, or skated together at group parties. Few went on dates. One college woman remembered that she and her fifth-grade boyfriend 'barely talked to each other, but we held hands a few times; we didn't do much for fear of teasing.'

The 'goin' with' relationships of fourth- fifth- and sixth-graders usually last only a few days, or at most, a few weeks. Third parties often carry out their dissolution, as well as their formation. David, who 'hired' a messenger to ask if Pam would go with him, said that after a few days, 'Pam's friend Jennie told me that Pam wanted to break up,' and that was the end of the liaison.

Gender, age, and sexual meanings

Same and mixed gender groups structure the early forms of active heterosexuality, and they assert an increasingly vocal taboo against other forms of sexuality. By fourth and fifth grades, 'fag' has become a widespread and serious term of insult. Unlike those who are heterosexual, lesbian and gay adolescents have no public, school-based rituals to codify and validate their desires: 'there are no affirming public markers about what they are feeling and thinking' (Gagnon, 1972: 238).

Drawing on Adrienne Rich's (1980) conceptualisation, the transition to adolescence can be understood as a period of entry into the institution of heterosexuality. While this transition brings new constraints and vulnerabilities for boys as well as girls, girls are particularly disadvantaged. Disturbing national statistics paint an overall picture of adolescence as 'the fall' for girls: compared with boys of the same age, and with themselves at earlier ages, girls who are twelve, thirteen, and fourteen have higher rates of depression, lower self-esteem, more negative images of their own bodies, and declining academic performance in areas like maths and science (Gilligan et al., 1989). These, of course, are statistical patterns; many girls fare well through this period of change, and some boys experience serious problems. But larger institutional forces, bound up in structures of gender, sexuality, and age, make this an especially difficult period for girls.

During adolescence both boys and girls come to be seen, and to see themselves, as sexual actors, but girls are more pervasively sexualised than boys. Athletics provides a continuous arena where at least some boys can perform and gain status as they move from primary through secondary schooling. But for many girls, appearance and relationships with boys begin to take primacy over other activities. In middle school or junior high the status of girls with other girls begins to be shaped by their popularity with boys; same gender relations among boys are less affected by relationships with the other gender (Schofield, 1982). In short, the social position of girls increasingly derives from their romantic relationships with boys, but not vice versa.

The sixth-grade girls' Hallowe'en preparations were a microcosm of a vast project that absorbs many teenage girls: bringing their personal appearance into line with idealised and sexual images of femininity. This involves learning the skills and practices of cosmetic culture, new modes of dress (pantyhose, heels, dangling earrings), and heterosexualised ways of moving and holding one's body. Propelled by strong cultural and commercial forces, many teenage girls learn to turn themselves into, and regard themselves as, objects.

The Hallowe'en scene also showed that there can be pleasure and creativity in this process. And sexual meanings can be a source of new forms of power. In the sexualised groups, some girls claimed space and exuded strength and energy. Girls may use cosmetics, discussions of boyfriends, dressing sexually, and other forms of exaggerated 'teen' femininity to challenge adult, and class- and race-based authority in schools (Anyon, 1983). But the pleasurable and powerful dimensions of heterosexual femininity contain a series of traps and double binds. The double standard persists, and girls who are too overtly sexual run the risk of being labelled 'sluts.' As Rosalind Petchesky (1984) has observed, teenage girls 'are in the anomalous position of being at once infantalised by the cult of virginity (codified, for example, in statutory rape and "age of consent" laws) and objectified by the media's cult of "Lolita"; at the same time, they have few real resources for independence.' Sexual harassment and rape are persistent dangers, and if they are heterosexually active, girls also run the risks of pregnancy and disease. In gestures that mix protection with punishment, parents and other adults often tighten their control of girls when they become adolescents, and sexuality becomes a terrain of struggle between generations. While some girls use active sexuality to declare their independence from parental and school authority, this challenge (if they are heterosexual) may 'ultimately and paradoxically' bring them under more direct control by boys; as Mica Nava (1984: 15) remarks, 'girls' most common form of rebellion serves only to bind them more tightly to their subordination as women.'

References

Anyon, J. (1983) 'Intersections of gender and class: Accommodation and resistance by working-class and affluent females to contradictory sex-role ideologies', in Walker, S. and Barton, L. (Eds) *Gender, Class and Education*, Brighton, Sussex: Falmer Press.

Canaan, J. (1987) 'A comparative analysis of American suburban middle class, middle school, and high school teenage cliques', in Spindler, G. and Spindler, L. (Eds) *Interpretive Ethnography of Education*, Hillsdale, NJ: Lawrence Erlbaum, 385–406.

Douglas, M. (1966) *Purity and Danger*, New York: Praeger.

Fine, G.A. (1980) 'The natural history of preadolescent male friendship groups', in Foot, H.C. and Chapman, A.J. (Eds) *Friendship and Social Relations in Children*, New York: Wiley, 293–320.

Gagnon, J.H. (1972) 'The creation of the sexual in early adolescence', in Kagan, J. and Coles, R. (Eds) *Twelve to Sixteen*, New York: Norton.

Gagnon, J.H. and Simon, W. (1973) *Sexual Conduct*, Chicago: Aldine.

Gilligan, C., Lyons, N.P. and Hanmer, T.J. (Eds) (1989) *Making Connections: The Relational Worlds of Adolescent Girls at Emma Willard School*, Troy, NY: Emma Willard School.

Gross, R.T. and Duke, P.M. (1986) 'The effect of early years versus late physical maturation on adolescent behavior', *Symposium on Adolescent Medicine*, **27**: 71–77.

Nava, M. (1984) 'Youth service provision, social order and the question of girls', in McRobbie, A. and Nava, M. (Eds) *Gender and Generation*, London: Macmillan.

Petchesky, R. (1984) *Abortion and Women's Choice*, New York: Longman.

Petersen, A.C. (1988) 'Adolescent development', *Annual Review of Psychology*, **39**: 583–607.

Rich, A. (1980) 'Compulsory heterosexuality and lesbian existence', *Signs*, **5**: 198–210.

Schofield, J.W. (1982) *Black and White in School*, New York: Praeger.

Walkerdine, V. (1986) 'Post-structuralist theory and everyday practices: The family and the school', in Wilkinson, S. (ed.) *Feminist Social Psychology*, Philadelphia: Open University Press, 57–76.

Commentary: Barrie Thorne

My interest in gender arrangements among children evolved from two life-changing events. The first began in the late 1960s when I was a graduate student in sociology at Brandeis University, near Boston, and was engaged in both activism and fieldwork in the movement against conscription for the war in Vietnam. The ideas of women's liberation began to circulate; I was drawn to them and joined a consciousness-group, which eventually became part of Bread and Roses, an early women's liberation organization.

Those of us in Bread and Roses who were shuttling between feminist activism and graduate work began to notice and question the absence of women's lives and experiences in our fields of study. Social theorists, such as Marx and Durkheim, assumed men as actors and placed women, at best, at the periphery. Women were relegated to footnotes in the study of work, politics, social movements, social organization, and other topics. The feminist question, 'Where are the women?' altered the course of my research, and I eventually wrote a chapter (which became my first journal article) about the subordinate position of women in the draft resistance movement. By 1971, when I took up my first faculty position at Michigan State University, I was adding yet-to-be-recognized specialties, the sociology of gender and women's studies, to my research and teaching interests.

The Brandeis graduate program emphasized ethnographic fieldwork and the study of everyday life and situated interaction. These were ripe approaches for studying the construction of gender, a topic I first explored through collaborative research on women's and men's uses of speech and non-verbal communication. Nancy Henley and I co-edited a book on this topic, and as we framed the introduction, we grappled with the challenges of thinking systematically about sex and gender (Thorne and Henley, 1975). That challenge gradually became an ongoing, even obsessive, pre-occupation in my teaching, reading, and writing.

In 1973 I became a mother – a second life-changing event that added fresh twists to my focus on gender. Having a child took me into social worlds that I still find entrancing, such as toddlers making contact with one another in public places (rather like Martians, finding their own kind), four-year-olds building forts out of sofa pillows and launching grand sagas of 'let's pretend that...', and snacktime in a day care center, where waves of giggling roll through. My husband and I often discussed the challenges of raising a son, and later a daughter, in a sexist society.

I began to look for social science research on children and found that it was surprisingly uneven. Work by sociologists was tucked into small pockets, framing children as learners (research on education), problems and threats (studies of juvenile delinquency), and victims (research on child abuse) – but not as actors in a range of institutions. I also began to notice the adult-centered assumptions of social and feminist theories and the absence of 'age' in the litanies of difference and inequality ('social class, race, gender') that critical scholars brought to view. Returning to earlier questions about women and knowledge, I began to ask 'Where are the children?'

In 1976, when my husband and I were visiting faculty at a university in California, we created and taught a course on the sociology of childhood. I also steered my research in the direction of children. For several years I had mused about the possibility of gaining access to groups of kids to find out how they thought about and experienced gender. I was inspired by the work of the folklorists, Iona and Peter Opie (1959), who watched kids on playgrounds with open-ended respect, documenting and trying to understand the social and cultural worlds that they create when they are relatively free from adult control.

I chose to observe in 'Oceanside' Elementary School for reasons of convenience; a friend put me in touch with a fourth–fifth-grade teacher who was willing to put up with a regular observer. *Gender Play* also draws upon a shorter stint of fieldwork that I conducted in a public elementary school in Michigan in 1980. That school was chosen by a school district officer who invited me to do gender equity 'needs assessment,' with an agreement that I could also gather data for my own purposes. Looking back, I now think of Oceanside as the close-up and inside story of the book, with Miss Bailey's fourth–fifth-graders at center stage. The data from the Michigan school feels more telescopic, crossing a wider range of ages, and involving regular mapping of school-wide patterns, for example, of seating in the cafeteria. Having two fieldsites alerted me to both differences and similarities in the organization and cultures of particular schools.

The back-and-forth of data-gathering and analysis

When I first entered the field, what were my starting questions or hypotheses? Nothing very focused or tight. I wanted to learn about children's experiences of gender, and I was curious about the dynamics of sex segregation in their friendships and play groups, a pattern that stood out in the preschool worlds I had visited with my son. At that time studies of children and gender focused on 'sex differences' and 'sex role development and socialization.' I wore those garments of pre-existing literature lightly, partly because psychologists had done most of the stitching. As a sociologist, I was oriented to group life and social relations rather than patterns of individual development, and the psychological literature on sex differences was stripped from the social contexts and situated meanings that are the stuff of ethnography. The emerging feminist literature on 'sex role socialization' was more up my alley, but I questioned the teleology of starting with end-points (unitary, somewhat stereotypic conceptions of masculinity and femininity) and then working backwards to ask how these 'outcomes' were produced. I wanted to be with and to learn from children in the present, outside the shadow of their presumed futures.

Gender was at the center of my awareness, and, with my orientation as an interpretive sociologist, I was on the lookout for social processes, nego-tiated meanings, and recurring patterns of social interaction. In effect, I was trying to find out 'how gender works,' with children's experiences and actions at the center. But how could I *locate* the amorphous, multifaceted phenomenon we call 'gender'? When I began observing in Miss Bailey's fourth–fifth-grade classroom, I recorded girls' and boys' seating arrange-ments in the classroom and cafeteria; the ways they formed lines; and their groupings on the playground. I noted patterns of inclusion and exclusion. And I recorded as much as I could of the things they did and said, unsure just what details might turn out to be relevant. (Fieldworkers have to culti-vate the virtues of persistence and faith, returning to the field and taking notes day after day, even when the purpose seems diffuse and the challenge of making-sense-of-it-all seems overwhelming.)

I knew I was onto pay dirt the first time a game of 'girls chase the boys' came into view, with a boy yelling 'Help! A girl's chasin' me!' and girls call-ing out, 'Let's get those boys!' Girls and boys arrayed on opposite and antagonistic sides, with individual names and other identities muted – this was Gender Intensified, and it drew me, and my note-taking, like a magnet. It was much harder to 'see' gender when girls and boys were in mixed gender groups, with individualized identities. As I puzzled about that gap and its implications for the dynamics of gender, it occurred to me that the salience of gender varies across contexts. This, in turn, led me to ask: What might account for the fluctuating significance of gender? That became one of many strands of questioning and analysis that I had in mind and contin-ued to develop (or, in some cases, eventually tossed out) as I observed, took fieldnotes, analyzed data, and eventually wrote up the study.

Fieldwork involves continual movement between the gathering of data and the process of analyzing and making sense of it. Pushing oneself to 'do sociology,' however modestly, while one is observing and writing fieldnotes helps draw concrete particulars into possible patterns (for a terrific discus-sion of this process, with 'how to' tips, see Emerson, Fretz and Shaw, 1995). For example, one day when kids were scrambling for seats on the floor of the auditorium, I noticed that girls and boys were more likely to sit together rather than apart if they were near a teacher. I jotted that observation in my fieldnotes and connected it to another pattern I had noticed: that in the absence of adults, especially in situations of witnessed choice (e.g. deciding where to sit in the lunchroom), kids were more likely to separate by gender. When a boy chose to sit by a girl, or vice versa, they were sometimes teased (the power of witnesses!) – a risk, I came to see, that might diminish in the presence of adults with the power to intervene and to shape children's groups.

Several years later, when I sat down to systematically code and analyze my piles of fieldnotes, I picked up on the scattered leads and hunches, and pursued them more systematically. As I ploughed through my notes, I was often grateful for long chunks of description whose purpose at the time I wrote the fieldnotes might have seemed vague or unclear. For example, when I worked on the theme of 'gender crossing,' I searched for instances of boys seeking non-disruptive access to girls' games. I discovered 'Brian' (as I called him in *Gender Play*), a boy in the Michigan school who popped up here and there in my fieldnotes, like Waldo in the *Where's Waldo?* children's books. Many years after I had observed and recorded them, I found a logic in Brian's movements.

Instances that seem to contradict an emergent pattern are especially valuable to think with (an argument Katz, 1988 develops in a discussion of the process of 'analytic induction' in qualitative research). Brian, for example, went against the grain of routinized gender separation, and figuring out his position helped me add nuance to my analysis of 'with-then-apart' gender patterns. As did my analysis of the dynamics of a group of eight to ten Oceanside kids, unusually mixed by gender and by age, who played games of dodgeball day after day during recess and lunchtime. They were all bilingual in Spanish, and many of them spoke little English. I theorized that in order to pull off lively games of dodgeball with the comfort of shared language and culture, these Spanish-speaking kids reached across lines of gender and age. Building upon the case of the dodgeball group and parallel situations, I shaped a more general observation: when another line of cross-cutting difference becomes highly salient, gender may recede from view.

In the course of fieldwork and writing, emergent lines of analysis (such as 'the variable salience of difference' and 'situations of witnessed choice') became like magnets that picked up the scattered iron filings of my reading, teaching, and casual conversations. By the late 1980s, when I was engaged in more concerted writing from the project, theories of gender had been reconfigured by poststructuralist theories of discourse (e.g. Walkerdine, 1986); by the interactionist concept, 'doing gender' (West & Zimmerman, 1987), and by Connell's argument (1987) that there are multiple masculinities and femininities, arrayed in continually contested fields. Gender had been theorized and studied through varying lenses – structural, discursive, individual, and situational (see Thorne, 2002). All of these advances provided tools to use and ideas to extend, rework, and critique as I wrote the manuscript that became *Gender Play*.

From gender play to growing up in Oakland

The fieldnotes I gathered for *Gender Play* are full of juicy details and strands of possible analysis that I wasn't able to pursue. Research, as I often tell my students, involves continual decisions; one simply can't include everything one uncovers. But some of the paths I didn't take have haunted me. One path has to do with issues of racial ethnicity, which I briefly addressed when I wrote about Jessie, the token African-American girl who skilfully moved between the somewhat separate spaces and activities of boys and girls in the mostly white fourth–fifth-grade classroom. I concluded my analysis of the matchmaking role that she assumed in heterosexual teasing rituals by writing that her navigation of gender relations 'was also a navigation of race relations in a situation of tokenism: gender and race were being mutually constructed' (Thorne, 1993: 128). Even as I wrote that sentence, I knew I had barely begun to demonstrate its generalizing claim.

I was also haunted by my social distance from the group of Spanish-speaking girls and boys who regularly played dodgeball on the Oceanside playground. The group was great to theorize with, but I watched them from a distance and didn't take the initiative to try to get to know the kids who were involved. At the time, I felt limited by my lack of language and cultural knowledge, but I was also reluctant to plunge into issues of racial-ethnicity and social class, because it seemed so complex, and I was afraid of getting it wrong.

Questions about children's experiences of immigration, racialized ethnicity, and social class came back into view when my family and I moved to Southern California in 1987. Driving around Los Angeles, we were amazed by the contrast between highly affluent and impoverished areas, and by the complex and rapidly shifting mosaic of cultures (at that time, due to high rates of immigration, 30% of children in California spoke a language other than English at home; over 20% lived in poverty, with widening gaps between rich and poor). I got an itch to return to the field – this time with children's experiences of immigration, racial-ethnicity, and social class at the forefront. In 1995 I began to organize an ethnographic study framed by the changing political economy of US childhoods, and focused on the daily lives of children and families in particular urban areas.

The California Childhoods Project reaches in a more structural and historical direction, but it also extends themes in *Gender Play*: children's experiences and interactions are at the center, as is the question, 'When, and how, does a difference make a difference?' In this work, gender and age are framed as pieces of a much larger mosaic highlighting social class, immigration, and racial ethnicity. I organized a multilingual research team to do fieldwork not only in schools, but also in households, neighborhoods, after-school programs, and other child-related sites in inner-city Los Angeles and in Oakland. (For preliminary reports from this work, see Orellana et al., 2001; Orellana & Thorne, 1998; Thorne, 2001.)

As I write this commentary, piles of fieldnotes, interview transcripts, and other data from the Oakland research site are arrayed in binders on the shelf across the room. Once again I'm enmeshed in the chaotic trails of back-and-forth, which – fingers crossed and with the exercise of faith and persistence – will eventually result in a coherent story.

References

Connell, R.W. (1987) *Gender and Power*, Stanford, CA: Stanford University Press.

Emerson, R.M., Fretz, R.I. and Shaw, L.L. (1995) *Writing Ethnographic Fieldnotes*, Chicago: University of Chicago Press.

Katz, J. (1988) 'A theory of qualitative methodology: The system of analytic field-work', in Emerson, R.M. (ed.) *Contemporary Field Research*. Prospect Heights, IL: Waveland, 127–148.

Opie, I. and Opie, P. (1959) *The Lore and Language of Schoolchildren*, New York: Oxford University Press.

Orellana, M. and Thorne, B. (1998) 'Year-round schools and the politics of time', *Anthropology and Education Quarterly*, **29**: 446–472.

Orellana, M.F., Thorne, B., Chee, A. and Lam, W.S.E. (2001) 'Transnational child-hoods: The participation of children in processes of family migration', *Social Problems*, **48**: 573–592.

Thorne, B. (1993) *Gender Play: Girls and Boys in School*, New Brunswick, NJ: Rutgers University Press.

Thorne, B. (2001). 'Pick-up time at Oakdale Elementary School: Work and family from the vantage point of children', in Hertz, R. and Marshall, N. (Eds) *Working Families*, Berkeley: University of California Press, 354–376.

Thorne, B. (2002) 'Gender and interaction: Widening the conceptual scope', in Baron, B. and Kotthoff, H. (Eds) *Gender in Interaction: Perspectives on Femininity and Masculinity in Ethnography and Discourse*, Amsterdam: John Benjamins, 3–18.

Thorne, B. and Henley, N. (Eds) (1975) *Language and Sex: Difference and Dominance*, Rowley, MA: Newbury House.

Walkerdine, V. (1986) *Schoolgirl Fictions*, New York: Verso.

West, C. and Zimmerman, D.H. (1987) 'Doing gender', *Gender & Society*, **1**: 125–151.

14

Children in South Africa Can Make a Difference: An Assessment of 'Growing Up in Cities' in Johannesburg

DEV GRIESEL, JILL SWART-KRUGER AND LOUISE CHAWLA

This paper was originally published as: Griesel, R.D., Swart-Kruger, J. and Chawla, L. (2002) 'Children in South Africa can make a difference: an assessment of "Growing Up in Cities" in Johannesburg', *Childhood*, 9(1): 83–100.

Abstract

The article presents the evaluation of two Johannesburg sites of 'Growing Up in Cities', a project that involves children in documenting and improving their urban environments, with respect to the effect of project participation. Participating children and their parents were surveyed or interviewed regarding the project's value and effect on the children. In addition, the children were measured on scales of self-esteem, locus of control and self-efficacy, and compared with control groups. The results of the evaluation are summarized, and claims about the value of children's participation in community development are critically reviewed.

Introduction

This article reports on an evaluation of the South African site of a project that was conceived during Sharon Stephens's direction of the Children and Environment Programme at the Norwegian Centre for Child Research: a revival of 'Growing Up in Cities' (GUIC). This action-research project involves 10- to 15-year-olds in low-income areas around the world in documenting their own perspectives on the places where they live and in developing ideas for community improvements. Initiated in 1970 by the urban planner Kevin Lynch (1977) in cooperation with UNESCO, the project was revived in 1995 in eight countries, with the support of the Norwegian Centre for Child Research and Childwatch International of Oslo. It was quickly adopted by the MOST Programme of UNESCO (Management of

Social Transformations) as well as numerous international and national organizations (Chawla, 2001; Driskell, in press). The project's methods for work with children and youth continue to spread to new locations (see descriptions at www.unesco.org/most/growing.htm). One country where GUIC has taken root is South Africa, where the project goal of child and youth participation in improving the urban environment coincides with the nation's urgent need to build a post-Apartheid civil society as well as address a legacy of poverty and housing shortages in the context of rapidly changing urban populations.

This article presents an evaluation of two GUIC sites in Johannesburg: Canaansland, an African squatter camp, and Ferreirasdorp, an Indian community. In keeping with the provisions of the UN Convention on the Rights of the Child, together with Agenda 21 from the UN Conference on Environment and Development, and the Habitat Agenda from the Second UN Conference on Human Settlements, GUIC pursues a number of objectives:

- Gaining an understanding of children's environmental interests and needs through participatory research;
- Applying this information to the design of programmes and activities to improve life quality for children and their communities;
- Pressing for effective urban policies for children;
- Organizing public events to draw attention to urban children's rights and needs;
- Increasing the capacity for participatory research and action among academic researchers and the staff of community-based organizations.

This article focuses on the influence phase of participatory action-research on the young people of Canaansland and Ferreirasdorp. Many claims have been made regarding the benefits of participation for children, including enhanced self-esteem, a greater sense of self-efficacy, an internal locus of control, greater awareness and appreciation of democratic processes, an increased sense of responsibility for their communities, and improved communication and problem-solving skills (de Winter, 1997; Hart, 1997; Stapp et al., 1996). Through describing the use of multiple methods of evaluation, which engaged both children and their parents, this article critically examines these claims.

Canaansland and Ferreirasdorp

The work of GUIC in Canaansland is one of the first detailed published studies of life inside an urban squatter camp from children's perspectives, and one of the first studies of children's responses to a forced eviction (Swart-Kruger, 2000, 2001). Squatter settlements represent a worldwide response to housing shortages, and form a refuge for many families seeking to escape extreme rural poverty or life on urban pavements. In South Africa, it is estimated that about 13 per cent of homes are shacks such as squatter housing (van Tonder, 1997).

As a thriving mining and industrial city, Johannesburg attracts large numbers of job seekers and is currently the most densely populated city in South Africa. Informal housing proliferates as people struggle to become financially secure. It is important to understand how these environments function for children. Therefore, GUIC was introduced in 1996 in Canaansland, the largest of 61 squatter sites in inner-city Johannesburg. Located on 1.48 acres of land with only one water tap and no sewerage or sanitation, the camp was home for about 1,000 people. The choice of this site was discussed with the mayor of Johannesburg and the chairman of the Executive Committee of the Transitional Metropolitan Council to ensure that some commitment would be made to implement ideas that the project generated. An official letter confirming the support of the Council was received from the mayor before work was undertaken with the children.

Fifteen girls and boys aged between 10 and 14 years took part in the full range of GUIC activities at this location. Because the activities took place during a series of Saturday morning workshops, the children quickly named the sessions 'Saturday school'. In addition to making drawings of their homes and neighbourhood, answering interview questions, taking the researchers on walks to show important places in daily life, role playing, and doing group activities to identify problems, envisage a better place to live and suggest changes to improve Canaansland, the children also took part in songs and games and shared refreshments. When these activities were completed, Mayor Isaac Mogase, of the Greater Johannesburg Metropolitan Council, hosted a one-day workshop at which the children presented the results of their work to the mayor, four regional mayors, city planners, representatives of donor agencies and young members of the city's Mini and Junior Councils. Following these presentations, the members of the audience drafted action plans to respond to the children's needs and the needs of squatter families as well as to urban children in greater Johannesburg as a whole.

Before improvements agreed to at the workshop could be implemented, and without the mayor's advance knowledge, the community was forcibly evicted with no notice and trucked 40 km away to a new location in empty veld, to land allocated for informal settlements by the Regional Department of Housing and Land Affairs. Several other inner-city squatter settlements were also dropped in this barren region known as 'Thula Mntwana' (Zulu for 'Hush my child'). Here the Canaansland families have had to begin the slow process of rebuilding their lives. GUIC project members have continued to work with them, including securing funds for the construction of a children's centre and adjoining playground in response to the children's identification of these needs. In May 1999, Mayor Mogase officially opened the children's centre on the new site. Named 'Ubuhle Buyeza' ('Good things are about to happen') by one of the project children, it now functions as a centre of community life for all ages. In February 1999, after the workshop and eviction and before the opening ceremony for the centre, 10 children from the original GUIC sample participated in a project impact assessment.

The children of the Ferreirasdorp location of GUIC, which was initiated in 1998, live in two high-rise apartment complexes inhabited by Indian families, just west of inner-city Johannesburg. These families are the remnants of a once large and vital Indian, African and Coloured community that suffered a series of evictions from the 1950s to the 1970s under the Apartheid policy of clearing Johannesburg for white residents only. A sample of 25 children, between 10 and 14 years old, was drawn from local primary schools to participate in the project. As in Canaansland, the children did drawings, interviews, role plays and walking tours of the neighbourhood, as well as group activities through which they identified problems and envisaged improvements in their community.

The children in Ferreirasdorp were evaluated after the end of this research phase, before they had a chance to present their results. The mayor's office was also aware of the work undertaken in Ferreirasdorp, so that when the children there completed their research, they were invited to report their findings in the official council chambers at the annual national meeting of junior mayors and councillors from throughout South Africa. As in Canaansland, the Ferreirasdorp children elected four representatives who presented their ideas. In response, junior councillors came up with a scheme to raise money so that some of the children's ideas could be realized. A group of junior councillors painted a large picture of the city, cut it up into 600 pieces, and sold each piece for 5 rand (US$0.50) during a morning in a mall. With the 3,000 rand (US$300) that they received, the children of Ferreirasdorp decided to fill an empty swimming pool in an old recreation area that had recently been opened to the public, charge 1 rand admission, and, with part of the money, increase security by paying destitute people in the neighbourhood to protect their school surroundings. Meanwhile, the children also submitted reports to the Metropolitan Council. About two years after the research phase, the newly appointed manager of the Child Friendly Cities Initiative in Greater Johannesburg invited a small team of councillors to undertake a guided walk in Ferreirasdorp, so that the children there could make their recommendations directly.

These GUIC sites represent processes of participatory action-research with the goal of designing programmes and places that set communities on paths of progressive self-improvement. In addition to the benefits to the communities themselves, how do these processes affect the children involved? Despite many claims made, there has been almost no systematic research to answer this question. The remainder of this article reports on a multi-method effort to explore the effect of these activities on the children of Canaansland and Ferreirasdorp. Because research of this kind is so new, the work that follows should be regarded as an exploratory initiative to determine measures that might most effectively assess this type of engagement.

Participants

The impact assessment procedures discussed in this article were carried out in January and February 1999, almost a year after young participants in Ferreirasdorp had undertaken an evaluation of their urban setting, and about 18 months after young participants at Canaansland had done so. Four of the original 25 participants from Ferreirasdorp had relocated, leaving 21 participants; 82 schoolfellows were available as a control group (see Table 14.1). Only 15 of the original 23 participants at Canaansland were involved in the full GUIC process until its completion, and after relocation, only 10 children from this group were available for the impact assessment study. They were compared with nine children from the larger settlement of Thula Mntwana who had had no previous exposure to GUIC.

English was the medium of communication in Ferreirasdorp. English and isiZulu were the two main languages used in Canaansland and Thula Mntwana; occasionally children asked for clarification in SeSotho.

Table 14.1 Summary of characteristics of participants

Group	Number	Description
Canaansland	10	Relocated inner-city squatter-camp children in GUIC programme
Thula Mntwana	9	Rural squatter settlement children with no GUIC exposure
Ferreirasdorp	21	Inner-city apartment children in the GUIC programme
Ferreirasdorp control	82	Inner-city apartment children with no GUIC exposure
Total	122	

Methods

The Convention on the Rights of the Child (CRC) addresses children's right to participation in two senses: their possibilities for engagement in the social life and physical world that surrounds them, and their opportunities to have a voice in more formal processes of democratic decision-making (Stephens, 1994). GUIC explores both dimensions. Through multiple methods of research, it seeks to understand how children use and value their localities, and through advocacy, it seeks to create formal channels through which children can be heard. Because it does this within the framework of the CRC, it was important for the project evaluation in Johannesburg to respond to different dimensions of this guiding legislation.

Stephens observed that the CRC is a document that assumes the universality of a free-standing, individual child who is to be protected and socialized into a culture according to liberal democratic principles (Stephens, 1995). The so-called 'participation articles' of the CRC (Articles 12–15), in particular, assume socialization into 'democratic principles of tolerance for diverse views and freedom of self-expression' (Stephens, 1995: 38). She noted that, as a consequence, critics have accused the Convention of cultural authoritarianism that subsumes all children into 'predominantly Western notions of normal childhood and child development' (Stephens, 1995: 36). Because of this, she was interested in the drafting and process of ratification of the African Charter on the Rights and Welfare of the Child, an instrument of the Organization of African Unity that came into force in November 2000. This takes into consideration both children's rights and children's responsibilities and was as influential in guiding the implementation of GUIC in South Africa as the CRC.

The paradox of Articles 12 and 13 of the CRC is that they simultaneously view children as objects of rights and as creative subjects.[1] Children are objects in the sense that the adults who drafted, adopted and are implementing this legislation have predetermined that children should have opportunities to exercise these particular rights, for predetermined reasons. To the extent that children creatively appropriate these rights, however, they become agents in imagining and reshaping the conditions of their lives. Another reason why it is critical to consider both adults' and children's expectations of participation is that any implementation of children's ideas – particularly in complex, contested urban spaces like Johannesburg – requires that adults and children work together to bring about change.

For these reasons, the exploratory evaluation of GUIC in Canaansland and Ferreirasdorp combined different methodological approaches. On one hand, it examined common adult claims regarding aspects of autonomous development that processes like GUIC should encourage: self-esteem, an internal locus of control (the belief that gains are dependent upon one's own actions) and self-efficacy (the belief that one can achieve the goals one sets oneself). To measure these benefits, standard psychometric measures were used: the Culture-Free Scale of Self-Esteem (Battle, 1981), the Nowicki–Strickland Locus of Control Scale (Nowicki & Strickland, 1973) and measures of self-efficacy that were especially created for this study.

In addition to these quantitative measures, which sought to evaluate universalized expectations regarding the benefits of participation for children, open-ended, qualitative information was also gathered through group discussions with the children who had taken part in the GUIC process. The discussions were not formal focus groups: eight thematic points were identified by researchers from the GUIC project, but participants were free to diverge from these themes. Using open-ended questionnaires, supplementary input was obtained from the children's parents. Since a number of the adults at Canaansland were illiterate, fieldworkers posed the questions verbally to the parents there and recorded their responses in writing. Since the parents of children from Ferreirasdorp were literate, they were not interviewed personally. Their questionnaires were distributed through the junior school and returned there for collection. Through these qualitative measures, the study sought to understand how parents believed that GUIC affected their children, as well as children's own experiences regarding the project's meaning and value. The set of different measures is listed in Table 14.2.

Table 14.2   Methods of evaluation used*

Type	Method	Description
Psychometric measures	Culture-Free Scale of Self-Esteem	Developed by James Battle (1981). A few items of the original scale were omitted and a few new items more relevant to the present study were added. In the end, there were 39 items to the scale, covering three areas of the children's lives: 7 social, 8 environmental and 24 personal issues.
	Nowicki-Strickland (1973) Locus of Control Scale	This scale was previously used successfully with South African children (Richter, 1989; Richter & van der Walt, 1996), and was based on that developed by Rotter (1966). A few minor colloquial adaptations from the original presentation were made.
	Measures of self-efficacy	A Likert-type scale of 42 items was developed, which tapped six areas of concern relevant to the programme; social issues and issues related to peer groups, school, independence, personal achievement and the environment. Children responded to each item twice: first in terms of the degree to which they considered it an ideal area of behaviour, and second in terms of the degree to which they personally matched this behaviour.
Qualitative measures	Group discussions	Project children took part in discussions about eight themes related to the project, as well as other project issues that they wished to bring up.
	Parent questionnaires	Depending on their literacy, the parents of children in the project responded to verbal or written questions about how GUIC affected their children.

*For details about the construction of the research instruments and a comprehensive report of results, see Griesel and Swart-Kruger (1999).

To adapt the psychometric instruments for the few children who did not use English as their mother tongue, the questions were translated from English into isiZulu and then back-translated, mindful of the requirements imposed by a constantly changing dialect. When it was not possible to make direct translations, where certain concepts were either not available or were differently applied in the two languages, the closest colloquial equivalent was decided on in consultation with the workers assisting with the translation. For each of the psychometric measurements, one of the two fieldworkers posed the questions to the group of children and ensured that the children understood the question and recorded their answers at the correct position on the answer sheet. Their answers were transferred to a database for scoring, calculating total raw scores and creating standardized scores for further analysis. For each instrument an item analysis and an estimation of the reliability of the measure was obtained for the total group of children. All quantitative data were analysed using the Statistica software package.

The measures of self-efficacy deserve special attention. One of the most frequently claimed benefits of children's participation is an increased belief in ability to achieve desired goals, described in terms of self-confidence, a sense of competence, or self-efficacy. The concept of self-efficacy, however, demands that this construct must be understood within a particular appropriate context (Bandura, 1997). Therefore one of the goals of this study was to create a measure that would be relevant to participatory processes of environmental change such as GUIC. For this purpose, a questionnaire with 42 items was created, based on discussions with the programme director and the fieldworkers who worked most closely with the children in Canaansland and Ferreirasdorp.

The questionnaire was applied twice: once by asking what a child perceived to be ideal areas of behaviour (measured on a Likert-type scale in five gradations from 'definitely not important' to 'very important'), and thereafter with respect to the extent to which a child believed that he or she personally met this ideal (measured in five gradations from 'always disagree' to 'always agree'). A visual aid was used to explain to the children differences in magnitude from the lowest to the highest ratings on the scale. An adjusted self-efficacy score was calculated for each item, which weighted the self-descriptive estimates in terms of the idealized estimates. If a child viewed a particular attribute as being maximally important and also fully personally met that criterion, the self-efficacy score was maximal. The reverse was also true: if a child viewed an attribute as being maximally important and personally only met that criterion minimally, then the self-efficacy score was adjusted downwards to a minimum. For each of the six areas of concern outlined in Table 14.2, the adjusted efficacy scores for the items under each heading were summed, and the total scores for each area were then transformed to T-scores based on the performance of the total group.

Results

Group discussions

In group discussions, children from both Canaansland and Ferreirasdorp spoke of how they believed that the GUIC process had affected their lives, and what they had learned from taking part.

Because the presentation by Canaansland children on the shortcomings in their urban environment had been favourably received by officials, they believed that the improvements they had recommended would be implemented. Instead, six months after their presentation and a year before the impact assessment was undertaken, all residents were relocated to a peri-urban area (Swart-Kruger, 2000). Their responses in group discussions showed that they conflated the positive outcomes expected from the urban workshop two years previously with recent improvements in their new setting – although some of these were introduced by GUIC and others by the regional Department of Housing and Land Affairs:

Everything we asked for in Braamfontein…we got it; now we are happy.

At both sites, the children said that their ability to communicate with each other had been enhanced by the GUIC process:

Kids here listen to each other, respect and share ideas. (Canaansland)

[It] taught us how to communicate with each other. (Ferreirasdorp)

They also felt that the process was not only fun, but helpful for gaining greater awareness of their surroundings:

Every single thing they taught us here is important. (Canaansland)

Growing Up in Cities helps us to know how to do directions. (Canaansland)

[It] helped us to learn about our areas. (Ferreirasdorp)

We enjoyed being asked questions, playing games, drawing, and talking about our environment. (Ferreirasdorp)

The Canaansland children were critical of the fact that the water at both the city and the new site was not potable, but commented favourably on the fact that disgusting environmental conditions in their city camp – such as stagnant water, foul smoke, mud, the stench of faeces, and dirt in general – which had provoked hostile reactions to them from passers-by, no longer permeated their lives. They reported that they had learned that 'to improve the environment in cities is to keep it tidy'.

The children from Ferreirasdorp were more explicit about what they had learned concerning the environment:

The project taught us how to care for our environment and keep it clean.

It taught us that people can help you change your life and change the environment in which you live.

They also claimed to have become more assertive about environmental issues:

It taught us that as children we have the right to give our opinions to improve our environment.

It taught me that the children of South Africa can make a difference.

Trapped as they are in the central business district of the inner city, the children of Ferreirasdorp were keen that rowdy local bars that disrupted the evening prayer hour should be replaced with parks and a swimming pool. Poignantly, they wished that it were less dangerous for children to ride bicycles and visit the movies, and that it was possible to feel safe at night. They expressed the hope that 'what we have learned here is passed on to others'.

Parents' questionnaires

Parents were generally positive about their children's involvement in the GUIC programme. Some described the benefit of the programme in terms of the learning opportunities it afforded, while others said that they had seen a general improvement in their children's behaviour and attitude:

They have become more mature and independent; they somehow feel proud of being heard.

He has become aware, independent, and respects his surroundings and his neighbours.

Parents especially thought that the project had been beneficial in motivating their children to learn more about the environment and to take care of it.

Taking part in this project has motivated her. She is very eager to learn about the things around her.

She now tells her friends about it, and makes them aware of the problems surrounding their environment, and how all of them should work together to make it a pleasant one.

They also noticed that their children showed increased caring in a concrete way:

She makes an effort to help in the environment in any way she can.

Before, she used to sometimes litter but now she picks up litter and throws it in the rubbish bin.

She talks about things that would make a difference for the betterment of the environment.

Some parents felt that children should take part in decision-making on environmental issues:

Children should be involved to some extent in decisions about their environment so that the environment can become a better and safe place for them.

In all, more than half of the parents identified specific areas in which their children had found benefit from the GUIC programme.

Self-esteem

Detailed information about the reliability of responses, the distribution of scores and the results of the statistical comparisons for each of the psychometric instruments are reported elsewhere (Griesel & Swart-Kruger, 1999). Because of the small numbers of children involved, it was not deemed desirable to rely on the statistical testing of results, but rather on analyses of variance. Post-hoc Scheffe comparisons were carried out to determine whether any statistically significant differences between groups were suggested.

On the Culture-Free Scale of Self-Esteem the reliability of the questionnaire as a whole was not very high. To estimate the extent to which the various items converge when a characteristic is measured, Cronbach's alpha is commonly used. Perfect convergence is indicated by an alpha value of 1. The Scale of Self-Esteem resulted in a standardized Cronbach's alpha of 0.55. The children's responses on social items, the environment and personal self-esteem were summed to give raw scores from 7, 8 and 24 items respectively.

The distribution of scores of the total group for each of these measures was reasonably normal. The scales could not easily be compared with each other because of the different numbers of items, so a standard metric had to be found. The raw subscale scores and the total raw score from the three subscales together were each converted to T-scores ($M = 50$; $SD = 10$) for the total group; and the relative T-scores for the four groups on the three subscales were then compared. Measured by these means, the Canaansland children had slightly lower self-esteem in terms of social issues but they, and their control group (the squatter group), had higher self-esteem than the inner-city apartment children, based on personal issues. The Thula Mntwana children who had not been exposed to the GUIC programme were slightly more satisfied with themselves in terms of their environment and on the full-scale measure. The groups did not otherwise differ from each other, and none of the comparisons between groups approached statistical significance.

Locus of control

The central characteristic of 'locus of control' is the degree of perceived internally located control over the world and its relation to the subject. For the Nowicki–Strickland Locus of Control Scale, the internal reliability in the total sample was not very high (standardized Cronbach's alpha of 0.56). After confirming that the distribution of raw scores across the total group was reasonably normal, the raw scores were converted to T-scores. The Canaansland group showed the lowest mean internal locus of control score, followed by the group from Ferreirasdorp which had also been exposed to the GUIC programme. The small group of rural squatter camp children had the highest mean internal locus of control score. However, these differences were very small and not statistically significant on an analysis of variance.

Measures of self-efficacy

As described earlier, adjusted self-efficacy scores were calculated based first on how important a child considered an item to be, and second in terms of its perceived applicability to him- or herself. When Cronbach's alpha was calculated across the items, a standardized correlation of 0.84 was obtained for the 'importance' version, 0.81 for the 'applicability' version and 0.81 for the adjusted scoring. These results suggest that the questionnaire was tapping a wide selection of aspects relating to a single construct (self-efficacy?) in a way that was internally reliable. The distribution of the summed scores for the 'importance' version was somewhat skewed to the right, suggesting that the majority of children regarded the items to be 'important'. But the distribution of the 'applicability' scores appeared reasonably normal – as did the distribution of the resulting adjusted raw scores. A common metric (T-scores) was adopted to allow comparison of these scores with each other and with other measures in the study. Then the four groups were compared on the summed adjusted scores expressed as T-scores (Table 14.3).

Taken together, the four groups differed from each other on this measure. A one-way analysis of variance of the four groups suggested a statistically significant group effect ($F = 9.61$, $df = 3$, $p = 0.0001$). There were also statistically significant differences among the groups, comparing one against each other in turn, using the post-hoc Scheffe test (Table 14.4).

Children in the control group at Thula Mntwana tended to consider themselves more efficacious than the other three groups. Though the one-way analysis of variance and post-hoc Scheffe test support this observation, it is important to remember that the small number of children in the Thula Mntwana control group may encourage an artefactual statistical significance in the group comparisons.

When the adjusted self-efficacy scores were examined in the six descriptive areas (social, peer group, school, independence, personal achievement and environment) much the same pattern emerged as with the total adjusted efficacy score reported earlier. The same caveat applies, however. In the area of social efficacy the Thula Mntwana control differed significantly from the two groups who had followed the GUIC programme and

Table 14.3   Summary table of mean T-scores on total ('adjusted') self-efficacy

Group	M	SD
Canaansland	51.90	9.80
Thula Mntwana	65.09	13.87
Ferreirasdorp	46.98	9.07
Ferreirasdorp controls	48.86	8.38
All groups	50.00	10.00

Table 14.4   Scheffe test of four groups on adjusted total self-efficacy T-scores

Group	Group 1 (M = 51.09)	Group 2 (M = 65.09)	Group 3 (M = 46.99)	Group 4 (M = 48.86)
Canaansland	–	0.02194*	0.58315	0.80079
Thula Mntwana	0.02194*	–	0.00005*	0.00003*
Ferreirasdorp	0.58315	0.00005*	–	0.87572
Ferreirasdorp controls	0.80079	0.00003*	0.87572	–

$*p < .05.$

they also rated themselves somewhat more efficacious than the Ferreirasdorp control children did. In regard to school-related items, the post-hoc test indicated that the two squatter settlement groups scored significantly higher than the Ferreirasdorp GUIC group. With respect to personal achievement and estimates of efficacy in the context of the environment, the Thula Mntwana control group rated themselves higher than did the two groups from Ferreirasdorp but the other groups did not differ significantly from one another. Nor did the groups differ significantly in respect of how efficacious the children rated themselves in the arenas of peer group relations or independence.

Discussion

The qualitative measures reported here indicate that the children for whom GUIC was run benefited from the programme. This study has highlighted the value of qualitative assessments in revealing the children's growth in skills and awareness, according to the children themselves and their parents.

As in many spheres of life, just the mere fact that one is being singled out for special treatment brings a certain psychological edge. Parents and children were specific about the benefits that they attributed to project participation, and their appraisals conformed to the project's goals for the children in terms of increased awareness of the environment and community needs, better communication skills, and a sense that they could express their opinions and make a positive contribution to their communities. Many children reported that the GUIC programme had sensitized them to the plight of the urban environment, drawn their attention to the place and role of others in their lives, and made them self-confident if not assertive. Most parents and children clearly championed the principle of the need for children to be heard, particularly in respect to plans to upgrade their environment or design new places to live. Therefore, the observations of both children and parents appeared to be directly associated with GUIC, rather than just a 'Hawthorne effect' due to special treatment.

Since these benefits claimed by the children and their parents can be expected to have an impact on psychological functioning, it is disappointing that the psychometric measures did not yield more substantive indicators of change in the children's lives. The contrast between the qualitative and quantitative results of this study invites a number of reflections.

As noted before, self-esteem, self-efficacy and an internal locus of control reflect what Sharon Stephens called the 'international modernist culture' of the CRC (Stephens, 1995: 39), with its emphasis on individual autonomy and achievement. Perhaps these constructs were not appropriate to the Islamic Indian culture of Ferreirasdorp and the African cultures of Canaansland. The study results suggest that the cultural relevance of these measures needs to be carefully considered within each project context.

It can also be argued, however, that these psychological characteristics are likely to be robust and unlikely to be greatly influenced by relatively short-term interventions. This factor also needs careful consideration in terms of the gains anticipated from any intervention programme.

It is noteworthy that the measure that yielded high reliability figures was the self-efficacy questionnaire, in contrast to the low reliability of the self-esteem and locus of control instruments. As Boyden and Ennew (1997) observe, questionnaires are most useful when they use ideas and words with which respondents are already familiar and build upon information gained from prior qualitative research. Although steps were taken to adapt the pre-existing measures of self-esteem and locus of control, it is possible that these measures still did not adequately relate to the study settings; whereas the self-efficacy questionnaire was specifically designed to fit the context of growing up in an impoverished and deteriorating environment. It is also interesting to note that the distribution of the children's self-efficacy scores was skewed to the right when the children rated the importance of the issues represented by the different items. That is, most children identified clearly that which society prescribes as desirable. This was more true for the Ferreirasdorp than for the Canaansland children. The fact that the children's application of the items to themselves yielded a nearly normal distribution supports the notion that the children understood the aim of the two questionnaires.

A shift in emphasis yielded different assessments of efficacy. In the present instance, it appeared essential to temper the assessment of achievement of the children in various arenas by referring to the extent to which they perceived such achievement as being important. Indirectly, this may reflect socially determined norms for such achievement. However, it may equally relate to the acceptance of such norms by the individuals. This should of course be contrasted with perceptions of the efficacy of the group as such. Instruments for assessing group efficacy, as seen by members of the group, have yet to be researched in relation to the efficacy of individuals in the group. These aspects deserve further research with similar groups.

The direction of the psychometric results raises questions regarding what reasonable expectations should be for participatory processes like GUIC. The children who experienced the intervention appeared slightly more driven by external forces, if the locus of control results can be accepted. On the 'application' measure of self-efficacy, the children exposed to GUIC also seemed slightly less sure of being efficacious than the control groups. Though these results were not strong, they do point to the fact that, although it was initially expected that the children would be more internally driven and feel more efficacious after their engagement with GUIC, the project was very much directed to sensitizing the children to their physical and social environment. Environmental changes based on the project depended on extensive collaboration among the children and between children and adults, rather than individual efforts. Perhaps projects like GUIC should be regarded primarily as experiences in collective efficacy rather than self-efficacy and internal locus of control. Typically, measures of collective efficacy ask members of a group to appraise the capability of their group as a whole (Bandura, 1997).

It should also be kept in mind that, as a rule, accurate self-appraisal and the accurate appraisal of difficulties increase with age (Bandura, 1997). Perhaps GUIC fostered a more mature sense of self-efficacy in terms of the real challenges of community development, and therefore downward-adjusted scores. The exact formulation of the aims of intervention studies clearly needs to converge with their content. In the present case it is not clear whether a more internal locus of control and a stronger sense of self-efficacy were the appropriate outcomes to anticipate.

The timing of the evaluations at the two sites also needs to be taken into consideration. As noted before, in some respects the move of the Canaansland group from their inner-city camp to an informal settlement on the city's edge was confounded with the GUIC programme. Some parents and children identified the GUIC programme – which had encouraged the development of environments in which children could be safer and happier – with the event of being relocated to a more remote but in some ways more acceptable place to live in Thula Mntwana. This impression seemed to have been reinforced by promises made at the mayor's workshop. The focus group remarks of the Canaansland children to a large extent support this observation. At the same time, the children found the ways in which city government works bewildering. They did not understand when the project director explained to them that the Metropolitan Council had to take an official resolution to assist them in the ways approved at the mayor's workshop, and that the resolution would only be discussed much later in the year. Similarly, the children in Ferreirasdorp could not understand why it should take council officials two years to bring up new bylaws for discussion and a vote. It is also important to keep in mind that the children in Ferreirasdorp were tested before the fundraising event run by the Junior Council.

The finding that children from GUIC showed a slightly lower degree of self-efficacy could be due to their conception that while local government and other official agencies had listened to what they had to say, the lack of concrete action by officials frustrated them. Johnson (1996: 7) has noted that both researchers and children feel disappointed when they have believed that their findings will make a difference, and then they do not. Although the causes of the lower scores are not clear, these results reinforce the need for ethical principles of participatory work with children and communities. The articulation of priorities for change needs to be followed by sessions with adults and minors jointly, to ensure that what remains to be done, and by whom, is clearly demarcated and that there are no residues of misunderstanding which might have a negative impact on young informants. These results also reinforce the importance of integrating into participatory processes some 'mastery experiences' that can be quickly implemented.

Further work to evaluate participatory programmes with children should allow for proper 'pre' and 'post' assessments and, whenever possible, repeated follow-up measures after increasing intervals of time. Given the time and resources required to initiate GUIC in South Africa, it was not possible in this case to focus on impact assessments until the process was well under way. Ideally, a pre/post design should be integrated into project funding from the start. It would also be desirable to ensure (as far as such factors can be controlled in real life) that the numbers of participants are higher and that the research is not confounded by too many factors such as relocation and sample attrition. Finally, more attention needs to be given to the translation, adaptation and creation of culture-sensitive psychometric instruments for non-western groups.

In summary, the goals of children in Canaansland and Ferreirasdorp, and the changes for the better that the children helped to achieve, may seem small compared to the magnitude of the environmental and social problems facing Johannesburg and many other cities of the world. According to statements by children and parents in the GUIC project, however, taking these steps gave the children a greater awareness of their environment and a greater sense of their rights and abilities to express their views and take action to improve their living conditions. In a world where an increasing proportion of the population lives in urban areas, it will be vitally important that urban residents have such an awareness and knowledge of how to take action. It is out of the activities of citizens in numberless communities like Canaansland and Ferreirasdorp around the world, that the foundations for liveable and sustainable cities will be built.

Notes

This study was made possible by funding from the Johann Jacobs Foundation, and by the enthusiastic effort of numerous people, including the project fieldworkers Maurice Mogane and Lineo Lerotholi in Canaansland, and Fatima Noor Mahomed and Afzal Noor Mahomed in Ferreirasdorp. Not least, we thank the wonderfully responsive children and their parents.

1. Article 12 of the CRC provides for children's opinions to be taken into account in all decisions made on their behalf, in accordance with their age and maturity; Article 13 provides children with the right to freedom of expression.

References

Bandura, A. (1997) *Self-Efficacy: The Exercise of Control*. San Francisco: Freeman.
Battle, J. (1981) *Culture-Free SEI – Self-Esteem Inventories for Children and Adults*. Seattle, WA: Special Child Publications.
Boyden, J. and Ennew, J. (1997) *Children in Focus – A Manual for Participatory Work with Children*. Stockholm: Rädda Barnen.
Chawla, L. (ed.) (2001) *Growing Up in an Urbanizing World*. London: Earthscan/UNESCO.
De Winter, M. (1997) *Children as Fellow Citizens*. Oxford: Radcliffe Medical Press.
Driskell, D. (in press) *Creating Better Cities with Children and Youth*. London: Earthscan/UNESCO.
Griesel, R.D. and Swart-Kruger, J. (1999) 'An Assessment of the Impact of the Growing Up in Cities Project on Children in Johannesburg, South Africa: Final Project Report submitted to Johann Jacobs Foundation', unpublished report.
Hart, R. (1997) *Children's Participation*. London: Earthscan/UNESCO.
Johnson, V. (1996) 'Starting a Dialogue: Children's Participation', *PLA Notes* [Participatory Learning and Action] **25**: 3–16.
Lynch, K. (ed.) (1977) *Growing Up in Cities*. Cambridge, MA: MIT Press.
Nowicki, S. and B.R. Strickland (1973) 'A Locus of Control Scale for Children', *Journal of Consulting and Clinical Psychology* **40**(l): 148–54.
Richter, L.M. (1989) *A Psychological Study of 'Street Children' in Johannesburg*, Report 89–01. Pretoria: Institute for Behavioural Sciences, University of South Africa.
Richter, L.M. and M. van der Walt (1996) 'The Psychological Assessment of South African Street Children', *Africa Insight* **26**(3): 211–20.
Rotter, L.B. (1966) 'Generalized Expectancies for Internal versus External Control of Reinforcement', *Psychological Monographs* **80**(1), whole no. 609.
Stapp, W.B., Wals, A. and S.L. Stankorb (Eds) (1996) *Environmental Education for Empowerment*. Dubuque, IA: Kendall/Hunt Publishing.
Stephens, S. (1994) 'Children and Environment: Local Worlds and Global Connections', *Childhood* **2**(1–2): 1–21.

Stephens, S. (1995) 'Children and the Politics of Culture in Late Capitalism', in S. Stephens (ed.) *Children and the Politics of Culture*, pp. 3–48. Princeton, NJ: Princeton University Press.

Swart-Kruger, J.M. (ed.) (2000) *Growing Up in Canaansland: Children's Recommendations on Improving a Squatter Camp Environment*. Pretoria: Human Sciences Research Council/UNESCO.

Swart-Kruger, J.M. (2001) 'Children in a South African Squatter Camp Gain and Lose a Voice', in L. Chawla (ed.) *Growing Up in an Urbanizing World*. London: Earthscan/UNESCO.

Van Tonder, D. (1997) 'The Road to Egoli', *MUNIVIRO* **13**(2): 6–7.

Commentary: Dev Griesel

Background

My colleague, Louise Chawla from Kentucky State University, attended a conference called 'Children in the City' in Italy, during 1994. Discussions there led to the idea of revitalising an existing UNESCO project called 'Growing Up in Cities' (GUIC). In the original programme there were various research sites throughout the world and the current GUIC programme, which Louise coordinates, is attempting to replicate the original studies. These original studies had failed to draw children into the research programme aimed at urban planning, (Lynch, 1997). In contrast, the current project emphasises children's participation, in keeping with the UN Convention on the Rights of the Child (1989), Agenda 21 of the 1992 Earth Summit and the 1996 Habitat Agenda.[1]

Louise pulled together an international research team that believed it was important to add a participatory dimension to research, creating routes for children to be drawn directly into urban evaluation and planning. Although the team was inspired by an apparent need for children's participation it could not be assumed that the children's participation was necessarily and wholly enjoyable, beneficial, effective or permanent for those involved. To ensure that the programme's aims were not confused with outcomes the research/interventions needed to be assessed and evaluated. We needed to know about the strengths and weaknesses of the intervention in order to build upon positive influences and discard, if possible, any less beneficial aspects of the GUIC programme.

Jill Kruger heads the South African end of the GUIC Project and is an acknowledged specialist in anthropological research related to children in South Africa. I am a psychologist based at the University of Natal and have been interested for many years in various psychological and neuropsychological aspects of child development. We wanted to find out if the GUIC programme in South Africa actually enhanced children's self-esteem and self-efficacy within a developing network of support and relationships with people and place. The dimensions we used to examine this are outlined in our article. We used a mix of quantitative and qualitative measures. We sought an 'everyday validity' when we conceptualised the research and it was initially motivated from the viewpoint of ordinary people rather than scientific theory. However, rigorous, scientifically supported methods and analysis were essential; hence the involvement of professional researchers with a background in the social sciences, particularly psychology and statistics, and experience in the multi-cultural milieu of South Africa.

'Real world' research

'Real world' research often means that the practicalities of the situation work against important assumptions of design in research and statistical analysis. One frequently has to make do with what is available and then assess the impact on the assumptions one would ordinarily have wanted to meet. For example, we were concerned about ensuring naivety on the part of our young people with respect to our testing procedures and group discussions (we needed personal input and not a reflection of the opinion of 'leaders' in the groups); the number of young people at our disposal was totally out of our control since many of them had moved away from the area where the programme had been implemented; not all the young people had participated equally in the original programme, in terms of commitment and motivation; and there was no way in which we could randomly allocate children to control and participant groups, nor could we ensure equal numbers in the groups.

By the time our impact study could be started, about a year had already passed since the implementation of the current GUIC programme. Because of this we were concerned that the original GUIC participants might not be available to take part in the evaluation. Attrition had occurred, particularly among the children from the squatter camp, Canaansland. This had been cleared and the inhabitants moved to a remote site. Children from the surrounding areas heard about GUIC programme and potentially provided a 'control group'. In practice they did not engage with the same high motivation as GUIC attendees. The inner-city children who had participated in the programme were mostly still available at the local school and many of their peers who had not been enrolled in the programme, for one or other reason, provided a comparison group for the inner-city dwellers.

A second issue was the possible dilution of any programme effects with the passage of time. Yet the delay allowed us to look for long-term effects – one of our ultimate goals. We believed that the comparison of the squatter-camp and inner-city children would still be valid.

The squatter-camp children were quite confused about having had to move and to some extent even thought that the programme was somehow connected with the positive aspects of the move. We were aware that there could be both benefits and disadvantages for each of the two sites. In some respects GUIC had been able to assist in making the new site more acceptable, e.g. by being instrumental in finding a sponsor to erect a play centre. As in all research, proper rapport with those taking part was of utmost importance and continual contact with the groups was necessary even when it came to issues not directly concerned with our assessment.

Obtaining approval

One of the problems that besets practical or field research is obtaining official approval from educational, civic and other authorities for carrying out the study and also for enrolling particular groups. Fortunately Jill had been in close contact not only with the children we were studying but also with their school and civic authorities over several years and was able to elicit all the necessary cooperation. Happily we were able to elicit the interest of the principal of the school of our inner-city group to the extent that he allowed the use of the school premises and sometimes of official school time. Many a study flounders because of not having followed the correct procedures to obtain all necessary permissions and cooperation. We also needed ethical clearance from the University of Natal before embarking on the research. In times past this requirement was stringently applied only in the medical field. With the emergence of democracy, personal freedom and human rights, the issue of research ethics has come to the fore to ensure that the interests of the participants are not compromised.

Talking the same language?

Many of the research instruments used in psychology and sociology have been developed in the 'western world'. We found that the availability of appropriate psychometric tools among South African cultural groups was limited, despite a long-standing tradition of world-class psychometric research within our country. Fortunately, the Battle 'Culture-free Scale of Self-Esteem' was available and we had previously used the Nowicki–Strickland 'Locus of Control Scale' successfully with South African children. When it came to the issue of self-efficacy we attempted to use a Likert scale. Likert scales offer structure and flexibility to responses to a stimulus, e.g. statements, photographs, drawings. For example, in response to the statement 'it is important that people listen to what you say' participants had to mark a scale (see the bottom line of Figure 14.1).

This led to a problem. Most of our respondents did not speak English and the Likert scale categories had to be translated into isiZulu. However, isiZulu is categorical about the truth and does not allow for a gradient of truth, as implied by a Likert scale. Either something is true or it is not true. To help the children understand the idea of a gradient when they scored themselves against the self-efficacy items, we constructed a large illustration (see the top half of Figure 14.1) and reviewed the scale with them until we

Figure 14.1 Illustration and Lickert Scale

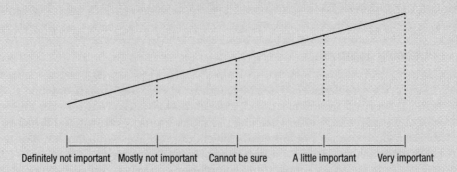

Definitely not important Mostly not important Cannot be sure A little important Very important

were sure that they understood what was expected of them. The illustration was kept before them throughout the administration of the test.

We also had more general concerns about communication. The inner-city children all spoke English, but not all were equally fluent and certainly the squatter-camp children differed in their understanding not only of English but also of the other languages being used. We had anticipated this during our early planning and attempted to overcome it by asking two university lecturers to translate the questionnaires into SeSotho and isiZulu. However, a small pilot study showed that children similar to those in our study could not understand the translations on their own. At the end of the day we found that we had to monitor carefully the children's understanding of our assessment procedures, and to be prepared to restructure our questions to elicit a response relevant to the issue we were addressing. A problem that arises when one does research across different cultural and language groups is that the concepts we often take for granted do not necessarily exist in the language of our subjects. Translating into the nearest similar meaning is also not necessarily sufficient. This is a difficult problem to deal with. We found that we sometimes had to restructure a question in order to elicit a response relevant to the broad issue we were wanting to address. We communicated through fieldworkers thoroughly trained in our procedures and fluent in the children's languages.

We were fortunate in our translation exercise insofar as the fieldworkers we employed were well educated in the use of English and could translate into the local languages with ease. We had to take care, however, that local dialects were adequately incorporated, since the isiZulu spoken in KwaZulu is 'purer' than that in Johannesburg. In fact the lingua franca amongst squatter-camp dwellers is extremely dynamic, being based on a generally used language but full of colloquialisms. We found that by discussing our translations with several users of both English and the local language as part of the back-translation process we were able to overcome this problem to a very large extent. Translation and back-translation, sometimes several times over, is absolutely essential when working across language groups.

You may wonder how essentially western researchers can conduct research with non-western groups. In our case we felt reasonably comfortable since we have lived in this country for a long time and have always had close contact both formally and informally with the groups we studied. From their side, the children were certainly not aliens in a western world. They have always had contact with western culture and have incorporated much of it (e.g. in dress, music, language and education). Further, our contact with them was through our research assistants, who came from a similar cultural background, spoke their languages and yet were part of our western culture. Research assistants with exceptional rapport with the children (by virtue of their prior positive contact with them over a long period of time, as much as because of similar cultural experience) were the backbone of the study.

We talked to children about GUIC in focus groups. Research assistants who were focus group facilitators were of critical importance in encouraging participation that does not bias responses. Because of the extreme reticence of some of the children, we invited all of them to participate, sometimes by suggesting that they address one of several key issues that the children had agreed amongst themselves should be discussed.

Reflections

The participants in our research were residents of a squatter camp. Throughout we were aware of the interrelationship of the research and the social intervention or pressure to intervene. At times the exposure of the researchers to the personal details and enormous problems of the participants' lives could be quite demanding. A related phenomenon is that of the community becoming involved in the research effort. This occurred out of curiosity and good-neighbourliness but sometimes in order to lay claim to some assistance in obtaining food. These experiences in the research field leave an indelible impression although they can bring considerable complication to the research. For instance, we benefited greatly when a local community leader could be persuaded to help by providing lunches for our participants but there were frequently children from the surrounding area standing around, watching the procedures, making comments or joining in the lunch queue.

The findings of the study left one with a sense of some frustration at the inequalities of society. A poignant wish of the inner-city children was that their environment should be cleaner, without bars and moving taxi ranks. They wished for a safer place for children where they could ride bicycles, go to movies and be safe at night. These were expressions simply documented by our 'scientific observation' of how we all yearn for a positive environment.

The children were less concerned with their own personal needs, being more concerned with the future needs of their society.

It was somewhat surprising to find that the squatter-camp children who had not been exposed to the GUIC programme revealed somewhat higher self-esteem than the children in the programme did. In this regard, the sensitizing role of the programme could be viewed as possibly having a negative spin-off. On the other hand it could indicate that the children in the programme had become more aware of the world's challenges and their own limitations.

Writing up the results of a study inevitably brings into question some of the assumptions and expectations one had prior to starting the work. This is illustrated in the present study by the Locus of Control results. We had expected that after their exposure to the GUIC programme the children would be more internally driven, but the programme was very much directed to sensitizing the children to their environment. Clearly, the exact formulation of the aims of intervention studies and their content need to converge. In the present case it is not clear whether increased internal locus of control was the most appropriate outcome, given the nature of the intervention.

Intervention in the 'Majority World' context needs to be scientifically documented to ensure that we move forward efficiently with our attempts to uplift our fellow human beings rather than simply earning 'Brownie points' for our good works. Related to this is the desirability of linking research to ongoing social efforts in order to monitor their sustainability. In the present study it was evident how the dynamic nature of society continually influences the effectiveness of interventions. Over the short time of our programme a social group was forcibly moved to alternative housing with far-reaching consequences not only for them but for our research project!

Participating in this project was personally rewarding. We assisted our participants with issues outside of the research. We were able to explore a new technique in assessing self-efficacy. We drew attention to the complexity of psychological constructs and the need for intervention programmes to build in assessment procedures. In the course of our work we have contributed to the development of our research assistants. Last, but not least, interaction with colleagues of a similar mind, in planning such work, carrying out and ultimately discussing and publishing the results has been most satisfying.

There is a serious problem in participatory action-research with children in South Africa. Government is not effectively delivering improvements to the children's living conditions. The fact that their recommendations have been invited and welcomed but then apparently ignored directly affects the children. It has taken six years for the children of Thula Mntwana to see basic services such as water, lights and sanitation approved for their living area. Those in Ferreirasdorp have had no feedback from local government on what changes might be made in their area; officials visited there in 1999 to be shown around by the children but since then nothing has happened.

Note

1 **The UN Convention on the Rights of the Child** was adopted by the UN General Assembly on 20 November 1989 and opened for signature on 26 January 1990. Sixty-one countries signed the document on that day, a record first-day response. By signing the Convention, a government indicates its intention to ratify, but this then requires the approval of national parliaments or other competent authorities. However, it took just seven months for the necessary 20 countries to ratify the Convention, and it entered into force as international law on 2 September 1990.

    Agenda 21 is a comprehensive plan of action to be taken globally, nationally and locally by organizations of the United Nations System, governments, and major groups in every area in which humans impact on the environment. Agenda 21, the *Rio Declaration on Environment and Development*, and the *Statement of Principles for the Sustainable Management of Forests* were adopted by more than 178 governments at the United Nations Conference on Environment and Development (UNCED) held in Rio de Janeiro, Brazil, 3 to 14 June 1992.

    The Habitat II Conference held in Istanbul, Turkey, in June 1996 was the first global conference in which representatives of local authorities and civil society participated actively in the formulation of the major outcome, **the** Habitat Agenda. The Habitat Agenda was adopted by 171 governments from around the world. The Agenda provides a practical roadmap to an urbanizing world, setting out approaches and strategies towards the achievement of sustainable development of the world's urban areas.

Reference

Lynch, K. (ed.) (1977) *Growing up in Cities*. Cambridge, MA: MIT Press.

Index